D0064677

Foundations and Applications of Group Psychotherapy

A Sphere of Influence

MARK F. ETTIN, Ph.D.

Private Practice
East Brunswick, New Jersey

Adjunct Associate Professor
Department of Psychiatry
UMDNJ—Robert Wood Johnson
Medical School

ALLYN AND BACON

Boston   London   Toronto   Sydney   Tokyo   Singapore

Library of Congress Cataloging-in-Publication Data

Ettin, Mark F., 1947–
    Foundations and applications of group psychotherapy : a sphere of
influence / by Mark F. Ettin.
        p.   cm.
    Includes bibliographical references and index.
    ISBN 0-205-13508-0
    1. Group psychotherapy.   2. Group psychotherapy—History.
3. Small groups.   I. Title.
    [DNLM: 1. Group Processes.   2. Psychotherapy, Group.   WM 430
E85F]
RC488.E88   1992
616.89′152—dc20
DNLM/DLC
for Library of Congress   91–33193
                                                                          CIP

Printed in the United States of America

10 9 8 7 6 5 4 3 2 1   96 95 94 93 92

Contents

Preface

Small-group work is a psychological as well as a cultural phenomenon—a constant juxtaposition between the "group-as-imagined" and the "group-as-lived." Any text on group therapy must necessarily assume a mediating position somewhere between pensive reason and a more interactive sensibility. The "group-in-the-telling" can be broached by discursive means, providing logical, scientific, theory-bound explanations of emergent collective phenomena while developing a logos of small-group practice. Logos provides food for thought by pondering the organizational structures, motive forces, objective relations, and linear development of the group process while relying on literal truths and rational explanations thought out consciously.

The group can also be approached by assuming a more storied, dramatic, narrative pose when recounting the mythos of small-group participation. Mythos proffers word of mouth by speaking to primitive processes, intuitive meanings, fantasied relations, and storied progressions while relying on metaphoric truths and figurative expressions often conjured up without conscious realization (Shelburne, 1988). If the telling is to approach the tale, then it is necessary to look to both the logic and order underlying the grouping process as well as to the participatory mystique and literary device marking the small-group advance.

The history of human groups, therapy groups included, begins in the oral tradition, an incantation to the human dilemma often phrased in a language of images and metaphors akin to mythic recollection. Socrates, in the fifth century before Christ, sought to move the group process from the persuasive and hypnotic to the convincing and logical, not by merely captivating the heart but also by enticing the mind. Yet Vernant (1988), in contrasting mythos and logos, warns against giving up too much to get too little. "It is as if discourse could win in the sphere of truth and intelligibility by simultaneously losing out in the sphere of what is pleasurable, moving, and dramatic" (p. 208). Becoming "a part of a group" requires a rationale for joining and remaining connected, in the form of a thoughtful individual motive; it also implies joining in and resonating to a more automatic,

thoughtless collective motif. Therefore, working with groups entails understanding the logistics of how people are brought, kept, and treated together
while appreciating the artistry born when individuals so combine. A group's
"sphere of influence" necessarily comprises both a pervasive logic and a
precocious aesthetic.

This book traces the logos of small-group practice by examining the
history, logistics, and specific usages of the developing group medium. It
also traces the mythos of small-group participation by highlighting the metaphoric language, dynamic configurations, and thematic concerns represented within the ongoing group drama. Sets of logical frameworks (paradigms) for telling human stories (vignettes) are expressed, when possible,
with the group's own evocative language (symbolic figures and recurrent
forms). By presenting a combination of theories, practical clinical vignettes,
and literary devices within each chapter, the reader views a full range of
phenomenological experiences in person and a compendium of interventional strategies in context.

Structure and Content of the Text

This book looks at providing effective individual treatment within psychoeducational and psychotherapeutic groups, and examines the structural
properties of such groups as organizational entities in their own right.
Foundations and Applications each make up two sections of three chapters.
The Foundations section covers the history and epistemology of the grouping process. The intent is always to learn exactly what ideas and techniques
have been used before and which notions still apply today. After considering important nuts and bolts issues, many practical and philosophical questions are examined. What do we actually mean when we say we are forming
a group or doing group therapy? What is the precise nature of the collective
endeavor and how might group interventions best be practiced with different aims in diverse settings?

The Applications section looks to specific psychoeducational and psychotherapeutic uses of the group medium. The reader can expect to gain
both an in-depth understanding of the human grouping process and a practical knowledge of how to organize, facilitate, and manage collective treatment regimens. How are naturally evolving group processes and dynamics
harnessed in the service of psychosocial insight and the amelioration of personal difficulties? What is the relationship between task and process
groups? What are the inherent tasks in process or psychotherapy groups
and how does one work with group processes in nonprocess groups? The
text is bookended by considering the logistics of small-group participation

and the mythic roots of small-group culture. Although each chapter and each section can be read as a discrete unit, they are linked and sequenced by recurrent motifs, consistent structural analyses, and a generalized perspective about collective dynamics.

Audience and Base of Experience

Both the subject matter and its treatment cross traditional interdisciplinary lines by introducing insights from anthropology, mythology, and the philosophy of science—giving the work relevance to the therapeutic circle, the task group, the classroom, and the managerial conglomerate. The book is therefore aimed at the varied audience of practitioners, students, academicians, trainers, and managers—all of whom must understand and work within collective settings. By moving across time, context, and modality, the text explores the many faceted universalities of group structure, formation, leadership, organization, and epistemology—always with a ready eye toward specific applications.

In addition to being informed by the collective wisdom of the group therapy literature, this project is influenced by 20 years of group therapy practice and training, membership in many organizations and task groups, and an active immersion as participant-observer in settings for the study of group processes and organizational life. These varied experiences within groups have engendered a respect for and an awe of both obvious and subtle collective dynamics; stated and hidden organizational agendas; and facilitative and dysfunctional groupwide structural processes. Understanding the intricate workings of groups in action has taken on a personal meaning as well as a cultural imperative. This book represents an individual attempt to understand and a social gesture to share just this group of truths and truth of groups.

Acknowledgments

The production of this book is of course a group effort and I wish to thank the various people who have aided or supported the process. Fritz Redl (1980) suggests that "first people" function as group leaders by initiating dangerous or difficult actions in the service of a larger cause. The first reader of a manuscript, as initial audience, engages in an act of courage when taking the risk of critiquing the preliminary draft. Thanks to Dr. Marsha Heiman for her honesty, puzzlement, enthusiasm, and concrete suggestions when previewing various chapters, sections, and overall plans in their initial conception and subsequent development. Her ongoing moral support, patience, and faith in the project are also greatly appreciated.

Many of the chapters are well traveled, having passed through various hands before returning for final revision. Drs. Donald Franklin and Barbara Dazzo lent good sense and wide perspective to the introduction. Dr. Jay Fidler was very encouraging, years ago, about publishing the historical material. Working through the most difficult epistemology chapters required the services of Dr. Bertram Cohen, who made sure the philosophy of science was sound, as well as offered many sage ideas about group process. My friend, Dr. Richard Michael, read and commented on these same chapters and the conclusion, providing timely suggestions and an enthusiastic response that supplied needed courage. Dr. Yvonne Agazarian and Professor Dorothy Whitaker graciously reviewed and generously gave their approvals to the group-as-a-whole perspectives.

I want to recognize the collaboration of Dr. Heiman and Dr. Steven Kopel, who co-authored an earlier version of Chapter 10. Drs. Eleanore Vaughan and Nancy Fiedler arranged the consultation group and co-wrote an earlier rendition of Chapter 9. Dr. Robert Dies patiently encouraged the many revisions of Chapter 12 for an earlier publication. Dr. Howard Kibel and Victor Schermer, M.A., reviewed the mythos of small-group culture, providing helpful comments on object relations, primitive mentality, and modern treatment considerations. Dr. Eric Villepontaux provided some needed anthropological perspective en route.

More generally, I want to acknowledge my colleagues in the New Jersey Group Psychotherapy Society, who for many years have provided a reference group and an experiential partnership for studying collective dynamics. Thanks to Professor Julian Jaynes for his kind encouragement and guidance when the whole process seemed so daunting. My colleague, Jeffrey Bowden, A.C.S.W., lent an ear, philosophical outlook, and mental space at key junctures by covering clients and groups while I sat over the keyboard. And certainly this work could not have been possible without the trust and sharing provided by the many clients and therapy groups who taught me the inherent logic of groups by telling and enacting their stories.

Final thanks also to my editorial consultant, Terry Schneider, for helping with permissions, manuscript development, indexing, and stylistic perplexities. Elydia Davis and Lynda Griffiths, with sensitivity to an author's concerns, aided in the final production of the book. And of course gratitude to Allyn and Bacon for publishing the work under the guidance of Mylan Jaixen and his assistant, Deborah Reinke. In many mentoring conversations, Mylan eased this rite of passage by talking through the publishing process and guiding me in making the decisions and judgment calls necessary to bringing this book to fruition.

PART ONE

Introduction

CHAPTER ONE
The Logos of Small-Group Participation: Structural Guidelines and Organizational Formats

To know something by way of logos is to have encompassing explanations and rational guidance systems. To change by way of logical processes means to question and alter the reasons, organizational structures, and conscious motives configuring and propelling events.

An exposition on the logos of small-group participation introduces the concept of grouping as both a universal collective tendency and a particularized format for psychosocial exploration. Various framing questions and logistic parameters are outlined in structural preparation for the theories and practices to follow. Psychoeducational, training, and psychotherapy groups are differentiated. Time determinations, group size, membership criteria, client selection, treatment planning, temporal and spatial focuses, and levels of group analysis are considered across modalities. When putting together a group, the facilitator must find effective ways to help members move from being seemingly lone operators to becoming bonafide participants in a shared process (Chapter One).

CHAPTER ONE

The Logos of Small-Group Participation: Structural Guidelines and Organizational Formats

We are descended from small bands of hunter-gatherers (Pfeiffer, 1985; Glantz & Pearce, 1989). The human time line goes back at least forty thousand years to when Cro-Magnon walked the savannas, steppes, and limestone precipices of the Upper Paleolithic period (Leroi-Gourhan, 1967; White, 1986). Our remote ancestors threw aside the restrictions of isolated experience by coming together in open clearings to form a social contract for the protection of the few and the benefit of the many (Rousseau,1987). Related by blood or bound by harsh circumstances, small nomadic groups formed with the collective purpose of surviving and proliferating. Limited resources and environmental dangers dictated coming together as one and for all. Clans became cohesive as members identified with common totems. Leaders emerged, and a social structure was roughly hewn out of the prehistoric tundra. In communion and in reciprocity, joining and belonging came to characterize the human condition.

It is still difficult to identify ourselves without naming the groups of which we are a part. We are born into families, tribes, races, religions, nations, and cultures. We move into territories, neighborhoods, communities, towns, cities, and countries populated however sparsely or densely by others of our kind. We join schools, teams, organizations, working collectives, professions, and peer familiars.

Seemingly, "no individual, however isolated in time and space, can be regarded as outside a group or lacking in active manifestations of group psychology" (Bion, 1961, p. 54). For all behavior must ultimately be understood within some social context and against some collective backdrop. Even the hermit lives in counterpoint to his societal grouping on the outskirts of an organized civilization and culture. Thus spoke Zarathustra! (Nietzsche,1968). Likewise, the ostracized and hallucinating schizophrenic carries a group in his head—a group from which he cringes and withdraws, and a group to which he addresses his most vehement soliloquistic protests.

With each grouping comes an increase in power and exploratory potential. Maxims such as, "There is power in numbers," "Together we stand, divided we fall," or the anthem, "One for all and all for one" abound. Many examples can be drawn from everyday life of the increase in efficiency and potency that comes from joining together—companies, classrooms, unions, money markets, political action groups, and think tanks all bring people into social contract, pooling labor and resources, influencing and propagating opinions, and brainstorming solutions to common problems.

Recent years have seen a proliferation of smaller groups purposely formed for problem solving, breaking habits, controlling impulses, coping with adversity, learning new skills, combating disease, interrupting cycles of isolation and loneliness, or seeking the support of others with similar injuries, maladies, concerns, interests, or happenstance. Together we give up alcohol and drugs; share grief to lessen the pain of a tragic life circumstance; support one another's hopes and dreams; exercise our bodies and build up or trim down; explore the nature of our interactions and personalities; and play, work, talk, and engage in all forms of focused, collective attentions. The encounter group movement of the 60s served to open up communication and humanize the values of the larger society. The self-improvement craze of the 70s brought people together to discover and celebrate inherent personal potentials. The self-help movement of the 80s culled out others with like problems for mutual support and encouragement. The 90s may bring people together around sustaining their environments, whether workplace, family, neighborhood, or nature.

The ability to function as part of a group is a skill essential to the conduct of social life. Giving and taking, speaking and listening, are distinctly human exchanges. Difficulty fitting into groups is a source of maladjustment and a root cause of discontent. With each successive grouping comes the opportunity to satisfy basic social and personal needs while accomplishing varied tasks. Differing aptitudes and attitudes about how familiar, intimate, open, involved, committed, attached, entwined, or invested to become influence the success or failure of our collective endeavors. Each subsequent grouping therefore finds its own level of care, chaos, cooperation, competition, comraderie, conspiracy, competence, cataclysm, or cultural achievement.

Groups can be exploitive as well as encouraging. Individuals are ill served when an aberrant collective ethos or a rigid organizational structure eclipses personal freedom and initiative or fails to recognize and respond to a special need. Staid collectives may conservatively hold to a status quo, branding and punishing more progressive elements as malcontented, misinformed, dissident, crazy, or incompetent. Negative group-induced messages solidifying the control of the collective, like "Big brother is watching" or "In the name of the the clique (gang, fatherland), all is condoned," are too easily expounded and enforced. Many examples of destructive group processes are found in the form of mob rule, mass contagion, scapegoating, martyrdom, ostracism, or social abandonment. Violence is endemic, whether directed within or without a group's constraining bounds, and the wounds that result may be physical and/or psychological.

To understand and harness the power of the group process, human collectivity must be approached from the encompassing perspectives of both the individual and the group. Dialectic compromise between the overlapping poles of identity—I and We—requires a synthesis of personal freedom with an appreciation of the common good. To work within groups means gainsaying some organizational structure while still providing for and protecting the individuals who make up the group. Constructive and synergistic potentials are thus maximized while destructive trends are challenged, controlled, or rechanneled. Certainly the world is in the midst of the startling breakdown of collective systems that failed to meet the requirements of their constituencies.

Small groups expressly formed for task accomplishment, self-exploration, personal enhancement, characterological change, or rapid recovery must also be responsive and answerable to the needs of its members. The aim of group work is always intersecting and twofold: the power of the collective is invoked to help individuals cope with or overcome personal problems, while the individual is simultaneously required to find satisfying and effective ways of fitting in and contributing to the group's overall aims.

Group Logistics

Although the human grouping process is universal and ubiquitous, the creation of a specific working collective requires developing a structure best suited for set purposes. A group's structure is made up of its internal organizational framework, consisting of formative constructions, dynamic proclivities, and operational decisions. This framework underlies and influences a group's ongoing developments, interactions, and goal-directed strategies.

A group's initial structure is influenced by certain backdrop issues such as the very nature of human collectivity—what generally happens when people come together—as well as by a particular group's foundation matrix (Foulkes, 1965) or overall societal and cultural context. Formative decisions concerning membership (who will actually take part in the evolving dynamic matrix [Foulkes, 1965] and the resultant logistics (how the collective will organize and operate) also help determine what becomes possible. Matriculated members bring their unique personalities, relevant social experiences, and pregroup expectations to bear on the ultimate shape of the proceedings. Early ground rules, boundary setting, and selective attentions result in the evolution of notable customs, conventions, and norms, which further determine the direction, focus, and purpose of the shared experience.

Very early in the group process, the collective begins to refine its general aims and specific tasks by working out the nature of participation and self-disclosure required; the skills and roles needed; the leadership sought and accepted; the degree of intimacy and confrontation possible; and the resources and topical material that is to make up the raw data of the group interaction. Will the group concentrate on productive endeavors, creative ideas, functional tasks, or self-analysis? Will the collective consider future plans, past experiences, and/or shared here-and-now concerns? Decisions concerning the relevance of a range of affect-laden fears, beliefs, memories, wishes, fantasies, images, dreams, and/or symbolic transformations will affect the quality, depth, and texture of the proceedings.

Structural guidelines can be outlined for any budding group enterprise in order to map the logistical parameters and organizational requisites of the proposed gathering. Framing questions in planning and facilitation include:

- What are the group's general purposes, specific aims, and relevant tasks? Why is the group being formed in the first place?
- What group protocol of operating rules and participatory practices will support set aims?
- What organizational format will best suit purposes and missions?
- What level of expertise and activity will the group require of its formal leadership? What managerial functions are needed? What aspects of leadership can the members-at-large provide for themselves?
- What are the group's built-in time requirements and/or limitations?
- What is the optimum group size for set purposes?
- What are the group's membership qualifications? What inclusion or exclusion criteria can be identified?
- What compositional aims and constraints should be taken into account? What level of group diversity is optimal?
- How will participants be selected, solicited, or accepted for group membership?
- What preparation, orientation, or special training will members re-

quire to maximize successful participation and satisfaction with the group experience?

- What, if any, individual adjunctive support or attention will members receive while participating as active group members?
- Once the group convenes, what tasks, processes, or topics will receive the focus of attention? Will the group work with impersonal concerns and topics? How much self-exposure and self-examination will be required?
- Will the group be person-oriented or task-oriented? Will the group focus on individual agendas or shared concerns?
- What level of exploration and depth of analysis will the group require to accomplish its work?
- What will be the group's temporal and spatial focus? For how long will the group meet in session and in what setting? Will the group be ongoing or time limited?
- As the group develops, what phases within the work can be identified, supported, reinforced, and specifically utilized in the service of collective aims?
- What individual tendencies, interactional proclivities, organizational structures, collective dynamics, and groupwide processes can be identified, built upon, and attended to in order to enhance individual progress and task fulfillment?

Organizational Format

Groups can be organized in a number of different formats chosen to match inherent purposes, aims, and task requirements. Various interventional strategies differ according to the selection of membership, the type of leadership mandated, the specificity of the treating regimen, the focus of attention, and the inherent ideology underlying collective efforts (Lieberman, 1990). Formats for addressing psychosocial concerns span from self-help, support, problem-oriented psychoeducation, training and process, to psychotherapy groups (Shaffer & Galinsky, 1974).

The level of expertise evident in these various collective facilitations ranges from leaderless self-help groups, to discussion groups with untrained facilitators, to paraprofessionals presiding within a supportive context. Professionals with special training in personality development, differential diagnosis, psychotherapy, and collective dynamics run process-oriented or clinically based groups. The more a group's aims move toward psychoeducation, training, or psychotherapeutics, the more likely a professional leader will be called upon as consultant, conductor, or teacher, or be regularly involved in the role of group therapist. Recognizable collective processes arise and transform within each conceivable group format. This book specifically addresses those combined endeavors that require formal expertise and an articulated, psychologically minded theory of practice (training, psychoeducation, and psychotherapy groups). See Table 1–1 for a comparison of the different types of groups.

Psychoeducational Groups

Psychoeducational groups usually work along a predetermined focal axis with a homogeneous population. The group's area of concentration can be a targeted problem, common concern, prevalent illness, psychiatric syndrome, life transition, situational crisis, or member-relevant theme. Psychoeducational interventions are facilitated by a diversity of professionals working in hospitals, mental health centers, child guidance clinics, and private practice. For example, Irizarry (1983) reports on hospital-based groups run by the nursing staff for obstetrical and cancer patients. Here, supportive and psychoeducational elements are incorporated within an active medical treatment regimen to address morale and to foster up-to-date care. Similarly, groups can be formed to help mental health patients cope with a variety of symptoms and syndromes, including depression, anxiety, anger, and relational difficulties.

A pure support group might resemble a social gathering. Members' affiliative proclivities are utilized to provide one another with advice or emotional bolstering in times of illness, isolation, trauma, life-cycle crisis, general confusion, or psychological distress. Professionally led efforts, however, often strive to include an educational and emotional processing component, taking advantage of the opportunity to instill knowledge and work through feelings about the phenomenology and personal impact of the targeted adversity.

Lieberman (1990) specifically contrasts the workings of self-help with professionally led groups. The self-help group tends to depend more on normal social exchange, empathy, and storytelling. Members talk about their own experiences, listen to each other, offer condolence and advice, while going through the problem or dilemma together, albeit often at different stages in the process. While perhaps fostering a philosophy of illness, no formal theory of psychopathology, diagnosis, or technical intervention is relied upon. The helpers and the helped are of the same ilk, prepared for their roles only by similar experiences and armed with varying interpersonal skills and differing bedside manners.

The professional group tends to be more directive and technically pitched, relying less on informal contacts and anecdotal exchanges than on the use of the collective format as a learning lab for teaching various skills, perspectives, and adaptive strategies. Informative didactic presentations are

TABLE 1-1 • Treatment Continuum

Type of Group	Self-Help	Support	Psychoeducational	Process	Psychotherapeutic
Function	Control Support Normalization	Holding Information exchange Socializing Support	Learning Adaptational development	Psychosocial insight	Amelioration Structural/characterological change Analysis Holding/containing
Derivatives	Anonymous groups Consciousness raising	Club-related Activities Discussion	Theme-centered Symptom-focused Issue/topic-driven Problem-centered Guidance Workshop Behavior change Industrial consultation	Training group Encounter Marathon Psychodrama Student study Human relations	Heterogeneous on-going Symptom-centered, ongoing (with time symptoms less of a focus)
Leadership	Peer	Peer/para or professional	Professional task leader	Professional facilitator	Mental health professional
Structure	Programmatic Habit formation Exercise/routine Discussion	Discussion Event oriented	Teaching/processing Didactics Exercise Discussion Lecture/lab format Seminar	Free flow Emergent developments and processes	Free flow Emergent themes and topics Recurrent/overdetermined problems and dynamics

Continued

11

TABLE 1-1 • Continued

Type of Group	Self-Help	Support	Psychoeducational	Process	Psychotherapeutic
Focus	Symptom/habit control Support Similar concerns	Support Social mingling Life transition	Issue/topic/problem understanding Mastery of symptom, diagnosis, life circumstance, demographics, milestone, critical incidence	Here-and-now interaction Group dynamics Part-whole analysis	Full spectrum of foci and dynamics (intrapsychic) (interpersonal) (group-as-a-whole)
Mechanism	Social confession Social control Social networking Social exposure	Social acceptance Social ventilation Social activation Social information exchange	Social learning Social adaptation	Psychosocial awareness	Psychosocial transformation
Time Frame	Ongoing	As needed	Short-term Time-determined Contracted	Time-limited Time-concentrated	Ongoing Contracted
Metaphor of Treatment	Religious Inspirational Indoctrination Illness Lifestyle	Familial Social animal Loss/recovery	School/academic Consumer education Emotional literacy Behavioral change	Evolutionary science Developmental Managerial	Medical Psychodynamic Interpersonal
Leader Role	Older sibling Task leader Fellow	Dutch uncle/aunt Discussion leader Emotional leader	Educator Topical expert Seminar leader Trainer	Facilitator Dynamic consultant	Psychotherapist (most other functions included)

often combined with more process-oriented interventions. The adjustable formula of how much information flows from the leader to members, in contrast to how much open exchange is built into the proceedings, determines how fixed, structured, or interactive the group will be. While still relying on a learning metaphor, the seminar format moves the group toward ready and mutual exchange. Exercises and focused discussions can also be introduced to highlight particular informational points and to facilitate critical skills, interactions, and behaviors. The leader, while still a central figure, provides structures that foster member-to-member exchange.

In psychoeducation, pathology is associated with being undereducated, ill-informed, or unprepared. Guidance groups, of a similar genre, assume that with rational counseling and direction, individuals will be able to function better with respect to numerous commonly faced dilemmas, such as childraising. The group aims to create a more enlightened context, which, as quickly as possible, is generalized to the home or work environment. Even in succinctly targeted and strictly programmed psychoeducational contexts, evolving group dynamics arise as a hindrance or a help.

Training Groups

Training or process groups with relatively open agendas and few set informational points or structured ground rules convene specifically for psychosocial analysis. Rather than offering a targeted, theme-centered, content-oriented focus, such groupings rely on the unimpeded evolution of collective processes and predictable incidence of emergent group dynamics. By concentrating on the here-and-now of the current process, members get to discover the regularities of their interpersonal styles, while coming to know the developing character of their group formations and collective memberships.

The process format is conducive to generic training in group membership that is relevant for other collective forums. The only preconceived homogeneity necessary for matriculation is a common willingness and the ability to participate. The phenomena under study are more diffuse and the resultant learning is more general than in psychoeducational groups. Recurrent topics, motifs, and focal conflicts do, however, spontaneously arise within the process (Whitaker & Lieberman, 1964). Particular affects and more pointed experiences may be elicited within an encounter group format or when transactional and communicational exercises are factored into the group protocol.

A significant component of a T-group or process model is the creation of a "cultural island" away from the preconceived role constraints of the outside society. Members come to the group as equal partners and naive participants. No one is really prepared ahead of time for what may emerge on site. The ongoing focus is on give-and-take interaction and observation, rather than on cure or amelioration of distress. Members are encouraged to work closely together without relying solely on an expert, teacher, or the provision of a predetermined emphasis or preprogrammed protocol. The group culture itself becomes the object of study. The formal leader functions more in an instructive, interpretive, and facilitative role by high-lighting emergent themes and interactions, helping the group with its self-analysis. In this context, the group-as-a-whole comes to recognize its collec-tive tendencies, whether facilitative or constrictive to the process.

Dual aims are studying the evolving organizational dynamics, on the one hand, while looking at individual reactivities and interpersonal skills and liabilities, on the other. Members learn what it takes to be an effective group member or even an emergent leader. They explore the tricky interface of maximizing personal authority while operating cooperatively within a collective setting. Participants are encouraged to reflect on how such in-creased facility and insight relate back to the effectiveness of the groupings from which they have come and to which they will shortly return.

Psychotherapy Groups

Psychotherapy groups are usually heterogeneously composed rather than limited in focus to single symptoms, conditions, or demographic groups. The evolving group process is specifically utilized as the context within which to address an array of problems, people, and issues reminis-cent of the diverse outside world. Those who apply to the mental health clinic, health maintenance organization, or private practitioner are treated with the dual aims of relieving personal distress while helping the individual function better in society.

The creation of a safe transitional space is critical to clinical care and recuperation (Winnicott, 1965). A holding environment is fostered wherein trust, continuity, and the establishment of enabling norms are encouraged so that the therapy group can progressively and safely work on deep issues of lasting personal import. Much of the treatment takes place around the group's boundaries and in the context of relationships to the other mem-bers, the therapist, and the group-as-a-whole. It is essential to foster and maintain closer boundaries than would be common in self-help, support, or even psychoeducational efforts. Everything occurring between members is considered group business, and outside group contacts are discouraged so as not to dilute within-session influences by creating uncontrollable group or subgroup dynamics. Yet, more flexibility is also needed than would be present in a strict process format. Increased individual attention is mandated by treatment goals which, by definition, are specific to the particular individual's idiosyncratic needs, particular vulnerabilities, and intrapsychic dynamics.

Traditional psychotherapy groups often work with recurrent and recalcitrant problems, expecting and encountering defense, resistance, acting out, positive and negative transference, and many ingrained problems of character, relation, and cultural malfeasance. Psychotherapy groups address symptoms and syndromes, as well as more diffuse difficulties in self-concept, object relations, ego strength, and adaptational strategy. Rather than dealing almost exclusively with morale (as in support groups), with isolation, competency, and skills acquisition (as in self-help and psychoeducational groups), or with social awareness (as in training groups), psychotherapy groups tackle the more ingrained "noxious and coercive elements of personality" (Balgopal, Ephross, & Vassil, 1986, p. 136).

Yalom (1970) identifies a prototypical set of curative factors present in group psychotherapy:

1. They resemble supportive functions such as the cultivation of altruism, universality, and belonging; the development of a group cohesion; the fostering of catharsis; and the instillation of hope.
2. Helpful components similar to those encouraged in psychoeducational groups include imparting information and developing socializing techniques.
3. Ameliorate factors reminiscent of processes present in training groups are the enhancement of imitative behavior and interpersonal learning.
4. Perhaps unique to a psychotherapy format, personal insight into etiology is fostered and the corrective recapitulation of primary family relations are transformed within the current group context.

Here, content and process are blended together in an ongoing stream of interaction and analysis. The psychotherapy collective becomes a ready peer group and a substitute family. Old patterns are encountered, explored, analyzed, and rechanneled in the service of lessening psychic pain and increasing adaptive functioning.

Time Determinants

Groups range from workshops, marathons, and single extended sessions to crisis interventions (1–5 sessions), short-term contracted courses of treatment (6–20 sessions), medium-length contracts (20–52 sessions), and long-term groups (over one year's duration). Kellerman (1979) writes of psychotherapy groups extending for as long as 10 years with each 2 years representing a generational cycle. Many of the clinical vignettes in this book are taken from four ongoing psychotherapy groups of 4, 6, 8, and 12 years duration. The two longest running groups have no original members. However, the group culture is preserved as the experiences of members, both past and present, are passed on to future generations. An ongoing group develops its norms over time and readily refers back to formative history in moments of crisis, confusion, or celebration. The invisible host of past members functions for the therapy group much in the way blood families rely on ancestors, roots, and lineage and the way the culture-at-large treats precursors, progenitors, and historical personages, both hero or villain.

Group therapy can be conducted in either an open-ended or time-limited fashion. In open-ended therapy, the group is begun with no fixed termination point in mind. Membership changes as clients drop out or graduate and as new participants matriculate to fill available spaces. Like many organizations, open-ended groups can completely change membership and/ or leadership and still continue to exist. The treatment setting often reflects on the longevity of the group. Clinics usually engage crisis and short-term groups, with the notable exception of continuing care programs for chronic populations. Social agencies and community organizations encourage fast turnover to accommodate the ever-pressing needs of other patients. Private practitioners tend to run long-term, open-ended groups as a matter of stability and profitability (Gans, 1990). Actually, the ambitiousness of goals ought to determine the length of the group experience. Focused psychoeducation or specific conflict-resolution groups can run their course in a relatively limited and defined space of time. Heterogeneous groups, formed to spur character change and provide a holding environment required to treat more severe and longstanding personality problems, require more flexibility and open-ended time parameters.

Long-term, ongoing groups operate in a psychological netherland of seemingly infinite time. Spans may occur between members' successively important life events. For example, a client may divorce, remarry, and have children in the course of his or her stay in group. Healthy individuals may become sick or disabled. Sick individuals may recover. Time may bring bounty or loss as members age together, passing through various phases of developmental growth and life transition. Traditional long-term treatments proceed as if time were, in fact, unlimited. Only at critical junctures of resource drain, changing priorities, or transitional crises do members become aware that they may be passing along or running out of the very medium through which the treatment proceeds.

By contrast, contracted, time-limited groups specifically make use of the limited time patients have together as the working medium. Such collective endeavors usually have beginning and ending points clearly specified so that natural existential and developmental processes are heightened and can be utilized as an inherent part of the therapy process. Because the time-limited group has a set temporal frame in which to accomplish its tasks, no illusion of infinite time is fostered. Rather, temporal parameters are continuously highlighted as the single most important variable influencing the treatment. The inherent anxiety and problems in beginning, sustaining, and ending the group must, by definition, be faced in short order. Time-determined therapy becomes enlivened from its very beginning and imbued with a certain tension and immediacy. Here, the ending takes on special significance as the affect around separation, loss, and independence is tangibly stimulated and therapeutically utilized in the course of treatment (Ettin, 1983).

Every group's procession mirrors the unfolding of the human life cycle from infancy, childhood, latency, adolescence, young adulthood, full maturity, old age, to death (Mills, 1964; Mann, Gibbard, & Hartman,1967). In contracted, time-limited groups, the collective most visibly moves through distinct stages together, from pregroup considerations to orientation ("forming") through rebellion and resolution ("storming" and "norming") on the way toward productive work ("performing") before reaching termination ("mourning" or "adjourning") (Tuckman, 1965; Tuckman & Jensen, 1977; Lacoursiere, 1980).

The affect and task requirements specifically associated with these natural passages can be built into group protocols to enhance the periodicity of the psychoeducational experience. In long-term, open-ended groups, distinct phase behavior is less linear and more pendular (Kellerman, 1979). Over time the group progresses and regresses, going in and out of equilibrium many times in succession. For example, the addition of new members to open-ended groups may spur a return to earlier processes and phases, as old members reexperience and reminisce, and as new members catch on and catch up.

Group Size

The size of any group will depend on what needs to be accomplished, by whom, in what period of time. Client demographics, such as age, will also influence how many clients can be accommodated. For example, the activity level and attention span of members of a children's group, moving around the room while playing out feelings, suggests fewer participants than a relatively sedentary adult group with superior ability to contain themselves, concentrate, think abstractly, and interact verbally.

The number of dyads possible in a group, as a measure of interactive potential, can be calculated by using the formula $1/2\, n\, (n - 1)$ (Osmond, Osmundsen, & Agel, 1974; Mann, 1990). A group of 4 would allow direct relations between 6 potential pairs, whereas a group of 8 would permit 28 separate dyadic configurations. The number of triads, quadrants, quintets and other subgroup innumerations makes the possible combination calculably larger. The addition of participants to a group geometrically increases the quantitative complexity of the proceedings. Significant size increases change the character and nature of the group by influencing the logistical potentials for interaction and intimacy as well as for isolation and withdrawal.

Very small groups of 2 to 4 may more resemble individual therapy, as members work in turn, often focusing specific attention on the therapist as helper. However, even in very small groups, collective dynamics are recognizable in dyads, triangles, and more complicated pairings. Since the potential number of dyadic configurations is limited, more constant pressure is put on the members and therapist to become directly involved by contributing material and more constantly interrelating (Cohen & Rice, 1985). Very small groups are also subject to the stress of attrition. An absent member or two for a larger group would be a disruption. Such an absence for a small group becomes a veritable existential crisis. The participants and the leader must decide how many members it actually takes to conduct a group session. What is the minimum group quorum?

Small groups of 5 to 9, the usual size of psychotherapy groups, allows for intimate relating of one to another. Such groups are small enough for members to be directly and actively involved or, alternately, to be more silent and vicariously related at various points in the proceedings. Group folklore has it that the optimum size for a small interactive group is 7 plus or minus 2 (in addition to a leader). It might be noted that many nontherapeutic groups such as cabinets, boards, and basic military units fall within this quantitative configuration. The basic unit of the Roman legion was 6 to 8, as are many commando groups, communist cells, and Mafia inner circles (Osmond, Osmundsen, & Agel, 1974, p. 180). This size allows both for a diversity of perspective and a division of labor to coexist with coordination of effort.

Midsize groups of 10 to 15 participants, often convened for training and workshop purposes, build in the potential for some closeness amidst the distance and anonymity necessary for conforming to a more impersonal didactic component and instructional learning format. Here, individuals become less prominent than the groupwide agenda. If a member or two leaves, the remaining group can more easily fill in around them and continue the process. Similarly, fragmentation is harder to prevent as personal needs are less adequately addressed. The group task must be sufficiently relevant and enveloping to hold the members in unison.

Median groups of 16 to 30 (Foulkes, 1975) are often used in milieu settings, such as day hospitals, where a whole community addresses its common problems (Rosie & Azim, 1990). Multiple facilitators may be involved as a way of evening out the leader-member ratio. When working with groups of 20, De Mare (1989, 1990) suggests that social context rather than primary relationships takes on increasing importance. The group culture itself arises as the most analyzable object in the room. Median groups move from family-like dynamics based on personal transference to more communal interactions based on subgroup dialogue and impersonal fellowship.

Large groups of 30 to 60 are convened as a standard exercise at human relations conferences. When a group gets to be this large, ambiguities abound. Tracking and containing all the forces present in the room becomes impossible, except by noting the conflicts between recognizable subgroups or by following the collective myths, images, and symbols that arise en masse. With less intimacy possible, more feelings of personal estrangement arise. With less certainty about procedures, more doubt and suspicion are engendered. Fantasy material often becomes a substitute for real-life relations. Massive regression and primitive psychic processes, including pronounced splitting, projecting, introjecting, displacing, mythologizing, and distorting, can be unleashed since it is impossible to really know everyone else's motivations (Main, 1985; De Mare, 1989). With added structure comes less anxiety, but also less potential for free exchange.

Very large groups of 100 or more reduce possible dialogue, as members speak to and are heard for their reactions to the larger system. A very large group can take on small-group dynamics as individuals become subgroup representatives, ambassadors, or negotiators, speaking to and for their larger constituencies. In a large group, members may be recognized more for their role than for their person.

Membership Criteria

Naturally occurring groups are often homogeneous in nature. People gravitate toward others with similar concerns or characteristics. Support, psychoeducational, and even analytically oriented groups may be formed based on similar demographics, developmental stages, symptoms, ego strengths, problems, life circumstances, converging diagnoses, or shared concerns. Depression, anxiety, borderline, or schizophrenic groups specifically address persons with equivalent psychological structures, common experiences, problems, and coping strategies. Such groupings are predicated on the assumption that individuals, at certain stages of life or in common predicaments, display developmental or situational similarities conducive to working in a combined treatment format.

For example, milestone groups can be organized to help children coming into adolescence, young adults about to leave home for the first time, mature individuals approaching middle-age or menopause, or older citizens soon to retire. Here again, the group combines a support-inducing climate that consists of others at a similar stage of life with a conscripted body of information offered as normative data for taking the uncertainty and confusion out of common passages (Sheehy, 1976; Levinson, Darrow, & Klein, 1978).

In every society, certain stressful life crises arise with some regularity. People experiencing divorce, single-parent problems, grief, or illness may be assembled together in a supportive exploratory forum. Stress-management groups may form to learn to cope with interferences to emotional stability or reactive physiology. Homogeneous groups are often more task-oriented, directive, and behaviorally focused than are more heterogeneous groups. They may also run for a shorter time. However, some support or theme-focused therapy groups are ongoing, especially as they serve severely dysfunctional or addictive populations.

Every group needs to be cohesive in order to accomplish its aims. Homogeneous groups have their identificatory focus built into the very purpose and structure of the gathering. The advantage is an easier way of relating, the ready exchange of pertinent experiences, the harnessing of collective influence in the service of self-control and personal enhancement, along with a support conducive sense of "Here I am." The disadvantage of such targeted groups is that the focus can become reified, the attention constricted, and the viewpoint doctrinaire, as the group locates its corpus of identity around encapsulated life circumstances, dysfunctional behaviors, or circumscribed sensitivities, thus proclaiming, "I am a single parent (a depressive, an alcoholic, an agoraphobic, a dysfunctional family member, an obsessive-compulsive, a senior citizen)."

Psychotherapy groups are often heterogeneous in composition, encompassing an array of problems, people, and issues. The advantage of such groupings is that members get practice in fitting in and negotiating amidst differences, contradictions, and uncertainties. Isolation is broken by ultimately finding out that "This, too, is me." Certainly, empathy bridges the narrow confines of "It takes one to know one." With time and in-depth exploration, superficial differences break down and deeper commonalities arise.

Nietzsche (1968) identified *truth* with the cultivation of a diversity of perspectives. The more points of view, styles of interaction, and basic emotions that can be expressed in a group, the more possibilities an individual has for restructuring self-concept and world view. Parts of the self that have been undeveloped, cut off, or underrepresented can emerge and grow by a member identifying with and learning from other members. The advantage of heterogeneous groups is just that ability to be expansive and consider the interlocking web of communications, transactions, transferences, and topical concerns that make up the human condition. The disadvantage of heterogeneous groups is that the focus is split, and so not as much specific attention can be spent on any one issue or task.

Client Selection

Not everyone off the street, on a waiting list, or in an overloaded clinician's caseload is appropriate for group therapy. Nor can the private practitioner form a group by merely convening his or her caseload. Thoughtful treatment planning requires thorough evaluation, selection, and preparation procedures. A successful psychoeducational or psychotherapy group begins with well-conceived selection decisions. Educated choices about group membership are especially important, since many individuals will be affected by each prospective member's group matriculation. Ill-advised decisions can be harmful to the individual client's progress while also adversely affecting the coalescence of a newly formed group. Similarly, an ongoing group can be unnecessarily impeded or may regress if an ill-suited newcomer is added.

Selection choices are not simple. Often those clients excluded are those who need and have the most to gain from a group experience. Reviewers of the group therapy literature (Rutan & Stone, 1984; Yalom, 1970; Francis, Clarkin, & Marachi, 1980) bemoan contradictory clinical claims and confusing conscription criteria. Further complicating the picture are the variety of potential group therapy experiences available across collective formats, therapeutic orientations, time parameters, and group compositional lines. A specific client may be quite suitable for a behavioral or homogeneous group meeting in a targeted, short-term contract but would "fail to thrive" given an open-ended, ongoing psychodynamic, or unstructured (Tavistock) experience.

Special client characteristics and potentials must "fit" the structural properties of the proposed treatment regimen. Selection criteria for relatively unstructured heterogeneous groups must be considered separately from requirements for focused homogeneous groups. Clients considered for such diverse ongoing groups must have the frustration tolerance, empathic sensitivity, ability for delayed gratification, and enough cognitive capacity to see connections and find meanings amidst the sometimes fragmented proceedings. Conversely, a homogeneous group can be cohesively built and specifically structured precisely along the fault line that might preempt participation in the free-for-all of the heterogeneous group. For example, a group experience can be arranged for psychotics, mentally retarded, psychopathic patients, or all those others with limited insight and extreme problems in relating or in social amenity. In either case, a client must be ready, able, and willing to participate in the particular group for which he or she is being considered.

Group Therapy Within a Treatment Plan

Group participation is a powerful form of treatment when properly timed and sequenced. Treatment planning consists of determining when and how a group might further therapeutic, training, or psychoeducational aims. Groups can be used as the sole treatment modality or can be added in after or during a course of individual work. The normal sequence is to provide some individual therapy, whether of an exploratory or preparatory nature, before accepting an individual into a group. Individual therapy may also be arranged coincidentally or even countersequentially in the face of an emergent crisis or when severe problems need immediate, personal, and direct individual therapeutic attention.

Oftentimes, group and individual therapy are used together as a potent combination that allows for more particular attention while providing an interpersonal forum closer in many ways to real life. In individual sessions, the member can explore idiosyncratic issues in depth before bringing them up in the group for further work. Individual therapy may suggest themes, topics, and dynamics to be specifically considered in group at a later time. In other instances, the group will stimulate reactions and engender conflicts that have yet to arise within the individual dyadic forum. Emergent feelings, thoughts, and memories can then be individually explored and subsequently taken back to the group for further collective processing. In either case, a fluid boundary between the two mediums is necessary to maximize the dual treatment format. Concurrent individual and group therapy can be with the same therapist (combined treatment) or with different therapists (conjoint treatment). In the later case, some coordination or at least consistency of outlook is necessary to avoid confusion, splitting, or cross purposes.

Temporal and Spatial Focus

A group's specific temporal or spatial focus follows directly from its general purposes and organizational format. Many choices are available to the facilitator and the group as various therapeutic dimensions can be differentially attended. The group works across a continuum of temporal possibilities. Attention can be focused on the discovery and analysis of past events, either recent or remote. Most psychotherapy groups return at some points in the process to the "then and there" formative determinants of current behaviors, styles, and attitudes. The group's activities can also be pitched more in the present moment, on the "here and now" of the collective experience, seeking to amplify and learn from current, observable relations and transactions. Training and process groups often rely almost exclusively on the stimulus and response of the ongoing group experience. Groups can also be a forum for anticipatory guidance and practice action, taking up a more "when and where" focus. The emphasis of psychoeducational and behavioral intervention groups is often on what can be done differently in the future. Roleplaying, shaping new expectations, cognitive behavior modification, creative visualization, fostering appropriate goals and wishes, and step-by-step skills enhancements and proscriptive devices lead toward generalizations to be applied within, after, and outside the formal group experience.

Similarly, the group may use life inside or outside the collective enclave as its material focus or relevant data points. Content drawn from participants' everyday experiences in work, love, or play may be brought to the group for discussion, understanding, and conflict resolution. Members seemingly say, "This is what's going on out there for me. Can you all sooth, figure out, support, or help me with this problem that I'm having with my boss (parent, child, partner, coworker, neighbor)?" Problem-centered groups often rely on bringing in outside experiences. The focus of the group can also be on the world specifically evolving and developing inside the group room. Here, the collective enterprise becomes a social microcosm for problems in relating. Nowhere is the potential for affective involvement and interpersonal learning so great as when members engage each other in the group.

In reality, some mix between in and out-of-group attentions may be necessary to mediate between immediacy and relevancy. Too much out-of-group material takes energy away from the present collective experience. Too much in-group focus makes the group less apparently responsive to outside, real-life concerns. Within an ongoing group, members have a need to know how others are actually doing "out there" in order to stay current, thereby informing the here-and-now process. In a psychodynamic approach, the group then works with affective reactions to the presented material in order to enliven these out-of-group concerns and transferentially work them through.

The therapeutic space takes on special significance as a circular matrix and sphere of influence. Within the boundaries, the group members get a respite from the outside world. The healing circle allows for exchange of pertinent material while providing a safe place for experiments in intimacy and collective endeavor. All told, the group becomes a predictable place to come together for work and play, a place to bring one's thoughts and emotions, and a holding environment for exploration and possible amelioration.

Seating arrangement also plays a part in how the group functions. On "The Bob Newhart Show," Dr. Hartley, in his role of group psychotherapist, was invited to present a talk at a group conference. His topic turned out to be the proper arrangement of office furniture. Consider, for a serious moment, the importance of the arrangement of chairs in the following example.

A community task force was organized to prevent development on a plot of wooded land. A public meeting was convened at a local church. In the meeting room, chairs were arranged within a small horseshoe in front of the room, with a larger auditorium-like row of seats lined up in the back. Those neighbors claiming chairs in the semi-circle ultimately held the seats of power, having the only authoritative voices in the meeting. Other equally interested and resourceful community members, relegated to the anonymous back rows functioned more as an audience. They raised questions but had no tangible impact on the ultimate decisions of the group. The chairs next to the leader often assume transferential and hierarchical significance and they are either sought or avoided, depending on the dynamics of certain members and particular groups.

Levels of Group Analysis

Once a group is formed and members take their seats, many transformations are set in motion. Personal concerns become social issues. Subjective responses are objectified within consensual realities. Private life becomes public living. The complex group experience can be considered on many different levels of analysis and meaning.

Each member brings his or her personality makeup and character structure to the group in the form of a host of familiar roles and styles; a basic temperament, sensitivity, and interpersonal skill; a certain intelligence, introspective ability, and ego strength; and a history of formative relations. All of these states and traits combine to make up the likely quality of participation of the person who steps lightly or brashly into the group room. Whatever the clinician's initial assessment of the individual's potential as a group member, the client also brings in his or her own preconceptions, along with a conglomeration of fears, hesitancies, excitements, and pockets of availability. Prior experiences in therapy, training, support, psychoeducational, family, society, job, or other real-life groups influence these predilections. The clinician ponders, "Can this individual benefit from group therapy?" Simultaneously, the member wonders, "Can I survive and meet my personal needs in this particular collective setting?"

As the group progresses, similarities and differences are uncovered in the interaction of dyads and in the forming of subgroups. Relationships are covertly mediated by budding transferences (you remind me of . . .); ongoing boundary negotiations (this is me, this is you); evolving interactional rules and customs (this is what we can and can't do here); and growing interdependencies (I need you to listen and affirm me, whereas you seem to crave my attention and solicitation). Members constantly evaluate, "Can I derive satisfaction from the other group members?" "Can I negotiate and learn from experiences in this interpersonal setting?" The therapist constantly reevaluates the mix, figuring how to help the individuals use their similarities and differences for personal gain and collective advance.

As the group itself evolves, a unified entity can be readily discerned by noting stated and unstated objectives, assessing overriding agendas and shared task behaviors, diagnosing collusive diversions, and observing emergent group roles and leadership patterns. Every collective develops its own level of cohesion and cooperation, based in part on the nature of arising conflicts and mediations, the successful or unsuccessful transition through phases and stages of development, the establishment of normative rules and procedures, and the attainment of secure and recognizable boundaries. Members come to refer to "we," "us," and "the group" as recognition and affirmation of the shared experience.

Emergent concerns are sometimes directly expressed within the group dialogue. Preoccupations may become evident indirectly as shared fantasies, group-inspired dreams, common images, and universal symbols. All forms of collective representation arise. The resultant group formation can also be characterized by its invested content, recurrent themes, evolving myths, practiced rituals, and growing cultural presence. The group-as-a-whole also takes on an affective dimension. Prevalent emotions, cathected positions, fluctuating mood states, and evident fusions and separations determine the imminent atmosphere or collective climate. The basic feeling tone or affective state of the gathering can be described at any point in time.

Group considerations also reflect on the cultural, historical, and linguistic levels of experience. Issues from time immemorial, including existential uncertainties and verities, as well as collective imperatives, are reexperienced and reenacted en masse. The group is, after all, a shared production of the ones among the many. Members ultimately use the collective format to discover transcendental truths—truths about themselves and each other, and truths about the human grouping process itself.

PART TWO

Foundations: History

When we examine the past, we realize through hindsight the wisdom of the ages, and can thereafter more knowledgeably direct our studies and practices through foresight. Many historical reviews begin with a throwaway line about Socrates' prototypical group efforts. These brief references to the philosopher suggested further study of the Platonic dialogues as dramatic records of group sessions in the making. In fact, Socrates' dialectical and interactive methods foreshadow a collective therapeutic approach based on analysis, insight, interpersonal interplay, and the coherent relationship between beliefs and actions. When he cajoled the citizenry of Athens, Socrates encouraged them to think for themselves by engaging them in the rational discourse necessary to fully consider human issues of universal importance (Chapter Two).

Two thousand years later, at the turn of the twentieth century, collective treatment again emerged as a logical exploratory context with the invention of modern group therapy. By serendipity, group treatment was found to be a viable psychoeducational procedure for the care and amelioration of somatic and morale problems. Early efforts often involved a distinctly didactic approach, with physicians enticing patients to learn proper medical and mental hygiene while working in ensemble to counter disillusion and social anomaly. As the theory of treating emotional, mental, and psychosomatic problems in a group format gained in exposure and popularity, a burgeoning literature on group psychotherapy, with distinct psychoanalytic influences, began to develop and mature. From 1906 to 1938, pioneers laid out, often in colorfully descriptive language, the basic rationale, parameters, and logistics of collective practice (Chapter Three).

The growth spurt of group psychotherapy in the decade from 1938 to 1948 extended the use of groups to include the treatment of diverse populations for a variety of problems. Treatment settings also expanded from hospitals to clinics to private practices. During this era of experimentation and popularization, creative facilitators fought the more conservative trends that denigrated group therapy as being the stepchild of individual treatment. It took the exponential advance of the group modality during World War II and the subsequent founding of two viable group therapy organizations as touchstones, to fully solidify, legitimize, and propagate collective treatments (Chapter Four). Questions posited in this section include:

- What are the formative ideas and social pressures that resulted in the development of group therapy?

Heritage by Nathan Cabot Hale (1967) (nickel silver, height 25″ × 5″). Collection, Hernon Art Institute, Indianapolis, Indiana. Walter J. Russell, photographer.

- *Who are the pioneers of the group modality, and what did they have to say about group organization and treatment?*
- *What can be learned about the advantages of group treatment from the profusion of group practices, curative factors, facilitative techniques, procedural norms, and therapy goals advanced in this inventive age?*
- *What practical suggestions about client selection, group composition, interventional contracting, size and frequency of meetings, and interface between individual and collective treatments can be considered valid today?*

CHAPTER TWO

Sitting in on Socrates' Walking Groups

Socrates often worked in groups. This intellectual progenitor of many of the western world's forms of thought, logic, and guided inquiry could be found daily in the Athenian Agora (marketplace) prodding, coaxing, and sifting through the collected citizenry. Socrates' dialectical and interactional methods expressly foreshadowed psychoeducation by focusing on specific themes of human importance. His technique also anticipated a psycho-therapeutic tradition vested in analysis, insight, self knowledge, and inter-personal interplay (Simon, 1978; Maranhao, 1986). Through challenging and fast-paced dialogues, Socrates wished to move with his contemporaries toward greater understandings, enhanced self-control, and a more exacting coherency between beliefs and actions (Halpern, 1963; Maslow, 1963). To do so, he invited others to join him in a searching alliance—a dynamic process and ongoing quest for the enduring principles underlying moral truth and rational living.

The Socratic method, in contrast to the more didactic approaches or the "influence peddling" of his day, did not intend to instill any particular conceptions of reality. Rather, it offered a way of coming together to con-tinually question and explore latent possibilities. Maranhao (1986) notes a similarity between "the Socratic consensus and the therapeutic rapport, [both of which] are . . . stratagems destined to keep the argument flowing towards a possibility of understanding, and not maneuvers to win over an interlocutor" (p. 188). The acquisition of understandings was never meant to reach bone-dry, intellectualized truths, but rather sought to enhance po-tentials for fluid behavioral change. Socrates believed that true belief had action potentials built in. Maslow (1963, p. 122), as noted by Yalom (1970), concurs. "I am convinced that knowledge and action are frequently synon-

Citations in the text from the Platonic dialogues are taken from E. Hamilton and H. Cairns (Eds.), *Plato: The Collected Dialogues* (Princeton, NJ: Bollingen Series LXXI, Princeton Uni-versity Press, 1985) and Penguin Classics Editions.

ymous, identical in the Socratic fashion. When we know fully and completely, suitable actions follow automatically and reflectively. Choices are then made without conflict, with full spontaneity.''

Although there is never a guarantee that the cultivation of different opinions will necessarily lead to new ways of being, engaging in active dialogue allows for new perspectives to be conceived and then be put into practice. The wished-for wisdom, in order to provide a stable resource, cannot be imposed or maintained from without. Truth and change must be coaxed forth naturally to become egosyntonic with one's personality, character, and style. The Socratic method represents a newly wrought model of learning—a basic change for the Greek sensibility—and a shift in the structuring of experience with many modern applications (Durkin, 1964). Rather than relying on mythos or *minesis* (the copying of preconceived realities), Socrates worked to establish *methexis* (a reorganization of categories of understanding conducive to the thoughtful integration of word and deed) (Maranhao, 1986).

Socrates himself resembled the master clinician who disdains writing but, by his work, sets standards of practice. Our most reliable knowledge of the philosopher and his method is wrought in the Platonic dialogues and in the reminiscences of Xenophon (1897, 1985), the general turned historian. For Plato, Socrates represented a sublime rationality, whereas for Xenophon, he was a most practical intelligence. Both chroniclers agree in their description of a tireless conversationalist ''who never wearied of discussing human topics'' (Dakyns, 1897, p. 5).

While decrying the mystery religions, Socrates credited Orphism and the teachings of Pythagoras with providing a model of life dedicated to philosophical inquiry and the improvement of the soul. The Pythagoreans sought to bring their lives and works into proper harmony, balancing warring opposites by attuning passion with reason and thought with action, thereby reconciling head, heart, and soul. Socrates emulated the Pythagorean's lifestyle—a daily, uninterrupted quest for wisdom, betterment, and the common good. Such personal discipline and consistency of character led both Plato and Xenophon to consider Socrates the best man of their time.

Socrates' daily discussions would likely have engaged those citizens within earshot and eyesight, as well as the more regular meandering members of the Socratic circle. Distinguishing between a crowd, to which one gives an exhibition, and a group, where one carries on a dialogue, Socrates sought the intimate and genuine involvement of the gathered participants. As represented in Plato's early dialogues *(Charminades, Laches, Lysis)*, a Socratic group could be quite interactive with the philosopher in the role of process manager as well as principal dialectician. Later dialogues find Socrates working more with individuals within the group, while never losing sight of the collective as an audience and a vicarious representational body.

Socrates has come to be viewed as an archetypal protagonist, the wraith of spirited inquiry. The prima facie of the philosopher is as recognizable today as it was in Athens during the fifth century B.C.

> *Across two thousand three hundred years we can yet see his ungainly figure, clad always in the same rumpled tunic, walking leisurely through the agora, undisturbed by the bedlam of politics, buttonholing his prey, gathering the young and the learned about him, luring them into some shady nook of the temple porticos, and asking them to define their terms. (Durant, 1954, p. 5)*

The pioneers of more modern group therapy certainly recognized Socrates' contributions as a stepping stone toward their discipline (Ettin, 1988a, 1989a). Moreno (1953) readily fell in with the Athenian's dramatic strides.

> *Socrates, in a curious way [is] the closest to being a pioneer of the psychodramatic format. His dialogues impressed me, not because of their content, but because they were presented as "reports" of actual sessions. . . . Socrates was involved with actual people, acting as their midwife and clarifier, very much like a modern psychodramatist would. . . . His audience became involved and the dialogue ended with a "dialectic catharsis." (pp. xxii–xxiii)*

Marsh (1935), also noting Socrates' antecedent footfalls, suggested:

> *Group therapy is not a new thing. The students who clustered about such ancients as Pythagoras, Socrates, Zoroaster . . . were partly seekers for knowledge, but they were also seekers for emotional help. Many of these early teachers conducted the so-called peripatetic schools, wherein the students walked about with the teacher as he taught . . . [making] a form of group therapy as well as a form of education. (p. 382)*

The Circumstance and Setting of Socratic Groupings

Legend has it that Chaerephon, a friend of Socrates, traveled to the Sanctuary of Apollo, set along the holy precipices of Delphi, to ask the Oracle if any man living was wiser than Socrates (Petrakos, 1977). The voice of the Pythia (priestess), speaking for the god, simply answered, "No one" (*Apology*, 21a). When told of this prophetic pronouncement, Socrates claimed puzzlement, since he felt no certainty about any of his beliefs and in fact considered himself ignorant about the world's most eminent eternal verities. Yet, he did hold with the common belief that a god can't lie. This paradox of divinely attributed wisdom and surely felt ignorance became the impetus for a lifelong search for stable truths.

Initially, Socrates sought to prove the god wrong by finding men among the polis of Athens who were wiser than he. To this end, he encountered all manner of men, from poets to politicians, from craftsmen to crafty sophists, from generals to the general public. In these groupings, Socrates found, to his chagrin, many pretenders to wisdom. He discovered that if he probed, he would inevitably discover inconsistencies and incoherencies in how men thought and acted. Even those he respected, like the craftsmen, did not seem to understand the nature of their arts, works, or words. By negating such men, he could affirm the god. Thus, with a touch of characteristic irony, Socrates concluded:

> *Well I am certainly wiser than this man. It is only too likely that neither of us has any knowledge to boast of; but he thinks he knows something which he does not know, whereas I am quite conscious of my ignorance. At any rate it seems that I am wiser than he is to this small extent, that I do not think that I know what I do not know.* (Apology, *21d)*

Neither discouraged nor disheartened, Socrates continued to search out those citizens with whom he might converse and whose knowledge he might test. His unabiding "interest was much . . . in the trading of ideas, and this pursuit took him to places where he might find individuals or groups ready and eager to talk" (Lang, 1978, p. 8). Both Plato and Xenophon spoke of the single-minded perseverance with which Socrates approached his pilgrimage or mission (*Apology,* 22a). Socrates "was always on public view; for early in the morning he used to go to the walkways and gymnasia, to appear in the agora as it filled up, and to be present wherever he would meet the most people" (Lang, 1978, p. 2, from Xenophon I.i.10).

Socrates' footsteps can be traced throughout the rolling terraced streets of the Agora, which lie at the base of the butt that houses the majesty of the sacred Acropolis. Spontaneous groupings were commenced: in the open streets and common areas of the Agora; at bankers' counters, merchants shops, and craftsmen's work spaces; in available crevices such as the orchestra pit of the theater where booksellers set their wares; and in and around a myriad of public buildings like the Stoa of Zeus, the Palestra of Taureas, the Lyceum, and the Thalos or common round house. On noted occasions, such as the celebrated Symposium, groups were held in conjunction with private dinner or drinking parties. Here, for instance, at the house of his friend, Agathon, on the Street of the Marble Workers, Socrates and seven others, including Aristophanes, the playwright, freely associated about love while lying on encircled dinner sofas that suspiciously resembled analytic couches (Lang, 1978).

Never leaving Athens, except on two military campaigns, Socrates spent his adult life walking the Agora—sometimes trailing along and exhorting passersby, sometimes leading an encouraging entourage, and sometimes being invited to sit and consider. Xenophon reported how on one such occasion, Socrates "chanced upon Aristarchus wearing the look of one who suffered from a fit of the 'sullens,' and thus accosted him. . . . You seem to have some trouble on your mind, Aristarchus; if so, you should share it with your friends. Perhaps together we might lighten the weight of it a little" (Dakyns, 1897, p. 70). On another instance Callias, upon seeing a looming and surrounded Socrates, entreated, "Would you like to make a regular circle . . . so that you can talk sitting down" (*Protagoras,* 317d). On a third occasion, Socrates described how a group formed spontaneously in the gymnasium. "Menexus looking in from his game court and seeing Ctesippus and me came to sit down with us, Lysis also followed at the right of his friend, and took a seat by his side. There came up, moreover, the rest of our party . . . a good sized group" (*Lysis,* 207b).

Such Socratic groupings often followed a fishbowl format, with interested onlookers craning to see and hear the ensuing dialogue. The larger group, as outlying audience, was critical to the societal setting of Socratic pursuit. Socrates explained the deeply personal and the public purpose of such open meetings. "I assure you, I pursue the argument chiefly for my own sake, and perhaps in some degree also for the sake of my other friends. For would you not say that the discovery of things as they truly are is a good common to all mankind" (*Charminades,* 166d). Socratic groupings were meant to foster forethought and ultimately to allow men to act well in consortium.

The mainstays of many of these groupings were prominent and precocious young adults who both actively participated and vicariously witnessed the questioning of their elders and betters. Socrates described his following: "A number of young men with wealthy fathers and plenty of leisure time have deliberately attached themselves to me because they enjoy hearing other people cross-examined. These often take me as their model" (*Apology,* 23c). While having no formal affiliation or organized tutorial with Socrates, his young *hetairos,* or associates, often presumed to informally imitate their master (Taylor, 1953). From his charge, it is understandable how the indictment of corrupting the youth might have readily arisen. In actuality, Socrates welcomed all and turned away no one from these groupings. "I have never set up as any man's teacher; but if anyone, young or old, is eager to hear me conversing and carrying out my private mission, I never grudge him the opportunity" (*Apology,* 33a).

Practicing a hands-on approach, himself, Socrates was particularly fond of meeting with and around the craftspeople. Just outside the boundary stones of the Agora lay the cobbler shop of Simon, where history has it that Socrates would often congregate with the aforementioned wise young men of the city. According to the writings of Diogenes Laertius, Simon took notes and wrote 33 so-called Cobbler's dialogues based on these Socratic discussions (Hicks,1925; Lang, 1978). Coming down to us is a letter to Simon from Aristippus of Cyrene, a follower of Socrates and the founding member of the Cyrenaic School, which praises the efforts of such august groupings.

> *I marvel and applaud, if being but a cobbler you were wise enough to persuade Socrates and the fairest, best born youths to sit with you— such youths as Alcibiades son of Clinias, Phaedrus the Myrrhinousian, and Euthydemus son of Glaucus—and men of affairs too, like Epistrates the Shieldbearer and Euryptolemus and the others. Indeed if Pericles were not involved in official duties and in war, he too would be with you. (Lang, 1978, pp.12–13)*

In the dangerous and unstable time of the Thirty Tyrants, when the Athenian democracy had been temporarily overthrown, Socrates was warned off from making muckraking debate. Critias threateningly ordered: "You had better be done with your shoemakers, carpenters, and coppersmiths. These must be pretty well trodden out at heel by this time, considering the circulation you have given them" (as reported by Xenophon, in Russell, 1964, p. 83). To this and other such entreaties, Socrates held his ground while following the Delphic proscription that the unexamined life is not worth living: "So long as I draw breath and have my faculties, I shall never stop practicing philosophy and exhorting you and elucidating the truth for everyone I meet . . . young or old, foreigner or fellow citizen" (*Apology,* 29d–30a).

Aristophanes, in Clouds, parodied Socrates' pace and intensity when he wrote, "You stalk along the streets, rolling your eyes, and endure, barefoot, many a hardship, and gaze up at us" (Hicks, 1925, p. 159). Surely the term *agoraphobia* must have originated as a fear of encountering this doggedly determined and clip-shod Socrates advancing along the cobblestones of the marketplace!

The Socratic Project for a Logical Psychology

With presence and persistence, Socrates ushered in a new era of rational discourse (Durkin, 1964). To comprehend fully the intent and implications of Socratic analysis, it is necessary to place the philosopher back within his own historical and intellectual context. The wizened teachers up to his time included the Homeric poets, the natural philosophers, and Socrates' sophist contemporaries. Each of these groups demonstrated differing objectives, manners of inquiry and disputation, and conclusions as to the matter of certainty. In his turn, Socrates borrowed from and contrasted himself with each of these conceptual and programmatic approaches.

The poets and rhapsodes of the Homeric narrative tradition (Ion) were sired by inspiration, succored by imitation, and schooled with lyrical license. To emulate the words of the poets was thought, at one time, to be the instructive path toward realizing the proper conduct of life and relationship. For Socrates, however, to imitate a written narrative or to rely on rote musings was to give up rational responsibility and pander to divine madness. Instead, he wished to find a more active, participatory, conscious, and reasonable route toward ethical and human understandings. Socrates did not believe that there should be any intermediaries, however inspired, between the seeker and the search.

Looking for a firmer basis on which to build his philosophical ediface, Socrates turned to the so-called physicists for epistemological distinctions. He quickly became disillusioned with natural philosophy, which took on a metaphysical bent while assuming metaphorical airs (Allen, 1966; Barnes, 1986; Shibles, 1971). In the firmament, as described by these physical philosophers, humankind was nowhere to be found. Thales expounded on water, Anaximenes on air, and Democritus on atoms as the primal materials underlying worldly matters. In Anaxagoras' concept of *Nous*, or Mind, Socrates thought he had found his ultimate guiding principle only to be disappointed by discovering a limited concept of a quasi-spiritual first cause, useless as an everyday working principle for guiding human endeavors. Rosenbaum (1978) points out that "Socrates, on the very day of his death, criticized Anaxagoras . . . for attempting to explain human and natural phenomena with the same principles" (p. 38). Yet the philosopher did adapt some of the physicists' questions and quests to his own devise. Relevant preSocratic concerns included the possibility of knowing ultimate essences, the reality and reliability of change and permanence, the relationship between parts and wholes, and the place of balance and harmony as regulating principles.

Socrates carried the quest for essences into the social sphere. Cicero makes much of Socrates' pragmatic intent and practical accessibility. "Socrates . . . was the first to call philosophy down from the sky and put her in cities, and bring her even into homes and compel her to inquire about life and ethics, and good and evil" (Plato, 1987a, p 15). Instead of looking for the metaphysical properties of matter, he sought moral patterns and ethical permanencies, as an enduring structure on which to base the conduct of life. Socrates disavowed Heraclitus' notion of a universe in constant flux and turmoil, rather patterning his thinking after Parmenides, who espoused that change was an illusion.

Adopting the idea of *logos*, or word/meaning/pattern, Socrates sought to bring changing particulars under the control of preeminent gener-alizations. Each human action might be judged against some abiding ethical principle. For example, the man who displays *arete,* or excellence in living, is the man who wisely grasps the logos or moral precept behind each in-stance or choice point and acts accordingly. Thus, practical virtuosity be-came equated with categorical understanding. Socrates held the view that no man would knowingly do wrong if he truly understood the implica-tions of his action. Misconduct and mental malady became equated with ignorance or mistaken belief, and philosophical insight, by definition, was considered ameliorative.

The curative process underlying Socratic inquiry involved clearing the mind of false assumptions and leaving it receptive for the imprint of real knowledge. Such a quest called for repeated and narrowed thrusts toward the pattern recognition of moral templates. Zeno's paradox of an arrow continually launched half way to its intended destination, ever approaching but never quite reaching, serves as apt allusion for Socrates' asymptotic efforts to hit upon such ultimate ethical truths. It was left to Plato to target specific essences like "the good" or "the just," thus firmly striking upon a penetrating theory of ideas, forms, and universal prototypes.

Like Empedocles before him, Socrates speculated about the mingling and separation of parts and wholes (Bakewell, 1907). Ultimately, Socrates believed that the whole was nothing more than the sum of its parts (*Theaetetus,* 205c-d). By helping the individual come to personal virtue, he aimed at providing for the security and productivity of the larger societal grouping. Morality in its most basic form was a cumulative notion. Socrates believed that the universe, at its best, was a rationally ordered structure, where each man had a set role and a function. Essential to individual pur-pose was cooperating so as to finely fit in and facilitate the workings of the group as a whole. Conversely, the larger group, to be representative of its constituency was required to make full and creative use of its participants. Again, Plato furthered these notions when he ascribed and reified a hier-archy of societal roles, tasks, and interactions in his manifesto, the *Re-public.*

In his more everyday meanderings along the Panathenaic Way, So-crates met up with itinerant teachers who also proved most interested in worldly affairs. In the wandering sophist who, unlike himself, commanded fees for instructing men in the rhetorical skills of argumentation, Socrates found a ready shadow figure and alterego. Sophistry flourished in the at-mosphere of democratic Athens, where men were called upon to protect their own interests and to defend themselves in the law courts. Socrates took vehement exception to the stated aims of such teaching, targeted toward persuasion and not toward truth. Since the skilled practitioner might easily argue either side of an issue without regard to true belief or verifiable knowledge, the sophist's art bespoke a cultural and epistemological relativism as well as a moral nihilism. For Protagoras held out against enduring values by making man the measure of all things. For the sophists, the search for truth was relegated to heuristics at best, and sculduggery at worst.

Socrates presumed a therapeutic metaphor when warning his young contemporaries not to be taken in by such rhetoric and false argumentation. "Beware of the 'peddlers of mental nourishment': some of them . . . may well be ignorant of whether what they sell is harmful or beneficial to the soul. And the analogy holds further true of their clients, unless one among them happens to be a 'physician with regard to the soul'" (*Protagoras,* 313d). Similarly, he chastised his protégé Hippocrates for not exercising sufficient caution in choosing a teacher.

> *If it were a case of putting your body into the hands of someone and risking the treatment's turning out beneficial or the reverse, you would ponder deeply whether to entrust it to him or not. . . . But when it comes to something which you value more highly than your body, namely your soul—something on whose beneficial or harmful treatment your whole welfare depends—you have not consulted any of us.* (Protagoras, *313a)*

While often maligned in his time, and comically branded by Aristophanes (Dover,1968) as a "cloud-cloned sophist," Socrates' ultimate aim was to find a better way to search out truth. He looked to find a method wherein the soul was vouchsafed, the psyche was vested, and the human vision was verified.

Principles of Socratic Analysis

Socrates believed that teaching and learning involved more than just inculcating values, convincing a listener, or instructing a disciple. Rather, active engagement in the process of inquiry became a necessary requirement of the Socratic method. To this end, Socrates invented *elenchus,* or the interactive dialectic method for soul and psyche searching by examination, back and forth argument, and logical inductive proof (Vlastos, 1983). Throughout the Platonic dialogues, Socrates specifically and critically contrasted this elenchenic process with *epideixis,* or a lecture/exposition/display designed to impress and sway an audience by discursive means and verbal flatteries. Likewise, he lambasted the practitioners of *eristics,* that heady concoction of verbal maneuvers and linguistic tricks forged solely to win arguments without regard to the truth value of assumed statements or positions. Socrates passionately argued against the kind of consensual reality won by hypnotic inducements, hysterical contagions, or affective appeals.

In counterdistinction to this sophistry, Socrates predicated his method on participants "saying what they really believe" and "refraining from making long speeches or monologues"—thus clearly identifying the cardinal sins of dialectical resistance: prevarication, circuitous argument, and monopolizing the discussion (Vlastos, 1983, p. 35). By insisting on such true opinion, concise response, and interpersonal interplay, the resultant philosophical inquiry took on an integrity of purpose, an economy of design, and a lively dynamic flow.

In any therapy or psychoeducational group, matters tend to organize into common concerns and topical foci. Members talk amongst themselves and shared issues categorically arise, which the leader identifies and amplifies. Members then inquire, disclose, and interact around these emergent foci at increasingly intimate levels of discourse. The group as a whole, by considering such common and universal themes, encourages each member to participate in and benefit from the wisdom of the collective. As each member freely gives input to the shared situation, a more encompassing and truer viewing is made possible. Each member first contributes to the forming of the wider view by offering up his variation of experience. The member then partakes of the pooled wisdom of the group by hearing other perspectives and reorganizing himself to take into account these more general and complete understandings. Such a reciprocal process is conducive to freeing up the individual's conceptual mechanisms, thereby allowing for a more flexible responsiveness (Ettin, 1985a, p. 23).

The elenchus proper was proceeded by just such an open discussion, which then led to a more formal comparison and analysis of viewpoints. Once particular instances of an ethical nature manifested and were identified, Socrates would challenge participants to come up with the quality that constituted their common denominator, essence, or *eidos*—that special trait that makes a thing that which it is. Thus, Socrates reminded Euthyphro of the general purpose of the inquiry.

> *Well then, do you recollect that what I urged you to do was not to tell me about one or two of these many pious actions, but to describe the actual feature that makes all pious actions pious?. . . . Then explain to me what this characteristic is in itself, so that by fixing my eyes upon it and using it as a pattern I may be able to describe any action, yours, or anyone else's, as pious if it corresponds to the pattern and impious if it doesn't.* (Euthyphro, *6d*)

Once a general definition was offered, Socrates would ask a series of questions, thereby repeatedly putting emergent views to the test of argumentation, implication, and logical challenge. Those beliefs that survived the tug and thrust of the *elenchus* would be further qualified and tempered in the search for coherency and a hierarchy of moral values.

In the course of the Socratic groupings, a variety of themes arose for such detailed consideration. Temperance, courage, virtue, friendship, intentionality, good living, love, wisdom, and piety, among other topics, made up the manifest content of the Platonic dialogues. According to Xenophon's reminiscences, self-mastery, brotherly affection, gratitude to parents, the meaning of work, and even the nature of madness were avidly discussed in Socratic conversation. Similarly, Simon transcribed Socratic dialogues on justice, honor, diligence, efficiency, pretentiousness, and the art of conversation (Diogenes Laertius, pp. 251–253).

Since these Socratic investigations concerned ethical and behavioral categories, inquiries involved much more than exercises in speculative philosophy. The insight gained through the dialectical process bore intimate relation to the happiness, adjustment, and self-control of its participants. Within the dialectical process, men were held accountable for their ideas and for their actions. They were expected to change for the better in view of new understandings. So conceived, Socrates' approach was suitable for examining real-life choices as well as eternal verities.

> *Thus elenchus has a double objective: to discover how every human being ought to live and to test that single human being that is doing the answering—to find out if he is living as one ought to live. This is a two-in-one operation. Socrates does not provide for two types of elenchus—a philosophical one, searching for truth about the good life, and a therapeutic one, searching out the answerer's own life in the hope of bringing him to the truth. There is one elenchus and it must do both jobs. (Vlastos, 1983, p. 37)*

Socrates' Leadership Style

By virtue of style and substance, Socrates qualifies as a charismatic leader (Rutan & Rice, 1981), being "inspiring, imposing, stimulating . . . [and having] a strong sense of mission" (Lieberman, Yalom, & Miles, 1973, p. 233). Alcibiades extolled, "The really wonderful thing about him is that he is like no other human being, living or dead. . . . Our friend here is so extraordinary, both in his person and in his conversation, that you will never be able to find anyone remotely resembling him either in antiquity or in the present generation" (*Symposium* 221c-d).

A mystique followed Socrates from birth. His father, the sculptor Sophroniscus, was told by an oracle to practice parental forbearance, letting his son take his own shape. "Let the boy do whatever comes into his mind, and do not restrain him but give him his head, not bothering him except to pray on his behalf to Zeus . . . and the Muses" (Lang, 1978, pp. 4–5). Socrates himself reported a personal *daimon,* or guide, that attended him since his youth. "I am subject to a divine and supernatural experience. . . . It began in my early childhood—a sort of voice which comes to me; and when it comes it always dissuades me from what I am proposing to do, and never urges me on" (*Apology,* 31d). Whether an allusion, auditory hallucination, or merely the voice of conscience, this open acknowledgment of a personal oracle no doubt added to his allure and authority.

Socrates also stood out as a living contradiction between physical ugliness and spiritual beauty, being alternately compared to a satyr and a saint (*Symposium*). His physical oddities are well documented—squat physique, considerable paunch, snub nose, bulging eyes, and thick and protruding lips. Peculiarities of demeanor and behavior are also noted—great endurance in talk, remarkable physical stamina and strength, and the ability to drink his mates under the table while still carrying on his sober dialectic. Socrates similarly demonstrated an almost hypnotic oblivion to climatic extremes, as he addressed the elements barefoot and scantily attired. More peculiar still were Socrates' cataleptic trances, where he would stop dead still in his tracks and remain thus transfixed for hours at a time, until just as suddenly resuming his normal rounds. Rumor had it that during these interludes, Socrates was either in active dialogue with his *daimon* or silently figuring upon some timeless question.

More consciously and more intentionally, Socrates assumed several metaphoric positions when working within his groupings. With the group as a whole, he followed his father and chipped away at the pretenses of the larger society—constantly flaking off staid assumptions while attempting to carve out a healthy disequilibrium. Socrates believed that he could best serve the public by creating such a "friction of minds employed in the joint pursuit of truth" (Taylor, 1953, p. 149). Ormont, a more modern-day Socratic-like provocateur, has spoken similarly when espousing that "therapy occurs at the level of resistance" (Ettin, 1985b, p. 1). The clinician is thereby required to work hard in order to maintain a slight and steady imbalance in the group, just the dissonance that holds forth potentials for change.

With this tactic in mind, and perhaps as a less conscious father transference, Socrates even sought to unsettle his ego ideals, the stone workers, those worthy imitators of divine prototype. He accosted them for complacency and lack of self-examination. "He used to express his astonishment that the sculptors of marble statues should take pains to make the block of marble into the perfect likeness of a man, and should take no pains about themselves lest they should turn out to be mere blocks, not men" (Diogenes

Laertius, p. 165 in Hicks, 1925). Changing the image slightly to a more molded casting of influence, Xenophon praised Socrates for his craftsman-like efforts. "Socrates gave a lifetime to the outpouring of his substance in the shape of the greatest benefits bestowed on all who cared to receive them" (p. 20).

Socrates' efforts were not always received so appreciatively. His groupwide role was often perceived as more pestilent than pedagogic. He was often shunned, abused, or avoided, just as one might ward off a gadfly that continually swarms and bites. Socrates acknowledged and embraced this less than flattering characterization of his persona. "God has specifically appointed me to this city as though it were a thoroughbred horse which because of its great size is inclined to be lazy and needs stimulation of some stinging fly . . . and all day long I never cease to settle here, there, and everywhere, rousing, persuading, reproving every one of you" (*Apology*, 30e). Elliot (1976), writing about active encounter group techniques, suggests that the "tradition of stirring people out of their prereflective complacency is as old as philosophy itself, but was first enunciated clearly by Socrates" (p. 56).

With the individual in the group, Socrates more followed his mother, the midwife, by pulling and pushing new conceptions to life.

> *Haven't you heard that my mother Phainarete was a good, sturdy midwife? . . . And have you heard that I practice the same profession? . . . Well, my midwifery has all the standard features, except that I practice it on men instead of women, and supervise the labour of their minds, not their bodies. And the most important aspect of my skill is the ability to apply every conceivable test to see whether the young man's mental offspring is illusory and false or viable and true. (*Theatetus, 148e–150c*)*

Whichever role Socrates chose to assume, he demonstrated a stimulating and eliciting effect on his fellow Athenians. Alcibiades gave witness to Socrates' more positive impact and influence.

> *Whereas we most of us pay little attention to the words of any other speaker, however accomplished, a speech by you or even a very indifferent report of what you have said stirs us to the depths and cast a spell over us, men and women and young lads alike. . . . Whenever I listen to him my heart beats faster than if I were in a religious frenzy, and tears run down my face, and I observe that numbers of other people have the same experience. (*Symposium, 215d–e*)*

Yet, Socrates seemingly rejected such idealized transferences and attributions of personal power by refusing to be paid as a professional teacher, and by consistently assuming an underdog position (Perls, 1969b). This stance was not merely an oracularly inspired, dramatic, or rhetorical ploy. Socrates knowingly took on the role of professor of ignorance in striking counterpoise to the more haughty sophists, and as a prerequisite to a search for knowledge that relied more on process than on person.

Meno had proposed a challenging paradox for just such an unenlightened seeker after knowledge (*Meno*). Simply put, how might a man come to know something about which he had no understanding? Socrates believed that the answer to this Sphinx-like riddle lay in the power of the investigatory process itself. "What is crucial to knowledge is that information has been acquired in the proper way, no less and no more" (Nehamas, 1985, p. 24). By actively avowing such unenlightened leadership, the Socratic group itself was induced toward *episteme,* or knowledge. In such a dialogic relationship, Socrates was not cast as expert/provider but rather became like the hierophants of old mystery religions, a participant/guide. He prodded and probed, led and followed with such constant and eliciting appeals as, "Do you believe this is true? Is it not possible? Can this possibly be?"

Socrates uttered constant warnings not to rely on him for answers. "You come to me as if I profess to know about the questions which I ask. . . . Whereas the fact is that I am inquiring with you into the truth of that which is advanced from time to time, just because I do not know" (*Charminades,* 165b). In describing the learning that takes place in therapy groups, from a systems theory perspective, Gray (1981) equates Socrates with the kind of teacher who understands that "learning is only possible if it is self-organizing, so the role of the teacher, then, is to share experience and understanding in such a way so that what he/she says will become organizing foci for a self-organizing process in the other" (p. 315). It was ultimately left up to the various participants in the dialogue to find truth within themselves. "The truth so 'learned' is reached by a personal 'discovery,' to which the 'learner' has simply been stimulated by his 'teacher,' and yet [the truth] is also 'recognized' as already implied in what the 'learner' has all along known" (Taylor, 1953, p. 149). Put into a more expressedly therapeutic context, The "Socratic philosopher could not persuade his interlocutor outright, the therapist, by the same token, does not argue with his client, he or she shows, indicates, but does not exhort" (Maranhao, 1986, p. 224). By so doing, the leader helps the group members attune to their own sensitivities while bringing out truths housed within their own learned organism.

However charismatic and influential, Socrates knowingly relinquished his personal authority in favor of this self-generation of truths. In Socrates' logical psychology, only such insight gained, tested, and tempered through the stringent dialectical process could assure consistency, responsible action, and *arete,* or right living. Socrates demonstrated his faith in the instrumentality of this *elenchus,* manned, as it were, by a mind newly honed with the power of logos and informed by the ability to make critical judgments.

Socrates' Therapeutic and Group Technique

Any group procedure is only as good as the adherence of its principals, and any psychoeducational regimen must handle inevitable resistances and process anomalies (Ettin, Vaughn, & Fiedler, 1987). An important part of Socratic *techne,* or skill or craft, was to understand, account for, and utilize those interactions that fell between the leader's intent and the members' reactivity. Socrates had to actively employ his wisdom, wit, and charisma to keep the *elenchenic* group moving and to protect the dialectic from derelict direction.

Socrates' knowledge of groups and his group management skills might be assessed by monitoring his metacognitions, the extent to which he recognized and made use of the evolving group process. In the *Lysis,* for example, Socrates provided a running commentary on his thoughts and decisions. As the discussion progressed, he became acutely aware that one of the group members was on the cut of a narcissistic injury, through embarrassment and premature exposure. Knowing this, Socrates decided to change direction. "I . . . was on the point of making a great blunder. . . . I then, wishing to relieve Menexenus, and charmed by the other's intelligence, turned to Lysis, and directed my discourse to him" (*Lysis,* 210e and 213d). Similarly, Socrates exercised his judgment and adjusted his tactics when Protagoras began to show hostility. "At this point I thought Protagoras was beginning to bristle, ready for a quarrel and preparing to do battle with his answers. Seeing this I became more cautious and proceeded gently with my questioning" (*Protagoras,* 333e).

Varied tactics with various protagonists produced a variety of results. With irony, humor, abrasion, obsequiousness, and feigning, Socrates could reduce his dialoguing partners to frustration, helplessness, outrage, and even negative transference. With understanding, kindness, encouragement, and courageous example, he could evoke creativity, joyful encounter, spirited inquiry, and positive transference. Both adverse and positive responses needed to be recognized and managed.

When members of his groups became dismayed, disillusioned, or resistant, Socrates might directly coax a response, sometimes with encouragement and sometimes with mockery; switch his thrust to a more available member; join the resistance with characteristic irony and profession of ignorance; appeal to the altruism of the participant by pointing up the vicarious needs of the group for edification; or, on at least one occasion, evoke the peer pressure of the group-as-a-whole by actually threatening to walk out of the room.

Socrates seemed to provide differential treatment, depending on the composition of his group. With the sophists, he could be brutally combative and noncompromising—treating them much as one might certain character disorder or sociopathic patients, with confrontation, peer pressure, shame inducement, and strict adherence to dialectical norms and boundaries. For example, when encountering the renowned sophist Gorgias and his pedantic student Polus, Socrates chastises the latter and entreats the former:

> *It is plain, Gorgias, that Polus is well equipped to make speeches, but he fails to accomplish what he promised. . . . For it is obvious from what Polus has said that he is much better versed in what is called rhetoric than in dialogue. . . . Would you be willing, Gorgias, to continue our present method of conversing by question and answer, postponing to some other occasion lengthy discourses. (Gorgias, 448d–449b)*

In another instance, when Protagoras also failed to provide short answers essential to the continuance of dialectical process, Socrates stood up to leave, only to be restrained by the members of the group at large. The heretofore less verbal members proceeded to talk out a conflict resolution amidst recognition of the competition between the two masters. Callias coaxed his fellows, "But it is not for us to be partisans of Socrates or of Protagoras. Let us implore them both alike not to break up the discussion in mid-career." Prodicus then intervened as task leader to reestablish cohesiveness and to reset positive norms for the ongoing engagement. "I add my plea, Protagoras and Socrates, that you should be reconciled. Let your conversation be a discussion, not a dispute. A discussion is carried on among friends with good will, but a dispute is between rivals and enemies. In this way our meeting will be best conducted." Hippias added his voice, further delineating the role and power of the group in resolving the conflict. "And so my request and my advice to you, Protagoras and Socrates, is to be reconciled, allowing us to act as mediators and bring you together in compromise" (*Protagoras,* 336e–338a). The group thereupon continued.

With young followers, who proved more responsive and less recalcitrant, Socrates was much more open and inviting—treating such participants as one might those going through a normal developmental transition, with a Dutch uncle's kindness and a gentle eliciting. In the *Phaedo,* Socrates sincerely invited exploration and questioning. "If you feel any difficulty about our discussion, don't hesitate to put forward your own views, and point out any way in which you think that my account could be improved; and by all means make use of my services too, if you think I can help at all to solve the difficulty'' (*Phaedo,* 84c). When Simmias took up this open invitation and protested a conclusion, Socrates responded by encouraging independent thinking and a deepened continuance of the discussion. "The fact is, Socrates, that on thinking it over . . . I feel that your theory has serious flaws in it. . . . 'Your feeling is very likely right, my dear boy,' said Socrates, 'but tell me where you think the flaws are''' (*Phaedo,* 85d-e).

At other times, Socrates was tested by having to manage a protégé's more positive feelings. In ancient Athens it was usual for an older and younger man to form a close relation in the mentor/novitiate mold. This companionship had realistic as well as transferential components, including the siphoning off of feelings from the actual father-son bond (Simon, 1978). Socrates received many such father transferences, as attested to by Crito at the the time of his master's impending execution. "For we felt just as though we were losing a father and should be orphans for the rest of our lives" (*Phaedo,* 116a).

While the acceptable boundaries of these friendships were clearly delineated by societal norms, the pressure to idealize and act out sexually often had to be faced and channeled. When the precocious Alcibiades tried to seduce him, Socrates had to find a way to rebuff and refocus these positive feelings. His chosen response recognized Alcibiades' affections, teased out his young follower's motivation, questioned his judgment, and encouraged a sublimation to higher values.

> *You must be a very sharp fellow, my dear Alcibiades, if what you say about me is true, and I really have a power which might help you to improve yourself. You must see in me a beauty which is incomparable and far superiour to your own physical good looks, and if, having made this discovery, you are trying to get a share of it by exchanging your beauty for mine, you obviously mean to get much the better of the bargain; you are trying to get true beauty in return for sham; in fact, what you are proposing is to exchange dross for gold. But look more closely, my good friend, and make quite sure that you are not mistaken in your estimate of my worth. A man's mental vision does not begin to be keen until his physical vision is past its prime, and you are far from having reached that point. (*Symposium, 218e-219a*)

Alcibiades reacted positively to Socrates' handling of his transferential feelings, with the ultimate result being the strengthening of the therapeutic alliance. Socrates' now humbled admirer revealed that of all men only Socrates had the power to make him face himself, feel shame, and question his indiscretions.

> *What do you suppose to have been my state of mind after that? On the one hand I realized that I had been slighted, but on the other I*

> *felt reverence for Socrates' character, his self-control and courage; I
> had met a man whose like for wisdom and fortitude I could never
> have expected to encounter. The result was that I could neither bring
> myself to be angry with him and tear myself away from his society,
> nor find a way of subduing him to my will. (*Symposium, *219d-e)*

Like most group therapists, Socrates was not always able to maintain
a positive alliance, nor could he resolve all the impasses that arose. He, too,
had to bear up under the stress of dropouts and premature terminations.
On one such occasion, Socrates lamented, "Either of their own accord, or
under the influence of others, they [followers] left me sooner than they
ought to" (*Theaetetus,* 150e).

Moreover, however, Phaedo attested to Socrates' group acumen and
staying power, by marveling at his master's ability to read and effect the
interpersonal climate.

> *I can assure you . . . that Socrates often astonished me, but I never
> admired him more than on this particular occasion. That he should
> have been ready with an answer was, I suppose, nothing unusual; but
> what impressed me was first, the pleasant, kindly, appreciative way in
> which he received the two boys' objections, then his quick recognition
> of how the turn of the discussion had affected us; and lastly the skill
> with which he healed our wounds, rallied our scattered forces, and
> encouraged us to join him in pursuing the inquiry. (*Phaedo, 88e–89a)*

Socrates led virtually thousands of group sessions, with multitudes of diverse participants, over many decades. Through personal providence and
persistent practice, he became an accomplished, albeit controversial, group
leader.

The *Laches:* A Demonstration Group

The *Laches* is an early Platonic dialogue thought to be one of the best representations of the actual process and technique of the Socratic groupings.
Here, Lysimachus and his son Aristides, and Melesias and his son Thucyd-
ides have just witnessed a public display of fighting with armor in the company of the famous generals Nicias and Laches. Desiring the best education
for their heirs, Lysimachus consults the military men about the value of
providing such instruction for their sons. Enter an evidently prowling Socrates. With his addition, a spontaneous grouping of seven forms up and
moves off into discussion.

Asked to assume the mantle of authority by providing expert advice about the question at hand, Socrates rather fosters a group interaction. In his first act of leadership, he chooses the role of process manager by setting a ground rule of open and honest participation. With characteristic Socratic evasiveness, he proffers:

> *I will endeavor to advise you, Lysimachus, as far as I can in this matter, and also in every way will comply with your wishes; but as I am younger and not so experienced, I think that I ought certainly to hear first what my elders have to say, and to learn of them, and if I have anything to add, then I may venture to give my opinion and advice to them as well as to you. Suppose, Nicias, that one or other of you begin. (181d)*

To this entreaty, Nicias and Laches, in turn, give contradictory opinions about the virtue of fighting in armor. Lysimachus then implores Socrates to cast a tie-breaking vote. Instead, Socrates challenges the notion of consensual truth, raising the discussion toward a higher notion of validity. "What Lysimachus, are you going to accept the opinion of the majority . . . because a good decision is based on knowledge and not on numbers" (184d-e). Once Socrates' objection to the process is noted and affirmed, he goes on to plunge the group deeper into discussion, while advising against premature closure. The philosopher suggests that an underlying question is yet to be uncovered and clarified. "But would there not arise a prior question. . . . I do not think that we have as yet decided what it is about which we are consulting" (185b). Socrates challenges the group to discover what basic end they wish to bring about in the youth, as prerequisite to deciding on its means of its attainment. In the course of the discussion, he comes to identify the collective's recurrent thematic concern, the inducement and nature of courage.

Now, taking more active and direct control of the process, Socrates challenges the participants to cite their own qualifications for being expert advisors on courage—what special experience or insight might they have about this subject. By so doing, the group assumes a less theoretical and a more intimate framing. Again, Socrates spurs interaction by imploring, "Make them tell you Lysimachus, and do not let them off" (187b). Lysimachus takes up the instruction, but when the argument comes to no practicable conclusions, he beseeches the generals to enter into dialectic alliance with Socrates: "Well then, if you have no objection, suppose that you take Socrates into partnership, and do you and he ask and answer one another's questions. . . . I hope you see fit to comply with our request" (187c-d).

Nicias, obviously acquainted with Socrates' style of inquiry, orients the less informed members of the group to expect an inherently personal inquest. He warns them that while the ensuing questions may appear hypothetical, each participant will, in fact, wind up exposing his own philosophies, feelings, and experiences.

> *Anyone who is close to Socrates and enters into conversation with him is liable to be drawn into an argument, and whatever subject he may start, he will be continually carried round and round by him, until at last he finds that he has to give an account both of his present and past life, and when he is once entangled, Socrates will not let him go until he has completely and thoroughly sifted him. (187e–188a)*

So saying, Nicias affirms his own willingness to take part in the process of inquiry.

> *Now I am used to his ways, and I know he will certainly do as I say, and also that I myself shall be the sufferer, for I am fond of his conversation. . . . To me, to be cross-examined by Socrates is neither unusual nor unpleasant. Indeed, I was fairly certain all along that where Socrates was, the subject of discussion would soon be ourselves, not our sons. (188b)*

Laches, a prideful man of action, also readily agrees to take an active part in the discussion. He seems undaunted by the personal aspects of the procedure, believing as he does in the Pythagorean tradition of harmonizing a man's words with his deeds.

Socrates now begins in earnest the task of defining the nature of courage. Clearly the views that emerge represent highly cathexted positions clung to with analyzable aspects of affect and character. Socrates refrains from examining the etiology of such beliefs (formal cause), but rather explores their logical implication, teleology, and final cause (Ettin, 1988b). The back and forth of the *elenchus* proceeds. Upon inquiry, Laches offers up a specific instance of courage in battle—the *behavior* of defending one's post by standing and fighting the enemy.

Socrates, at this point in the process, is interested in more general understandings. Demurely, he assumes responsibility for the insufficiency of Laches' answer. "I was to blame in having put the question badly, and this was the reason of your answering badly" (191c). Socrates clarifies his intent. "I was asking about courage . . . in general. . . . What is that common quality, which is the same in all cases . . . which includes all the various uses of the term"(192b). Laches catches on, and replies that the universal nature of courage is a special quality of *character*—"a sort of endurance of the soul" (pp. 192b-c). Socrates and Laches work their way through the implications of this belief. Socrates leads the general through a labyrinth of questions and answers and ultimately comes out showing inconsistencies in the proposed definition. Laches and Socrates further qualify the definition, and another dialectical exchange follows that likewise leads to a muddle of logical absurdities. The discussion reaches an *aporia,* or a state of confusion and helplessness.

Socrates recognizes that the proud and high-spirited Laches is becoming perplexed, sullen, and disheartened. In a brilliant metaphoric maneuver, Socrates allies with Laches' resistance and pushes him past the impasse.

> Socrates: *"Suppose, however, that we admit the principle of which we are speaking to a certain extent?*
> Laches: *"To what extent and what principle do you mean?"*
> Socrates: *"The principle of endurance. If you agree, we too must endure and persevere in the inquiry, and then courage will not laugh at our faintheartedness in searching for courage, which afterall may frequently be endurance. (193e–194a)*

Socrates realizes that, despite being assuaged, Laches could not now withstand further questioning. Catching him in continuing contradiction would surely lash at his pride and provoke a defensive counterattack. He decides, instead, to involve Nicias and thereby simultaneously continue and enrich the dialogue by switching participants and perspectives. "Come then, Nicias, and do what you can to help your friends, who are tossing on the waves of argument, and at the last gasp. You see our extremity, and may save us and also settle your own opinions, if you tell us what you think about courage" (194c).

Nicias readily takes up the group gauntlet and suggests that courage is actually a kind of *knowledge*—the wisdom of that which inspires fear or confidence. Again, Socrates orchestrates interaction, leading one member to address another. "Do you hear him Laches?" (194d). Clearly Laches does and seizes the opportunity to displace some of his frustration on Nicias, intimating that his now rivalrous peer is making strange and silly assertions. Socrates tries to avert a direct confrontation, holding to task by telling Laches forthwith: "Suppose that we instruct rather than abuse him" (195a). Nicias, however, is quick to retaliate by suggesting that since Laches has already spouted nonsense, he only seeks company in his folly and embarrassment. A heated exchange between the generals follows.

While continuing to foster dialogue, Socrates uses all his interpersonal skills to avert a premature end to the debate. He supports and confronts each in their turn. At one point Laches threatens to drop out of the discussion and testily challenges Socrates to question Nicias himself. With alacrity, Socrates firmly replies, "That is what I am going to do, my dear friend. Do not, however, suppose I shall let you out of the partnership, for I shall expect you to apply your mind, and join with me in the consideration of the question" (197e). Laches capitulates and gives up his resistance. "I will if you think I ought" (197e).

As this discussion nears its end, the group requests, again, that Socrates make a tutorial on courage. While declining, the philosopher suggests, instead, that they are all in need of further exploration and should find a way to continue these pursuits, for their own sakes as well as for that of their sons. For insight, wisdom, and change come from a willingness to engage in and continue an ongoing dialogic process in life as in group.

Last and Lasting Groups

Plato, in theory, and Socrates, in process, laid the groundwork for some of the more modern practices of Joseph Hersey Pratt, the founder of psychoeducation, and for the pioneers of psychoanalysis, Sigmund Freud and Carl Jung (Halpern, 1963; Simon, 1978; Maranhao, 1986; Stevens, 1982; Shelburne, 1988). Socrates might be considered the first "psyche" analyst, given his active concerns for matters of the soul, spirit, and mind. The philosopher even anticipated a "talking cure," when suggesting that "the cure of the soul . . . has to be effected by certain charms, and these charms are fair words" (*Charminades,* 157a).

Both Socrates and Freud began their treatment process with a free association based on the axiomatic belief in the necessity of self-examination. Socrates explained the process: "If a man has any feeling of what is due to himself he cannot let the thought which comes into his mind pass unheeded and unexamined" (*Charminades,* 173a). Both Socrates and Freud believed that knowledge thus gained could ultimately dispel psychic pathology. To this end, Socrates sought to bring hedonistic tendencies and untamed passions under the control of reasoned sublimation, by way of rational discourse. Likewise, Freud was intent on bringing id impulses under the enlightened reign of the conscious ego, by way of probes into the unconscious. In theory, both Socrates and Freud readily relinquished dogma and personal authority in favor of this insight-oriented, self-generation of truths. However, the personae and practices of both philosopher and psychoanalyst, to an extent, occluded such methodological innocence.

Differences between Socrates and Freud might be understood, in part, as due to the state of mind encountered in their respective historical epochs. The philosopher came along during a progressive evolutionary age, new to conscious consideration and rational thinking (Jaynes, 1976), a time of moving from a mimetic oral culture to a literate and logical legacy. Socrates' system, by historical necessity, overrelied on cognitive considerations. Freud, by contrast, came along at a time of obsessive intellectualizations, where highly developed rituals and reasons often obfuscated underlying affective realities. For Freud, working in the Victorian era required a methodology that allowed for a regression from the logical and literate back to a more oral, primitive, affectively inspired mind.

Pratt (1934) writing of the intimate interplay between logic and emotion, cites Plato's parable about how

> *the chariot of life was drawn by the white horse of reason and the black horse of passion. If the black brute gets out of control trouble results and the chariot will be dragged off the road. This is what happens to the psychoneurotic . . . [the understanding that] nervous disorders are due to abnormal states of feeling has led to successful treatment by suggestion, persuasion and reeducation (p. 10).*

Wilson (1969), also working in a psychoeducational group context, warns of too excessive a tendency toward heady argument.

> *One can easily conjure up the picture of an interesting but exclusively cerebral group functioning along the lines of Plato's* Symposium, *given to all sorts of intellectual legerdemain, with the leader comfortably ensconced in the role of Socrates. This obvious pitfall has to be carefully avoided from the onset. However, to my surprise, I soon discovered that the group itself is very quick to raise objections when a session begins to take on this complexion; there are immediate complaints that "There wasn't enough going on—we just sat around discussing things." (*Ruitenbeek, 1969, p. 274).

Stereotype aside, Socrates' groups were anything but dry discourse. Even in the course of the *Symposium,* Alcibiades broke through Agathon's doorway drunk, and interrupted the group's orderly panegyrics on love, thereby creating a new and challenging group dynamic. It is certainly true, however, that in psychoeducation or psychotherapy groups, the twin steeds of emotion and reason, gut and head, process and processing, unconscious and conscious, and mythos and logos must always be coaxed on together. The group setting, with its unbridled affects and varied perspectives, allows for a bridging and harnessing of many of the dualities of human nature— often in the form of conjoining experiences and collective meanings.

The search for ultimate, general, or universal patterns, practiced by Socrates and concretized in Plato's theory of ideas, anticipated Jung's more transcendental notions. Jung openly credited Plato with preconceiving of archetypes as "active living dispositions, ideas in the Platonic sense, that preform and continually influence our thoughts and feelings and actions" (Jung, 1960). Unlike Plato, however, both Socrates and Jung remained equivocal about whether the forms they sought were a priori metaphysical

concepts reanimated through remembrance and participation in the netherland of a collective unconscious (Shelburne, 1988), or rather prototypical
human structures brought to life by existential expediency. In either case,
Jung speculated about the way in which the archetype configured the individual while Socrates and Plato wondered at how the individual imitated
and participated in the ideal.

For Jung, experiences of deep meaning, whether personal, cultural,
or archetypal, became available as visualizable images, symbols, or myths.
When plumbing the depths and heights of the psyche, attention to preconscious contents took precedence over considerations of more conscious
processes. Jung essentially returned to a preSocratic view of reality and
human affairs. Snell (1982), for example, relates how, like Jung and Empedocles, "Heraclitus also wants to penetrate to an invisible core, to a reality which needs to be uncovered. . . . The truth which Heraclitus has set
himself to unveil cannot be expressed in any other way except through an
image. Heraclitus shows us the meaning of the 'necessary metaphor''' (p.
220). So conjured, Thales' "water" might take on significance as an underlying psychological symbol for the unconscious basis of life. Similarly, An-
aximes' "air" could represent the basic human need for inspiration. In a
Jungian model, mythos rather than logos once again gains supremacy.

While speculating widely on the place of the individual in society and
the relationship between individual problems and more common concerns,
neither Freud nor Jung ran groups in their clinical practices (Illing, 1957;
Kanzer, 1983). In fact, these early practitioners believed that psychoanalysis
should be carried on in a seemingly secluded and private setting. In contrast, Socrates engaged in a fully public process. He did not believe that
insight and excellence in living could or should be achieved in isolation. For
Socrates, the very act of reasoning "had its origin in people's practice of
meeting together to reason on matters" (Bakewell, 1897, p. 95 from Xenophon IV, 5, 12). Personal improvement demanded the stimulation of many
minds working in concert to uncover what is particular to some and common to all. Coming to personal and social understandings was in prelude
to enacting these insights in one's public life.

Such inquiry into the relation between the specific and the general,
the part and the whole, the particular and the universal, the person and his
or her society bears intimate relevance to the work of group psychotherapy.
Aristotle suggested that Socrates' two most distinctive contributions to the
science of inquiry were the employment of inductive arguments and the
formulation of universal definitions (Copleston, 1985, p. 3). Group psychotherapy, at its simplest, represents an epistemologically inductive process wherein the therapist helps the group members compare their experiences, derive helpful generalizations, and thereupon adopt more
enlightened and adaptive particularizations.

Socrates, and Plato after him, took the relationship between the individual and the group even further, believing that one's inherent function or essence might only be appreciated deductively, according to how one fits into the larger culture. Scheidlinger (1952) points out, "To Plato, the ideal state, cast on the model of the individual soul, became the basic condition for the development of man toward perfection" (p. 3). Moral knowledge and ultimate happiness came down to knowing and acting in accordance with both one's self and one's setting. Thus, the interrelationship of the individual and the group was crucial to both the means and the ends of Socratic pursuits.

Even on his last days, awaiting the fatal dose of hemlock, Socrates was surrounded by a group and engaged in dialectical group process. "The picture in the Phaedo is of Socrates' friends gathered together with him in the prison on the last day of his life. The group was rather large; fourteen are mentioned by name and 'some others' passed over anonymously may have brought the total up to eighteen" (Lang, 1978, p. 26). Through question, answer, and discussion, this terminating session sought to bring conclusion a life of inquiry and to reconcile reluctant and mournful followers to the now inevitable fate of their leader's leave taking.

CHAPTER THREE

The Invention of Modern Group Treatment at the Turn of the Twentieth Century

The consensus among historians of psychotherapy (Thomas, 1943; Corsini, 1955; Dreikurs, 1959; Rosenbaum, 1978; Shapiro, 1978; Sadock & Kaplan, 1983; Rutan & Stone, 1984; Lubin & Lubin, 1987) is that group psychotherapy literature began formally in 1906 with the publication of Joseph Hersey Pratt's "The 'Home Sanatorium' Treatment of Consumption." Over the next 25 years, clinicians working in clinics, hospitals, and private practice experimented with and wrote about the theory and technique of group psychotherapeutics. It is an enlightening exercise to go back and read these pioneering works. By so doing, the root concepts of a burgeoning theory and the basic logistics of a formalized practice are revealed.

These early works tell us much about the purposes and possibilities of the psychoeducational and psychotherapeutic groups. The pioneers, in presenting their approaches, explicate curative factors and therapy goals; group size; composition and membership criteria; the length, frequency, and structure of meetings; the interface between individual and group treatment; and the techniques and role of the leader. (See the Appendix at the end of this chapter.) Such practical advice from the near past can certainly inform our more modern pursuits.

This chapter reviews the written works of some of the inventors of group psychotherapy over its first quarter century, with an eye toward practical application. The writings of the psychoeducators—Joseph Hersey Pratt (1906, 1907, 1908, 1922, 1934, 1945), Edward Lazell (1921, 1930), and Cody Marsh (1931, 1933, 1935)—who used the group for medical and mental education, and the therapeutic endeavors of the early analysts—

An earlier version of this chapter appeared the *International Journal of Group Psychotherapy,* 38 (2), 139–167, Copyright 1988. Reprinted with permission of the American Group Psychotherapy Association.

Sigmund Freud (1922) (in theory), Alfred Adler, Rudolf Dreikurs (1956, 1959), and Trigant Burrow (1927, 1928)—who used the group for intrapsychic and interpersonal analysis, are reviewed. In summarizing these seminal works, an attempt is made to convey the substance, spirit, and flavor of these early writings.

The Psychoeducators

Joseph Hersey Pratt

Joseph Hersey Pratt is often credited with being the father of group therapy. If so, the pregnancy was unplanned. Pratt, an internist from Boston, began working with groups of tuberculosis patients in 1905 in an attempt to indoctrinate them into following the rigorous disciplines of home hygienic care. As with many other scientific discoveries, Pratt (1922) indirectly came to realize the potential of groups for the treatment of medical, psychosomatic, and psychoneurotic problems:

> *I originally brought the patients together as a group simply with the idea that it would save my time, that of my associate and of the social worker. It was planned as a labor saving device. I did not have the time to instruct or encourage the patients individually. Advice, encouragement or admonition given to one I hoped would be heeded by all. (p. 403)*

Initially, Pratt held "health classes" in Emmanuel Church in Boston and was apparently influenced by the psychological and religious leanings of the theologians Elwood Worcester and Samuel McComb. This connection led Pratt's early work to be deemed the "repressive-inspirational class method."

At first, Pratt denied that psychological factors, such as the group influences or his own dynamic personality, accounted for the improvement of his patients. However, it is clear from later publications that he came to realize that the class itself was an important part of the treatment regimen. Pratt (1922) described the essentials of the tuberculosis class:

> *The weekly meeting is the distinctive feature of the class system. A fine spirit of camaraderie has been developed. They never discuss their symptoms, and are almost invariably in good spirits. Frequently our graduates drop in at the meeting to get weighed and to greet their old associates. . . . The favorable cases that are making rapid progress toward recovery infuse a spirit of hope in all. . . . I usually give the*

class as a whole, some advice or encouragement during the meeting, but such talk is always short, never more than two or three minutes in length. (pp. 403–404)

Pratt's early class method induced such ameliorative collective variables as cohesion and belonging, the power of positive identification, while establishing a supportive climate conducive to the exchange of information and encouragement. Groups had a maximum of 15 to 20 patients and were homogeneous for disease and heterogeneous for demographics, character, and social status. To lessen early resistance and assure compliance, matriculation was made dependent on the acceptance of strict group rules and norms. "Before admission to the class is granted the applicant must promise to give up all work, to live the out-of-door life, and to obey all the rules of the class" (1906, pp. 211–212).

The actual group process utilized patient testimonials much as Alcoholics Anonymous groups were later to do. "If a candidate for membership is present, one of the 'star' patients is frequer ly asked to tell what the rest treatment has done for him, and usually he bears testimony to the value of rest with an enthusiasm that exerts a powerful influence on the newcomer" (1922, p. 404).

Pratt (1922) proudly wrote of the applicability of class treatment for other medical patients; groups were begun for undernourished children in 1908, diabetics and cardiac patients in 1915, and obesity patients in 1922. In 1930, Pratt established a clinic in Boston for the treatment of psychosomatic illnesses, and subsequent writings (1934) took a sharp turn toward treating the emotional causes of physical and psychoneurotic disorders. He now actively explained how the idea that "nervous disorders are due to abnormal states of feeling has led to successful treatment by suggestion, persuasion and reeducation" (1934, p. 10). Pratt began to espouse a distinctive psychotherapeutic approach advising that, "unless the patient's state of mind improved, the therapeutic results were far from satisfactory. . . .In order to cure patients suffering from functional nervous disorders, the first and most important thing was to get hold of their morale, in other words, to practice psychotherapy" (Pratt, 1945, p. 85).

The class for treating disorders of psychic origin was named the "Thought Control Class" by one of its members. Pratt explained the novelty of this program where "psychotherapy is given not to individual patients but to a group" (1934, p. 11). Hour-long meetings were held with an initial five-session contract requested. The dropout rate after the first meeting was 45 percent. Assigned seating based on attendance, old members paired with new members, initial deep muscle relaxation, imagery exercises, a 10- or 15-minute orientation talk by the group leader, and patient testimonials made up the process of the group class. Individual therapy complemented the group treatment.

Pratt's last article, published in 1945, represents the full maturing of his thoughts about group therapy. Of 500 cases referred to the Medical Clinic of the Boston Dispensary, over 30 percent were diagnosed as functional nervous disorders. All such cases were referred to thought control classes.

Pratt summarized his group efforts by saying, "Patients in the class have usually recovered more quickly than have my private patients. This I attribute to hope of recovery awakened by being in the presence of those who were sick and now are well, and secondly to faith in the class and its methods as well as in the directing physician" (1945, p. 91).

Although Pratt's paternity of group therapy may have been accidental, he did help initiate and guide this fledgling treatment modality toward its psychological maturity.

Edward Lazell

A psychiatrist working at St. Elizabeth's Hospital in Washington, DC, Edward Lazell believed that institutions should provide patients with more than just custodial care. In 1920, Lazell reported on a didactic group method, based on psychoanalytic principles, actually begun prior to World War I. Informally known as the "Etiology Spiel," this group-lecture method sought to reeducate patients suffering from dementia praecox and manic depression.

Lazell believed that certain universalities of experience could be addressed in a group format.

Every psychoanalyst recognizes that the problems of the patient are individual ones, specific to the patient. But it is not the nature of the problem that varies, it is the coloring matter, the stage setting as one might call it. There are certain groups of facts that might be given to such patients in lecture form. . . . The nuclear conflict, the Oedipus problem, and the problems of sexual development are the basis of them all. (1921, pp. 169–170)

The topics of the 1921 talks and their representative developmental issues included:

Talk	Topic	Developmental Issues
1	The fear of death	Confusion
2	Conflict	Regression
3	Reactivation of emotion	Reactivation of infantile wish fulfillment

Continued

Talk	Topic	Developmental Issues
4	Common hallucinations	Ego-ideal correction
5	Masturbation	Narcissism
6	Self-love	Substitution or sublimation of narcissism
7	Homosexuality	Homosexuality
8	Inferiority	Rationalization of inferiority
9	Usual causes of flight from women	Projection of inferiority rationalization
10	Overcompensation for inferiority	Overcompensation
11	Explanation of hallucinations and delusions	Conscience and infantile wish
12	Daydreaming	Constructive activity

Initially working within a Freudian paradigm, Lazell (1921) wrote of the "submissive homoerotic fears" stirred by individual psychotherapy. He cited the specific advantages of a group methodology. In the structured collective setting, the fear generated by an exclusive relationship with the analyst was greatly reduced. A normalization process ensued as patients realized that others also feared death and ruminated about sex. This lessened their own feelings of guilt, shame, and difference. Lazell found that many severely disturbed patients who were believed to be inaccessible to treatment heard and retained much of the material, despite fantasizing or talking to themselves through the whole of the lecture. He observed that patients discussed the presented material with one another for some time after the talks, which increased socialization and helped in the assimilation of the material. Lazell added that many patients developed a more positive "transfer" to the leader and later asked for individual assistance.

Treatment began by taking an individual diagnostic history. Early groups were composed homogeneously, initially by symptoms, and then by etiological categories. In the group, lecture material was presented simply, using repetition and review to emphasize important psychological information. Lazell realized that the talks might initially stimulate regression and agitation but argued that "these episodes are constructive, since their occurrence shows that the lecture has touched the vital spot, the patient's problem, and that he will emerge from the conflict on a higher level" (1921, p. 175).

The sequence of talks was meant to recapitulate and work through concerns particular to the normal stages of human development. Anticipating later developments in psychoanalysis and ego psychology, Lazell stated,

"The patient who recovers with insight and really conquers himself passes through the stages of development the libido originally should have passed through" (1921, p. 170).

In a 1930 article, Lazell reported that he had expanded from using 12 to 30 lectures and had moved from a strictly Freudian to a more Jungian perspective. Material pertaining to mythology, totemism, and other archetypal themes demonstrated Lazell's belief in the universal substrate of human experience. Lazell professed a holistic body-mind concept of mental illness. He began leading other homogeneously and heterogeneously composed classes. Groups for patients suffering from extreme hyperthyroidism were organized around Cannon's (1920) work on the physical effects of emotion. A more heterogeneous class group composed of patients with mild *dementia praecox,* anxiety neurosis, hysteria, neurasthenia, and psychasthenia was facilitated. Also reported was a class for service-connected epilepsy. These latter lectures were given once a week with the full series taking six to eight months to complete. Lazell reported better results with patients who stayed longer and experienced more of the lecture sequence.

Lazell summarized his work by stating:

> *It is not contended that the group method should supplant individual psychoanalysis, nor that the lectures as outlined are all that could be wished. . . . It is hoped that this work will be taken up by other psychotherapists working in hospitals where the group method is possible and the results reported so that some statistics may eventually be gathered. The writer feels that the group method in the hands of competent psychotherapists of the psychoanalytic type will prove a great advance over the methods now in use. (1921, p. 179)*

Cody Marsh

As early as 1909, Cody Marsh, a cousin of "Buffalo Bill" Cody, and a former minister turned psychiatrist, began giving academic and inspirational group lectures to psychiatric patients. The experience of serving as a morale officer during World War I in an American hospital in Vladivstok, Siberia, further reinforced Marsh's proclivity toward active encouragement of the weak and weary. In 1931, Marsh first wrote of his large-group and intensive class work at Kings Park State Hospital on Long Island. There, he attempted to utilize the theoretical notions of Freud, Le Bon, and McDougall, as well as the psychoeducational methods of Lazell, to stimulate group emotion and to encourage a more active and involved adjustment for the hospital's largely psychotic population. Yet, contrasting himself to Lazell, Marsh gave more weight to the process of the group class than to the specific content of the lectures.

Lazell seems to be solely concerned with selling a program of mental hygiene, for he makes much of the lecture material and includes in his class patients with but one diagnosis. Personally, I am less interested in the lecture material. . . . The aim is to extrovert all energies at the social level. The patient passes through a psychological revival meeting, where he is converted from introspection, phantasy, bitterness, shame, inferiority. . . . to extrospection, constructive planning, cheerfulness, assurance, security. . . . In short, I do not think it makes a particle of difference what the subject is, so long as it is instructive and constructive and can be given an inspirational polish. (1931, pp. 341 & 334)

While obviously drawing on revivalist techniques, Marsh disclaimed religious objectives. Rather, he traced the philosophical roots of his approach to the "walking groups" conducted by Pythagoras, Socrates, and Zoroaster.

Marsh subsequently moved to Worcester State Hospital, where he was given "carte blanche to use group methods wherever . . . they might be indicated" (1933, p. 396). There he organized a myriad of "social-educational-industrial" groups for hospital personnel, patients, and the community-at-large, including discussion groups on each ward. Recognizing the power of the aggregate and recommending a "milieu therapy," Marsh professed, "I suppose every psychiatrist is tempted to some one generalization to explain mental disease. The Freudians lean to sex as such an explanation. I lean to a social-emotional explanation, and beg to quote . . . the motto on my psychiatric shield: By the crowd they have been broken, by the crowd they shall be healed" (1933, pp. 406–407).

Marsh lobbied for medical training to include group work and he rotated interns through the wards as discussion leaders. While expressly interested in stimulating group process, the heart of Marsh's approach did include a lecture series. He explained that "something like seventy-five percent" of the material considered with individual patients is general enough to be presented in a class format to a group of patients. Individual work, when required, could serve as a supplementary treatment where more intimate and personal details might be discussed.

Marsh's 1931 series of 30 lectures included adjustment to hospitalization, religion and philosophy, problems of growth, reality, problems of work and relaxation, adjustment to family, problems of sex, emotions, people and social customs, self-expression, inward drives and the physical world, adequate and inadequate methods of adjustment, reeducation, current events, conscience, superstitions, the human nervous system, good sense, how to raise a baby, constructive self-examination and criticism, the insecure personality, insight and judgment, the will to balance serenity and happiness, behavior patterns, ward notes, and successes. The last two classes consisted of the relating of personal experience by recovering patients and a final examination on the material presented in the series (1931, pp. 335–336).

A later series at the Re-educational Institute in Boston, founded in 1932, included family situation, foundations of personality in childhood, economic equipment, emotional life, social life, religious life, sex life, abnormal people, and normal adult personality" (1935, p. 385). Marsh supplemented his lectures with homework, readings, singing, roleplaying and other dramatic procedures, group exercises, patient co-teaching, testimonials, and a question-and-answer period. He reported how frank students were in asking personal questions that very clearly related to their own difficulties. He would often refer such questions to the group for opinion and consensus. By doing so, "it was not long before each class developed a sound mental hygiene point of view. The class thus became a democratic, educational project wherein the instructor was rather a moderator than a lord" (1935, p. 386).

Marsh spoke of the special benefits of group treatment—enthusiasm unlikely in private contact, more rapid recovery, and more willingness to accept a new point of view. He also spoke of the advantages of group transference over the individual transferences that arose in private therapy.

By the time he published his results in the early 1930s, Marsh had worked with a number of kinds of groups, including those composed of "frankly psychotic," prepsychotic, and psychoneurotic patients. At the Re-Educational Institute, he facilitated groups of "normal persons, physicians, clergymen, educators, teachers, nurses, college students" (1935, p. 384), as well as more pathological patients. He often combined normals and psychiatric patients in the same group, believing that group participation created a common level of experience and uniformity of interests and progress. Marsh also espoused the use of the group method for homogeneous medical groups such as "cardiac, orthopedic, asthmatic and hay fever, gastric ulcer and diabetic cases" (1935, p. 392).

Upon request, he would sometimes conduct brief individual treatment with group participants during the course or after they had finished the lecture series. Even in these cases, the educational metaphor was never abandoned. Marsh believed that the dignity of the individual was preserved by using the class method and treating participants as students rather than as patients. Individual therapy was ever embedded in the prevailing educational model when referred to as *tutoring* or *coaching,* terms later adopted by family therapists.

The Early Analysts

Sigmund Freud

In 1921, Sigmund Freud published a monograph entitled *Group Psychology and the Analysis of the Ego*. Stimulated by the work of McDougall and Le Bon, he sought to explain group phenomena by way of psychoanalytic theory. Freud (1967a) differentiated between transient and permanent, homogeneous and heterogeneous, and natural and artificial groups. He believed that the empathic relations evident in the group were derivative of more basic identification processes.

Special attention was given to the role of the leader. Members' libidinal ties to the authority figure served to cohesively bind one to the other, and imbue the collective with ego idealistic value. Cessation of such ties could readily elicit neurotic fear, anxiety, and panic. Freud presented a striking analogy for the breach of the group's cohesion that comes with a leader's incapacitation. "The cry went out, 'The general has lost his head!' and thereupon all the Assyrians take flight" (1967a, p. 29). The relationship with the leader, however, was far from ideal or free from conflict. Freud considered group rebellion an inevitable and symbolic representation of the primal horde's killing and eating of its leader in order to secure instinctual aims. Such latent rebellion might account for why prospective group therapists often experience such anticipatory terror.

Member-to-member relationships also demonstrate a basic ambivalence, with hostility and aversion present, but often repressed. Freud (1922/1977) passes along Schopenhauer's famous simile as a model of group interrelatedness:

> *A company of porcupines crowded themselves very close together one cold winter's day so as to profit by one another's warmth and so save themselves from being frozen to death. But soon they felt one another's quills, which induced them to separate again. And now when the need for warmth brought them nearer together again, the second evil arose once more. So they were driven backwards and forwards from one to the other, until they discovered a mean distance at which they could most tolerably exist. (1967a, p. 33)*

Freud never ran therapeutic groups in his psychoanalytic practice, though clearly recognizing the curative value of group participation. He explained that "where powerful impetus has been given to group formation neurosis may diminish. . . . Justifiable attempts have also been made to turn this antagonism between neurosis and group formation to therapeutic account" (1967a, p. 74).

Some (Kanzer, 1983; Roth, 1991) have likened the famous Wednesday evening meetings of the Viennese Circle (1901–1907) to the first long-term psychoanalytic group. In these gatherings, Freud steadfastly upheld his role as leader and model of analytic authority. These expressly educational and albeit emotionally charged gatherings, terminated in rebellion and controversy between Freud and Alfred Adler. Such ferocity and revolt may have prefigured Freud's convictions about the destructive power of the primal horde.

Alfred Adler

Alfred Adler, focusing on the social context of human behavior and sensitive to the needs of the working class in Europe, established guidance clinics practicing family and group techniques. Dreikurs (1956) suggests that Adler's theory represented the first democratic concept of man and, as such, provided the basis for interpersonal group treatment. "Social interest became the yardstick of social functioning, inter-personal relationships the prime focus of interest, interaction the key to an understanding of each participant" (Dreikurs, 1956, p. 120).

Adler initially began counseling families before an audience as a training aid for mental health and social service workers. Participation from onlookers was encouraged and incorporated into the treatment of the family. With subjective observers serving as auxiliary therapists, the dynamics and experiences of the group-at-large were brought into otherwise closed family systems as an open, interactive curative variable.

> Adler's work departed from Freudian psychoanalytic concepts: In contrast to the psychoanalytic assumption that only through exploration of the deepest depths of man's unconscious can he be understood and cured, the social orientation points to the individual's movements, his goals, and emphasizes what is taking place between him and others. The element of privacy, a pre-requisite for introspection into deep intimate feelings, appears in a new light. Secrecy is well justified in a cultural setting of emotional isolation where each one is afraid that his deficiencies will be discovered. A lack of mutual trust and a restricted feeling of belonging keeps people in distance. The desire for privacy, therefore, so long assumed as essential for therapy is no longer considered as essential; in many instances it is an expression of a neurotic attitude. (Dreikurs, 1956, p. 122)

Adler's first actual psychotherapy group is reported to have begun in 1921, the year of the publication of Freud's group manifesto. Collective therapy, based on Adlerian principles, was practiced in Vienna and elsewhere in the early decades of the twentieth century.

Rudolf Dreikurs

Rudolf Dreikurs was a follower of Alfred Adler, an enthusiastic practitioner of group therapy, and a chronicler of the early group therapy experiments in Europe at the turn of the twentieth century. He brought with him to America Adler's family counseling methods and a faith in treatment within social settings. Dreikurs woefully reports that much of the group therapy work done in Vienna and elsewhere was not reported and was thus lost to posterity. Hence, the early group work of Metzl (alcoholics), Wetterstrand (collective hypnosis), Rosenstein (mentally retarded), Herschfield (sexual deviants), Guilarowski (obsessive-compulsives), Schubert, and Ozertovsky remain largely unavailable to group historians and theorists.

Dreikurs does report on his early work with Adler, where the social context of behavior was clearly the focus of treatment. Beginning with family work and soon encompassing groups with unrelated others, treatment in a collective context was viewed as the natural setting for psychotherapy. Dreikurs admitted that Adler and he were unaware that they were experimenting with a new form of treatment. " 'Collective Therapy' as it was called at that time, was merely a by-product of our general therapeutic orientation" (1959, p. 884).

Dreikurs' first group therapy publications were recorded in German in 1928 and 1932. By 1927, he practiced collective therapy with alcoholics and is credited with being one of the first to use group methods with psychiatric patients in private practice, beginning as early as 1929. He reported on this work to the Individual Psychotherapy Association of Vienna in 1930. In a 1932 publication translated from the German in 1959, he describes how:

> *The characteristics and lifestyle of a patient are shown with emphatic clarity in the course of Collective Therapy. In the joint discussions with several other patients, each learns to know himself better because he is able to learn from his observations of others. Once the first resistance against taking part in a group formed for the purpose of therapeutic treatment has been overcome, much ground has been gained toward a quicker and more thorough recognition by the patient of his own personality. Above all, this method eliminates any last remnant of a personal battle with the therapist. (1959, p. 886)*

Initially three or four patients formed a group, with later work accommodating more participants. Where possible, group members were also treated concurrently in individual psychotherapy. Initial individual sessions were used to collect a detailed case history. Dreikurs began group sessions by describing disguised case histories of various patients, thereby opening up impersonal discussions of varied dynamics and pathologies. He found patients to be quite frank in their discussion, as the clinical material attracted wide participation and the group worked toward psychological insight. Later groups, under the impetus of patients' requests, appeared more free flowing and direct in the consideration of personal problems. "They all wanted to talk about whatever came up in therapy. Everything was discussed, after some hesitation, including sexual problems" (1932, p. 888).

Group dynamics, interactions among patients, and cohesion making became intimate parts of the treatment process. Dreikurs believed that it was important to work in a setting where patients could be directly observed in their dealings with others. By emphasizing the primacy of member to member confrontations, he demonstrated a less authoritative role for the physician. "One of the most important aspects seems to be that in collective therapy the physician is not the center of all activity. It is different when one patient recognizes the maneuvers of another than when the physician discloses them" (1932, p. 888).

Dreikurs reported that such group work lessens personal isolation by destroying the feeling that symptoms and problems are unique. His rationale for the use of group therapy included practical as well as clinical considerations. Collective therapy is "the only way in which psychotherapy can be introduced when large numbers of patients are involved, as in health insurance clinics for workers" (1932, p. 889).

Trigant Burrow

In 1909, a young M.D. and Ph.D., Trigant Burrow, had occasion to meet the great European analysts Sigmund Freud and Carl Gustav Jung during their trip to the United States to lecture at Clark University in Worcester, Massachusetts. Captivated by psychoanalysis, Burrow followed Jung back to Zurich to study. In 1910, Burrow returned to the United States and began practicing psychoanalysis, becoming one of the founding members of the American Psychoanalytic Association.

Influenced by Adolf Meyer and the work of the Phipps Psychiatric Clinic at Johns Hopkins Hospital, Burrow came to believe that the emphasis psychoanalysis put on individual dynamics was misplaced. "The esoteric practice of closeting a patient in our private consultation room in order to hear a story of ineptitudes and maladjustments that are due to social interpositions and substitutions common to the race . . . has, I think, nowhere its counterpart in any sphere of scientific procedure" (1927, pp. 271–272).

With irony, he later recounted,

For many years it was my daily experience in personal analyses to pursue diligently the secret phantasies and symbolic irrelevancies of the individual unconscious, hunting them out from their remotest crevices with meticulous painstaking. And there is no doubt that the

entertainment afforded my patients . . . was in many cases suffi-
ciently diverting to constitute what is commonly called a cure. (1928,
p. 204)

Burrow eventually abandoned the rudiments of psychoanalysis to emphasize a "phyloanalysis," aimed at discovering the universal principles and societal influences behind both pathological and normal behaviors. He rejected the assumption that humans should be viewed and treated solely as individuals in favor of an emphasis on the analysis of people as "social organisms." This rarely cited but relatively prolific writer (68 articles and 5 books) coined the phrase *group analysis* and in 1928 first used the concept of a *group as a whole.*

Burrow began conducting private psychotherapy groups as early as 1925. His groups initially contained as many as 20 patients but were later limited to 10. Patients with a wide variety of psychiatric diagnoses were included. Sessions were held once weekly for one hour. Treatment often began with a course of individual sessions, and intermittent private sessions continued after group analysis began.

Burrow's groups stressed spontaneity, immediacy, here-and-now interaction, bridging the gap between words and feelings, and exploring the meaning of nonverbal behavior. He reiterated that "group or social analysis is the analysis of the immediate group in the immediate moment" (1928, p.198). A colleague of Trigant Burrow at the Phipps Clinic, Hans Syz, underscored the rudiments of the here-and-now approach by suggesting that the group moment represents an isomorph and repetition of earlier conflicts. Not withstanding the emphasis that psychoanalysis placed on reminiscent events, Syz concluded, "The elements which in the past or in any situation outside the immediate group-moment have obstructed a unified and direct function are identical with those factors which are observable in the contradictions and interferences of the immediate social situation" (1928, p. 147).

Burrow (1928) encouraged his groups to search out the meanings behind more manifest and casual social interchange. He believed that underlying many diverse behaviors were universal interpersonal variables that could account for psychopathology and symptom formation. Appraisals and criticisms of others often represented a social transference wherein the donor's social images, reflexes, and values were expressed through projection and interaction. Thus, in social analysis, the group might examine the process behind apparently straightforward questions by pondering: Who is the person making the inquiry? What is his or her background? Why has he or she asked this particular question at this time? How will the answer be received and used? Why does the inquirer seek out this or that person? What is the relationship between the questioner and the questioned? What relation would the questioner ideally like to have with the person they've just engaged?

Burrow argued that patients more naturally demonstrated a diversity of behaviors in the group setting, and that in therapy groups dramatic changes could occur for various psychopathological types.

> *Under these conditions we have experienced again and again how much more readily the schizoid, for example, resting in his intrauterine lethargy, is roused from his dreaming inactions and learns to enter the objective immediacy of the surrounding actualities; how much more radically the hysteric is ousted from his egocentric reveries and at length lends himself to the day's constructive demands; and, finally with what greater dispatch the cyclothymic surrenders his bi-dimensional mood alternatives in favor of an adaptation to life that represents a symmetrical unitary effort. (1927, p. 274)*

In the second decade of the century, Burrow experimented with the intensive residential setting as a workshop for group analysis. The Lifwynn Camp in the Adirondacks was an early incarnation of the encounter and T-groups of the 1960s and 1970s. Normal amenities were largely dispensed with as various work, social, and mealtime interactions became the source of study and analysis. A here-and-now focus was adapted and maintained throughout.

Burrow further specified the importance of the patient as "observer" and "responsible student of our common human problems" (1927, p. 276). In fact, Clarence Shields, a student and research assistant, played an important part in the development of Burrow's work. Burrow believed that group analysis precluded dependence on the physician, neutralized transference, and dissolved resistances by reducing the isolation from one's own conflicts. His work certainly represents an early experiment in interpersonal psychotherapeutics, and it in fact influenced the later practices of the interpersonal school of psychiatry as represented by Harry Stack Sullivan, Karen Horney, and Irwin Yalom. Samuel Slavson's archives, housed at the headquarters of the American Group Psychotherapy Association, contain many reprints of Burrow's writings. Though underacknowledged, Trigant Burrow's work represented an innovation in the treatment of individuals as social beings.

Looking Back and Looking Ahead

The inventors of group therapy displayed an enthusiasm and wonder that can only accompany first-born efforts. In discovering the group as a viable treatment modality, many problems of convenience and practicality were resolved, adding an air of relief to more aesthetic sensitivities. The psychoeducators, for example, devised a methodology for highlighting the common problems and adaptations of their charge. By forming groups, they efficiently communicated salient information to individuals made increasingly available and amenable to influence by being seen together. These same physicians, turned mental practitioners, specifically commandeered the group dynamics naturally amplified in collective settings. Mutual suggestion, persuasion, stimulation, socialization, inculcation of values, inspiration, and reeducation were the processes that largely contributed to forming ameliorative cultures based on enlightenment and the adaptive aspects of social conformity.

Yet these early leaders soon discovered that the power of psychoeducation did not simply depend on conveying information. Moving away from a strictly didactic, medically based model, Pratt (1907) recommended, "The social aspects [of group treatment] need to be developed. They are quite distinct from the medical side. Students of sociology should join heartily with medical men in this work" (p. 479). Marsh (1933) readily concurred, "Physicians who study psychiatry should have wide social training and be able to handle patients in groups, both in order to reach the larger number and in order to take advantage of the compulsion to work in crowd psychology" (p. 415). These great grandfathers of group psychotherapy foreshadowed and foretold the elements still essential for the conduct of contemporary groups with patients brought together by disease, disorder, or dysfunction. Support, self-help, problem, theme, or symptom-focused groups; collective guidance, counseling or nursing regimens; behavioral management, habit control, and addiction protocols; milieu therapy; and site-centered, morale building, industrial consultations hearken back to the pioneering work of the psychoeducators (Lieberman, 1990). Pratt, Lazell, and Marsh provide the modern practitioner with both a faith in the grouping process and the rudiments of a programmatic approach geared for mass consumption.

With the entry into the group field by clinicians of psychodynamic persuasion and practice, the emphasis further evolved from one of collective influence to one of learning by interaction and psychosocial insight in ever smaller units of application. Movement went from podiums and audiences to circles of horizontal equidistant relations. The interstimulation of one member with another, while still reminiscent of more general or universal principles, became the object of attention. Freud realized that group participation could at least distract from more personal preoccupations. Adler and Dreikurs sought to use the social context to do psychotherapy work in public, enjoining people to come together at a level of mutual resources and collective compromises. Burrow, well ahead of his time, maximized the occurrence and analysis group dynamics by way of a here-and-now focus, ever searching for phylogenetic insights. It is not surprising that both he and Lazell turned to Jung for inspiration, thereby emphasizing cultural rather than intrapsychic transformations.

Jung, however, concentrating on the individuation process as the primary goal of psychotherapy, depreciated group treatments.

As a physician, I consider any psychic disturbance, whether neurosis or psychosis, to be an individual illness; the patient has to be treated accordingly. The individual can be treated in a group only if he is a member of it. If he is, this should be a great help, since, being submerged in the group, he apparently escapes his self to some degree. The feeling of security is increased and the feeling of responsibility is decreased when one is part of a group. (Illing, 1957, p. 78)

This lack of endorsement for forming stranger groups with specific therapeutic intent delayed Jungians, until the near dawn of the encounter movement, from expressly applying their knowledge of symbol formation, archetypes, mythology, and collective dynamics to group practice (Hobson, 1959, 1964; Whitmont, 1964; Willeford, 1967).

The early analysts, Adler, Dreikurs, and Burrow, who did experiment with collective treatment, capitalized on group therapy's social and interactive potentials. The psychoanalytically inspired innovators of the next generation, Louis Wender, Paul Schilder, Alexander Wolf, Samuel Slavson, and Lauretta Bender with children, sought to bring the main therapeutic emphasis back to the level of the individual member. While the participants sat in a circle, the thrust largely encompassed vertical analysis of patients' intrapsychic worlds. Members took turns being the center of the group's attention. Thus, the next generation, with the notable exception of Jacob Moreno, who straddled many worlds both old and new, sought to apply dyadic psychoanalytic principles to the treatment of individuals in groups.

Appendix to Chapter 3

TABLE 1   •   Group Therapy Pioneers: Type of Group and Treatment Advantages

Group Leader	Type of Group	Advantages of Group Treatment
Pratt	Psychoeducation "Repressive-inspiration" "Thought-control class"	More economical Practical use of time Group energizes helpful emotions Vicarious treatment provided Hopeful influence of patients who have overcome symptoms and regained mental tranquility
Lazell	Psychoeducation "Etiology Spiel"	Economical Practical Increases accessibility of disturbed patients Fear of the analyst and homoerotic fears removed Socialization provided Fundamental problems common to all cases can be addressed (nuclear conflicts, Oedipal problem, sexual development)
Marsh	Psychoeducation "Milieu Therapy" Social-educational-industrial groups	Pragmatics—more patients reached (75% of material to be presented to patients is common material) Mental illness is a social disease caused by the group and it must be healed by the group Group method is a necessary part of each case A mental hygiene compulsion is at work in a group Many patients are unavailable to individual therapy
Adler/ Dreikurs	Family Therapy Guidance Groups "Collective Therapy" "Collective Counseling"	Democratic concept of therapy Effective training aid for mental health workers and social service personnel Quicker treatment modality Practical treatment for health insurance clinics Group treatment in the social setting is the natural environment for psychotherapy

TABLE 1 • *Continued*

Group Leader	Type of Group	Advantages of Group Treatment
		Eliminates personal battle with therapist
		Physician is not the center of all activity
		Patients can't evade issues as easily
		Can observe patients dealing with others
		Characteristic life-style of patient shown with empathic clarity
Burrow	"Group Analysis" "Phyloanalysis" Intensive residential workshops	Man is a social being and the group is the natural focus of treatment
		Transference to and dependence on the physician is precluded
		Interaction stimulates change
		More diversity of behaviors manifest
		Reduced isolation from one's own conflicts

TABLE 2 • *Group Therapy Pioneers: Curative Factors*

Therapist	Setting	Curative Factors and Therapy Goals
Pratt	Boston Emmanuel Church Boston Dispensary	Reeducation
		Camaraderie
		Healthy emulation (modeling and imitation)
		Instillation of a spirit of hope
		Raising morale
		Suggestion (mild hypnotic combined with relaxation)
		Persuasion
		Correcting destructive habit patterns
		Stir up and redirect emotions along healthy lines (reorientation— replace bad emotions with good)
		Instillation of common sense
		Confidence in physician and class
		Develop new habits of thought (power of positive thinking and

Continued

TABLE 2 • Continued

Therapist	Setting	Curative Factors and Therapy Goals
		repression of dysphoric emotions and life views) Convince neurotic patient of the emotional cause of physical symptoms
Lazell	St. Elizabeth's Hospital, Washington, DC U.S. Veterans Bureau, Denver, CO	Reeducation Socialization Universalization of issues Character building Working through normal stages of human development Insight Mind-body holism Directing instinctual demands into normal channels Removing obstructions to the onward flow of libido
Marsh	Kings Park State Hospital, Long Island, NY Worcester State Hospital Re-education Institute, Boston	Reeducation Inspiration Increased morale Social-emotional growth and adjustment Group process Group enthusiasm and work compulsion Group transference (impersonal) Understanding Instillation of happiness Integration of mind, emotion, and motor activity Emotional release Conversion from introspection, fantasy, bitterness, shame, and inferiority to extrospection, constructive planning, cheerfulness, assurance, and security Extroverting energies at a social level Acceptance of principles of mental hygiene Bonding Working out social difficulties
Adler/ Dreikurs	Guidance Clinics in Vienna Private practice	Destroying uniqueness of symptoms and personal problems Fostering cooperation and social harmony

TABLE 2 • _Continued_

Therapist	_Setting_	_Curative Factors and Therapy Goals_
		Breaking emotional isolation
		Establishing trust and belonging
		Learning from others
		Knowing self better through psychological insight
		Cohesion
		Social interest enhanced
		Understanding group dynamics
		Affirming the creativity and the wholeness of each individual member
Burrow	Phipps Clinic, Johns Hopkins Hospital Private practice Lifwynn Camp	Spontaneity
		Immediacy
		Here-and-now interaction
		Bridging the gap between words and feelings
		Exploring the meaning of nonverbal behavior
		Analyzing the universal substrate of behavior
		Bringing to consciousness latent and repressed meanings behind manifest and casual social exchange
		Seeing own neurosis reflected in others
		Neutralizing individual expression of illness by revealing social nature
		Uncovering complexes
		True expression of divorced social images

TABLE 3 • Group Therapy Pioneers: Practical Applications

Therapist	Type of Patient	Exclusion Criteria	Homogeneity	Heterogeneity	Individual Therapy
Pratt	Tuberculosis Psychosomatic Psychoneurotic Undernourished Diabetes Cardiac Obesity	Psychosis	For disease	Demographics Character Social status	Concurrent to talk about difficulties, failures, and unresolved problems
Lazell	Demetia praecox Manic depression Hyperthyroidism Mixed symptomatology (mild dementia, hysteria, neurasthenia, psychasthenia, anxiety neurosis) Service-connected epilepsy		For symptom or etiology		Concurrent (at times)
Marsh	Psychotics Juvenile psychotics Prepsychotics Psychoneurotics Normals Relatives of patients Community at large Students Hospital personnel Recommended special classes for epileptics, deteriorated cases, organics		Recommended for medical groups: cardiac, orthopedic, asthmatic, hayfever, gastric ulcer, diabetes	Normally to promote common experience	Some concurrent or consecutive "tutoring" or "coaching"
Adler/ Dreikurs	Families Alcoholics Outpatients Neurotics Mothers		For problems		Concurrent individual therapy whenever possible
Burrow	Psychoneurotics Normals			Mixed symptoms and demographics	Initially, then intermittently during group

TABLE 4 • *Group Therapy Pioneers: Comparison of Techniques*

Therapist	Group Size	Length and Frequency of Meetings	Techniques/Procedures/Processes
Pratt	15–20		Initial individual history taking Pregroup contracting (rules and norms) Explanation of mind/body theory given Individual case management in group setting (case status, prescriptions, treatment planning) Address to class as a whole by leader (advice, encouragement, orientation, questions and answers) Appeal to emotions of patients Patient testimonials (old patients return to give inspiration) Pairing old members with new members for encouragement and information giving Deep muscle relaxation exercises Imagery exercises Social reinforcement Cognitive behavior modification (thought control)
Lazell	Large	1 a week 6 to 8 months	Taking individual diagnostic history Group lectures from Freudian and Jungian perspective Repetition and review Bibliotherapy Patients discuss lectures with each other
Marsh	Large		Lectures from a social adjustment perspective Discussion Patients relating personal experiences Question-and-answer period Notetaking, homework, and tests Roleplaying and dramatic procedures Group exercises Patient co-teaching Testimonials Morale building and encouragement Bibliotherapy Orientation to hospital lecture Pairing dialogues Singing and dancing

Continued

TABLE 4 • Continued

Therapist	Group Size	Length and Frequency of Meetings	Techniques/Procedures/Processes
Adler/ Dreikurs	3–4 at first, larger later		Initial individual sessions to collect detailed history and to do group preparation
			Overcoming resistance to group participation
			Fostering interaction
			Participation from the audience and use of auxiliary egos
			Family therapy
			Emphasize individual goal setting and goal directedness
			Focus on social context of behavior
			Interpersonal discussions of dynamics and pathologies
			Begin sessions by describing distinguished case histories
			Free-floating discussions of personal problems
			Focus on group dynamics and cohesion
			Encourage member-to-member confrontations
Burrow	Initially 20, later up to 10	1 a week 1-hour session	Initial individual sessions
			Encouraging spontaneity, immediacy, and here-and-now interaction
			Bridging the gap between words and feelings
			Exploring the meaning of nonverbal behavior
			Analyzing universal substrate of behavior
			Encouraging true expression of social images
			Bringing to consciousness latent and repressed meanings behind manifest and casual social exchange
			Analyzing interactions and communication
			Analyzing universal phylogenetic issues

CHAPTER FOUR

The Growth Spurt of Group Psychotherapy:

Innovations Prior to World War II

The decade of the 1930s and early 1940s prior to World War II saw the rapid growth of group psychotherapy (Corsini, 1955, 1956; Dreikurs, 1956, 1959; Z. T. Moreno, 1966; Wolberg, 1976; Rosenbaum, 1978; Shapiro, 1978; Bender, 1979; Rosenthal, 1983; Sadock & Kaplan, 1983; Schiffer, 1983; Rutan & Stone, 1984; Lubin & Lubin, 1987). Following closely upon the earlier efforts of the psychoeducators—Pratt, Lazell, and Marsh—and expanding on the pioneering work of the early analysts—Freud, Adler, Dreikurs, and Burrow—group therapy began to gain acceptance in hospitals, clinics, and private practice. The emerging literature reflects the diversity of the collective treatment modality applied to widening populations in varied settings, accompanied by a burgeoning sophistication of theory and technique.

As group therapy grew in popularity and technical refinement during its growth spurt, further understandings accrued concerning advantages, curative factors, and therapy goals; optimum group size, composition, and membership criteria; the length, structure, and frequency of meetings; the interface between individual and group interventions; and the technique and role of the leader. (See the Appendix at the end of this chapter.)

An earlier version of this chapter appeared in the *International Journal of Group Psychotherapy, 39* (1), 35–57, Copyright 1989. Reprinted by permission of the American Group Psychotherapy Association.

Various Schilder quotes throughout this chapter are from *Journal of Social Psychology, 12* (1940): 83–100. Reprinted with permission of the Helen Dwight Reid Educational Foundation. Published by Heldref Publications, 4000 Albemarle St., N.W., Washington, DC. Copyright © 1940.

The Second Generation of Group Analysts

Louis Wender

Seeking to apply psychoanalytic principles to the treatment of "hospitalized psychoneurotics," Louis Wender wrote of the group work begun in 1929 at Hillside Hospital in Hastings-on-Hudson. Wender wished to differentiate his method from the "large sociological and philosophical implications" of Trigant Burrow and from that of earlier inspirational psychoeducators like Joseph Hersey Pratt. Wender's later practices drew from the contemporary efforts of Paul Schilder and Lauretta Bender.

Wender saw the small group as a naturally interrelational and interdependent setting from which the individual patient might learn to adjust to society at large.

> *Place this individual who has failed in the more complex setting into a small group which is friendly to him and which is composed of others suffering from allied disturbances, and he will become enabled when he learns to understand the problems of others—to associate himself with them, to release his aggressive tendencies, his hates, his loves and his wishes, without accompanying sense of guilt. By working out his difficulties and achieving adjustment in the small group, he becomes able to face the large group (the world) and to handle his emotional problems, social or other, on a normal basis. (1940, p. 708)*

Wender observed that, in the hospital setting, "problems are frequently analyzed and discussed among patients with greater candor than with the physician" (1936, p. 55). He sought to harness these natural exchanges to foster a competition to remain well rather than merely allowing group gripes to result in infectiously toxic "symptoms orgies" (1936, p. 55).

Wender considered his approach specifically psychoanalytic, talked of the hospital as a "substitute family," and suggested that transference readily occurs with the therapist as the symbolic parent and other patients representing siblings. "The entire group set-up provides a kind of 'catharsis-in-the-family,' with an accompanying resolvement [sic] of conflicts and the displacement of parental love on to new objects" (1936, p. 59).

Wender (1940) encouraged patient-to-patient transferences to spur identifications and lead to a widening of interests and the spread of socialization. Evolving group interactions served to break individual isolation while acting as a consensual forum for evaluating the nature and scope of personal problems. Wender wrote about the processes of insight and the "working through" made possible by the group setting. The presentation of new material consistently suggested old adaptations. As members viewed the constraints of their peers, they came to understand the nature of recurrent problems. Eventually participants accepted interpretations about themselves as well as about the other group participants. Through continual repetition, patients began to recognize their neurotic symptoms and problematic behaviors as compensatory defensive structures for their emotional difficulties.

Wender's groups were composed of six to eight men who met two to three times a week for one-hour sessions. Nurses ran women's groups, with the anticipation that carefully selected mixed-gender groups would be formed as more was learned about collective treatment. Wender suggested that group treatment is "applicable only to disorders in which intellectual impairment is absent and in which some degree of affect is retained" (1936, p. 56). Group treatment was specifically recommended for schizophrenics in whom the disease was of recent onset and who were without systematized delusions, hallucinations, splitting, or blocking; depressives without marked retardation; and psychoneurotics with the exception of those manifesting longstanding compulsive neurosis. Group treatment was preceded by a thorough evaluation and preparatory individual sessions. Intermittent individual sessions were held throughout the course of the group, at the patient's request. Group participants were also encouraged to talk together and sustain friendships outside the group therapy sessions, while still maintaining confidentiality in relation to the general hospital population. Group treatment, which lasted approximately four to five months, was initially close-ended. Subsequently, however, new patients were admitted as ready. Wender (1940) found that reviewing the mechanisms and principles of group treatment for the benefit of the newcomers was helpful to all.

Seeking a "synthesis of intellect and emotions," group sessions often began with lecture material such as "a simple exposition of why we behave as we do, a description of primitive instinctual drives, conscious and unconscious elements, significance of dreams, early infantile traumata, reaction formations, repressions, rationalizations, etc." (Wender, 1936, p. 27). Later groups, while at times relying on psychoeducation, more closely resembled modern collective therapy methods, as the psychiatrist might simply begin a session, "Come on, Jack, tell us about yourself" (Wender, 1940, p. 716). A group patient of Wender's further elaborated on the process:

> *Well, Jack didn't seem to mind, nor did one or two others whose symptoms, histories and private lives were shamelessly exposed. Then, all the neurotics suddenly became psychiatrists. Anyone who desired to asked questions, highly personal questions of the patients under discussion, and advanced theories as to the causes of his particular ailment or breakdown. When the doctor finally propounded his own ideas on the subject, he did seem to shed some light on the specific case of one or another of the patients "on the carpet." (1940, p. 716)*

Wender prescribed the wider use of group psychotherapy in and out of the hospital setting with a more active involvement advised for the therapist. He summed his appeal. "It is the belief of the writer and his colleagues that it would be far better if every physician were able to assemble his patients once or twice weekly, to consciously become part of the group he is treating, instead of merely making rounds in a dignified manner" (1940, p. 715).

Paul Schilder

From his influential position as Clinical Director of Bellevue Psychiatric Hospital and Research Professor at New York University in the middle to late 1930s, Paul Schilder practiced, speculated about, and helped legitimize the practice of group psychotherapy in the United States. At the invitation of adolf Meyer, Trigant Burrow's mentor, Schilder came to America in 1930 with a background in psychiatry, neurology, and Viennese psychoanalysis in association with Sigmund Freud. Early work in Europe touched on the use of hypnosis in groups by providing direct suggestions for alleviating symptoms and problems. Schilder later gave up this practice because it created inordinate "erotic submission to the leader" (Bender, 1979, p.1). Yet he remained fascinated by the prevalence of various religious movements which used direct influence and public confession to relieve suffering.

As early as 1931, Schilder advocated more active treatment for psychosis, including psychoanalysis and group therapy. In the late 1930s and until his death in 1940, he collaborated with Louis Wender, whose application of psychoanalytic principles to group treatment he greatly admired. Influenced also by his wife, Lauretta Bender, Schilder began using art therapy in groups, working with such creative productions much as one might with dream material. He also advocated the wide use of occupational and avocational methods with the adult population at Bellevue. In advancing the widespread use of collective interventions, Schilder stated, "Hospital groups as groups need psychotherapeutic assistance. Such assistance (groups) should be organized" (1940, p. 96).

By 1933, Schilder had actually begun practicing psychotherapy, proper, in groups. He concurrently recommended doing research on "groups in action" with special attention to formative processes, to ongoing dynamics, as well as to members' unique experiences as participants. Schilder retained a scholarly, intellectual, and philosophical bent amidst more clinical pursuits. He believed that the isolation and secrecy of neurotic life adjustments should not be duplicated in the treatment situation. He argued that individual psychoanalytic therapy is an artificial situation in which the analyst, by silence, becomes "a more or less mythical figure."

Rather, Schilder advocated an approach that demystified the therapist and created a more open setting for mutual exchange. "From a purely theoretical point of view it would be advisable to change the set-up in order to see the problems appearing in the psychoanalytic situation from a new angle. It would [be] interesting to see a group which is less restricted than the psychoanalytic unit in its making" (1940, p. 93).

Schilder hinted at the principle of repetition compulsion and pointed the way toward working through elements of character, by talking of how changes in the structure of patients' experiences could be fostered by treatment in groups. "When the individual dives down into his personal experiences or brings them forward in the group the crystallized individual development comes into flux again which allows a new adaptation to the situation" (1940, p. 94).

An early form of group treatment called *analysis of ideologies* was suggestive of values clarification. In this treatment regimen, patients' aims, views, goals, attitudes, and beliefs were explored and compared in the group setting. Schilder's special interest in body image made its way into the discussions. Questionnaires were be selectively introduced to stimulate interaction around such topics as (1) body and beauty; (2) health, strength, efficiency, superiority, and inferiority in a physical sense; (3) aggressiveness and submission; (4) masculinity and femininity; (5) the relation of sex and love; (6) the expectation for the future; and (7) the meaning of death (Bender, 1979, p. 3). Paradoxically, this conscious and reasonable approach often took patients back to less conscious and more concrete etiological experiences and universalities.

Schilder wished to help patients realize that feelings and thoughts believed to be shamefully unique were actually common to all. So saying, he actively worked to help members associate to each other's life experiences as a way of fostering social insights through interpersonal exchange. "The deeper understanding of the universal problems of life . . . is an important part of every psychotherapy and can be conducted in a group. . . . It takes the problem out of the sphere of individual aberration and suffering . . . and breaks the isolation of the individual which is an important part of his neurosis" (1936, pp. 612–614).

As Schilder's group work progressed, more psychoanalytic influences became evident. He paid special attention to the patients' relationship with the therapist, describing vividly the positive and the negative transferences sure to develop in the collective setting.

The physician appears as the love object and the positive transference almost always finds an open expression and it is particularly astonishing how open the expression of hate can be. The complaint that the analyst does not give enough attention, that he is too much interested in the scientific side of the problem, that he is heartless and experiments, comes in a great number of instances. It can be easily shown that these complaints are dependent upon the parental situation in childhood. Very often the attitude of hate expressed by one patient finds a sympathetic response from other patients. Very often there is also a defense of the physician by other patients. Very often the patients project their own problems into the physician and have the feeling that he must have gone through them, and finally identify themselves with the physician as the man who has solved problems identical to theirs. (1940, p. 99)

Schilder further commented on member rivalries and competition for the leader's attention and implied that there were distinct stages in the group's development. In session, the group members were encouraged to associate freely to one another's biographical material as well as to actively interpret each other's symptoms and dreams. In the analytic tradition, he explained how "psychoanalytic insight was utilized in this group treatment. In every case the life history of the patient was discussed and elucidated in detail and early infantile material was particularly studied" (1939, p. 89).

Schilder's groups met once or twice a week with two to seven patients of the same gender. Treatment started with individual sessions in which patients were taught the principles of free analysis and dream analysis and wrote detailed individual biographies. Individual sessions were continued concurrently with group meetings. Often the groups were co-led by a physician-in-training. Inpatient groups were run with psychotic patients. Selected for outpatient groups were patients with diagnoses of severe neurosis, including social and obsessional disorders, anxiety, hysteria, hypochondriasis (not helped by treatment), depersonalization, and depression, as well as some characterological and schizophrenic disorders.

Schilder staunchly advocated that group therapy could become a more constructive replica of society than could individual treatment. In groups, hostility and aggression could be diverted into cooperative efforts, thus fostering sympathy and a common bonding between individuals. With the founding of the Schilder Society, his work was carried on after his death. His student, Donald Shaskan, came to prominence by further popularizing the use of group therapy during World War II.

Alexander Wolf

In 1949 and 1950, Alexander Wolf published, in serial presentation, a now-classic monograph entitled "The Psychoanalysis of Groups." He actually reported on group therapy efforts begun a decade earlier and continued in the army during World War II, a formative context for many group practitioners. "In 1938 I started an experimental group of four men and four women. So promptly were my uncertainties about group analysis dispelled, that within one year I had telescoped most of my practice, and in 1940 I was working with five groups of eight to ten patients each" (1949, p. 525).

Influenced by the writings of Wender and Schilder, Wolf adapted the Freudian techniques and concepts of dream interpretation, free association, analysis of resistance, transference, and countertransference to the collective setting. His approach most resembled individual analysis in a group, with patients alternating between being the direct focus of treatment and being auxiliary therapists. The group became a re-creation of the original family and an isomorph of society in general. Consequently, Wolf argued, "If treatment constitutes primarily the analysis of transference, is it not wiser to place the patient in a group setting in which he can project father, mother and siblings as well?" (1949, p. 526).

While utilizing homogeneous groups in his army experience, Wolf ultimately advocated the use of heterogeneous groups. "They reflect a microcosmic society and, of course, tend to reproduce that much abused institution—the family, which, since it probably ushered in the patients' neurosis, is the logical agency for checking it. . . . The battle is best won where it was apparently lost" (1949, p. 527).

Wolf advised excluding psychopaths, alcoholics, retardates, stutterers, hypomanic patients, and hallucinating psychotics from group participation. He typically practiced in open-ended groups of optimally 8 to 10 participants meeting for 90 minutes three times a week. Alternate meetings without the therapist were encouraged, with patients convening at each other's homes, so that they might discharge feelings about him in ways which they would be too inhibited to initiate in Wolf's presence. He found that participants brought back to the officiated meetings the highlights of these peer consultations. Schlachet (1979) suggests that this practice may have begun when Wolf, as a neurology student, organized a get-together with his analysts' other analysands—a move that ultimately brought interpretation and restrictive sanction. Wolf, however, retained a deep respect for members' abilities to understand each other as well as recognizing participants' ongoing need for peer support. He adamantly advised that "patients cannot be underestimated for their intuitive perception and adjunct analytic facility" (1949, p. 532).

To elucidate the process and clarify the technique of analytic group psychotherapy, a series of six overlapping treatment stages were formulated. Progress of individual patients and the movement of the group itself could be delineated by following this linear progression.

1. *Preliminary individual analysis.* Following an initial interview, a series of 10 to 30 individual preliminary visits were accomplished. To aid with proper evaluation, psychological testing was concurrently recommended.

> *In this preparatory phase the therapist explores present difficulties, biographical material, dreams, present, recurrent and former nightmares, gets an impression of the patient's day-to-day activities and strives to prepare him for group analysis by explaining something of its history and practice. The patient is told, as early as possible, that he is being groomed for group analysis. His fears and doubts are studied. (Wolf, 1949, pp. 533–534)*

2. *Rapport through dreams and fantasies.* The first interactive group process was for members to recount a dream or waking fantasy and then for the whole group to freely associate to the manifest content, thereby personalizing and interpreting the material. "The whole group becomes engrossed in dream analysis with its attendant associations, catharsis, sense of liberation and mutuality, all of which contribute toward the group unity which is so important in the first stages of treatment" (Wolf, 1949, p. 542).

3. *Interreaction through interpersonal free association.* In this phase, patients spontaneously and in uncensored fashion free associated about each other. Interpersonal feedback and open expression of feeling and fantasy were explicitly encouraged. Under the leader's direction, members worked toward identifying and avowing perceptions that "hit the target," while sorting through distortions and projections. Wolf suggested that "out of this technic, which elicits the most electric kind of unpremeditated interaction, a number of dynamic processes emerge. [The patient] comes to know just where he stands in the eyes of his fellows and why" (Wolf, 1949, pp. 544, 546). Association and feedback procedures might be formalized in a group "going around," with each member specifically asked for his or her feelings about every other participant or for opinions concerning the problem under discussion. Wolf explained the ultimate purpose of such interactions. "The groping of each individual to identify the character structure of his neighbor is a process that slowly outlines the basic personality by increments of ventured thrusts or flyers beneath the surface of the outer self" (1949, p. 550).

4. *The analysis of resistance.* As a result of the free-associative process, resistances began to emerge within various group members. The group leader worked persistently to bring members' attention to any activity that was nonpsychoanalytic in character. "In this stage these defenses are discovered, studied, delineated and the forces that support them are examined" (Wolf, 1949, p. 550). Wolf cataloged a number of individual resist-

ances specific to group therapy, including transfer of love from the therapist to another group member, compulsive missionary spirit, going blank, voyeurism, hiding behind the analysis of others, diffident discussion of sexual material, and the use of ritualized historical recital. In this phase of resistance analysis, Wolf clarified the place of personal history in the ongoing group process.

> *History has the greatest significance when evoked and recalled by the discovery and analysis of resistance and transference in the moment of their occurrence—that is, when history has a bearing on the present which is meaningful to the patient and the therapist. The present neurotic behavior is envisioned as a photograph of the significant past. Careful scrutiny of the immediate moment will recall pertinent traumatic events. Personal flashbacks may be vividly illuminating, and the exploration and understanding of the past in terms of its influence on the present is essential to the creation of a wholesome present and future. (1949, p. 554)*

5. *The analysis of transference.* Wolf also gave vivid descriptions of transference phenomena in the making. He suggested that the therapist educate the group about the unconscious, repetitious, and compulsive nature of these familial projections, with their inherently constraining influence on freedom, reality testing, and ultimate psychic health. He recommended that transference analysis make up the "largest single area of group concentration," and instructed that "transference must be dealt with in the moment of its occurrence" (1950, p. 18). The members' varied personalities actually stimulated multiple transferences. "The multiplicity of ways in which a patient dresses up the other members accurately reanimates the old family, disclosing in the action both his history and the richly divergent facets of his personality" (1950, p. 18).

6. *Conscious personal action and social integration.* The last stage of group analysis involved integrating learning and converting insights into behavioral changes and characterological shifts. Patients became more able to spot their own transferences and resistances, and do active battle with their overdetermined, compulsive strivings. "As patients grope for the solid side of themselves, transferences atrophy from disuse, and the irrational emotion of earlier meetings is gradually replaced by mutual friendliness and realistic regard" (Wolf, 1950, p. 29).

Wolf talked at length about the role of the group therapist and his respect for the wisdom of the group process. He summarized by saying that the group therapist's "effectiveness lies in his deep contact with each member, in his ability to integrate them, in his skill in foreseeing the historical course the group takes and in his confidence in the potential resources of the various members" (1950, p. 34). Wolf's early writings still represent one of the clearest and most elegant expositions on working with the individual-within-the-group.

Lauretta Bender

Versatile psychiatrist Lauretta Bender, perhaps best known for the Bender Visual Motor Gestalt Test, began working with groups of children in the mid-1930s. Bender (1937) described the work done at the Psychiatric Division of Bellevue Psychiatric Hospital, where ward activities were used for group therapy. While initiated as a measure of convenience, the staff soon found that collective activities allowed the children to express their emotions and act out their impulses for aggression or love, which resulted in the relief of anxiety and the lessening of apprehensions. By communing with the staff and other children, the individual child experienced a socializing effect that fostered interactive adaptations.

Milieu treatment represented a therapeutic replication of the nuclear family and became a specific forum for targeted group interventions. Bender described various formats for group work, including normal unit activities, rhythm and music classes, art therapy, schoolroom routines, puppet theater and discussion, and group treatment via staff conferences, as well as more traditional discussion and play therapy groups. Throughout her writings, she stressed that any regimen of group activities for children must be "based upon the natural rhythms of the child's growing organism. . . . The rhythm must adapt itself to age level, to intellectual maturation, to the motility problem and the attention span" (1937, p. 1156).

Adolescent therapy discussion groups were homogeneously organized by gender, age, and specific developmental problem. Group composition was planned so that problem youngsters could participate and be positively affected by modeling their more normal peers.

> *We have found that even the most intimate problems of the child are best discussed in groups. . . . A group of adolescent girls will actually discuss their sex problems, describe their own experiences, talk about masturbation, and ask more questions in groups than they will individually. Similarly a group of boys will discuss every problem freely. The further advantage is that one shy, completely repressed child can be added to such a group and benefit by the experience and gradually start to talk. (Bender, 1937, p. 1166)*

Play therapy with small children made use of the naturally induced social stimulation and the children's lack of repressive defenses in the group setting in order to open up avenues for encounter, exploration, and discussion. Bender (1937) reported how children could be ruthless with each other. Yet their naive honesty allowed each child to be "jibed by the others on his peculiarity, which made it possible to discuss these things freely and laugh over them" (p. 1167).

Bender and Woltman (1936) utilized a puppet theater to elicit and simulate various age-appropriate issues and conflicts. In the puppet plays, various characters came to represent parts of the child and/or people in the child's family. Thus, Casper became the child as hero, while Charlie the monkey portrayed the youngster's more primitive side. As the play progressed, cheering and jeering allowed for cathartic release.

> *Group discussions on the various problems which are brought out in the puppet play have been most successful in getting expressions on all problems, both of aggression and love. . . . Also the puppet shows are an excellent source of material for the physician to use in individual treatment. They may be used as dream material is used. The child never retells the show as it is produced, but modifies it in the telling to suit his own emotional problems. (Bender, 1937, p. 1161)*

Bender avowed the special advantages of the group situation for speeding children's individual treatment and for handling the inevitable rise of crisis and confrontation. She suggested that it is usually better for children in the midst of strong emotions to work out these feelings in a group setting. Any child working individually may be too overwhelmed or inhibited to express himself or herself, especially if those emotions are directed against the therapist. In contrast, "among a group of children there are enough who can simultaneously threaten and revile the physician without the individual child himself having to feel too much guilt and anxiety for the revolt. If the revolt is not justified, someone in the group will surely sense it and express it for the group" (Bender, 1937, p. 1157).

Bender's professional association with and marriage to Paul Schilder, in 1936, synergistically influenced both of their approaches to group therapy.

Systems Builders

Samuel Slavson

For more than half of his 91 years, Samuel Slavson was a prominent proselytizer, prolific writer, and vigilant watchdog for the field of group psychotherapy. In 1972, *Family Health,* in listing the "100 Most Important

Leaders in the World of Health," named him "Father of Group Psycho-therapy." This claim is worthy, given Slavson's discovery of "activity group therapy" in 1934, his founding of the American Group Psychotherapy Association in 1943 (the AGPA officially considers its founding date as 1942), his originating the International Journal of Group Psychotherapy in 1951, and his 192 publications, including 16 books on group-related matters.

Slavson was born in Russia in 1891 and emigrated to the United States with his family in 1903. His professional training was as an engineer, though he became familiar with groups through volunteer work with children and a later professional involvement in progressive education. From 1919 to 1927, he worked as a curriculum consultant for the Walden School in New York City, and later, from 1927 to 1929, served as Director of Research at the Malting House in Cambridge, England. Slavson was a self-taught psychoanalyst with no formal mental health training, although he claimed the distinction of having been psychoanalyzed by a student of Freud's.

His group psychotherapy experiments began in 1934 with latency age children at the Jewish Board of Guardians in New York City. There, he first introduced a creative recreation program for maladjusted girls, which utilized a small-group format (AGPA Committee on History, 1971). By 1935, Slavson was holding weekly training seminars for staff, which developed into the first group therapy program associated within a community agency, and which eventually led to an active consultancy and the beginnings of a formal group therapy organization.

Activity group therapy, Slavson's most innovative treatment contribution, was especially geared for working with overaggressive and excessively withdrawn children. In a permissive and accepting therapeutic atmosphere, children were allowed to interact in a manner conducive to free play and regression, which Slavson believed were the essential conditions for subsequent character reformation. In a manner reminiscent of Franz Alexander's "corrective emotional experience," the activity group therapist chose interventions tailored specifically to the needs of the particular child. Thus, the shy child might be courted, whereas the acting-out child was planfully ignored. Slavson observed that children naturally demonstrated their issues in an action language. He described the lively processes that unfolded in activity groups.

> *The opportunities for personality interaction are much more numerous. The members of the group work together; they quarrel, fight—and sometimes strike one another; they argue and haggle, but finally come to some working understanding with one another. Sometimes this process takes six months or more, but once it has been established, it becomes a permanent attitude on the part of the individuals involved. (Slavson, 1940, p. 39)*

Slavson's work with children was characterized by a permissive belief in freedom of self-expression, whether that expression initially yielded hostility or creative interaction.

Throughout his association with group therapy, Slavson held to a traditional line, urging that treatment be based on thorough diagnosis and sound psychoanalytic principles. Despite being a lay practitioner himself, Slavson advocated strict standards for the qualification of group psychotherapists. Later in his career, he had great difficulty accepting more active and affective treatment regimens. He lamented, "Particular violators in this area are the practitioners of the new groups of various types known under the generic term 'encounter groups,' whose specialties are massive regressive games and rather callous dealing with feelings in the name of catharsis, openness, and uninhibited relatedness" (1971, p. xxii).

Surprisingly, Slavson's own theorizing did show considerable flexibility. Under his auspices and tutelage, a diversity of groups were organized and supervised in clinics, mental hospitals, industry, and private practice (Slavson, 1971). Activity, analytic, para-analytic, and guidance groups were provided for delinquents, unmarried mothers, geriatric patients, addicts, alcoholics, stutterers, mental hospital patients, and couples with sex and marital problems (Slavson, 1971). Slavson explains the rationale for offering practically oriented guidance groups.

> *In considerable numbers of persons, feelings of discomfort and deviant conduct do not necessarily stem from neurotic states, they are rather the results of habit, early conditioning, imitation, or identifications. They should not be unnecessarily submitted to disturbing analytic procedures. There are greatly less strenuous and briefer methods available for them, both in individual and in group approaches. Such therapy is usually described as counseling, guidance, or psychonursing. (p. xvii)*

For psychotherapy, proper, Slavson strongly suggested that therapists carefully construct their groups. Some initial individual work, psychological testing, including the Rorschach Ink Blot Test, thorough diagnosis, and careful client selection, were integral parts of the grouping process. Slavson believed that many potential problems could be prevented by attention to pregroup concerns. "The chief skill a group therapist must possess . . . is the ability to recognize the suitability of patients for group treatment, and—what is even more difficult—to combine them so that they may be mutually helpful to each other therapeutically" (1971, p. xv).

Homogeneous groupings of patients based on the specific nature of their pathology was recommended. "Homogeneity of the patients' basic pathology or syndrome favors discussion of common problems and more intense therapeutic interchange . . . increased empathy, vicarious catharsis, and spectator therapy" (1964, p. 202). Slavson warned against including neurotic and character disorders together in the same group since "such individuals operate from completely different psychic sources and irreconcilable frames of reference" (1971, p. xiii).

While inventing the term *group dynamics* in 1939 with reference to nontherapeutic groups, Slavson actually advocated that in psychotherapy such collective dynamics should be nipped in the bud. He vigorously maintained that therapeutic emphasis must be kept on the individual patient and not displaced onto the group as a whole. Similarly, Slavson eschewed the usefulness of the group's reaching a cohesive state. "Cohesiveness is contraindicated in a real therapy group. . . . Each member must retain and exercise his idiosyncrasies, individuality, and ego functions so that they may come under the scrutiny and analysis of group members, the therapist, and the patient himself. Such helpful insights would be denied in a cohesive group" (1971, p. xiv).

Holding to a traditional line, Slavson believed that the group was merely the "technical instrument of psychotherapy"—a treatment regimen to be carefully patterned on psychoanalytic principles. Likened to a collective version of Freudian analysis, group treatment involved analysis of transference, catharsis, identification, insight formation, reality testing, and sublimation. Patients' "social hunger" spurred them to participate, while the group setting itself served to stimulate individual dynamics. Although true free association was not possible in the group, its derivative, "associated thinking," was widely encouraged, revealing as it did various members' intrapsychic problems. Episodically, Slavson might stretch the model by introducing more active strategies such as didactics, paradigmatic maneuvers, and mild confrontations, or by directly eliciting such helpful behaviors as assertiveness (Rosenthal, 1983).

He maintained that groups should have no more than eight patients, but actually functioned better with only five or six. A champion of group methods in general, he was careful to qualify their utility. Slavson believed that neurotic patients ultimately required the consolidated transference neurosis available in dyadic therapy. When group therapy was indicated, sequential (individual then group) or combined (individual and group) would often be recommended as the treatment of choice. Slavson's conviction that real personality change could best be accomplished in early intervention might have contributed to his continued interest in working with children.

Slavson's name remains irrevocably linked with the discipline of group therapy, as officially commemorated by the American Group Psychotherapy Association's naming him as its President Emeritus. Prominent students have included Saul Scheidlinger, Emanuel Hallowitz, Mortimer Schiffer, and Leslie Rosenthal. Helen Durkin and Henriette Glatzer were also directly influenced by Slavson's early work with children. His force of conviction and power of personality made Slavson a figure with whom to be reckoned.

Jacob Moreno

Jacob Moreno truly believed that "the world is a stage." He staked claim to the paternity of three group-related offspring: sociometry, psychodrama, and group therapy proper. Moreno may have begun experimenting with group methods as early as 1908 in Vienna. In 1913, while a medical student, he organized and led group sessions for Viennese prostitutes. Eight to ten women met two to three times a week. Moreno later reported, "We began to see then that 'one individual could become a therapeutic agent to the other' and the potentialities of a group therapy on the reality level crystallized in our mind" (1953). Before emigrating to the United States in 1925, he had established "The Theater of Spontaneous Man," an attempt to represent the dramas of life by therapeutic staging. By the time he reached Ellis Island, Moreno had already written several articles and a book on group-related matters.

In 1928, Moreno began demonstrating group action methods at Mount Sinai Hospital in New York City. Between 1929 and 1932, he ran psychodrama demonstrations three times a week at Carnegie Hall. He organized a group therapy program at Sing Sing Prison in 1931, using extensive sociometric ratings of prisoners based on actual behavior rather than on psychiatric diagnoses. In 1932, he made a presentation on group methods at the Annual Meeting of the American Psychiatric Association. Attracting the attention of the esteemed psychiatrist William Alanson White, Moreno began practicing sociometry and psychodrama at St. Elizabeth's Hospital in Washington, DC, in 1934, with the first official psychodrama stage being built there in 1940. In 1934, Moreno published the first edition of his opus volume on sociometry and group psychotherapy, entitled *Who Shall Survive* (Moreno, 1953), in which he expounded many of his interactional notions and action techniques. The first society specifically for group psychotherapists, the American Society for Group Psychotherapy and Psychodrama, was formed under his direction in 1942, and Moreno served as its inspirational leader and first president.

He began editing efforts in1918 with the monthly magazine *Daimon,* and continued with the journal, *Impromptu* (1931), the subsequent publication of *Sociometry* (1938), and later *Sociatry: Journal of Group and Intergroup Therapy* (1947), renamed *Group Psychotherapy, Psychodrama, and Sociometry* in 1954. Luminaries in psychiatry and social psychology served as editors and contributors to the various journals. For example, the lead article in *Group Psychotherapy, Psychodrama, and Sociometry's* inaugural issue was the now famous, "The Prediction of Interpersonal Behavior in Group Psychotherapy," by the infamous Timothy Leary with Hubert S. Coffey. Here, Leary introduced the "interpersonal wheel," the culmination of his social psychology research at Harvard. This interactive schema for understanding human behavior was quite consistent with Moreno's own notions about complimentary relationships and the mutual influence of dynamic pairs, whether husbands and wives, leaders and followers, fathers and sons, mothers and daughters, or therapists and clients.

Moreno made many of his own contributions to the language, practice, and understanding of group therapy. He coined such terminology as *encounter* (1912), *interpersonal communication* (1918), *group therapy* (1931), *group psychotherapy* (1932), and *group catharsis* (1937). His practice of roleplaying, role reversal and rehearsal, and his concepts of enactment, auxiliary ego, vicarious therapy, social atom, and group structure greatly influenced practice across a wide range of therapeutic schools from American behaviorism to British group analysis.

Moreno, himself, identified the beginning of group psychotherapy with the founding of the science of sociometry, the study of the quality and direction of interpersonal relationships within groups. He describes sociometry's early reception and intent.

> *For many who were satisfied with psychoanalytic explanations of group formation or with influencing the group from the outside, for instance, by means of lectures or motion pictures, my approaches appeared then as startling. But in order to study and change the group from within, I had to develop an exact science of the group, sociometry. I did not develop sociometry for its own sake but to give group psychotherapy a tangible anchorage. Without its study of socio-and-action dynamics the modern advances of group psychotherapy would hardly be what they are. (Moreno, 1950, p. 136)*

Moreno (1950) compared the sociogram to a "social compass," that could guide the therapist "through the intricate maze of group structure" (p. 125). In the course of following the group's ongoing direction, those emotional contagions and forces that threatened cohesion and development might be identified and redirected.

A "spatial proximity hypothesis" underlay the mapping of the interpersonal domain. Physical proximity, real and imagined, helped determine the nature of social bonds and mutual attractions. By noting nonverbal, spatial relations—who approaches or avoids whom—the facilitator could assess how the group arranges and organizes itself. Likewise, following a "temporal proximity hypothesis," the leader observed the precise order of social attentions—who talks when and what is taken up at which times. Moreno found that, generally, here-and-now material commanded initial attentions, followed by considerations from the past and the future in descending order (Wolberg, 1976). Later interpersonal scaling procedures (Bales, 1950; Hill, 1977) derive directly from Moreno's work in sociometry.

An early and vocal advocate of group dynamics, Moreno, in contrast to Slavson, held that groups necessarily assumed a life and personality of their own marked by varying degrees of cohesion and equilibrium. Participants related to the group by taking on various roles such as "star," "isolate," or "rejected member." Role formation served as the link between individual personalities and the group's social psychology. Moreno also recognized subgroup phenomena such as pairing and chaining. Group composition became essential to a successful process, with members' similarities and differences carefully matched to foster relatedness and wide-ranging interaction.

An admirer of Freud but a staunch adversary of psychoanalysis, Moreno believed that *analysis* and *psychotherapy* were antithetical. He rebuked Freud for ignoring "the *fluid ever-changing* constellations of actual groups." Moreno pointed out, "He had never studied groups. . . . He postulated a group psychology which was to be accepted on its philosophical merits" (quoted in Wohlberg, 1976, p. 9, from Moreno, 1957, p. ix). With his own emphasis on spontaneity, creativity, and here-and-now interactions, Moreno added, "One thing is certain: Freud's resistance to 'acting out' was a block to the progress of psychotherapy" (1953, p. xxvii). He criticized more substantively.

> *Inter-personal relations in the couch situation is a misnomer because of the one-sidedness of the therapeutic focus. Only the patient is on the couch; the doctor is not. It was with group psychotherapy and psychodrama that the genuine meaning of inter-personal relations became realized, one therapeutic agent facing the other on equal terms and with an equal opportunity for communication. (1950, p. 122)*

In practice, Moreno directed groups as small as two members and as large as the audiences accommodated in psychodramatic format. He suggested that, in psychotherapy proper, "groups should be so constructed in size and type so that every member is able to know every other member intimately" (1932, p. 64). A usual size for a psychotherapy group was 7 to 10 participants. Technique demanded an involved group and an active leader. Groups often began with a "warm-up process" and relied on the empathic or "tele" relationships between various members to further stimulate interaction. Moreno hearkened back to ancient Greek theater to explain the use of auxiliary egos and mental catharsis, while pointing out the vicarious growth possible for the spectating members. Moreno likened the psychodramatic theater to a world in miniature where "all situations and roles which the world produces or may produce are interacted" (1937, p. 25). In sociodramas, Moreno sought to replicate and transferentially remedy by small group methods the society-at-large's cultural and inter-group problems:

Moreno summarized his thoughts about groups. "Group therapy is the result of well calculated, spontaneous therapy plus proper social assignment. . . . Psychological treatment is projected away from the clinic into real life situations and techniques for a proper procedure [are developed] on the spot. The leader is within the group, not a person without" (1932, p. 94).

Moreno's group therapy efforts represented a combination of novel ideas, tireless energy, and loftiness of purpose. His work continues to have influence both in and out of the practice of psychodrama. The International Association of Group Psychotherapy, which in 1951 developed out of the American Society for Group Psychotherapy and Psychodrama, remains a viable umbrella organization for containing and disseminating diverse group therapy perspectives.

Remaining Questions

This era of diversity and innovation raised many legitimate questions about the nature and use of the group as a treating medium that would be taken up in detail by the next generation of group practitioners and theorists.

- Question 1: *Is the group, per se, merely the setting for individual treatment or does the collective, as such, develop into a viable social system of personal, cultural, and organizational import?*

Breaking from a strict dyadic treatment model, the innovators of group psychotherapy's second generation shared an underlying assumption that humans were in fact social beings. As such, individuals demonstrated a hunger to be with each other (Slavson), a need for socialization (Wolf), a benefit to breaking isolation and secrecy (Schilder), an ongoing connection with the dynamics of their families-of-origin (Wender), and a distinctive social psychology when congregating together (Moreno). In the spirit of reconciliation, Schilder suggests that "the group [as social microcosm] is a step nearer reality as opposed to the classical analytic twosome" (1938, p. 178).

Yet, in actual practice, the innovators ranged on a continuum from a more traditional hold out for a strict emphasis on the individual, to a focus on the group as an evolving system that might be measured and manipulated to therapeutic advantage. At one extreme, Slavson believed that the group setting merely catalyzes and highlights individual dynamic proclivities by precipitating regression, weakening defenses, loosening resistance, and maximizing reality testing (Rosenthal, 1983). The action remained in understanding each patient's intrapsychic structure, unique dynamics, nuclear problems, and maturational position in order to devise individualized treatment strategies to be actualized in milieu.

At the other extreme, Moreno espoused that groups became entities in their own right, with specifiable tendencies manifest in evident attractions, repulsions, and interpersonal enactments. As unique organizational entities emerge, opportunities for exploring and changing the socializing tendencies of the individuals so gathered and the group so formed are hastened. The group itself becomes a therapeutic agent, as collective norms and values are specifically cultivated for the benefit of the assembled participants (Wohlberg, 1976). Perhaps Schilder's traditional approach to group psychotherapy, combined with his steadfast belief that human collectives and their leaders cannot help but convey and instill ideologies, values, mores, and normative expectancies, represents a viable middle ground.

- Question 2: *What is the distinction between individual and collective processes, and do therapeutic gains lie in working with intrapsychic or group dynamics?*

Attention to and recognition of individual and collective dynamics depends on one's stance regarding the legitimate focus of treatment. Rosenthal (1983) argues that Slavson was more rigid in his writings when considering the presence or utility of whole-group phenomena than he was in practice or supervision. Even in theory, Slavson recognized the utility of cultivating adaptive collective dynamics in normal groups, where members shared a common goal. However, in therapy groups, where individuals experience separate problems of distinctive origin, he considered such collective dynamics a form of negative transference—or "acting out in unison." Therefore, the therapist's task was to interfere with evolving groupwide processes in order to keep individual dynamics in the forefront by keeping the group at bay.

Wolf concurred that patients only come together in "pseudo-mutuality" as a way of heading off fears of rejection and/or abandonment. The tendency to sacrifice personal perspectives and individual needs by forming symbiotic bonds disallows members from recognizing and effecting their unique capacities of self, as distinct from more socialized aspects. Although initially believing that groups went through particular stages, Wolf later concluded that group development was actually an artifice created by the therapist. Only individuals could engage in progressive maturational advance. Therefore, if the group was responding in a unified, stereotypical manner, Wolf might interrupt this process by initiating a go-around to elicit more individualized responses.

Moreno, once again, represented the resounding counterpoint, the emerging trend toward cultivating the group in order to influence the individual. He believed that the intrapsychic sphere or projective system, including transference phenomena, represented only one of the collective's viable treatment dimensions. Problem-solving capacities equated with reality factors and tendencies to accept or reject one another noted by sociometric measures provided two additional venues for exploration and enactment.

- Question 3: *What, then, is the place of group formation and cohesion in collective treatment—as an ameliorative factor or as an individual resistance?*

Coming to group cohesion can be viewed as a sign of progress, an analog of the therapeutic alliance, or even a curative variable (Yalom, 1970). Coming together, in unity, can also be seen as a defense against interpersonal struggles and individual diversities. Slavson believed that cohesive groups artificially blocked the necessary discharge of aggressive urges and negative feelings, thereby preventing catharsis, sublimation, and working through. Individual progress and psychic equilibrium only follow when intense struggles within and between individuals are unimpeded by conventional trends. The cultivation of a cohesive group represents a "status denial," a false sense of equality, and a stifling unanimity that prevents the expression of envy, hostility, or competition (Shiffer, 1983). Thus, any overt tendencies toward holistic formations or the assumption of groupwide emotions constitute a resistance to a more individualized treatment perspective.

Wolf also believed that cohesiveness was an acting out of symbiotic urges. He specifically resisted groupwide interpretations so as to not foster any false sense of "pseudo-cohesion" that would distract individuals from their more particularized work (Schlachet, 1979). Wolf and Schwartz (1962) later decried the potentially deleterious effects of group standards and conformity pressures.

Moreno intimated that groups, superordinate to individuals, formed distinctive social systems that could and should be cultivated with therapeutic intent. "The most important discovery was that every group had a structure of its own with varying degrees of cohesiveness and depth and that no two groups were alike, that the structure of groups could be explored and determined and that groups are phenomena which can be scientifically studied" (Moreno, 1932, p. XI, quoted in Wolberg, 1976, p. 10). By coming together as a whole and by recognizing formative tendencies, individual patients might change their behaviors and influence their intimate connections at the stage of current relations.

- Question 4: *What is the proper venue and object for diagnosis, analysis, and interpretation, the individual intrapsychic sphere or the group-as-a-whole?*

Debate continued, as Slavson (1951) later warned that the "placing of primary focus on treatment of the group as a unitary entity, rather than on individual patients, is a development which may prove to be a major crisis" (quoted in Rosenthal, 1983, p. 4). For him, group treatment represented a modification of individual treatment, not a novel modality with its own theory or rules of engagement. Rosenthal (1983) reiterates Slavson's preoccupation with individuals by noting his persistently asked supervisory query, "What are the nuclear problems of each member of your group?" (p. 4).

Wolf also believed that all analysis was essentially individually oriented and intrapsychic by design. Alternating attention was given to individual patients who might sequentially complain about their problems or even relay a dream. The other participants would then join the therapist by sharing associations and offering observations, feedback, and interpretations to the exposed member. The group provided an interpersonal forum for stimulating, demonstrating, and analyzing individual proclivities. The focus remained on figuring out how and why the individual member was reacting to the therapist and to the other participants—as a form of transference diagnosis.

Moreno assumed a more contextual approach wherein the individual could not be distinguished from the roles he or she assumed within the collective setting. Diagnosis, as in the science of sociometry, would evaluate an individual within the actual scope of his or her ongoing relations and interactions. Group involvement, whether in psychodrama or psychotherapy proper, brought out the creative, not merely the regressive aspects of individuality. The psychological products that emerged from such collective efforts were valued as qualitatively different from the formative dynamics and oft-repeated contents of the individual contributors.

- Question 5: *What is the essential nature of transference phenomena as they occur in the group setting?*

Slavson believed that the group served to dilute transference by creating multiple objects onto which to project personal conflicts. More nuclear problems with a host of familial figures could be reflected upon. The group itself became a natural metaphor for the family-of-origin. Wender believed that the therapist was viewed as a symbolic parent, while the members became transferential siblings. Wolf (1950) beautifully described the nature of parental transferences thrust upon the therapist, while also recognizing the potential for sibling rivalries and peer support.

Schilder sought to equalize the therapeutic relationship by humanizing the therapist in the role of group leader, rather than abject authority figure. Transference phenomena were thereby mitigated, as the facilitator became more of a real person, lowering the analytic screen by sharing some of his or her own values and morals. At least when working with ideologies, Schilder insisted, "The physician does not have the right to remain completely impersonal in such a group. He must reveal his own ideology and also justify it" (Schilder,1936, quoted in Bender, 1979, p. 5.). Yet Schilder realized that therapist self-disclosure, directive interventions, and the group's comparative activities lessened the potential for individual insight. He believed that group work more importantly fostered insights about the deep similarities in the human experience.

While the plot of many psychodramas reiterated familial conflicts, Moreno argued that the group-in-the-making did not necessarily duplicate the family-in-the-living. A distinctive organization, with open-ended potentials all its own, was created as a combination of individual tendencies and groupwide trends.

It is certainly true that in the group setting there is the possibility for many and varied identifications and transferences. Members will readily find parental stand-ins in the person of the therapist, by way of his or her role, education, and authoritative position, however open and candid the facilitation style. Likewise, various members readily represent all those significant others—brothers, sisters, friends, husbands, wives, and children— who populate the outer and inner world. But what of the group itself? Can the collective-as-a-whole be the actual object of projections and transferences? Slavson (1964), in later years, did suggest that the group functions "in loco maternis." It remained to be conceived if and how the group proper might serve as container and holding environment for individual affects, projections, and dynamics. It would be left for future generations of group therapists to explore this and other provocative questions.

Invention and the Mothers of Necessity

Group psychotherapy reached toward maturity just in time to respond to the pressing need for an efficient mental treatment for servicemen ravaged by the stress of World War II. Shaskan (1978) noted the wartime efforts of

Wilfred Bion, J. D. Sutherland, S. H. Foulkes, and Maxwell Jones among other British practitioners, as well as praising the contributions of many American group therapists, most notably Samuel Hadden. Shaskan suggested that during the war years, "the ground work for present group therapy was established." He added that "many authors of that period have progressed as well known group therapists [and] many authors became known in other fields of mental health" (p. 7).

In describing a match made of necessity, Shaskan observed that "the Army with its multiple individual soldiers, subjected to identical environment and training with an identical goal, afforded opportunity to give collective treatment" (Shaskan & Jolesch, 1944, p. 571). Perhaps the official endorsement of group therapy as a viable psychotherapeutic modality came in 1944, when the Army issued a bulletin professing that the favorable response of patients to comparatively brief treatment in groups warranted the widespread adoption of the regimen.

By 1943, both the American Society for Group Psychotherapy and Psychodrama (founded by Moreno) and the American Group Psychotherapy Association (pioneered by Slavson) gave group psychotherapy stable and recognizable bases from which to thrive and expand. During the first annual AGPA Conference, held in New York in 1944, active efforts were made to coordinate group therapy referrals for ex-service personnel. Discussion groups were organized and other clearinghouse activities were begun, including the collection of information and articles on group therapy. Moreno (1950) reminisced:

> Group and action methods began to spread with such rapidity, emerging in so many diverse minds and places that individual contributions were washed away, the anonymity of the movement becoming one of the greatest spurs to its rapid dissemination and acceptance. World War II made "group psychotherapy" and "psychodrama" phrases used in daily coinage everywhere and in the last years since the war's end, the number of workers in these areas have gone into the many thousands here as in Europe. (p. 137)

The growth spurt of group psychotherapy was over and the postwar literature boom had begun. Much of the work of the following generations of group theoreticians and practitioners, both during and after the war, served to clarify the nature of the two-way exchange between members and the group. An epistemology of the emergent grouping process was forged with special attention given to the distinction between individual and collective needs and trends. The prevailing question became: In what ways was it possible to relate and treat a member in the context of the group of which he or she was a part?

Appendix to Chapter 4

TABLE 1 • Group Therapy Innovators: Type of Group and Treatment Advantages

Therapist	Type of Group	Advantages of Group Treatment
Wender	Psychoanalytic	Applicable to wider group of patients
		Shorter in duration
		More financially feasible
		The human individual is a group animal
		Inhibitions and repressions motivated by mores of group
		By working out his difficulties in the small group he is able to face the large group (world)
		Group is a natural interactional setting
		Provides substitute family and milieu for hospitalized patients
		Takes advantage of normal patient groupings (problems are analyzed and discussed with greater candor among patients than with physician)
		Uses gregarious impulse therapeutically
Schilder	Psychoanalytic "Analysis of ideologies"	Group therapy does not recapitulate neurotic isolation
		Provides constructive social replica
		Human experiences in their deeper levels are very similar
		Group setting is nearer to reality
		Cooperation possible between patients with hostility mitigated through exposure
		Capacity to learn from others—imitation
		Basic need for a common bond between individuals
		Individual history is tied up with other human beings
		Research tool for studying group formation and action
		Efficient treatment modality
Wolf	"Psychoanalysis of groups"	Method of treatment for low-income patients
		Group is a microcosmic society

TABLE 1 • Continued

Therapist	Type of Group	Advantages of Group Treatment
		Patients can be auxiliary therapists
		Multiple transferences are possible
		Way to treat patients with heterogeneous problems
		Availability of "double Oedipal situation"
		Genuine socialization experience for patients
		Availability of consensual validation or invalidation
Slavson	Activity group therapy Analytic and para-analytic groups Guidance groups "Situational therapy" "Compensatory therapy" "Substitutive therapy"	Destiny of man tied up with groups Group life a potent force in personality organization Basic need for group relatedness-social hunger Groups are extension of biological life and an integral part of nature Small groups are replicas of family Group serves as "loco maternis" Compensation or substitute for traumatic relationships More and deeper insights possible with people in similar situations Direct and meaningful interactions stimulated Cooperation, fusing, merging are ascendant patterns of social life Group stimulates the formation of problems and thoughts Forum for multiple transferences and objects of identification Group catalyzes individual dynamics, accelerates regression, loosens resistances, and provides matrix for reality testing.
Moreno	Psychodrama Sociodrama Sociometry Group therapy	Group provides true interpersonal setting Treatment in "open social space" One patient therapeutic agent for another Possibility for vicarious growth Possibility for mental and social catharsis Therapeutic theater akin to world in

Continued

TABLE 1 • Continued

Therapist	Type of Group	Advantages of Group Treatment
		miniature
		Act or live out real situations
		More generalization to real life than with couch
		Synergistic effect of the group
		Group dynamics manifest
		"Tele" (empathic) relations manifest
		Equalizes therapist and patient, with leader in group
		Protects and stimulates self-regulatory mechanisms of natural groups

TABLE 2 • Group Therapy Innovators: Curative Factors

Therapist	Setting	Curative Factors and Therapy Goals
Wender	Hillside Hospital, Hastings on Hudson	Interrelation and interaction
		Adjustment to society
		Release of aggressive tendencies (hates, loves, wishes, and guilts)
		Emotional release
		Working through difficulties and adjustments in small group
		Lessen the fear of adjustment
		Generalization
		Competition to remain well
		Familial transference
		Symbolic catharsis in the family
		Displacement of parental love onto new objects
		Partial reorganization of the personality
		Diverting impulses into positive channels
		Socialization
		Identification
		Cutting isolation
		Consensual reality
		Insight
		Intellectualization
		Contagion
		Understanding unconscious trends
Schilder	Bellevue Psychiatric Hospital, New York	Logically thinking through and correcting ideologies and beliefs
		Discovering the genesis of various

TABLE 2 • *Continued*

Therapist	Setting	Curative Factors and Therapy Goals
		ideologies and beliefs
		Working through elements of character
		Making new adaptations to old problems
		Breaking the isolation of the individual
		Identification
		Imitation
		Insight into premature solutions and crystallization in developmental history
		Hostility and aggression diverted into cooperative efforts (work, nature)
		Fostering sympathy and common bonding
		Delve into the meaning of words (abstract ideas connected to concrete experiences)
		Transfer insight from one person to another
Wolf	U.S. Army Private practice	Catharsis
		Liberation and mutuality
		Group unity
		Mutual understanding
		Empathy
		Sympathy
		Sorting through interpersonal distortions and projections
		Personality and character description
		Analysis of resistance and defense
		Insight
		Reality testing
		Actively encouraging behavioral change
		Group as a buffer against despair
		Uncovering disparate parts of self
		Social rewards for constructive work
		Learn to trust own judgments
		Recreation of the original family (belonging)
		Feedback (microcosmic laboratory)
		Vicarious therapy

Continued

TABLE 2   •   *Continued*

Therapist	Setting	Curative Factors and Therapy Goals
		Practice group for intimacy and deep rapport
Slavson	Jewish Board of Guardians, New York	Empathy Catharsis Vicarious catharsis Spectator therapy Regression followed by character reformation Personality interaction Insight Reality testing Identifications Working through transference and resistance Fostering group solutions to problems Sublimation Effect changes in the structure of personality Build ego Provide unconditional love Redirect pathology Foster leisure interests
Moreno	Mt. Sinai Hospital, New York Demonstrations Carnegie Hall St. Elizabeth's Hospital Washington, DC	Spontaneity Improvisation fosters creativity Cohesion Enactment Expand available choices of behavior Stimulate less developed factors in each other Emotional expansion Foster relatedness and wide ranging interaction Problem solving Mental and social catharsis Group dynamics Vicarious therapy Impact of the group as a "Greek chorus" Mutual ability to bring each other to a level of completion and balance

TABLE 3 • Group Therapy Innovators: Practical Applications

Therapist	Type of Patient	Exclusion Criteria	Homogeneity	Heterogeneity	Individual Therapy
Wender	Hospitalized psychoneurotics Early schizophrenics Depression	Intellectual impairment Insufficient affect Long-standing compulsive neurosis	For sex		Intermittent Conjoint Concurrent
Schilder	Inpatient psychotic Outpatient severe neurosis (social, obsessional, hypochondriacal [not helped], depersonalization, depression, hysteria) Some characterological Some schizophrenic		For sex		Individual preparatory sessions taught principles of free association, dream analysis, and wrote detailed individual biographies Concurrent individual therapy
Wolf	Mixed outpatients Service personnel Married couples	Psychopaths Alcoholics Retardates Stutterers Hypomanics Hallucinating psychotics Psychosomatic	Age	For sex balanced homogeneity	Pregroup individual analysis Ongoing individual sessions available on request as escape hatch

Continued

TABLE 3 • *Continued*

Therapist	Type of Patient	Exclusion Criteria	Homogeneity	Heterogeneity	Individual Therapy
Slavson	Children Parents Outpatients	Insufficient ego strength or resiliency/flexibility to withstand stress Difficulty with time sharing, emotional stimulation, or contagion Children who are habitual stealers, neurotic delinquents, actively homosexual, compulsively homicidal, orally aggressive	For pathology or syndrome Don't mix neurotic and characterological		Some prior individual, sequential, combined, concurrent Individual therapy for deepest problems
Moreno	General outpatient General public Prisoners Inpatients Viennese prostitutes School children		Social classification system based on sociometric ratings, and demographics Sex, age, "tele" attractions, acquaintance, ethnic composition Matched for reaction types (i.e., prepared reactors, spontaneous reactors)		

TABLE 4 • *Group Therapy Innovators: Comparison of Techniques*

Therapist	Group Size	Length and Frequency of Meetings	Techniques/Procedures/Processes
Wender	6–8	2 to 3 times a week 1-hour session 4–5 months Initially closed, later open	Initial individual evaluation Initial individual therapy and group preparatory sessions Patient to patient transferences Initial lecture material Discussion of personal problems Dream interpretation Diverting resistance Repetition of material Education of mental mechanisms Indirect analysis and interpretation (not referring directly to patient)
Schilder	2–7	1 to 2 times a week	Life history and early infantile material discussed and elucidated Patient biographies prepared Initial preparatory sessions Exploration of values, aims, goals, beliefs, and attitudes Exploration of universal problems of life Working with negative and positive transferences Free association to others' biographical material Interpretation of symptoms and dreams Repetition and working through Art therapy and analysis
Wolf	8–10	2 to 3 times a week 90 minutes Open ended	Preliminary individual analysis (10–30 sessions) Dream and fantasy interpretation Free association Analysis of resistance Transference and countertransference analysis Interpersonal feedback Working with immediate moment (here-and-now analysis of resistance and transference) Analysis of group process shifts Flashback method of evoking per-

Continued

TABLE 4 • Continued

Therapist	Group Size	Length and Frequency of Meetings	Techniques/Procedures/Processes
			sonal history and memories "Going around"
Slavson	5–6 best		Thorough diagnosis, identification of nuclear problems, and carefully determined goal setting Some prior individual work Associative thinking (one member relating to another's issues) Fostering corrective emotional experiences Effect structural changes in personality Individual analysis in group Transference and resistance analysis Interpretation of individual dynamics Free play and social period (activity group)
Moreno	7–10 (therapy group) Audience for psychodrama, sociodrama 2 for dyadic therapy	2 to 3 times a week (therapy group)	Sociometric evaluation Careful group composition Warmup process Here-and-now interactions Roleplaying and role reversal Enactment and dramatization of conflicts Analysis of psychodramatic interactions Free association of acts Free discussion Dream in action Auxiliary egos Psychodramatic techniques (self-presentation, soliloquy, projection, mirroring, interpolation of resistance, double ego, role practice)

PART THREE

Foundations: Epistemology

An inquiry into the very structure of the grouping process is necessary for a full appreciation of the potentials of the collective medium. Because of the profusion of collective treatments developed during World War II and in the decades after, it became necessary to take a step back and examine the special context that develops when individuals are brought together for the express purpose of sharing treatment. There are three epistemological processes by which individuals can be grouped together as a whole: (1) inductive group building, (2) deductive rendering, and (3) depictive representation. Each chapter in this section will explore one of these processes.

- Process 1: *Both the idea and experience of the group-as-a-whole can be reached by inductive, bottom-up, empirical-additive processes.*

Distinct levels of group analysis are possible when focusing on separate individuals in collection, interactive relations and transactions, and/or holistic arrangements and groupwide dynamics. These levels demonstrate isomorphic relationships and can be worked together in a full ranging group therapy. Progressive attempts at conceptualizing a "group-in-the-mind," while simultaneously facilitating a "group-in-practice," led to an inductive theory for building a group up from the free associations and idiosyncratic contributions of its individual members (Chapter Five).

- Process 2: *Both the idea and experience of the group-as-a-whole can be reached by deductive, top-down, theory-bound processes.*

The figure-ground relationship between the members and the group can be reversed when considering the overriding influence of collective dynamics in determining individual reactivities. Groups can be considered viable cultures, formative matrices, or influential backdrops that actually give shape and meaning to subsequent member contributions. The group itself becomes the object of primary attention, requiring epistemological reckoning while taking into account the unique properties inherent in its collective dynamics. In order to examine adequately the very complex and synergistic formation of the group-as-a-whole, one must assume a deductive mind-set, searching for exemplary episodes in order to render groupwide events intelligible by putting them in context (Chapter Six).

- Process 3: *Both the idea and experience of the group-as-a-whole can be reached through intuitive, holistic, depictive processes as expressed in analogies, metaphoric images, and symbolic representations.*

Solidaritá by Lorenzo Cascio (1985) (bronze, height 10 1/2″ × 7″) Collection of author. Ted Hewitt, photographer.

Once the group-as-a-whole is acknowledged as an entity for study, analysis, and therapeutic rendition, the problem becomes one of developing a language capable of describing collective phenomena and their inherent part-processes at each possible level of conceptualization. A perspective is advanced here for intuitively attributing meaning to the ongoing group process by depicting intrapsychic, interpersonal, and collective events in the form of mental images and metaphors. The formative forces thus depicted are enlivened, amplified, and transformed. The collective itself can take on stable meanings and a predictable transpositional form through the assumption of the overriding symbolic perspective of the "mother-group" (Chapter Seven).

Relevant inquiries raised and explored in this section include:

- *What constitutes a group and to what levels of collective organization can interventions be addressed?*
- *What is the relationship between individual participants and the group-as-a-whole, and how does the collective develop from and relate to its part-processes?*
- *How can the group and its constituent membership be known, spoken to, and progressively influenced?*
- *What fleeting roles and projections and what stable images and symbols can be highlighted by the leader to describe current purposes and to express the lasting meanings inherent in the emergent group endeavor?*

CHAPTER FIVE

A Group Is a Group Is a Group?

Building a Collective Experience Through Inductive Processes

About the only way of tracking the proliferation of group psychotherapy theory and practice since World War II is by organizing the work according to the specific structural properties of the treating medium itself. What actually constitutes a group? How is the grouping process viewed and used by the members and by the leader? What built-in configurations and pieces of the process lend themselves to useful analysis and purposeful intervention? In what ways is it possible to conceive of treating individual patients while they are all joined together?

The word *group* is a singular noun that inherently implies multiple parts and relations. In order to define a group's structure, one must ascertain just how the conglomerate is composed and managed—in what way its various elements can be isolated, interrelated, or meaningfully organized. Similarly, various group therapy regimens can be understood only by comprehending the level and nature of group structure implied within the treatment format, so that relevant attentional foci can be clearly specified and therapeutically accessed. Wilfred Bion (1961), a British analyst and group therapy pioneer who came to prominence during World War II, suggests, "The term 'group therapy' can have two distinct meanings. It can refer to the treatment of individuals [in] special therapeutic sessions, or it can refer to a planned endeavor to develop in a group the forces that lead to a smoothly running cooperative activity" (p. 11). Just so, one's overall conceptualization of *groupness* determines how one views and intervenes in the psychotherapy group—whether the therapist concentrates his or her efforts on the individuals so gathered or on the group itself.

The Group as a Trinity: Intrapersonal, Interpersonal, and Group-as-a-Whole Levels of Analysis

The word *group* actually suggests three levels of organization that reflect on the varied tenor and tasks of group psychotherapy. Each dictionary definition focuses on dissimilar features of the assemblage, and denotes a different order of relationship between the parts and the whole. The first-level definition of *group* simply refers to a quantitative clustering of individuals. Free from built-in connections or necessary byplays, this grouping comes about when individual entities are seen simultaneously in the same space at the same time. Here, the focus remains on the intrapersonal nature of experience.

The second-level definition of *group* assumes some presupposed or preplanned ordering and interaction inherent in the combining of individual parts. An isolated assortment of single entities becomes a collection when individual objects are held in common and in relation to one another. Here, the emphasis is drawn to the interpersonal nature of experience.

The third-order definition of *group,* a more radical sense of joining together, indicates the creation of a qualitatively new and superordinate entity more than and distinct from the simple sum of its parts. At this synergistic level of combination, individuals in varied configuration serve as constituent and subsidiary components of a specifiable aggregate. The resultant group-as-a-whole encompasses, defines, and influences the relation of its individual members and subgroups. The parts are relevant only as they form a meaningful organization or gestalt. Here the primary attention is given to the nature of collective enterprise (see Table 5.1).

Various approaches to group psychotherapy can be distinguished by the level of group definition that each implies. Although all the levels of conceptualization and intervention ultimately share the aim of treating an individual within a group of individuals, theoretical assumptions, methodologies, and techniques vary according to how the therapist conceives and addresses the constituent parts (members) in interaction with each other (relationships) or in recombinant collective unity (group).

Group as a Collection of Discrete Individuals

The first-order definition of *group* is "an assemblage collected without any regular form or arrangement." The salient characteristic of this

TABLE 5.1 • *Three Levels of Group Intervention*

	Individual	*Interpersonal*	*Group-as-a-whole*
Group Definition	A collection of discrete members with no regular form or arrangement	A collection of related members having a certain order or arrangement, or having some common characteristics	A collective arrangement having common characteristics in form, structure, and focus
Salient Feature	Members' noninteractive proximity	Members bound into patterns of meaningful homogeneity and interaction	Formation of a holistic entity with properties comprised from, yet independent of, its individual parts
Geometric Corollary	Point	Line	Sphere
Group Function	Setting for individual work	Agency of or field for interrelating	Object; matrix, or entity of therapeutic attentions
Level of Organization	Simplex	Duplex	Complex
Energy Patterns	Entropy	Magnetism, tropism, attraction/ repulsion	Synergy, syzergy, synchrony, homeostasis
Theoretical Stance	Classicist Individualist	Transactionalist Interpersonalist	Integralist Holistic Practitioner
Analytic Emphasis	Vertical analysis	Horizontal analysis	Isomorphic/ existential analysis
Attentional Focus	Leader centered	Member centered	Group centered
Participatory Pattern	Member < >leader	Member < >member	Member < >group
Member Role	Person	Member	Spokesperson, voice
Role of Others	Auxiliary ego Stimulant Vicarious analysant	Self-object Peer Transference object	Containers Projective screens Parts of whole

Continued

TABLE 5.1 • *Continued*

	Individual	*Interpersonal*	*Group-as-a-whole*
Focus on Attention	Transferences	Cohesion	Group themes
	Resistances	Cooperation	Group conflicts
	Libidinal ties	Competition	Group atmosphere
	Instincts	Communication	Boundaries
	Frustrations	Linkages	Tasks
	Defense mechanisms	Member roles	Developmental sequences
	Compromise formations	Patterns	Rituals
		Perceptions	Symbols
	Regressions	Commonalities	Universalities
	Wishes	Interconnectedness	Group roles
	Fears	Attractions	Group norms
	Nuclear conflicts	Repulsions	Focal conflicts
	Character structure	Joining/pairing	Group voices
	Narcissistic vulnerabilities	Splitting	Spokesperson reactions
		Bonding/ affiliations	Overall trends
		Transactions	Collusions
		Object relations	Group defenses
		Peer transferences	Subgroup dynamics
		Parataxic distortions	
Theoretical Perspectives	Strict Analytic	Sullivanian	Tavistock
	Classic Gestalt	Rogerian	Systems
	Psychodrama	Object Relations	Group Analytic
	Behavioral	Encounter	Group-as-a-whole
	Redecision	NTL	Focal Conflict
		NeoFreudian	Invisible Group

definition is that of a throng of discrete entities in nonessential and noninteractive proximity. Relationships between members of the assemblage are not specifically addressed nor does the ultimate form of the collection take on any significance. The group is simply the "setting" in which to conduct the individualized work (Kauff, 1979). The medium of attention implied at this first level of group organization is the *simplex* characterized by the single element or action that receives the focus of attention. The individual entity or object becomes the point of concentration, as personal strivings within the group become the idiom of treatment.

We have here the image of freestanding trees in a wood; each tree is distinct and separate. To be fully appreciated, a particular specimen must be viewed in isolation from proximate flora—analyzed according to its rooted structure, nutrient soil, and evident growth or stunting. Specific attention is given to the individual plot. A member of a level-one group has the gratification, at critical times, of being undividedly tended by the therapist.

With this attention comes the pressure of transference and the heat generated when transplanted under the artificial glare of the "hot house." The group therapist who follows this first order definition has the advantage of not being distracted in his or her analysis of the individual specimen by the interactive or combined properties of the conglomerate. This same group therapist runs the risk of not seeing the forest for the trees.

Group therapy was preceded by individual treatment, and "classicists" (Parloff, 1968), if using group methods at all, apply concepts derived from their dyadic work (Ethan, 1987). Impulses, defenses, compromise formations, resistances, impasses, stages of ego development, character structure, and other individual regularities, anomalies, fixations, and regressions are analyzed and worked through. Individual associations, dreams, fantasies, wishes, and fears supply the manifest content for therapeutic attention. The group's development prompts individuals to reexperience and rework their own maturational stages, thereby recapitulating, for example, boundary negotiations, pulls toward and away from dependency, needs for self-assertion, desires and fears of intimacy, and eventual loss of important objects. As the individual patient progresses through the varied group experiences, the goal becomes stimulating insight, increasing adaptive capacities, and building more resilient, differentiated psychic structures within stronger, more enlightened and mature persons (Fried, 1982).

In the first-level group, as an assemblage of individuals, the focus remains on "vertical analysis" of intrapsychic processes. Members are selected for group participation on the basis of individual inclusion and exclusion criteria. The group process itself takes on a turn-taking tactic, as single members work with the therapist in authoritative sequences marked by relative inattention to and separation from each other. The individuals in first-level groups are prone to look specifically to a leader for order, recognition, purpose, and direction.

Each progressive group phase suggests a range of specific authority relations to be mediated, from overreliance to rebellion, from participatory dialogue to fearful dismissal. This selective attention is often consistent with members' initial untutored expectations about the group experience. For example, a newly recruited participant believed that the therapist would actually be seated in the middle of the room, the literal hub of the group's proceedings. He vaguely imagined the presence of others somewhere off on the unattended periphery. His fantasy was that the outpourings of individual group members functioned like a quartz heater, searching out the one central human object, the therapist, to absorb emergent energies and focus the heated exchange, thereby giving back with warmth and individualized enlightenment.

The tasks of the therapist in a first-level group include making sure each individual is participating and thus partaking of possibilities for insight and change. Even when a member is silent or seemingly uninvolved, the leader looks for nonverbal reactions to the various stimulations inherent in the group setting. The therapist assesses how and when real and imagined life problems are being rediscovered in the group. The emotive tugs and pulls of transference and countertransference are especially attended, as the persona of the therapist becomes the receptacle for projections of both unacceptable and overvalued parts. In bouts of splitting, the therapist may alternatively be seen as a kind and/or a cruel parental authority. In fits of despondency, patients may bemoan and mourn not having the constant unconditional care and undivided attention they desire. It is often instructive to various members to see just how differently they all view the therapist, at the same moment, in reference to the same group occasion.

Bennis and Shepard (1974) suggest that, "principal obstacles to valid interpersonal communication lie in rigidities of interpretation and response carried over from the anxious experiences with particular love and power figures into new situations where they are inappropriate" (p. 152). As various projections onto the therapist are enlivened, the group becomes crowded with an invisible contingent of formidable outside personages. Their shadowy presence is demonstrable by attuning to the meaning of varied reactivities, coaxing out familiar internal dialogues, and recognizing the unchanging face of stable identificatory introjects, whether soothing visages or gargoyle-like apparitions. A large part of the intrapersonal group process is made up of sorting out what memories, projections, and free-floating pieces of the past are actually being conjured up in the present. The unique formative history and resultant ego structure of the individual member takes up the therapeutic focus.

The group therapist, working on the individual level of analysis within the group, consistently wonders who he or she is becoming for each of the members, as well as what is wanted and what is feared. Alexander and French (1946), working with individual patients, went so far as to suggest that as a "corrective emotional experience," the therapist ought to become for the patient the kind of loving figure that was needed but not forthcoming while growing up.

Of course in group therapy, the facilitator cannot turn chameleon, responding to each pull or provocation. However, the therapist can maintain a steady, flexible presence while accurately timing and targeting responses to individuals as their particular dynamics require. While not artificially becoming something he or she is not, the facilitator can use all parts of himself or herself to understand introspectively just what is expected by each member—a formidable range given a group of 6 to 10 participants. By reacting with care, honesty, and an analytic attitude, the therapist does not usually confirm misguided expectations. The therapist's ulterior motives and interior responses do not often conform to what members project.

Put on the spot, the group leader does not fall apart or prevaricate; faced with attack he or she does not burn with rage and retaliate. In the presence of conflict, the therapist does not blatantly take sides or equivocally disappear; given a competitor, he or she does not overreact and go in for the kill. Provocations are contained, metabolized, and/or interpreted, not acted out in return.

When recognizing strong countertransferential trends or while detecting projective identifications (pulls to identify with and act out that which is projected), the therapist must use internal responses to understand better and to respond back to the patient in a nontoxic fashion (Horwitz,1983). The therapist's aim is to work within himself or herself to be clear, genuine, and strong enough to step away from distorted projections and transference demands. By reacting out-of-step to a member's heretofore untold and often catastrophic expectations, once perhaps accurate and protective, out-of-date mobilizations can eventually fall away as they no longer receive a fresh supply of confirming evidence. Agazarian and Peters (1981) suggest that "therapy begins when self-fulfilling prophecies fail" (p. 129).

In the normal course of the group, the therapist must also predict and recognize personal vulnerabilities, thereby assuaging and treating inevitable hurt feelings and narcissistic injuries as close to the moment of their occurrence as possible. In cases where the therapist has unintentionally wounded a member, it is important to take responsibility by acknowledging the hurt or unrequited need, however unrealistic, while making amends in order to repair the therapeutic alliance. While always good practice, helping members save face in the group is especially important, since public settings always present the possibility for embarrassment, shame, and humiliation.

As responses and reactions are sorted out, individual defenses and character resistances are identified and encountered on the way toward understanding underlying perceptions, drives, and impulses. The therapist helps the various members clarify the intent of their actions while decoding manifest behaviors in sequences of free association and subsequent interpretation. The therapist looks for points of inertia or entropy, just where the particular member is blocked, turned off, or stuck, and works to free up energy and increase the availability of alternate channels for active response or sublimation. The overall goal of intrapersonal intervention becomes fostering individual maturation and developmental progression.

As Freud (1967a) suggested about tribal, political, and cultural collectives, first-level psychotherapy groups, too, are organized around libidinal ties to the therapist and remain leader-centered throughout their course. Members compete for the therapist, much as they did for their parents, as individual accommodations made to the limited time and space of the shared setting reflect on critical "then-and-there" relations. While multiple transferences and sibling-like reactions are certainly possible, in the group as a collection of disparate individuals, relationships among members are not specifically encouraged or explored. When collective pressures inherent in the group setting are recognized as such, these dynamic processes are used only as an entry point for investigating individual reactivities and formative etiologies to connect the present with the past in interpretive couplings. Slavson (1971) went so far as to recommend that the "dynamics in groups are [to be] nipped in the bud . . . for just as soon as they are analyzed and related to their emotional sources they no longer operate" (quoted in Whitaker & Lieberman, 1964, p. 5).

The observation of other group members' work may aid individual analysis by providing some vicarious therapy or by loosening the observer's defenses. However, other group members function largely as stimulants, auxiliary egos, or a "Greek chorus" that underlies and sounds out the strivings and achievements of the working member. The focus on member-therapist relations remains primary and consistent throughout the treatment course.

Prototypical methodologies for working primarily with the individual-in-the group include strict psychoanalytic (Slavson, 1957; Locke, 1961; Wolf & Schwartz, 1962), classical Gestalt (Perls, 1969a; Ruitenbeek, 1970; Fagan & Shepard, 1970), redecision therapy (Goulding & Goulding, 1979), protagonist-focused psychodrama (Moreno, 1953), and behavioral treatment regimens (Wolpe & Lazarus, 1966; Shaffer & Galinsky, 1974).

Group as the Interpersonal Relations Among Members

The second-level definition of *group* notes and highlights the binding of individual members into patterns of meaningful relationship. Thus group becomes "an assemblage . . . in a certain order or relation . . . having some resemblance or common characteristics" (Urdang, 1972). The salient feature of this second order definition is the new and unique integration of previously separate entities. Here, participants are not considered in isolation but rather seen for their similarities to and differences from one another. The group itself is conceived as an interactive *agency* (Kauff, 1979), in which the interrelating of heretofore separate entities becomes the essential ingredient of the therapeutic process. The medium of attention implied at the second level of group organization is that of the *duplex,* brought about by dialogue and mutual exchange between members. The relationship between individual entities becomes the line of inquiry.

We have here the image of an arboretum as a collection of trees to be studied and cared for. Each tree is categorized and arranged by kind and in contrast. To be fully appreciated, the individual tree must be considered in relation to its neighbors. To capture the essence of specimens in active interaction, the trees can be seen to affect one another, as when blocking the sun or putting out shoots that encroach on its neighbors' space. A member of a second-level group has the advantage of gaining support in cooperative arrangement, while bracing against the storm winds of competitive peer or sibling-like confrontations. The group therapist who follows this second order definition has the advantage of comparative analysis. This same group therapist runs the risk of missing the unique qualities of each tree when distracted by others of its genus or by the turning leaf, bark, and peel of proximate species.

"Transactionalists" (Parloff, 1968) and "Interpersonalists" utilize the interactive potential and exchange of this group of individuals as the treating medium. Whatever particular intrapsychic concerns engendered matriculation, each person in the group shares the common need to maintain personal integrity while relying on others. Social hunger and a basic need for interconnection are implied. The nature of evolving affiliative ties, communications, transactions, and interpersonal relations become the central concern of treatment. The group's cohesive jelling is critical to the process, as dynamic relationships form and serve as transformative agencies.

The focus remains on *horizontal analysis* of the relational field. In the course of being with others in the group, overdetermined internal relationships serving as templates or prototypes for the current interactions are revealed and treated with scrutiny. The therapist, working within the relational field, uses his or her expertise as participant-observer, to facilitate the exploration of commonalities and differences, linkages, pairings, roles, reactivities, splits, communications, attractions and aversions, and competitions and cooperations. Members are specifically selected and groups carefully composed to reflect either a diverse heterogeneity reminiscent of the outside world, or a built-in homogeneity of task or problem that will assure relatedness of purpose and/or experience. The group process itself takes on a spontaneous flow as members freely choose when, about what, and with whom to converse. The members of a level-two group are likely to look to each other for acceptance, fulfillment, and mutual understanding.

The tasks of the therapist of a level-two group include looking to how each member is affecting every other, while making sure that transactions are inclusive enough by encouraging as many dyadic lines of communication as possible in the act of "bridge crafting" (Ormont, 1990). Even when participants are not specifically talking to another member, the leader looks to potential linkages and evident patterns of attraction and repulsion. The therapist wonders how any two members might relate to or feel about each other with respect to the particular content or process stimulated by the current group events.

Members may initially seek out others with superficial likenesses, such as similarities in age, appearance, marital status, education, or job title, as a way of finding comfort and familiarity within the group. Only later do they discover deeper affinities and discrepancies based on history, culture, defensive structure, morality, or character (Saravay, 1978; Agazarian & Peters, 1981). Resultant pairings are often reciprocal, bound up in dyads most resembling prototypical or member-specific male-female, husband-wife, mother-son, father-daughter, or rivalrous sibling bonds.

Following Leary's (1957) interpersonal wheel, opposite personalities stimulate equal and opposite reactions—as depression brings out hostility, dominance invites submission, introversion suggests extroversion, and leadership evokes followship (Rioch, 1975a). Members split into stereotypical roles—the reticent and the reactive, the passionate and the thoughtful, the selfish and the selfless. Here, the core of members' identities is located in the most exaggerated or flagrant parts of themselves and others. Participants may act misguidedly as if a particular trait or role comprises the whole of their own or each other's personality structure and interpersonal repertoire. Participants can also join each other more generally for work, play, or avoidance when more specifically pairing up around particular beliefs, viewpoints, and/or emotions. Discovering that "Yes, I too feel this way" is a powerful interpersonal antidote. Conversely, concluding that "I am nothing like him, her, or them" can be quite daunting and alienating.

The therapist assesses how all this pairing, counteracting, splitting, and joining re-creates real and imagined problems in relating in and outside the group. When are the dyadic machinations defensive in nature? When do they tell only part of the story or distort the data by dismissing others out of hand in an attempt to push away what is too painful in themselves? Alternately, when do members conform to, identify with, model, copy, or emulate what is appealing but missing within? The ready availability of varied transferences across gender, age, circumstance, and topical concern transforms the transactional field into an arena for taking stock of valued and despised attributes of both self and others. In ambivalent instances of acceptance or rejection, other members may be alternately seen as special or spoiled. A member may speak about how much or how little he or she is getting from being with another member, as others become mirrors reflecting back narcissistic needs and gaps.

It is often enlightening to compare how the various participants view one another during any sequence of the group interaction. Differing reactions reveal just who each member represents for every other group member. The group becomes an active forum for contrasting perceptions of self and other with those impressions held by peers, as the power of consensual reality is invoked. By working out relationships within the safety of the group agency, problems with outside persons in actuality and in internal representation are reworked transferentially. True empathy eventually becomes possible as members see and accept each other more for who they are rather than as targets or projective screens for their own internal dynamics (Saravay, 1978).

Yalom (1970) suggests that groups stimulate images of the primary family. As here-and-now relationships come to life, the group room becomes crowded with hosts of meaningful others placed in familiar roles and impossible situations. One man sees his wife in the chair opposite, while the same woman hears her boss across the thin divide that separates inside from outside, fantasy from reality. A large part of the interpersonal group process is made up of sorting out issues of closeness and distance, likeness and difference, accurate perception and parataxic distortion (Sullivan, 1953). Relational capabilities, proclivities, and styles of interaction become the focus of therapeutic activity.

While interpersonal forces operate throughout the whole course of the group experience, joint ventures are most prominent in the working or production phase of the shared endeavor. Fidler (1989), in elegant simplicity, suggests that members' attentions evolve from a preoccupation with the leader, themselves, and each other, to concern about real significant outside persons to whom they will be returning when the group ends. This progression actually replicates the normal family cycle of attachment to parent, self, family, and social world. As members sequence through the group together, they are required to wrestle with such basic interpersonal dichotomies as dependence/independence, trust/distrust, intimacy/isolation, cooperation/competition, and generativity/stagnation (Erickson, 1950). The therapist works to help members come to acceptable middle ground, thereby giving up extreme roles and dysfunctional interpersonal stances.

For example, in the course of the group work, interpersonal defenses and resistances, such as manic-like immersions and schizoid-like withdrawals, are identified and encountered. These contradictory strategies are compared as the members find that they are capable of either "hiding within the womb of the group [or] hiding out of sight of the group" (Bennis & Shepard, 1974, p. 146). It is assumed that the very sense of self that underlies and guides these overt interpersonal behaviors derives from interactions with and appraisals of "significant others" (Sullivan, 1954). Formative relations certainly help shape members' current feelings of safety, integrity, entitlement, difference, and/or deprivation. Basic identity issues are well exposed and duly available in the form of transactions with one another within the immediacy of the group setting.

In the course of group treatment, members become "self-objects" for each other. They mirror needed confirmation in a supportive and affirming context, thereby presenting the more hopeful possibility that emergent group relations can change the person by changing his or her relationships before the eyes of both self and other (Kohut, 1971; Tuttman, 1984). Members also serve to confront each other by providing feedback about the impression one creates and the effect one has on others. The therapist helps members to come to recognize their weaknesses and to appreciate and bolster their strengths, while learning to work together.

While doing so, the therapist consistently looks for evident magnetisms, effigies, and tropisms, just where a particular member is attracted or repulsed. The group itself becomes a reparative workshop in which to plane and hone the rough edges of character and relation, as members experiment with different ways of seeing and comporting themselves. As changes are made within this social microcosm, members are better able to develop more stable, satisfying, and realistic object relations and real outside contacts. In the normal course of treatment, the therapist must also predict and manage conflicts, thereby lessening inevitable misunderstandings that result from trying to meet personal needs in a world of separate others. For any move toward interdependence means compromise or giving up some of oneself, and is therefore fraught with potentials for narcissistic injury—the going price for binding up the wounds of isolation and ostracism.

Treatment approaches that most heavily rely on working with the individual-in-relation include Sullivanian (Yalom, 1970, 1985), neoFreudian psychodynamic (Scheidlinger, 1952, 1980; Rutan & Stone, 1984), object relations (Ganzarain, 1989), transactional analysis (Berne, 1958), Rogerian (Rogers, 1961, 1967), encounter (Schutz,1967; Solomon & Berzon, 1972), and National Training Lab (NTL) methods (Bradford, Gibb, & Benne, 1964; National Training Laboratories, 1962).

The Creation of a Group-as-a-Whole

In the third-order definition, the group itself emerges as a coherent entity with existent properties and dynamics independent of and superseding the qualities of its several members either in isolation or intimate relation. The collective becomes "an assemblage having some common characteristics in form and structure" (Urdang, 1972), which taken together make up the total gestalt that is perceived as a unity or group-as-a-whole. The salient feature of this level-three definition is of the group as a holistic entity composed of, yet qualitatively differing from, its constitutional elements. Individual constituents gain importance as they represent, contribute to, or partake of the whole. Particular strivings and relationships between members of the group receive attention as they signal or embody specifiable groupwide trends, developments, norms, themes, or dynamic processes.

Here, the group becomes the perceived *object* (Kauff, 1979) or referential *matrix* (Foulkes, 1964) of the psychotherapeutic inquiry. The medium of group organization implied is the *complex* or the system of interrelated ideas, feelings, moods, memories, symbols, impulses, defenses, needs, fears, or cultural imperatives that give rise to or delimit particular group-wide events. The overall dynamic properties of the group-as-a-whole are specifically cultivated as the relevant sphere of influence.

We have here the image of a forest. Any member of a third-level group can enjoy a sense of belonging and a freeing anonymity when fully encompassed and camouflaged as part of a larger configuration of trees. That same participant may alternately experience the disturbing disorientation of losing sight of individual boundaries when lost within the wooded maze. The group therapist who follows this third-order definition has the advantage of generalization, universality, and metacognition. This same group therapist runs the risk of overabstraction and fostering depersonalization by losing touch with the tangible essence of the individual tree amidst the forest.

"Integralists" (Parloff, 1968) recognize and focus on the therapeutic aggregate. Work is accomplished within the structural frame provided by the groups' ongoing development and in accordance with formal properties that result from successive accommodations to group boundaries, tasks, goals, and "barometric events" (Bennis & Shepard, 1974). More simply, whatever participants' individual problems may be, they now come together by sharing in the common pressures and possibilities specific to the joint endeavor. A social cosmos emerges from the synergistic blending of individual perspectives and energies.

The participatory experience of contributing, belonging, and discovering universalities of experience is, in itself, curative. The very life and progress of the group provides problems to be solved over and above the individual members' out-of-group concerns and relational patterns (Bennis & Shepard, 1974; Saravay, 1978; Beck, 1981a). In a reciprocal process, the member first contributes instances of his or her unique perspective to the shared experience, and then partakes of the collective wisdom to reorganize and reassess his or her own developmental solutions to analogous personal problems and nuclear conflicts. The therapist helps by identifying and clarifying group-level themes and focal conflicts (Whitaker & Lieberman, 1964) as they consume the group's attention. Emergent trends mirror more universal and primordial concerns, while also mimicking member's specific out-of-group issues. Even when a member is silent, he or she is still affected by the emotional eddies swirling within the group mix.

An important therapeutic task is to assess how the collective tides make up or stir up individual currents. For example, the client struggling with commitment and intimacy must find ways to stay engaged in the psychotherapy group, with all its fullness, travail, and close confines. Such a task is essential to both social living in general and to succeeding within particularly potent outside groupings, whether family, job, or peer.

In the course of the groupwork, collective defenses and resistances are identified and encountered. Every group can be characterized according to its emotional climate, overriding concerns, state of organization, level of cooperation, and success in accomplishing its tasks. The momentary character of the group itself constantly takes on surplus meanings. A host of unacceptable or overvalued parts and attributes are seemingly projected, intermixed, exchanged, amplified, and stored with the group-as-a-receptacle. The collective becomes crowded with the flotsam and jetsam of the members' combined psyches. For example, preemptive worries and anxieties, as well as flattering and unflattering attributions of self and other, are given over to the group for holding, consideration, and eventual remonstration. During this time, the group itself may be perceived as dangerous and/or fulfilling, and thereafter devalued or inflated. These now collected qualities and shared aspects consume much of the therapeutic focus, as members explore what the group means and is becoming for them.

The group-as-a-whole therapist must look to synchrony of individual events and homeostasis of the collective environment, working with the forces that sustain growth as well as those that foster constrictions, misdirections, and regressive patternings. Yet paradoxically, in this nondirective approach the strict group-as-a-whole leader provides little active structuring or precise suggestion as to the group's ongoing direction. Any individual attention is given with the dynamic context of the whole group always kept in mind. The group itself is studied and addressed as it evolves in harmony or perturbation. The task of the group-level therapist is to create an optimum therapeutic environment (Rothberg, 1984) by identifying and interpreting emergent collective processes, while encouraging the group-as-a-whole to work through inevitable impediments to its progress.

Group-level work allows *isomorphic and existential analysis* of the individual. It is surely impossible to change the course of a stream without affecting its tributaries. As the group works through developmental crises, so do the involved individuals. The goal remains individual treatment; a systemic frame of mind must be cultivated so that the collective might serve as the transformative vehicle for personal change. In a strict group-as-a-whole approach, members are selected who can abide by lower levels of direct attention, overt structure, and personalized care. The group process takes shape as members speak for and against each collective turn of events and as the therapist credits each member's contribution for its social import.

In the normal course of treatment, the therapist must predict and manage threats to the group's integrity and viability, thereby instilling trust in the process, vouchsafing boundaries and norms, while protecting the therapeutic medium from decay. Members of a level-three group join together to form an identificatory bond—a "we-ness"—and thereby gain a sense of purpose and self-importance from their mutual involvement.

Interventional methods most nearly following a strict group-as-a-whole approach include Tavistock (Bion, 1961; Rioch, 1970) and A. K. Rice (Colman & Bexton, 1975; Colman & Geller, 1985), group analysis (Ezriel, 1982; Foulkes, 1964; Pines, 1983; Borriello, 1976), focal conflict theory (Whitaker & Lieberman, 1964), and the invisible group (Agazarian & Peters, 1981).

Multivaried Attentions

In practice, few group therapists stay focused on only one level of the group structure—exclusively attuning to individual, relational, or group-level phenomena. In reality, an informed leader must be sensitive to each of the three levels of group experience, responding to the individual-in-the-group, the members-with-one-another, and the group-as-a-whole. Just so, the group therapist follows each member's psychodynamically inspired intrapersonal excursions, advances, and retreats in interpersonal relationship, all in the context of the group's progressive or regressive phasings. A fully functioning group is made up of such sequences of reaction, interaction, and enactment.

Traditional wisdom has it that during the early group meetings and around normative or boundary crises, such as members coming and going, confidentiality concerns, and outside group contacts, it is essential to address the shared level of group experience. At other junctures, group-level processes, while always operating, may form a backdrop for individual and interpersonal exploration. In the face of narcissistic injury or on the verge of personal insight, individuals may command the focus of attention. Involuted interpersonal conflicts or irrepressible attractions may call out for clarification or mediation. The therapeutic task is actually even more complicated since each level of the group experience participates in and structurally predicates every other. As Ezriel (1980) aptly points out, both group-wide and individual particularizations of experience must be understood and interpreted as the group members move together in common and uncommon union.

Working with the varied levels of group process is akin to visualizing chess. Each of the eight (four pairs) major pieces begins in a certain position with inherent capacities (intrapsychic structures and ego developments) and a prescribed range of motion (interpersonal repertoire and personal style) acted out concurrently over a myriad and hierarchy of issues, themes, and life circumstances. The movement of individual pieces is enabled or constrained, in turn, by the position and movement of the other pieces, as well as by the forces and counterforces (Lewin, 1951) on the whole of the playing surface (group-as-a-whole). The development of the overall grouping represents a fluid and momentary ebb and flow between protection and vulnerability, advance and retreat, strength and weakness, shared strategy and individualized encounter. The leader, while avoiding undo manipulations, is still the prime mover and must know where matters stand—in what direction to focus energy and resources—and when to retreat and protect a position or an exposed piece. As in life, the more the individual pieces can work in combination, the greater their chances for success. The more the total grouping can achieve coordinated unison, while still retaining the special character of rooks, knights, bishops, and royal pair, the more effective the total grouping—which then inherently reflects back on the security and resiliency of the individual pieces.

More than an act of gamesmanship, models like this are needed to chart the complexities of the multilevel group process. The group leader must think about the possible movement of each member in separation and in combination. What is best responded to at this time lest the opportunity for advance be missed? What pairings or subgroups, in intimate association or opposition, can be played up? Where will any such series of moves leave the whole of the group? Fidler (1979) suggests that psychotherapy takes place within the head of the therapist. What separates the amateur group leader from the professional facilitator is just this constant assessment and analysis of the proceedings. The group therapist works between interventional moves, even when silently mindful, to follow and figure the complexities of the ongoing process. In chess, life, and group psychotherapy, timing, contextual appreciation, foresight, and flexible response are the tools necessary for fashioning an effective maneuver in the context of a well-founded game plan.

An ongoing, open-ended psychotherapy group was experiencing an episode of a long-standing conflict between two female members that reverberated through the whole of the system. Lauren had gradually been separating from her boyfriend of two years. Despite every indication that he was not interested in a serious commitment, she clung desperately to the relationship, feeling too weak to risk a conflict or to break ties completely. In group, Lauren constantly critiqued what Charles had or had not done for her over their time together. A woman with distinct narcissistic tendencies, Lauren simultaneously portrayed a sense of vulnerability and hostile entitlement.

As the cataloging went on, Molly was seen to bristle, squirming in her chair but trying not to speak to her feelings. When the therapist suggested that Molly was holding back strong emotion, all hell broke loose. Molly burst forth and bombarded Lauren for being so judgmental and selfish. Unkindly, she remembered Charles's various declarations of limited intent. "He was always honest and never led you on." Lauren, hurt written all over her features, meekly protested that there were many mixed signals and specifically turned to the therapist for confirmation and protection. Molly kept on with snide quips. However accurate the feedback, understanding was precluded by the aggressive and vengeful nature of the offerings. Lauren, in characteristic fashion, then assiduously avoided further interaction by tearfully begging off, saying that this was not a good time for her, a familiar plea for leniency and dispensation. Molly responded by assuming a stubborn stance and childlike withdrawal. "If she's not gonna talk, neither am I."

Molly, in fact, shared many of Lauren's concerns, but experienced from a reciprocal point of view. While Lauren expected too much from others, Molly expected too little. She was often taken advantage of by men and in fact was jealous of Lauren's ability to find, if not hold, a man. Molly's mother had been very much like Lauren, automatically expecting others to do for her while showing little appreciation for their efforts. Molly often felt unattended and was just coming to recognize her own deep-seated rage about not being taken seriously.

The rest of the group vacillated between fomenting and forestalling the heated exchange. Paula quickly came to Lauren's aid. In her usual shooting-from-the-hip style, she accused Molly of always taking the man's side. Paula was in fact still raw and enraged about her own ex-husband, whose affair precipitated the end of their marriage five years before. Simon, a psychiatrist, who Paula sometimes likened to the group therapist, was living 3000 miles away and raising their 11-year-old son, whom Paula felt she couldn't support. Mixed with her evident hostility at men was a heavy dose of guilt for abandoning her child. Thus, in the current scenario, it was possible that Paula was experiencing both sides of Lauren's dilemma, simultaneously abandoned and abandoner. Paula also shared many of Lauren's intrapsychic dynamics around dependency and shaky sense of self, although her ready defense was to fight rather than flee.

Dennis cringed noticeably as soon as the current hostilities in the group began. A man from an alcoholic family with a violent father, he shied away from direct conflict. While reporting violent fantasies, such as "blowing away drivers who cut him off," Dennis demonstrated an affected laugh and an obsequious, fawning behavior that belied his own struggle to contain reactive rage. On this occasion, he sat self-contained, encircling his gut with his arms, looking incredibly uncomfortable while remaining silent.

Josh immediately tried to mediate the conflict. By logically analyzing the situation, in obvious parody of the therapist, he hoped to bring Lauren and Molly together. In his characteristic quest for "fairness," Josh spoke equally to both sides of the disagreement. When neither party in the dispute responded to him or budged from their entrenched positions, he became hurt. How like in his own family, where no matter how hard he tries to be reasonable, somehow he winds up invisible, unimportant, and without impact. Behaviorally, Josh's presenting symptom was impotence.

Pam, recently released from the hospital in response to a recurrent battle with major depression, this time marked by a suicide attempt, assumed a fetal position. Seated between Molly and Lauren, her body literally radiated with the heat of the conflict. She feebly tried to intervene on a few occasions, when invited by the therapist to speak to her own feelings. Pam reported being terrified by the emotions in the room. In her own family, no overt arguments were allowed, no matter the degree of tension. Her father would merely disengage while her mother, reminiscent of Molly's behavior, would seethe. For Pam, the only viable target for her anger was herself, castigated for being different by a history laden with self-inflicted wounds.

Milt reacted strongly to Paula's verbose downgrading of men. Struggling with his own inability to commit to a heterosexual relationship, he had come into therapy depressed after a woman friend broke off their five-year love affair when he could go no further. Milt was currently seriously dating someone else and was having familiar doubts and hesitations, which he regularly spoke about in the group. With the freshly emergent encounter between Paula and Milt, the group's attention switched to a newly troubled interactional split. Paula, less frightened than Lauren, readily volunteered herself to take on Milt, who in many ways resembled "the Charles" whom Lauren had so often described to the group as perfectly nice but noncommittal. The group readily diverted their attention to this pairing which, however volatile, was once removed and seemingly less toxic than the precipitating conflict still simmering between Lauren and Molly.

At stake for the group-as-a-whole were norms around openness, the ability to face and resolve conflicts, and the viability of the therapist's role in protecting or confronting patients—a delicate balance between moving the group forward or redressing individual injury. As the session drew toward a close, Lauren blasted the therapist for not urging the group to back off, despite her various warnings. She reported being close to walking out the last half hour and threatened not to come to the next meeting. In fact, she did not show up, leaving a vague message with the answering service after the group was already in session. The very safety and boundary integrity of the group was now directly challenged.

At what level does the therapist deal with this resounding individual, relational, and groupwide event? The many possibilities can be daunting. Like the chess master, the group therapist must be able to conceive of and work at the various levels of the group simultaneously. Thankfully, the action of the members within a group bears some logical correspondence to the behavior of the group-as-a-whole, while the group's overall tendencies necessarily influence the motive forces of its various members.

Induction: The Combining of Elementary Experiences

Given the complexities of the group interaction, the therapist can attempt to understand the proceedings only if he or she finds a way to group separate phenomena into meaningful wholes. Building a theory and building a group-in-the-mind are surprisingly similar endeavors. Discrete aspects of experience, whether individual participants, fundamental facts, or basic events in protocol are taken up together—as a unity of purpose, explanation, or action is wrought. Both theory-building and group-building are paradigmatic activities; both require defining the basic units of experience or the data points of initial interest, formulating hypotheses about how these elementary units are connected or combined, and fashioning generalizations about the particular group in analysis. Part-processes can be bridged by connective acts of association, fusion, conglomeration, or cohesion. The group therapist can reach summary judgments by adopting a mind-set that wonders, above all, What is the common quality, the essence of what is now happening? What wishes or fears bind the whole of the membership? What is everyone doing or saying, albeit in his or her own way?

Structuralists see the whole of the group as the inevitable result of this natural, cumulative process of organization. "If left to act together, any group of living parts will autonomously form themselves into a whole. In actively striving to achieve individual function they will improvise and consolidate group functions" (Durkin, 1981, p. 37). Thus, groups spontaneously consolidate by the adhesion and coordination of the proximate entities. In the organization of the psychotherapy group, these formative processes take place in the shared therapeutic space. Members inevitably move through this intermittent space, colliding, coalescing, and forming more complex object relations and configurational conglomerates (Schlachet, 1986; Ettin, 1989c). A language of boundaries, inclusions, exclusions, exchanges, attractions, and repulsions is suggested. To work with the group as a basic form of organization is to look at its organizational proclivities and to see how the process of grouping occurs and ultimately affects the integrity of the various parts. The formulation of the group-as-a-whole can be accomplished by a number of step-by-step processes.

• Process 1: *Both the idea and experience of the group-as-a-whole can be reached by inductive, bottom-up, empirical-additive processes.*

Following inductive logic, reasoning proceeds from the part to the whole—the group is built up out of basic, irreducible, and discrete impressions of its members (Angles, 1981, p. 110). In an inductive paradigm, one moves from the individual figure toward the more complex group-as-a-whole configuration.

General conclusions and summary hypotheses about collective regularities are reached by first observing particular instances of group behavior. In an inductive paradigm, members "offer up" parts of themselves to form the whole of the group experience—manifest as the resultant group culture. Meaning is inferred by understanding how the group context evolves from its part processes—how the interminglings and cohesions of the individual members determine the shape and admixture of the resultant conglomerate. The utility of inductive procedures comes from the organizational and explanatory power of generalizations and categorical abstractions. General conclusions are valid to the extent they adequately explain, predict, or encompass individual cases and particular instances; they are helpful to the extent that they allow the group to come together by working out individual problems in context. Group-building by inductive processes parallels the scientific method by formulating hypothesis about individual instances leading to generalized understandings.

The inductive process is therefore a way of building a whole from its more elementary working parts. Bottom-up approaches essentially rely on trial and error and learning from experience. Here, the group leader might wonder how it is that the members are joining together to come up with certain consistencies, whether rules, norms, topics, conflicts, and/or affective configurations. Likewise, the members might experience themselves as a cumulative body whose task it is to progress by combining resources, styles, and opinions, thereby solving problems by way of mutual associations and eventual consensus. Members might wonder: "How does each of us feel about the problem at hand? What experience have we each had with this sort of difficulty? What might we agree upon as a way of mastering these concerns? What conclusions or resident truths can we come to or find together?"

Whitaker and Lieberman (1964) offer a representative inductive paradigm for the building of the group-as-a-whole. In the normal course of the psychotherapy group, individuals contribute their opinions, feelings, and reactions to a common pool. An associative flow is initiated as members immerse themselves in this shared process and as problems are discussed and affective reactions are stirred up by simply coming together. Every individual has a story to tell, an idea to evince, an emotion to express, an injustice to enumerate. As members freely interact, individual "nuclear conflicts" become apparent, arising in the form of personal resistances, characterological defenses, rigid role repertoires, and dysfunctional views of self and world. Members "chain" together their reports and reactions by introducing material familiar to others in manners that are reciprocally stimulating. Individual concerns and personal meanings reveal relevant topics, prominent issues, emergent themes, resonant conflicts, and shared process anomalies. The group members progressively move from idiosyncratic private concerns to common public problems. Whitaker (1989) explains,

> *Group focal conflict theory is based on the recognition that successive comments and behaviors of participants in a group have a free associ-*

ative quality and that these associations build and develop into themes which characterize the group as a whole. Themes are generated by what persons say, nonverbal behaviors, paralinguistic behaviors, pace and timing, and of course sequence (p. 226). . . . A therapist who has focal conflict theory in mind will watch and listen to the associational flow and seek to understand the themes and issues which are gradually created by and through that associational flow. The therapist will notice how different patients contribute to evolving group events and how they seek to influence the character and directions of the group. (p. 230)

In a young-adult group, Dawn vented personal frustrations about how ongoing strife between her long divorced parents interfered with either of them helping her with college expenses. Each parent demanded the other to pay, as an acknowledged obligation and as an act of contrition. Dawn could not go to mother or father without being passed off. She was particularly aggravated with her father's evasions of responsibility and absenteeism. Members attentively listened to Dawn's story and associated to their own situations.

Bob expressed resentment about having had to take care of himself since he was 17 years old. Todd explained how his own wealthy father resists entreaties for help, but then assists unsolicited. Carol talked of trying to rely less on her family. Sam told Dawn how unfair her parents were being while admitting to no such difficulties in his own family. Yet his own father had severe mental difficulties, and was often unreliable or away in a hospital. In response to Dawn's dilemma, various participants gave their versions of the same story as an empathic gesture and as an amplification of underlying focal conflicts. The group therapist highlighted common issues of dependency and rage. He further pointed out the father focus emerging in the session.

About halfway through the group, the members spontaneously switched their interest to interpersonal relationships with peers. Todd was asked how his date went the previous weekend. He reported having a good time but was told by the woman he went out with that she didn't want a romantic involvement. The group became very animated as a common theme emerged about whether men and women could "just be friends." Participants talked openly about what they sought in a lover and what they wished for in a supportive friend. The therapist believed that a connection existed between the session's two predominant issues: unresponsive parents and responsive friendships. It was suggested that in the group's wisdom, they advocated a generational shift. "Perhaps, the resolution of Dawn's problem lies in forming satisfying peer relationships as a support and an antidote to dependency on parents." The fluid dialogue between members in response to Dawn's dilemma enacted that very solution within the group.

This session followed a week when the group therapist was absent and was replaced by a substitute. This was a new experience for many of the members.

During that meeting, one new member railed against the therapist in his absence. She reported how he had gone off to meet his own needs while ignoring hers. The theme of going back and forth between parents (the usual and the substitute therapist), and the rage at abandonment and thwarted dependency needs certainly related to the group's own workings. Members sought to solve problems created by their simultaneous desire for and anger at the missing therapist by actively turning to each other, making the leader less important in the process. The group now was able to join together to directly explore its own parenting.

Thus, as members share time, space, and self, individual problems transform into groupwide dilemmas, and groupwide dilemmas spur individuals to find more apt personal solutions. Whitaker (1987, 1989) writes of the resonances, including transference phenomena, projections, and identifications that bridge the gap between individual and group dynamics. Foulkes and Anthony (1965) concur that, "each member of the group . . . will show a distinctive tendency to reverberate to any group event according to the level at which he is set" (p.152), or according to his own needs, preoccupations, and maturational prerogatives. The ongoing group then serves a "condenser function" for the individual members, bringing together and amplifying heretofore separate and idiosyncratic reactions. Under the pressure of accumulated affects, ideas, and developments, individual resistances are lessened and the group-as-a-whole actively collects and discharges its now pooled fears, fantasies, and dreams (Foulkes & Anthony, 1965). By cohesion, members conform to the group's focal conflicts and shared initiatives.

The inductive progression continues as nuclear dynamics are continually expressed through associations that group into topics. Recurrent topics define prevalent themes, which are elaborated by collective attentions. Difficult themes, reflective of more basic struggles, configure as shared focal conflicts. The group-as-a-whole then invokes varied solutions to resolve its common conflicts before the membership comes to consensus about how to move on. Normative decisions become generalized as rules of engagement that influence future interactions. The combination of the group's trials, errors, and workable solutions define a common culture that continues to develop and change over time.

Winnicott (1965, 1971), as reviewed by Schermer (1991), intimates a similar developmental progression as the infant moves from inner need to outer engagement. The "facilitating environment" of the mother-child merger initially provides the physical and contextual staples needed for personal survival. Given normal frustrations engendered by temporary maternal absences, the child becomes identified with a "potential space" reflective of both inner impulse and outward anticipation of care. With the discovery of the "transitional object" or "first not-me possession," the child claims and fills surrounding space with a tangible and fantasied object, opening up to the world of illusion and interactive play. The use of toys and the imaginative projection of fears and satisfactions into playful activities allows for eventual self-soothing and personal coherence in the absence of an all-giving parental figure. Sublimations of basic needs are fashioned, a middle ground between provision and deprivation is found, creative compromises with self and others become possible, culminating in societal adaptations and cultural achievements.

The group itself may be seen to follow a similar path as members come out of themselves to work together when inductively building a therapeutic society. When recognizing the general flow from individual to shared concerns, specific questions can be formulated to identify the buildup of group-related adaptations.

- What are the common denominators of the group's experience? What are the members interested in when together? *Members may be sharing in the process of trying to become more intimate. They may also be attending to their own protection.*
- What expressive choices and attitudinal variations present themselves to the group and what choices are being acted upon? *The collection of members may variously experiment with how honest and direct to be during any one sequence of the group interaction. Personal attitudes and behaviors may concur or conflict around the safety or danger of self-disclosure.*
- What is the current mood or motivation of the group? *The group may find that a free dynamic exchange of views is exhilarating, cathartic, and hopeful. Or the group may cringe in the face of such exposure and become stuck, perseverative, constipated, or fixed, taking up a mood of stultifying reserve, overwhelming fear, or helpless passivity.*
- What tasks, themes, dynamics, or subgroup ambivalences are being defined and resolved by the group? *Some members may be trying to find a way to come together constructively for mutual gain and acceptance, while others may be more concerned with warding off feelings of competitiveness, envy, or greed.*
- With what existential issues are the members having to come to terms? *Some commonly experienced universal issues arising time and again include individual interests versus the common good, sharing versus hoarding, merging versus separating, autonomy versus dependency, hope versus despair, and holding on versus letting go.*
- What resistances and transferences are combining to produce the group's common tensions (Ezriel, 1982)? *Members may adopt a joint storm front with respect to the therapist in order to ward off submissive tendencies in response to fearful expectations that the facilitator will unduly lull them into dangerous compliance.*

- What is allowed and what is disallowed within the process? *Constant self-effacing may be responded to negatively. Direct approval seeking may be marginally tolerated. Member silence may be condoned for a time. Monopolizing can be subliminally encouraged. Feedback may be ambivalently welcomed. Altruistic interpersonal ventures might be directly rewarded.*
- What shared concerns are evolving and gaining in expression? *The group members, during a time of member crisis, may silently wonder or explicitly voice concerns about whether they can solve their individual problems in the shared setting. They may also wonder whether anger, disgust, or sexual attraction can really be expressed and accepted in the group.*

In summary: How is the membership coming together and by so doing what are they coming up with? How is the group perceiving itself and its purpose at this time? The therapist's unique role is to help the members make sense of the shared events and perceptions as they take shape and to encourage the membership to deal with conflicts as they arise. From observations about how individuals comport themselves in the group—how they "participate in, are distressed by, cooperate with, challenge and retreat from" such shared endeavors—the therapist "builds an increasingly full picture of each person" and, by a recombination of elements, understands the resultant group formation (Whitaker, 1989, pp. 231–233).

Focal Conflict Theory: The Synthesis of Disturbing Motives and Reactive Fears into Shared Solutions

Facing common circumstances in groups brings out varied solutional attempts. Initially, individual nuclear conflicts, along with their overdetermined, automatic, or usual solutions, are brought to bear on progressively evolving shared concerns and task requirements. Whitaker (1989) specifically defines pathology as the "preponderance of disadvantageous, disabling, rigidly maintained personal solutions" (pp. 228–229) that the individual then recapitulates in the group. For example, faced with competitive feelings, one member may become characteristically aggressive—having witnessed and experienced that, at home, shouting and forcibly taking over was the only way to be heard and acknowledged. Another member, given the same group stimulus, might withdraw in fear, having learned to cower and retreat from anything even resembling a hostile grasp for favor. A third participant might seek vicarious satisfaction by identifying and emulating the therapist's powerful position, having developed the unconscious strategy of seeking special attentions by becoming the parental child, mother's helper, or daddy's favorite. These individual stances reflect need-satisfying positions assumed in various members' formative groupings, which are now acted out anew within the psychotherapy group. Additionally, members espousing these various conflicting strategies now vie for group support.

Out of this sea of individual material and response, various groupwide "focal conflicts" arise and configure. Whitaker (1989) explains,

> *In order to feel comfortable (or even to survive), each patient can be expected to try to establish preferred personal solutions, whether those be preferred defenses, characteristic roles and interpersonal positions, or ways of viewing self and the world. Group focal conflicts may emerge which resemble nuclear conflicts and which become a powerful imperative for the person to reexperience, in derived focal form, these early conflicts. (p. 229)*

Whitaker and Lieberman (1964), following French (1952), believe that the group-as-a-whole specifically organizes itself by formulating its diverse energies into dialectical dilemmas characterized by a common wish or impulse ("disturbing motive") opposed by a shared fear or guilt ("reactive motive"). Such bipolar, ambivalent conflicts predominate notable sequences of the interaction. The group members as a whole want to express or attain something while simultaneously fearing the consequences of acting on this need. For example, members may want a special relationship with the therapist but fear the competitive ire of others if they court such individualized attention. Such dialectical conflicts propel the group forward by successive approximation to seek synthetic collective compromises and mutually agreeable solutions to problems engendered by sharing space and time. Deriving functional solutions allows the members to survive together and move forward within the group context.

Some solutions, upon trial, turn out to be restrictive, alleviating the fear component of the conflict without satisfying the implied wish or need. For example, a group may struggle with the shared wish to be helped by revealing personal problems and ventilating dysphoric emotions. They may share the concurrent fear that in doing so they will lose face by looking stupid, crazy, or selfish in the process (Whitaker & Lieberman, 1964, pp. 121–122). In a *disabling solution,* or shared resistance, the group may decide, with silent consensus, to censor more turbulent emotions by hiding shameful difficulties. Thus, the reactive fear of foolishness would be successfully prevented by such disguise, but the accompanying disturbing motive of receiving help through self-disclosure would be unrequited. Such a group is stuck in a nonproductive equilibrium.

Here, the leader might intervene to identify the poles of the focal conflict. He or she might then urge the group to work toward a more *enabling solution*—one that quells the fear but also acknowledges, explores, and at least partially gratifies the heretofore hidden wishes, needs, agendas, or shared impulses of the collective membership. In this case, the group might control the pace and timing of disclosures, and simultaneously encourage, reward, and contain genuine expressions.

A *solutional conflict* may arise if a member or subgroup assumes a deviant position by taking exception to or impeding the adoption of an pending solution. Here, the group will likely turn its efforts to working through the objection. If failing in this persuasive endeavor, the group may modify its proposed solution in order to encompass the member's or subgroup's objection, thereby hopefully finding an alternative way to move on with all of its participants intact and in tow.

Progress as Successive Approximation and the Accumulation of Enabling Solutions

Progress is often achieved by successive approximation and trial and error. Various solutions are tried before one is found that satisfies all of the membership, alleviating participant anxieties while giving some resolution to a prevailing impasse. For example, a group might wish to express its resentment about the infrequency of the therapist's interventions, yet simultaneously fear that being so critical would only result in total abandonment or even in retaliation. An initial disabling solution might be for members to adopt the restrictive tactic of halfheartedly agreeing and complying with every sparsely offered interpretation or procedural suggestion, no matter its merit or relevance. Such an unconscious strategy gainsays the reactive fear of retaliation by adopting a seductive, seemingly nonbelligerent, grateful—feed me anything but feed me anyhow—stance.

Yet, this attempted solution does not give vent to inherent dissatisfactions, nor does it necessarily demand, identify, or specify the group's actual leadership needs and desires. Still frustrated and unrequited, the group may now band together and vent anger on a substitute target, likely a quiet, passive, or uninvolved member representative of the leader's shadow persona. Some of the angry affect contained in the disturbing motive is thereby released. However, such a displaced, indirect confrontation may stir up additional reactive feelings such as sadness, impotent rage, or guilt surrounding the scapegoating. Still frustrated, members may now begin to complain about distant outside authorities whose poor bedside manner or notable lack of guidance and support prevents them from thriving or doing their jobs properly. The parallels with the perceived noncaring stance of the group therapist become readily apparent or can be pointed out by the leader—no longer a silent or neglecting partner in the process. By trial and error, the group works toward more encompassing and enabling solutions—those that allow increasingly direct and honest encounters with the group psychotherapist, as acts of assertion and autonomy. As progressively helpful and expressive solutions are found, the group is freed to move on to other related themes and focal conflicts.

Trial Solutions as Progress Within an Evolutionary Framework

Gustafson and Cooper (1979) describe a similar process wherein small groups seek to solve problems within their midst by an ordered, logical progression of trial, error, and error elimination. In the course of the interaction, members reveal to each other their individual goals, troubles, and interactive strategies. The group then acts in concert "like a single author arranging their stories together" (p.1046). In accordance with now shared unconscious goals and task requirements, the collective sets up an approximate order in which difficulties will be revealed and confronted. Gustafson and Cooper suggest that the resultant mass movement involves the continual equilibration of growth with safety.

All we can predict at the start is how it [the group] will work on its problems . . . by making them prominent in a certain order that allows the principal dangers to be adequately controlled, while solutions are being sought (p. 1057). . . . Group planning coordinates control of group defense with deepening involvement and capability, so that deepening occurs progressively as it is safe to do so. (p.1043)

These authors coach against impatience and recommend a respect for the inherently planful and necessary sequence of the group's step-by-step trial solutions. By taking into account its available resources and constraints, the collective goes through what it must to come up where it will. The leader's role, in this paradigm, becomes helping the group articulate its goals and solutions, while treating errant compromises as desirable way-stations toward more adequate adaptations.

Taken together, the group's dialectical impasses and subsequent compromise formations make up the essence of the group-as-a-whole's therapeutic life and progressive developmental sequence. As successive focal conflicts, raised over time, are more or less resolved in line with the collective wisdom, shared understandings arise and working norms and cultural configurations are built up. By progressive flurry and advance, the group's collective adaptations contribute to defining its unique collective personality, group mindfulness, and distinctive *modus operandi*. The group-as-a-whole develops into identifiable configurations of "mood, atmosphere, shared themes, norms, belief systems, cohesiveness, structure, boundaries, roles, role distribution, conflict consensus, and developmental stages" (Whitaker, 1989, p. 225).

A well-functioning group becomes increasingly more articulate in specifying its needs, less fearful of negative consequences, and more creative in finding satisfying compromises. This evolution continues as basic themes, recurring under expanding cultural conditions, are reexperienced, reexamined, and reresolved. The group-as-a-whole thereby gains in complexity, capacity, scope, and texture.

By consortium and by contagion, everyone joins in this shared process. By participating in the inductive resolution of groupwide focal concerns, members simultaneously and transferentially address their own underlying nuclear conflicts. An instrumental goal of the focal conflict paradigm is to specifically use shared events to help the individual members. Horwitz (1977) suggests that the group begin by concerning itself with "individual, idiosyncratic and characterological issues" (p. 433) and only then, by way of inductive procedures, determine groupwide trends.

Therapeutic goals can be further specified as helping the individual to: (1) find a place in society by freely contributing to the larger grouping, (2) learn to recognize and manage a full range of affects and impulses *in situ*, (3) participate in the adaptive solution of evolving groupwide focal conflicts, (4) form more complex wholes by contributing to the representative culture's ability to formulate creative structures and solutional guidelines, and (5) generalize from the group experience to change individual problem-solving repertoires.

What begins as individual problems and styles are successively donated to the group proper for consideration and resolution. Members are induced to participate in and experiment with various basic human dualities such as expression and suppression, passivity and activity, reason and passion, dependence and independence, affection and hostility, self-esteem and self-abasement. Whitaker and Lieberman (1964) believe that "the individual is likely to experience the full range of personal conflicts if the group culture is dominated by enabling rather than restrictive solutions" (p. 164). In fact, their whole therapeutic approach manifestly strives to induce a curative culture from which individual members can restructure the building blocks of their own personalities and relationships.

As a result of such brainstorming, comparing, and interacting, the group-as-a-whole develops an optimal sense of togetherness which, by participation and generalization, affects members' inside and outside adaptations. From their engagements together, members come to consensual understandings about how to satisfy themselves better while being more fully with others. Whitaker and Lieberman (1964) suggest that a progressive group culture provides members with a special form of safety, wherein genuine feelings (disturbing motives) can be expressed and where disastrous results (reactive motives) are unlikely to occur. The individual patient can then test out his or her own maladaptive behaviors (disabling solutions) and risk more efficacious compromises (enabling solutions) (p. 166). As understandings and integrations build up, the group and its constituent members successively formulate into more integrated wholes.

Lauren and Molly Revisited

In light of general understandings about inductive group-as-a-whole theories and the focal conflict paradigm in particular, let us return to the quagmire of Lauren, Molly, and their group. When we left them, Lauren was absent, Molly was steaming, Paula and Milt were in battle, Josh was sulking, Dennis was hiding, and Pam was cowering.

In focal conflict terms, Lauren and Molly represent two poles of a dilemma around which the whole group revolves. Lauren represents the desperate wish to be taken care of at all costs. Molly represents the fear of being abandoned and deemed insignificant or unworthy of such attentions. The rest of the members join in the conflict, according to their own issues of attention seeking or abandonment, thereby lining up on either side of the divide.

In Dennis's house, catching his father's eye was unpredictable at best and downright dangerous at worst. So Dennis disappears behind a smile and a shrug and avoids any chance of encountering another's anger or his own retaliatory rage. Abandonment is prevalent and even more current for Paula and Milt, so they fight it out, trying to decide who is right and who is wrong. Only one it seems, in relational separations, can emerge victorious and unscathed. Pam considers it her lot in life to be left alone and so openly suffers in the face of her fate, while perhaps even pushing others away so as not to be ultimately disappointed by them. Josh's bids for attention get ignored, and so he sinks into the role of victim and the state of demoralization.

Transferentially, all these diverse passions play out in members' relationships to the therapist. When the conflict breaks out, all look to how the leader will respond and whom he will support. The competition for the therapist's ready attentions is most pronounced between Lauren and Molly. Each wishes confirmation and protection and each fears abandonment or criticism. Both withdraw in anxiety so as not to find out what the therapist actually will or won't do. Paula and Milt momentarily distract the group by displacing the tension onto themselves, thereby protecting everyone, including the therapist, from facing the real conflict between Lauren and Molly (restrictive solution #1). Pam and Dennis close their eyes and hold their breath. Josh melts into confused huff and guffaw, but not before wondering aloud if the therapist really knows what he's doing.

The group's next failed attempt at a resolution (restrictive solution #2) to the dialectical dilemma (focal conflict) between the desperate wish for care (disturbing motive) and hopeless fear of abandonment (reactive motive) is to split up and fight it out. They can then actually see who will be protected and supported and who will be abandoned. While failing as a final resolution, this trial-and-error attempt does succeed in bringing up the considerable affect tied to the issue of ultimate loyalties. However, the fighting solution is soon abandoned as too dangerous and is replaced by silence, as if to say "See no evil, fear no evil." The group now chooses the collusive defense of fleeing, marked by Lauren's actual escape and other members' noted refusal to address the issue at hand (restrictive solution #3). The problem, and the inherent fear of being abandoned by the leader, are temporarily avoided but the pressing need for authoratative recognition remains unmet.

The therapist chooses to begin the next session, addressing the collective as a body, by pointing out what is at stake for the group-as-a-whole and for the individuals involved in the shared impasse. The group is reminded that crisis, however unnerving, provides an opportunity for growth and advance. The therapist urges the collective to find a more progressive and creative solution to its stalemate, one other than fighting or fleeing. He suggests that to begin, each member might take personal responsibility by speaking to the vehemence of their own response during the previous session. "What was set off for you by what happened? What did you think about the group since last week?" By assuming a facilitative posture, the group therapist neither abandons nor takes sides. Rather, he gives care by crediting the strength and meaning of each member's reaction and empathically coaxing the group to use its relationships for personal insight and mutual benefit.

Following the lead, Molly considers the source of her rage. During the preceding week, memories and dreams flooded her concerning a retarded brother who was shunted off to an institution 32 years ago, only to die of kidney failure after 2 years of custodial care. Johnny would have been 40 just this month. Her parents explained at the time to 6-year-old Molly that her older brother had to be sent away so that they could attend to her with less distraction. Molly is overwhelmed with anger at this guilt inducement and the realization that her brother's absence made virtually no difference to her level of care. She railed, with cathartic force, about how both she and her brother were virtually abandoned. Molly's reactivity to Lauren's learned helplessness and seemingly shameless demand for care, even as a competent adult, might now be better understood with respect to her own hostile acceptance of the neglected position. How dare Lauren demand to be attended to when neither she nor her brother, even as helpless children, could harbor any such hope or maintain any such expectation? Molly's targeted revenge was not so coincidentally related to Lauren's position as a social worker with a retardation agency, a fact commonly known but a topic too toxic to touch until this point.

Lauren was prompted in an individual session, and later upon returning to group, to look at her own part in the interaction. What precipitated her defensiveness during the session? Was her subsequent absence in self-defense or retaliation?

Lauren came to realize, however grudgingly, that walking away from group, although with provocation, failed to take other members' needs into account. They were left holding strong feelings that could not be worked out without her present. How could she, in reality, expect to be taken care of by others when she offered so little consideration or inducement in return? Paradoxically, by walking away hurt and unresolved, Lauren was left feeling weak by not facing up to her problems. Having to leave someone, Charles in particular, she acted out by leaving the group instead.

Other group members likewise looked at their reactivity and stake in the proceedings. By exploring these individual nuclear conflicts, the group was able to come to partial resolution (enabling solution) and move on to other related issues and emergent preoccupations. Constructive group processes were forged around facing anger as an instance of norm setting, and meaning was derived from struggle as an enlivened occasion for cultural transformation.

Regularities in the Ongoing Group Process

Members' encounters surely build experience anew out of the group's more basic happenings. Emergent group themes are reflective of the panoply of individual life problems and attempts at solution redefined and recapitulated by the collective group impetus. Members inevitably move together to determine "the character of the therapeutic enterprise, the relations among patients and between patients and therapists, the boundaries on the expression of affect, acceptable content and acceptable modes of interaction" (Whitaker & Lieberman, 1964, pp. 97–98).

Induction, while an experiential process, yields generalizations upon retroactive analysis. There is some predictability of themes and processes across time and across groups. Whitaker and Lieberman (1964, pp. 121–123) observe a set of prototypical reactive and disturbing motives, and naive solutional attempts, as a product of clients' early expectations and the group's initial structure. Early on, members may wish to reveal "faults" and still be accepted, be helped by talking about difficulties, be seen as unique and favored by the therapist, or exclude or destroy rivals for the leader's attention. Participants may simultaneously fear looking foolish; exposure to attack or criticism from other clients; abandonment, retaliation, or disapproval of the therapist; or conversely hurting others by venting one's own destructive impulses. Attempts at finding a compromise solution between reactive extremes may serve to induce each other to admit some problems; get the therapist to provide care, direction, and control; develop the defensive fantasy that the therapist is making unreasonable demands; and/or come to the tentative conclusion that some analysis can be helpful.

Later and more subtle developments may be harder to specify in advance of their occurrence. Yet, Beck (1981a, pp. 330–332), based on empirical study, suggests that members of a therapy group regularly go through a set progression of shared tasks from beginning to end, including:

1. Making a contract to work on becoming a functional group

    a. By beginning to recognize each member, clarifying individual and group goals, and identifying limits and expectations
    b. While settling the issue of who will be members

2. Establishing a group identity and direction

    a. By clarifying goals and subgoals and delineating the limits of operation in a process of establishing mutually acceptable norms with regard to leadership, style of communication, and competition
    b. While experimenting with role differentiation and stereotypic relating

3. Exploring the group identity and direction

    a. By recognizing individuals and exploring their issues
    b. While developing effective communication skills, establishing equality and a cooperative interactive work mode

4. Establishing intimacy

    a. By coping with sexuality in personal relationships and expressing tenderness and closeness in the group
    b. While creating a shared space for play and fantasy

5. Exploring mutuality

    a. By working out how dependency needs, hostility, and frustration, as well as needs for personal space, will be handled within the peer relations
    b. While making a new and stronger commitment to the other members

6. Achieving autonomy through the reorganization of the group's structure

    a. By restructuring leadership and moving from therapist domination to peer primacy in the service of the self-directedness of the group
    b. While incorporating the task leader as a member

7. Confronting self and achieving interdependence

   a. By intensively working on individual issues in the process of sharing with and supporting each other
   b. While developing fluid role relations

8. Transferring learning through interdependent acts

   a. By reviewing issues dealt with in the group and extrapolating from what has been learned
   b. While rehearsing the development of relationships outside the group

9. Terminating and separating from significant persons

   a. By completing unfinished business
   b. While sharing the meaning of the experience with the other participants

The group thus builds upon its time, transforming by going through a more or less complete experience—a whole sequence of events and processes comprising many related parts. The membership moves as a unit from initial tentative contact through contract completion and ultimate termination. This locomotion precipitates a change in organization, from simple to complex structures, and yields natural developments subsumed under the scientific rubric of progress and evolutionary advance.

In the normal course of nature, elemental particles combine and adhere to form complex substances. Subatomic and atomic particles link together to form cells. Cells combine to form organs. Organs interface to comprise organisms. Organisms join together to procreate, and larger groupings form for mutual protection and the satisfaction of common and basic needs. Groups, once formed, become entities, in their own right, with recognizable compositions, properties, shapes, cultures, boundaries, moods, energy pathways, fantasies, projections, and patterns of interaction involving rules, norms, procedures, explicit and implicit goals, hierarchies, leadership and membership roles, communication styles, alliances, allegiances, and aversions. Place eight strangers in a room together and a social conglomerate can be created which, when properly tended, contains all the elements and interactions necessary for catalyzing a psychotherapeutic reaction.

CHAPTER SIX

The Epistemology of the Group-as-a-Whole:

Relying on Deduction to Render the Group Intelligible

It has been argued that there are several levels of meaning for the word *group,* and that a collective entity can be built up from individual constituencies through inductive processes. Still, there is much diversity and confusion about the nature of the most complex definition of *group*—the elusive and yet ubiquitous *group-as-a-whole.* This is the grouping whose presence must be implied or imputed from the synergy of the conglomerate—the grouping that exists as a shadow phenomenon always lurking, hardly seen, yet ever in evidence, the grouping that provides the common ground in which the individual members come to figure (Rice, 1969; Pines, 1985).

There are many times in a group's life when nothing seems to add up. Rendering a simple exposition of the proceedings appears impossible. In disheartening instances of confusion, looking for cumulative explanations yields no ready commonalities, renditions, or focal conflicts. The group process is much too fragmented as members go off on their own, acting out who-knows-what. A participant's behavior may appear out of context, and a group's shift in mood may be sudden, unexpected, and unfathomable. The therapist may conclude regrettably that what is being witnessed in the group room bears little explicable resemblance to the occurrences and associative flow to this point. In fact, members' reactivities may seem so disparate and unconnected, that there is hardly a sense of group at all.

Such times of seeming dispersion and chaos are disturbing for member and leader alike. No coherent explanation or foreseeable intervention serves to pull matters together. Rather, the group's diffuse energies, a product of splitting and rampant part-process projections, resists containment.

Cohesion breaks down and the group medium itself seems a questionable excuse for a therapeutic milieu. This is a point similar to when group therapy supervisees arrive in panic or in shame, and excitedly or reluctantly talk about how "my group is falling apart" or how this or that crazy, manic, self-absorbed, or depressed patient is ruining things for everyone. Symptomatically, group therapists often report feeling confused and divided, with no inkling of how to respond or without any real hope of making sense of the proceedings. The gap in understanding and the distance necessary to pull things together seems too wide to fashion a bridge.

With a leap of faith and by way of a figure-ground reversal, it is time to begin speculating about the invisible forces that, while at first appear to pull the group apart, must actually be holding it together. By an act of abstraction, while in a sleuth-like frame of mind, the facilitator adopts the assumption that connections can be found or hypothesized that will show how matters are tied together and members are intertwined. However puzzling the particular course of events, a conviction must be courageously maintained that the occasions that emerge bear meaning and relation to the whole of the group enterprise. The therapist looks for clues—those pockets of energy and action where something of import is afoot. To see members' behaviors as separate, unrelated acts is to see them out of context. Here, the therapist's job is to hold the group together in conception and in reality by supplying the contextual meaning for what, on the surface, appears meaningless.

The classic paradigm for understanding part-whole relations—the logical interface between particulars with universals—can help us understand how the pieces of the group process fit in with the process-as-a-whole. *Particular* refers to *some* as distinct from *all*. The particular has built into it the possibility of standing alone and of being subsumed under a larger category or structural whole. In a simple sense, the particular is defined as a self-contained unit of experience—whether a person, an object, an action, or a phenomenological aspect of experience. In a group psychotherapy context, the particular unit of concern is a member, a bit of group behavior, or a circumscribed occasion. Here, we have the raw data of the group collage, arrived at by direct observations and intuitions about individual persons and discrete events. A scattered, disintegrated proceeding is yielded when only viewing each instance of group business as a separate piece of experience.

The idea of universal presupposes the possibility of logical combination when suggesting a general category, concept, characteristic, quality, or property shared by or subsuming a number of particular persons, objects, or instances. *Universal* implies belonging to all of a group. Here, we have the more abstract level of the group, arrived at by formulating hypotheses and generalizations about collective themes, moods, behaviors, organizations, dynamics, conflicts, or motives. Mediating variables seek to link particulars together in order to explain the content, affect, action, structure, process, and/or overall agenda of the collective experience. Such abstractions point to something common that is repeated or exemplified in a number of single instances. To imply a universal is to organize particulars "according to classes, genera/species, properties, unities or wholes" (Angles, 1981). Therapy groups can be viewed according to their discrete happenings or can be seen for their combined, holistic properties.

True, holistic phenomena that make up the group's shifting essence and affect often form complex and confusing configurations. But these instances of interaction intimately reflect on overall group dynamics and developmental processes. A pattern can be found and/or supplied to parsimoniously explain group events. The therapist, in an educated attempt to make sense of the collective process, wonders at each point in time what the group is actually straining to express through its varied member reactivities and subset of relationships. An alternative mental set to the inductive paradigm would begin with the a priori assumption of a meaningful connectivity between events and among persons. Pragmatically, the therapist moves the group toward an understanding of its groupwide tendencies by investigating the meaning of manifest occasions as they occur. Though certainly not limited in utility to such critical junctures, deductive reasoning provides a crucial logic for rendering the group intelligible.

- Process 2. *Both the idea and experience of the group-as-a-whole can be reached by deductive, top-down, theory-bound processes.*

Following a deductive paradigm, reasoning proceeds from the whole to the parts, from the universal to the particulars. Working from a general understanding of group-level phenomena leads down to a specific understanding of the meaning of an individual instance of group behavior. In a deductive paradigm, one moves from the explanatory level of the group-as-a-whole to its representative part-processes, as demonstrated in resultant member or subgroup themes and dynamics.

It is assumed that reactivities within the membership unconsciously reflect groupwide trends. Members often take direction from the whole of the group enterprise when formulating particular responses in the service of the collective. Meaning is derived from understanding what member behaviors represent for the larger group context. The utility of deductive procedures comes from being able to employ general understandings or universal concepts about groups to interpret individual or particular occasions. Conclusions about individual events are assumed valid as they coherently explain, re-create, foreshadow, reconstruct, point up, or refer back to groupwide trends. Deductive conclusions are deemed pragmatically helpful as they bring diffuse energies back together so that members can appreciate the relationship between their personal motives and the group's overall motifs.

In this top-down approach to the group, the meaning of part-processes is deduced from the overall conception of the whole. In a psychotherapy group, the therapist might ponder how various members are affected by or are acting in response to the group's current tensions, cultural imperatives, dynamic pressures, and hidden agendas. Similarly, the members might experience themselves as being actually pulled and pushed by the group. An inherent task for the participants would be to clarify and analyze their positions in the overall scheme of things.

- What is the meaning of my feelings and behaviors in the context of this group?
- What is an accurate perception of my position in the emotional field (Bion, 1961, p. 45)?
- What are the currents that I am being subjected to and what are the forces impinging on me?
- What is going on here and how do I fit into this process?
- Given the way I am being affected here, what does this really say about me and my position in society-at-large?

It is the leader's distinct role to aid in this process of attaining organizational insight. A vignette may help to clarify the assumption of a top-down, groupwide, deductive perspective.

A senior female member and former president of a statewide group organization was late for an executive committee meeting. In her absence, the subgroup of other women unanimously criticized her role in the organization as being too authoritative, and wished that she would be less dominant, more personal, and increasingly retiring. Each woman, in turn, talked of her own difficulties with this active leadership style.

Upon entering the room, the senior woman was confronted en masse by the females, while the male members sat still, silent, and dumbfounded. At no time during the group's six-plus years together had Carla received such negative feedback about her dominance or the distracting nature of her group presence. Why now? What was the meaning of this turn of events? Was it simply that the lateness spurred a confrontation? Perhaps an accumulation of unsaid feelings had built up over the years? Was the feedback, in fact, justified and a long time in coming? Was the group's ability to confront one of its members a sign of health and maturity, marking a phase of open conflict and potential conflict resolution?

Looking to the group-as-a-whole's recent history and overall struggle provided an alternative and more encompassing contextual explanation. After three succes-

sive female presidencies that spanned 6 years, both the new president and presi-
dent-elect were males. Furthermore, the operative task commanding the group's
attention was upcoming changes in the structure of the Board. An as yet faceless
and unspecified number of executive members would soon be expected to rotate
off in order to make room for "new blood," thereby more directly involving the
membership-at-large in the governance of the organization.

The Board was stable, cohesive, and notably resistant to the imminent change.
Since it was still to be decided who was out and how orderly change would occur,
the "blood letting" of Carla can be understood as a piece of the group's generational struggle—a ceremonial termination ritual or symbolic execution. To date,
the group had resisted more directly confronting, personalizing, and specifying its
needed change, and had continuously postponed decisions about who in fact
would leave and how to call for resignations. Talks had been tabled, and the group
had conveniently found other less disturbing matters with which to distract itself.
Even the confrontation of Carla put off a more direct, reasoned approach to the
impending change. The group acted out its conflict and its mission in a way that
exposed its difficulties in effecting a transition without killing off members. Another
older female Board member recently left precipitously after a contracted period of
mutual misunderstandings and subsequent scapegoating.

Perhaps the most apt explanation for the turn of affairs can be found within this
groupwide context. Carla served as president some 20 years ago, following a long
line of male leaders in what was then a distinctly patriarchal organization. She
successfully created a space for women within the organization, most clearly symbolized by the recent run of female presidents. That line had ended and a new
generation of men were again assuming prominent positions. By rising up as one,
the women reasserted their power and acted out their fears of displacement and
renewed male domination. Yet, paradoxically, they attacked one of their own, their
heretofore readily acknowledged senior spokeswoman. As subgroup sacrifice, it
was demanded that Carla step down from her role as head woman in the service
of the larger female body. Untold others must also literally step down, as the future
shape and tenor of the Executive Board was in question. Perhaps the women in the
group were simultaneously serving the larger collective purposes by precipitating
needed shifts, while signaling the anger and anxiety inherent in changing times.

By joining together to dethrone the senior female while competing for her
space, the women were reasserting the power of a new matriarchy in the service
of the organization. The outspokenness of the female members and their drive to
take out the old guard facilitated the generational shift, albeit in a manner that
hastened wounds and left unclaimed many hidden agendas. The silence and impotence of the males was also noteworthy. Taking a deductive perspective, it could
be argued that the struggle for organizational survival overtook and overdetermined the behavior of individual members and subgroups who then unknowingly
carried out its varied implications. For the group to move on intact, members would
have to more knowingly avow and face their new task and status. The group would

have to find its full voice, with the men joining back in, in order to maximize resources and elicit a more encompassing perspective. All of the group experience, including recognitions about formative history, was needed to use the whole of the process effectively to more consciously shape the evolving reorganization.

The Group as a Superordinate Structure Influencing Its Individual Members

Freud (1967a) believed that individual psychology intuitively presumed a group psychology. Every theory of individual behavior must account for the influences of the group as a shaping context, whether residence is taken up in the family, the community, the small-task group, or the society-at-large. Bion (1961) suggests, "Acceptance of the idea that the human being is a group animal would solve the difficulties that are felt to exist in the seeming paradox that a group is more than the sum of its members" (p. 133). He argues, "The explanation of certain phenomena must be sought in the matrix of the group and not in the individuals that go to make up the group" (p. 133). Most simply, he defines group as "the pool to which anonymous contributions are made . . . and through which desires implicated in these contributions are gratified" (p. 50). Here, in a deductive paradigm, the task becomes to study how, when, and in what fashion inevitable group processes unfold in the course of any particular group's experience.

Charismatic leaders throughout history have known how to allow the group to rise above its members. Mesmer (1980), experimenting with social influence techniques, hypothesized about an animal magnetism akin to mass hypnosis. Le Bon (1977), patterning ideas after the hysteria of the French Revolution, decried the barbaric and instinctual acts of which humans are capable under the irrational and heightened emotionality of the crowd. He identified three properties of large groups to explain their awful transformative power. A sense of "invincibility" encourages acting on instincts that are more normally constrained. "Contagion" of hypnotic magnitude leads to sacrificing personal for collective interests. An atmosphere of "suggestibility" summons an impetuous and unconscious group personality linked to racial history and reminiscent of primitive, untamed humankind. Le Bon's notions were quite consistent with Freud's later ideas about repression, id, and the violent rise of the "primal horde."

Anzieu (1984) agrees that "the group situation is perceived essentially in terms of the most archaic phantasies" (p. 117). Fears of annihilation and dismemberment can give vent to drastic and dangerous restorative efforts. Paradoxically, it is just that collection of individuals fearing for its integrity that is capable of coming together most divisively, through paranoid projections and splitting the world into polarities of good and bad, us and them.

McDougall (1973) saw the group's potentials for fostering more positive behavioral change in its individual members. Through active, constructive leadership and the adoption of progressive organizational structures, the group could take the form of a purposeful and specialized working unit. McDougall coined the phrases "mental homogeneity" and "reciprocal influence" to explain such collective transformative group agencies. His thinking about group organization clearly foreshadows the facilitator's harnessing of group-as-a-whole phenomena to enhance the accomplishment of progressive therapeutic tasks. De Mare (1989) concurs that large groups, through dialogue, are capable of more positively transforming into a culture that supports fellowship, progressive development, and effective communication.

Bion (1961), working with small study and psychotherapy groups, insisted that groupwide phenomena are a universal and primary feature of the human condition. Originally following an inductive path—by attending to his *Experiences in Groups*—Bion eventually envisioned a set of prototypical patterns, that taken together, express the elementary formative tendencies of every group. Three basic patterns of collectivity reanimating phylogenetic imperatives are specifically identified. In the so-called *basic assumption* groups, the combined membership behaves "as if" they were meeting to fulfill some primordial survival need, in addition to accomplishing whatever is overtly defined as their express purpose or task.

Groups conform "as if" to fight or flee—with members nervously rushing to secure boundaries or to escape from intrusions and aggressions from within or without—thus mimicking adaptive strategies for protection against internal and external threats. Fight/flight groups are infused with vitality, averse to understanding, compelled by immediacy, and belligerently suspicious or withdrawing by nature.

Groups conform "as if" to secure dependency needs from the leader—with members helplessly waiting to be told, directed, or guided—thus approximating species-specific requirements of primary bonding and child rearing. Dependency groups are drawn to historical precedent, attracted to authority, and mired in the past, while producing members who are depressed and immature by nature.

Groups conform "as if" to foster pairing needs—with members actively or vicariously joining in consummate relationship in order to produce creative offspring—thus recapitulating the conditions necessary for sexual reproduction. Pairing groups are driven to heal part-object splits, compelled to find hope and salvation, oriented toward the future, and overly optimistic by nature.

Turquet (1985) suggests that groups can also form "as if" to experience oceanic feelings of wholeness and well-being—with members giving themselves over to the collective, or otherwise passively surrendering to higher powers and omnipotent forces—thus activating deeply held mytho-religious tendencies and traditions.

Bion (1961) also describes the antithesis of the basic assumption group or the special case of the "work group," which is organized around a specific task and is geared toward progress and learning from experience. Members of a task group conform for the express purpose of solving interactive or environmental problems that threaten the security of the tribe, culture, or race—thus allowing the group-as-a-whole to evolve by working through problems and conflicts in the service of the common good. Work groups are concerned with development, aided by understanding, covetous of change, and grounded in reality.

All of the basic assumption grouping tendencies can be characterized by their timelessness and instinctive nature (Kibel & Stein, 1981). According to Bion, no special preparation, practice, or skill is needed for the members to assume a fight/flight, dependency, or pairing culture. The group-as-a-whole unconsciously slips in and out of the various regressive basic assumptions automatically whenever it seeks to ward off anxiety or bypass threat. All told, basic assumption groups deplore development, do not learn from experience, and seek ready-made solutions to life's diversity of problems. No matter what members may say about their overt purpose for being in the group, the ready assumption of a collective mentality suggests other motives. It is just this collective mentality or regressive culture that is the object of deductive speculations. Bion (1961) suggests that "if a group affords splendid opportunities for evasion and denial, it should afford equally splendid opportunities for observation of the way in which these evasions and denials are effected" (pp. 49–50).

In any group gathering, basic assumption mentality coincides with potentials for more adaptive functioning. In fact, the relationship between regressive and progressive trends is complex and overlapping. Basic assumptions feed into, underlie, lend emotion to, alternate with, or impede the group's ability to carry out its stated business and work function. Specific skill and progressive learning require the assumption of a more consciously intended work group posture. Here, the collective must specifically cultivate individual competency and cooperative endeavor. Higher-order relations are forged in order for the group to accomplish its developmental tasks responsibly, while undertaking its fully acknowledged overt purposes.

Finding the Group Through Its Organizational Regularities and Superordinate Structures

Agazarian and Peters (1981) offer a representative deductive paradigm of the group-as-a-whole based, in part, on Bion's notions. They distinguish between the inductive "visible group" made up of combined and observable member contributions, and the deductive "invisible group," "a group that can be seen if we don't see it in terms of people" (p. 95), but rather in terms of group roles, dynamics, and developments. This is the group that can only be deduced from the presence and trace of its inherent functional relationships, organizational regularities, and collective perturbations. This is also the grouping that is presumed to exist, but that we seemingly see and hear only as a movement, a stirring of the common pool, or as a representative vision or vibration. Here, the individual member is viewed as a dynamic or subsystem of a larger macrosystem or shaping context (Agazarian, 1989).

The movement and meaning of the deducible group-as-a-whole can be located by identifying the collective's fluctuations and regularities, explicit and implicit goals, driving and restraining forces, developmental and maturational phases, and ongoing historical progressions and regressions. To recognize these holistic processes, it is necessary to approach the group itself as a meaningful collective entity, ever ready to manifest itself in its part processes. To detect groupwide dynamics, Agazarian and Peters ask themselves questions like: "What is the group-as-a-whole doing? What is the membership acting 'as if' it were trying to accomplish? What explicit and implicit goals and agendas can I infer that explain evident collective behavior?"

Following general systems theories (Bertalanfty, 1968) and field (Lewin, 1951) theories, Agazarian (1989) identifies many metaconceptions that define and predetermine a group's intrinsic structuring process. Inherent organizational principles are essentially taken a priori and applied anew to conceive of each group's unique developments. The resultant, discoverable, collective proclivities of any particular group is, in this sense, universal, theory-bound, mathematical, hard-wired, and predetermined.

Agazarian (1989) suggests that systems are organized hierarchically, ranging from the superordinate group-as-a-whole, through the interpersonal system of subgroups forming and dissolving incessantly around similarities and differences, and down further to the subordinate intrapersonal field comprising individual members responding to overriding forces. Each system within this overall structure can be theoretically identified and simultaneously separated according to its own boundaries, however permeable or impervious to the outside influence. Varied influences occur with the penetration of concentric relations by higher or lower-order subsystems.

The group-as-a-whole, as the highest level of the system, functions as the formative shaping environment under whose influence all subordinate systems operate and conform. What comes down is ultimately acted out by interactive subgroups and individual members. The systems group therapist "focuses attention on the dynamic maturation of the group-as-a-whole"

(p. 132) as the most efficient way of finding out about and reaching down to all of its membership. It should be remembered, however, that every group is part of other higher-order systems and that even the psychotherapy group is subject to normative influence of the predominant culture in which it operates, whether the clinic, the private practice, or the encompassing society's foundation matrix (Foulkes, 1964).

Agazarian (1989) suggests that "a primary function of the systems group therapist is to maintain the group boundaries "around each subsystem whether concentrating on the intrapersonal, interpersonal or holistic group field" (p 138). When maintained in a state of internal equilibrium, each constituent part of the process is most available for problem solving, goal achievement, and maturational striving. First, functional exchanges are directly facilitated at each level of organization—amidst the group-as-a-whole, between the members-in-relation, and inside persons-onto-themselves. Once each systems level is secure in and of itself, the therapist's task changes to that of examining and consulting to the boundaries between systems. Specifically, once individual members feel secure enough within themselves, then their relations to others can be encouraged and probed. Similarly, once relationships are evident and viable, the meaning of overall alliances and groupwide developments can be considered. Information between systems flows more freely as transactions open up. The inherent task of each subsystem is ultimately to exist in consort with its environment, while at the same time subsuming all subordinate parts into a coherent whole—people in intimate relation and enculturation.

Group Problems Become Individual Problems

This so-called invisible group must ultimately make itself known through its members, since the collective as a theoretical entity has no expressive organ of its own. Like a skilled ventriloquist, the group speaks through its would-be representatives, whether lone participants or allied subgroups. Through a syntax of group roles and voices, spokesperson phenomena, and subgroup sentiments, the collective lets its agendas, dynamics, developments, desires, and fears be known. Through role suction, individuals are induced to portray various emotions and take on certain collectively inspired positions. The group thereby acts out its prerogatives through its members. Bion (1961) further specifies group mentality as "the unanimous expression of the will of the group, contributed to by the individual in ways of which he is unaware" (p. 65). Members exchange affects, ideas, and psychic contents in a mobile language consisting of notable projections, empathic identifications, and subsequent reintrojections. Unclaimed and unwanted elements are cast out just far enough to be encapsulated and redeemable from within the repository of a particular member or pulled from the reach of the otherwise silent mass.

Agazarian (1989) recommends that "the systems group therapist watches the patterns of behavior and listens with the third ear to hear how each member's voice speaks for the subgroup dynamics of the group-as-a-whole" (p. 136). He or she wonders, "How is this particular subgroup interaction serving the viability of the group-as-a-whole?" (p. 143). The individual member is more likely to be aware of his own state (intrapersonal level) or the state of his relationships to one or more of the others (interpersonal level), than to his relationship to the state or dynamics of the group-as-a-whole. Thus, it is the special skill and responsibility of the therapist to be cognizant of the contextual aspect of group life. The leader may or may not make such group-relevant knowledge explicit, depending on the general purposes of the gathering (therapy or training) and/or the needs, requirements, and momentary abilities of the members to learn.

Clinically relevant and epistemologically couched questions now become:

- What of the whole do the parts express?
- If a particular member or subgroup is speaking for the group-as-a-whole, what might he or she be saying?

In object relations terms:

- What have the group members been asked to carry on behalf of the group?
- What is being deposited in each member for the others?
- What split-off or projected parts and attributes is the individual holding and expressing for the group? (Wells, 1985).

The group-as-a-whole can also come together as one by assuming collusive defenses when direct expression of its needs seems prohibitively dangerous. Agazarian (1989) specifically identifies four group-level defenses:

1. Denial—cutting off anxiety by banishing material behind a barrier permeable to conscious recognition but not to open acknowledgment ("The emperor has no clothes")
2. Acting out—taking contradictory needs and sentiments out against one or another part of the system ("I can't tell you but I'll certainly show you")
3. Splitting—externalizing and holding off differences currently too threatening to be organized and integrated ("What, me worry when you're the one with all the problems?")

4. Scapegoating—choosing a target or container to carry the onus of unacceptable attributes ("Better you than me, but better still to drive you away or kill you off lest we catch your disease")

Keeping unwanted feelings close at hand, the group may tacitly enlist, allow, or encourage a monopolizer to express its own obsessive concerns. Pushing unwanted feelings further away, the group may designate a victim who is then charged with being the group sacrifice, carrying in shame, demise, or extrusion the collective's underside, shadow qualities, and awful, unassimilated, or split-off parts. When a member is under group attack or quarantine, the therapist specifically assumes a protective and sheltering function. He or she "encourages the patients to see the problem as belonging to the group rather than to the person who is under pressure from the group" (Whitaker, 1989, p. 235).

The group therapist is not immune to the collective's more primitive, unconscious, and manipulative ministrations. While questioning projections that negate his or her therapeutic role, the leader can also serve as an overflow container for the group's good and bad parts. He or she can take over for safekeeping the chaos and differences too dangerous or toxic for individual members or subgroups to presently hold. The therapist remains open to the group experience by nondefensively allowing for transference and confrontation without retaliating, displacing, or splitting. Hostile projections thereby remain available for the group to eventually reconsider and for individual members to subsequently reintegrate.

It is often easiest to identify a groupwide configuration during a time of boundary and norm disruption or when something in the group's process or a constituent member's behavior seems exaggerated, at risk, or out of control, phase, or alignment. For example, during a time of group insecurity, a patient unabashedly expressed a panoply of underlying and heretofore unsaid paranoid suspicions and fears. The group was initially unable to accept, as their own, these overtly terrifying sentiments. Here, the therapist translated seemingly tangential, out of bounds, frightful feelings back into the language of the more recognizable groupwide struggle. Group members were encouraged to recognize, avow, and ultimately take back their projections. "Joe is expressing for the group its suspicion that everyone here is being judged negatively and its fear that, as a result, the group will dissolve as individual members are killed off." Such a therapeutic tact helps the seemingly peripheral or deviant member to reintegrate, while encouraging the group itself to come closer together by working through emergent process material in context.

As long as the targeted member contains the unwanted emotions, attributes, or behaviors of the other group members, the social system

> *goes unexamined. As a result, other members of the group collude to*
> *distance themselves from personal responsibility for examining how*
> *their own behavior has resulted in the feelings experienced by the tar-*
> *geted or scapegoated member. (Bion, 1961, p. 306)*

When focusing on a member's service to the community, the targeted individual's contribution to the whole is acknowledged, while simultaneously relieving the person cast in the deviant position from bearing total responsibility for the disturbing affects in the room. Individual reactions and provocations, however outlandish or outrageous, can thus be brought back within the confines and contexts of the group business. For example, the blatantly narcissistic patient whose unconscionable greed enrages and alienates others can serve the group by putting others in touch with their own interpersonal hunger, vulnerability, and struggle to get personal needs met within collective settings. To prevent the emergence of a black sheep, a smooth and fluid two-way exchange, between targets and donors (Cohen & Epstein, 1981), between give and take back, between feedback and food for thought, must be part of the group's working norms. No matter how seemingly objective a reaction to a targeted member may be, the other participants must wonder at the vehemence or indifference of their reactions, and ponder the contextual significance of the manifested behavior and emergent group stance. The questions can always be raised: "Why are you so excited by or so uninvolved in all of what's going on? What about the part of you that is just like Joe? Can you speak from your own suspicious or fearful side?"

Like parts in a play, the group-as-a-whole needs certain actions to be performed and various words to be spoken. With the aid of its group representatives, mood states are reflected and specific transactions are carried out (Rice, 1969). Thus, various members arise from within the ranks to carry forth the group's ongoing concerns. Leadership within an organization such as a therapy group is sometimes assumed by a knowing and skillful act of competency. At other times, the point man or woman assumes his or her position unknowingly. By role suction (Redl, 1982; Gemmill & Kraus, 1988) and projective identification, individual members may be induced to enact the drama of the larger proceedings. A recruited member may wonder just how he or she got into this uncomfortable position and bemoan what has come over him or her.

Taking Back Projections and Responsibility

Group-level roles emerge as individual members express the group's required voices and as representative subgroups vitalize competing tensions and aims. A member, in the dual role of agent for both the self and the group, bridges the gap between individual need and collective demand. The group can find in a member's activities and in their emotional relationship to him or her a common rallying point.

Redl (1982) writes of various members who might act as the "central person" "around whom the group's formative processes take place . . . the crystallization point of the whole affair" (p. 21). The psychotherapist might point out to the group what issues it wishes to work through by hard pressing a particular member.

A group is encouraging Bill to monopolize the session by talking about his marriage and directly facing up to his difficulties in relation to his wife. No one else is claiming similar relational concerns. Seemingly, this is only Bill's problem; on the surface, it appears as if the group is being quite magnanimous in allowing this fellow so much time and targeted concern. However, the "helpful" members are demonstrating, in tone and nonverbal mannerisms, much unspoken feeling, and Bill is becoming increasingly uncomfortable under the exclusive spotlight. The therapist might interrupt the interrogation by reversing the normal perspective and paradoxically stating, "Bill is being quite helpful to the group by allowing members to work out feelings of powerlessness and avoidance through him. However, it is unclear, here-and-now, who is avoiding what. It might be more helpful if members talked about their own similar issues, as related to their outside lives and current group experiences."

Beck, Eng, and Brusa (1989) identify four recurrent leadership roles within the group that can be filled either in stable configuration or in variant succession. The *task leader,* most often the therapist, functions as the work group leader. The *emotional leader* is played by the member most able to meet the group on its own terms. The person assuming this role is usually well liked, widely imitated, and serves to directly elicit and support the feelings of the other group participants. Less popular, but equally important, is the *scapegoat leader,* the member seen as most threatening or different. The person in this role often becomes the target of unspoken negative feelings or outright attack. Yet the scapegoat can be of great help to the group in clarifying ongoing conflicts, underlying affects, and outright prejudices. Coming to terms with the scapegoat means facing the darker side of oneself while overcoming the regressive elements in the group. More openly opinionated and troublesome, the *defiant leader* serves to evoke directly the group's conflicts and ambivalences around self-assertion, conformity, dependence, and openness to the evolving process. The Socratic gadfly, devil's advocate, or rebel in search of a cause often functions from the defiant position.

Within the course of any group's development, certain stereotypical impressions of particular members may be formed and perpetuated. Agazarian (1982) distinguishes between member roles and group roles. In assuming a *member role,* the individual takes a position in the group relevant to his or her own intrapersonal experience, transferential needs, and dynamic issues. In assuming a *group role,* the member's "spokesperson reaction" has more to do with collective needs and dynamics than with individual prerogatives. A selected participant may be the only one in the group allowed to carry a certain attribute or express a particular emotion. In the face of such prescribed or unalterable roles, the members-at-large might be queried about their consignment of traits and responsibilities. For example, it might be asked:

- Do the rest of you wish to place all the active competence in the room within Milt and hold for yourselves only passive incompetence?
- Is Lauren really the only person here who feels self-protective and who takes better care of herself than she does of others?
- Why is Dennis expected to be happy all the time while the rest of the group is allowed to demonstrate a variety of moods and feelings?

In the course of the group process, many issues also get worked out in relation to the leader. In a Tavistock or a dynamically oriented psychotherapy paradigm, the consultant does not always assume the directive role of task or emotional leader. While providing necessary orientation and structural guidance around boundaries and norms, he or she more responds to the group dynamics than leads in any predetermined, directive, or overt way. Group members may certainly attempt to compel the consultant to act like the nurturing father or mother or even the all-knowing deity they really wish him or her to be. The facilitator's job is then to interpret that wish and transferred authority in therapeutically useful ways. What members want the leader to be reflects their own expectations, participant anxieties, and response to prevalent groupwide forces and pressures. The therapist might wonder: Of what leadership abilities, positions, or facilities is the membership in search? Where within its own body might such qualities be found?

Following a deductive paradigm, theorists look for general group dynamics that play out in individual member instances. Foulkes (1964) goes so far as to suggest that group-level processes determine all part processes. The therapeutic aims of this deductive group-as-a-whole approach are: (1) identifying the groupwide forces played out though the medium of its members; (2) encouraging members-at-large to recognize and take back projected and unwanted feelings and role attributions; (3) helping members accept and integrate their own contradictory and less than perfect parts; (4) cultivating personally useful skills, roles, and leadership potentials applicable to the needs of one's formative groupings; and (5) in a reciprocal process, asking, How do we now better understand group trends by the illumination of members' behaviors?

Member Valence and Subgroup Sentience

The member serving as group spokesperson or protagonist is not an arbitrary selection. Participants volunteer or are enlisted according to their latent ability to carry out the specific role that the group requires at the time. In a sense, members are typecast. Certain individuals have a higher *valence* or "readiness for entering into combination with the group in making and acting out the basic assumptions" or current needs of the collective (Bion, 1961, p. 116). The member whose nuclear concerns best match the group's holistic issues becomes the likely candidate for group spokesperson. It is as if the group-as-a-whole unconsciously decides, "We know Joe tends to be _____ and so we can count on him to express _____ for us." and not so surprisingly, Joe often does.

Within the confines of the groupwide exploration, individual members can be helped to recognize and alter their exaggerated or stereotypical responses. At any point in the proceedings, individuals can be asked:

- How do you feel about the role you seem to be stuck in here?
- Do you realize how you keep eliciting this same group response?
- How did you contribute or collude in getting this reaction from the others?
- Is there a reason why you set yourself up in this difficult position?
- What overdetermined, automatic, or dysfunctional patterns of interaction are being reexperienced here and now?
- How do you act similarly in this group to the way you act in your current family and/or family of origin?
- Do you always want to express the group's and, for that matter, everyone else's anger, disappointment, or evident anxieties?

The group voice is not always carried by an individual. Subgroups may form as members join to express various aspects of the group's overall concerns. The group's prevailing views and overdetermined emotional commitments have been subsumed under the intermediary concept of *sentience* (Rice, 1969). Subgroups may be thought of as pockets of prevailing group sentience that vie for influence over the direction of the proceedings. For example, the group-as-a-whole may be represented by warring subgroups, holding out for different boundary regulations or rules of engagement. The conservative sentiment may strongly wish to keep the group closed by admitting no new members or novel perspectives. The liberal subgroup may argue for the need to increase membership and thereby bring in new energies and diverse ideas. This struggle can be conscious, verbal, and overt, or appear as an unconscious, unspoken, and covert battle of hidden agendas. Of course the subgroup affiliations chosen are fueled by individual boundary requirements and intrapersonal dynamics.

It is important to account for all the energies in the room before reaching conclusions about the group-as-a-whole's position with respect to any issue or affect. Bion (1961) tended to interpret silence as an "avowal and consent" of the most overt, vocal, and specifiable group trends (Sherwood, 1964, pp. 124–125). Horwitz (1977) recommends caution when relying on "nonverbal reactions, attentiveness, seeming approval or disapproval and knowledge of patients to avoid overgeneralizing from one or two patients to the whole group" (pp. 429–430). Quiet members, as a silent majority, may truly be in support of their more vocal and active representatives. However, they may just as well simply signify an untapped minority and silent sentience. When in doubt, it is always possible to poll the group to see if they agree with the ideas or share the feelings being expressed. So for example, the therapist might raise the question: Is it true that the group wishes to put off the time for new members to join us?

Group voices and roles and subgroup alignments invariably arise and conflict, thus providing the tension necessary to move the collective process by mediating overriding concerns. As individuals and/or subgroups identify and vocalize the different parts of the group process, a more encompassing whole is sought—one capable of contradiction while still being able to contain the bulk of available energies and perspectives alive within the room.

> The systems group therapist focuses on the dynamic maturation of the group-as-a-whole as the major path to the goals of the therapy— treatment of individual members. . . . The phases in the group-as-a-whole development, and its phase specific maturational challenges, provide the stimulus and the context in which individual members' developmental issues are revisited. (Agazarian, 1989, pp. 150–151)

Compromises may be wrought and complexity gained as varied views seek expression, acceptance, and accommodation. Similarly, the inherent conflict between individual needs and groupwide requirements brings the call for intermediaries—a lively interplay between the speech of individuals and the voice of the group.

Inferring and Affecting the Group-as-a-Whole

Knowing, communicating with, and affecting the group-as-a-whole is a task akin to dancing with an alternatively benign and malevolent ghost. How do we infer its shadowy presence? What fleeting translucency do we wish to touch, lead, and move? How can the dance be of life and developmental integration, rather than a regressive stepping toward destructive potencies and organizational disintegration?

James (1984) describes the group-as-a-whole as "ameboid, constantly fluctuating and changing shape and focus [while] representing a dynamic matrix" (p. 656). Bion (1961) describes what he calls basic assumption cultures, regressive collective formations dominated by dependency, fight/flight, or pairing in fantasy-bound collusive dyads. Whitaker and Lieberman (1964) suggest the presence of disabling solutions to common problems that impede the group from gaining satisfaction and moving on with its shared life. These resistive group stances readily meld into one another, shifting and coexisting with more progessive, task-bound or working configurations. More elusive still, it must be remembered that the group-as-a-whole is but a necessary abstraction that can be constructed or deconstructed but never quite realized.

Bion (1970) likens the task of describing the group, by understanding and interpretation, to the Kantian notion of approaching the "the thing-in-itself." We can only use our categories of understanding to model the ultimate truths inherent in the group configuration—truths in continuous and elusive flux, truths ultimately of our own making. Every group-as-a-whole theorist, in reality, engages in an "as if" enterprise (Vaihinger,1876, summarized in Curtis & Greenslet, 1962). "Even the most sober scientific investigator . . . cannot dispense with fiction, he must at least make use of categories, and they are already fictions, analogical fictions. . . . Fiction is indeed, an indispensable supplement to logic; or even a part of it; whether we are working inductively or deductively" (Curtis & Greenslet, 1962, p. 23).

The thoughtful group psychotherapist must constantly ask:

- What do my imaginative speculations suggest about the unfolding group processes?
- What operative dynamics am I understanding and taking into account and what am I missing?
- How do I know what I think I know?
- What is the evidence for my current construal of the group?

To avoid clinical hubris, the introspective group analyst must be concerned with the source, essence, and application of his or her groupwide conceptions. The practice of working with groups requires a methodology that ascertains, speaks to, and transforms group dynamics.

- Praxis 1: *Group-as-a-whole configurations can be observed, inferred, and diagnosed by examining both external and internal processes.*

Groups can be viewed in their regularity or in their perturbation from both outside and inside the process. Groups, at any point in time, can be characterized as smoothly working, stalled, regressed, or in flux. By catching downcast eyes or watching exuberant interchanges, the group's emotional climate can be diagnosed or described. By listening to group sentiments as expressed through representative member reactions, and by witnessing trends, groundswells, preoccupations, and contagions, holistic regularities can be heard and seen. The analysis of emergent role formations and subgroupings allows indirect access to the issues and feelings around which the group is forming. The associative flow and the configuration of themes and developmental sequences suggest the presence of particular focal conflicts (Whitaker & Lieberman, 1964) and common maturational tensions (Ezriel, 1982). The group's use of language, including emergent images, metaphors, and symbols, reveals relevant motifs, comparative analogies, and cultural contexts. The observation of organizational patterns, like boundary regulations, inclusions and cutoffs, leadership behavior, and interactional rules and norms, gives clues to the group's formative structures and ongoing dynamics.

As the therapist experiences the group with empathy and "free-floating attention," his or her own feelings and fantasies provide an additional source of data. Bion (1961) suggests,

> *It can be justly argued that interpretations for which the strongest evidence lies, [are based] not in the observed facts in the group but in the subjective reactions of the analyst. . . . In group treatment many interpretations, and amongst them the most important, have to be made on the strength of the analyst's own emotional reactions. . . . These reactions are dependent on the fact that the analyst in the group is at the receiving end of . . . projective identification. (pp. 148–149)*

The group leader holds a special role within the proceedings. He or she is not outside the group, but hopefully maintains secure footing in external reality. As a participant-observer, the therapist is subject to the emotional eddies and tides of the experience. Yet at the same time, he or she is removed enough to analyze and use subjective reactions in the service of the group's work.

Arcaya (1985) further suggests that since group psychotherapy essentially involves a hermeneutical process—with the group interaction providing a text to be understood—the creation and attribution of meaning depends on the analyst's unique position as a listening-experiencing-construing-interpreting member. "Rather than being located outside (i.e., objectively) or inside (i.e., subjectively) the therapist, perceived reality exists *between* the analyst and the patient(s)—mediated by the kind of language that they jointly establish in speaking about [the group experience]" (p. 20). Similarly, a semiotic perspective suggests that the group presents itself as a series of interactive puzzles and holistic paradoxes to be deconstructed (Eco, 1984). Overall meanings can be deduced by decoding the symbology of the proceedings.

The group's oscillations of mood and need can be sensed as palpable yearnings and designs. An impression is made by pressing demands and subtle expectations directed toward the leader or toward a member. The steady or staccato rhythm of the group can be felt in the pace and the cadence of the proceedings. It is important for the group analyst to be open to receiving these nonverbal, affective, metaphoric, and preconscious messages from the group. Bion (1970) describes the process of reception. "Let us imagine that when a number of people collect together . . . there are stray thoughts floating around trying to find a mind to settle in. Can we, as individuals, catch one of these thoughts . . . give it a home and then allow it to escape . . . in other words, give it birth" (p. 187).

While carefully guarding against the pressure to act out countertransference, the impact of the collective forces on the group facilitator as another human being must be noted and understood in context. By seeing between the lines, hearing beyond the words, and feeling amidst the process, the leader uses emotional sensitivities as well as creative and intuitive processes to assess the group's needs and fashion ameliorative responses.

• Praxis 2: *The group-as-a-whole can be affected through both literal and figurative communications.*

Once the group's momentum is manifest, the leader must decide what to interpret and what to leave alone. Common wisdom suggests that the group analyst only intervene to challenge resistance, directly enhance the work in progress, or interpret the group's ongoing dynamics in the service of more mature integrations. To do so, the therapist must not only recognize the group's ongoing dynamics but also attribute meaning to the proceedings. The significance and direction of groupwide trends can be inferred by assessing the nature, utility, direction, or implications of the group's behavior (Ettin, 1988b). Bion (1961) suggests that "the interpretation itself is an attempt to translate into precise speech what I suppose to be the attitude of the group to me or to some other individual, and of the individual to the group" (p. 143). The group's attention is thus directed to that common preoccupation that lends collective coherency and shared emphasis to the work, and that reflects back on members' core dynamics.

Once regularity and meaning has been attributed to the group process, and once the decision has been made to intervene, the relevant question becomes: What is the most effective means of communication? Possibilities range from literal statements that simply and reasonably call the group's attention to its dynamics, to rather abstract, figurative sphinx-like pronouncements that provoke affective and unconscious stirrings. Foulkes (1968) recommends avoiding the use of technical terms and "plunging interpretations," instead fashioning interventions that have a "conversational and simple quality" (cited in Whitaker, 1987, p. 214). In contrast, Banet and Hayden (1977) compare one class of Tavistock intervention to the Zen practice of satori. Here, the facilitator calls immediate attention to the absurd or dysfunctional nature of a current collective dynamic by passing a pithy or pointed remark. For example, he or she might say to a group mired in a dependency culture while idealizing the leader, "Today I am viewed as a constellation on high; what will the group do tomorrow when my star falls?"

Interventions can be alternately declarative, rhetorical, suggestive, quizzical, questioning, reactive, or any such expressive device. Borriello (1976) suggests that the nature of "interpretation language depends on the therapist's theoretical persuasion" (p. 3)." He (1976, p. 150) suggests wordings such as:

"The group seems to subscribe to the myth that . . ."
(all will be well here if we astutely avoid conflict)
(the group therapist is the only one who has had any experience in the matters under discussion, etc.)

"The group seems to want to disregard what is happening and instead cling to the illusion that . . ."
(John is the only one here having angry feelings)
(matters will magically work out on their own so that no active decisions are required from the group, etc.)

"Mr. Morris has willingly become the repository of the group for its . . ."
(fear, avoidance, anger, sadness, confusion, etc.)

"The group acts as if all its members are . . ."
(incompetent, lazy, uncaring, unreliable, cured, etc.)

Such interventions follow the laws of hypothesis formation and the giving of contributory evidence. The therapist first attends to the data arising from within-the-group context. He or she then forms a hypothesis to best explain the group-as-a-whole's current functional position. The hypothesis can be shared with the group, along with the data that led to its formulation. Thus, Bion might say, "I think the group has got together in the last five minutes to . . ." (p. 60). He would then supply the occurrences that led him to this conclusion. Here, the interpretive task is to call out the peculiarities of the group situation, including the evident basic assumptions, how various members contributed to the prevalent group culture, and how emergent task leaders were chosen and treated (p. 70). The group is now free to respond to the hypothetical generalization by incorporating the information given and changing the pattern of interaction, or by supplying more data which substantiate, qualify, or contradict the conclusions.

Schermer (1985, p. 148) suggests that whereas Bion's original interpretations of group-as-a-whole processes "were obsessional and intellectualized," he later went on to use "virtually autistic, psychotic thinking and highly abstract meaning" (p. 148). Rioch (1991), in fact, recalls that "Bion was the most obtuse man I ever met and he didn't really mean to be that way." She raises the possibility that perhaps obscure wordings were an artifact of Bion's thinking process or communicational style and not a cornerstone of his method. In any case, language is such a flexible instrument that it is possible to intentionally intermix levels of meaning amidst direct yet suggestive phrasings. The group analyst can use secondary and primary processes together to communicate to the group. Agazarian (1989) concurs that the language of consultation "is the language of emotion, condensation, metaphor, and paradox" (p. 147).

A group was struggling with members' inability to control self-destructive impulses. Carol, a particularly vulnerable group member who was trapped in a sadomasochistic relationship, told the convoluted story of how, while having a good time on a date with a new man, she felt compelled to leave early to seek out her old boyfriend for comfort and companionship. Another member, Jack, talked of his struggle in abstaining from drugs, describing how at a recent rock concert he decided to do "just a little bit" to enhance the experience. The revelations were couched in denials and repressive innocence.

Other group members related easily to these disclosures with a sense of urgent introspection. The facts were clear to all—Carol rarely got comfort from her old boyfriend, and Jack never stopped at just a little. Rather than confront these members directly, a tact likely to precipitate shame and invoke resistance, the therapist made a groupwide interpretation. He stated empathically to everyone in general and to no one in particular, "They say that elephants have tremendous memories. But then they can afford to, they have such thick skins!" Shortly afterward, Carol remembered how, as a child, she excitedly sought out a group of playmates who then consistently beat her up. Jack was able to speak about his usual pattern of getting hooked. He recognized how he invites self-destruction (by taking drugs) as a way of avoiding facing his fears about going on with his life. Jack was now able to more directly face and explore issues of judgment, repressive defenses, self-abasement, impulse control, and masochism. The group-as-a-whole could also consider what type of playmates we would be for each other. Would we ignore, condone, or confront nihilistic behaviors?

In another instance, in a hardened group of male drug offenders, John tested time boundaries by coming consistently late to group. After many sessions of leader and peer pressure, John showed up on time for a meeting. The group immediately responded with derisive clapping. An apt interpretation might have addressed the ambivalent nature of the group sentience as evident in their resounding here-and-now response. Thus, the therapist could have said, "The group's clapping is a two-handed gesture. On the one hand (making an effeminate movement with the left wrist), the group mocks conformity, fearing that following the rules is merely a prissy form of cowardice and surrender. On the other hand (making a raised fist power sign with the right hand), the group applauds John's responsible action as well as celebrating its own success and power in coming together."

- Praxis 3: *The transformations of the group-as-a-whole can be regressive and countertherapeutic or progressive and therapeutic.*

Within any one session, the group-as-a-whole may slip in and out of work and resistance. Progression, regression, and digression, as well as fantasy, reality, repression and insight, coalesce, overlap, and tag-team through the experience. In every group, free-associative processes coincident with the group's evolving enterprise, arise, metabolize, and disintegrate, leaving behind both helpful and harmful residues.

Bion (1961) suggests that resistance and regression are set in motion precisely when progression is demanded of the group or the individual members. Thus, countertherapeutic forces are built into the collective fabric of the ongoing experience (p. 127). "When the pressures of reality and the effort required to maintain a sophisticated, rational viewpoint are too great there occurs a regression . . . a static and insulated retreat" (Bion, 1961, p. 89). In these regressive formations, development is eschewed, individuality is lessened, constituent members are not used to their full authoritative capacities, and primary process and flights of fantasy are engaged as a source of instant gratification. Whitaker (1987, p. 200) defines just these restrictive developments as "times when members collectively maintain some solution that prevents full exploration of the wishes and fears involved in the group focal conflict . . . [thus fostering] shared collusive defenses."

When a group is so allied as to block constructive efforts, it organizes itself around disabling norms, neurotic stabilities, characterological rigidities, hidden agendas, covert purposes, defensive avoidances, restrictive solutions, and undiagnosed role constraints. Resistance may take the form of shared denial, acting out, splitting, scapegoating, or role lock (Agazarian, 1989; Whitaker, 1989). Such a group may appear loosely organized with chaotic, uncertain, and fluctuating boundaries and behaviors, "more colloquially . . . not knowing who, or what belongs where" (Rice, 1969, p. 573).

This type of group formation is often accompanied by labile affect and considerable panic associated with fears of disintegration. Alternately, a resistant group can also appear highly organized, recalcitrant, and cohesive, as disabling solutions and regressive patterns consolidate into collusive climates, restrictive norms, bureaucratic rules, and dysfunctional cultural imperatives. For instance, a group may appear defiant, as it assumes a distinct paranoid position (Klein, 1946), stubbornly refusing any consultation while engaging in collective fight behaviors.

The group-as-a-whole is also capable of following a progressive developmental sequence wherein the collective evolves in order to master its work in its allotted time and space at ever higher levels of integration. To foster such a work group atmosphere, those aspects of the group functioning that are directly concerned with accomplishing the psychotherapeutic task must be reinforced. One essential aspect of groupwide therapeutic change is simply bringing to members' awareness the difference between *resistance* (i.e., basic assumption behavior) and *work*. This kind of insight is cultivated as the therapist calls attention to regressive phenomena while they are hot and operative. He or she thus makes it possible for participants to apprehend, in the immediate present, their defensive patterns. Resistance, properly regarded and managed, is an intrinsic part of therapeutic progress.

Progressive group transformations also entail the development of suitable organizational structures and task-focused leadership; representative group sentience; cooperative membership patterns; capacities for experimentation, feedback, and constructive criticism; and a reality testing that takes into account time boundaries and spatial constraints (Rioch, 1970). Digressions from the task or regressions in the developmental sequence are pointed out for active examination or are directly challenged, as the group is guided back toward therapeutic goals. More facilitative group organizations and richer cultural transformations characterized by less "ambiguity, contradiction, and redundancy" are specifically encouraged (Agazarian & Peters, 1981, p. 47). Bion (1961, p. 50) defines a good group spirit and a positive group culture as,

> *(1) having a common purpose; (2) a common recognition of boundaries in relation to larger units or groups; (3) capacity to absorb new members and relinquish old ones without fear of the group disintegrating; (4) freedom from rigid internal subgroups; (5) recognition of the value of each individual for his contribution; and (6) capacity to face discontent and cope with it in the group. (cited in Brown, 1985, pp. 194–195)*

Agazarian and Peters (1981) reiterate,

Thus a mature group has increased complexity and flexibility of function; diversification of roles; permeability of boundaries between systems, inputs and outputs that convey information through a communications system that has a high potential for organizing it. Negative and positive feedback, in the mature group, serves to keep the group in balance between over-organization and under-organization, and thus in a state of free energy to work through developmental tasks (which in a group is never-ending) and to solve problems (which in living systems are ever-present). (p. 89)

Taken as a whole, the group represents a malleable formative context. The therapist's special role is to foster a safe and constructive working environment, while analyzing restrictive group configurations, so that growth can occur amidst the here-and-now of the collective's shared endeavors. The seriousness of the task should not preclude the playfulness of encounter (Winnicott, 1971). The essence of the work requires freely using collective formations, spirited interactions, progressions, and regressions alike, all in the service of psychotherapeutic change. By so doing, the conglomerate works through resistance and works toward more integrated wholes, both in the group proper and in the individuals who make up the shared experience.

The Isomorphy of Parts and Wholes

Individual, interpersonal, and group-as-a-whole processes are, in reality, intimately related since the issues of life and death, inclusion and exclusion, affiliative relation and autonomous separation, and meaning and void are common to all levels of organization. Following the principle of isomorphy, group-level processes are believed to mirror individual-level processes, while individual processes can stand in for group-as-a-whole phenomena. As in holographic imagery, the whole can be projected from a part, and the part can be reflected in the whole. Rice (1969) writes of the intimate interrelation between the parts and the whole: "Since each part of the enterprise has its own primary task and thus requires an organizational model itself, the organizations for the whole will be constrained by the need to integrate the organizations of the parts, and the organizations of the parts will be constrained by the need to fit into the whole" (p. 569).

Similarly, Brown (1985) suggests that "individuals speak for the group and the group for individuals. Individuals personify aspects and attitudes of the group, often initially disavowed by others, and represent polarities which may later become reconciled within individuals and the group as a whole'' (p. 214). Thus, for example, when a reticent participant plays out his or her own resistance, the group is expressly affected by contrast or by identification. By directly addressing such an individual, one indirectly addresses the group; conversely, by speaking directly to the whole assemblage, the therapist indirectly speaks to a particular member, dyad, or subgroup. Various targeted therapeutic comments to particular members reverberate through the whole of the membership by addressing more universal, existential realities.

The psychotherapeutic implication of the belief that the various levels of group organization are isomorphically related is that interventions at any level of organization affect every other level. Agazarian (1982) argues that increasing one's understanding or bettering one's functioning at any level of a system will increase understandings and capacities at every other level. Group-as-a-whole therapists address most, if not all, of their attention to group-level phenomena. By influencing the most complex strata of an organization, the group itself, it is believed that the most encompassing influence reverberates throughout the whole of the system, thereby affecting all of the members.

CHAPTER SEVEN

The Art of Depiction:

Finding Meaning in the Collective Process

The course of group treatment often revolves around the attribution of meaning and the transformation of psychic structures. How we see ourselves, imagine each other, and view the world around us goes a long way toward determining our unique sphere of influence. Like an inveterate photographer, we all develop and carry a ready portfolio of still lifes and moving pictures—a formative viewing of ourselves and important others in both isolation and interaction. Within the collective montage that is the psychotherapy group, it is possible to see and directly experience our own and each other's positions, projections, and representations. In private showings, within this theater of multiple, public screenings (Foulkes, 1965), distinctive visions can be previewed and edited, as pictures of reality change with contextual shifts, varied frames, and increased exposure.

Certainly it is possible to picture the intrapsychic structures and relational styles of the varied characters who populate our therapy groups (Millon, 1981). We can vividly imagine the dependent person's obsequious gaze and fawn; the paranoid's furtive glances and careful plottings; the histrionic's overblown reactivity and scattered attentions; the narcissist's difficulties seeing others through the contracted lens of his or her own needs and reflections; the schizoid's emotional vacuity, hesitation, and removal from the center of the stage; the obsessive-compulsive's incessant ambivalence, judgments, rituals, and pseudoscientific categorizing; the passive-aggressive's subtle traps and persistent disclaimers; and, of course, the borderline's varied images of merger, distress, breakdown, catastrophe, and violent separation.

Some material in this chapter is adapted from an earlier article in *The Journal of Mental Imagery,* 9 (3), 19–44. Copyright 1985, published by permission of Brandon House, Inc., P.O. Box 240, Bronx, NY 10471.

We all have these pictures and parts more or less within—visions that are projected, displayed, recognized, and reintegrated during the normal life course of the psychotherapy group. Various organizations of the psyche can be characterized and cultivated by forming mental images of internal and external reality. Perhaps structural repair consists of reconstruing a more balanced and healthful imagery—the schizoid in relation, the obsessive in certainty, the passive-aggressive in assertive confrontation, and the borderline in calm assurance and structural integrity.

Ann, a woman with schizoidal proclivities, captured her style of relating by the image of *floating away*. Using this image as an anchor, Ann was given the task of identifying when she began to drift in the group. She was also asked to observe where she floated. During one session, Ann began to mentally wander; she found herself alone in the basement of the building. Another member quickly identified with the image of "putting oneself down" when unable to respond adequately to social demands. Ann was now invited to reemerge and look at her imminent fear of the group's expectations that led to her flight.

Jake, a member with distinct paranoid tendencies, found himself violently angry at the group. He felt overwhelmed by aggressive impulses, and characterized himself as an "electric spark." Using this charged image as a guide, Jake's anger could be explored explicitly along the dimension of its sudden volatility and undirected nature. He could also look at what in the group process short-circuited him, while visualizing the dangerous conflagrations that might lie ahead. Some sessions later, Jake spoke about beginning to learn how to differentiate his friends from his enemies. He reported not reacting as instantly or as violently to everyone.

Pines (1989) expounds on the epistemology and utility of metaphors in psychotherapy.

> *Our human thought processes are largely metaphorical; there are metaphors in our conceptual systems and metaphors bind elements into coherent systems. The "as if-ness" of things is a key element of our therapeutic endeavor. . . . Through this we are able to move our patients into a new mental space where the dynamics of therapy intermesh with the internalized dynamics of the patient's life development. Progress in psychotherapeutic theory is fundamentally our capacity to devise new metaphors which hold and contain our experiences and make them intelligible to our peers. (p. 213)*

With the help of such metaphoric vehicles, ambiguous data can be transformed into coherent objects with descriptive, visualizable properties of their own. With the help of timely projections, the core or essence of the individual and of the interactive experience can be succinctly captured by way of analogy, symbol, and/or a whole host of comparative relation and linguistic device. Metaphoric images and symbols are of the same expressive genre. Persons, object relations, transactions, and emotions can be represented by vivacious mental pictures. The inherent qualities of relationships, with both self and others, which would otherwise remain vague, fleeting, or inexpressible, are thus made directly available for study and change.

For the purpose of this analysis, Wheelwright's (1962) distinction between image and symbol, based on frequency of usage and communicative acceptance, is adopted. An *image* becomes a *symbol* when it is "capable of undergoing recurrence" and develops a stable and repeatable character. To prevent conceptual confusion, *imagery* is differentiated from the more comprehensive term *fantasy,* which includes verbal reports of such diverse mental processes as wishes, fears, expectations, and hypothesis. Such fantasies may or may not be expressed as mental pictures.

The group's search for meaningful connection produces a range of image forms, which are the shared product of operative group dynamics. Images of personal integrity, boundary maintenance, self-concept, essential view of and relation to others, crisis evocation and resolution, closeness and distance, part-whole relations, and groupwide motifs around containment and/or splitting characterize the nature and meaning of the proceedings.

There are so many times in working with groups when personal characteristics and patterns of interaction become clouded within layers of seemingly unimportant content relayed by way of dry, staid, or intellectualized verbiage. Members are also capable of following the group process in more poetic and preconscious narration. Imagery and symbolization are the natural language of such ongoing preconscious processes (Kubie, 1961). Symbolic and metaphoric images naturally arise or can be summoned to the surface to creatively specify various personal attributes, relational patterns, and groupwide configurations. What emerges is a collective picture that is representative of the energies and patterns existing within the group. The image represents events in a gerund language that is capable of movement and change. It simultaneously denotes ongoing aspects of reality, just as it connotes the fluid emotional and meaning components of experience.

Group therapy is differentiated from other forms of psychotherapy by its complexity and potency. Given 8 people and a leader, 72 dyadic, 720 triadic or Oedipal configurations (Mann, 1990), and a conceptually boundless number of more complex and holistic relationships are possible at any one point, with respect to any of an infinite number of issues, feelings, or thoughts. As the formula gets more complicated, a two-dimensional bipolar model or even a triadic dialectic progression fail to follow the myriad of interactions or to reflect fairly the intricacies inherent in members' relations to themselves, each other, and the whole of the group. In fact, no nosological term or noun taken from standard vocabulary is mobile enough to follow and describe the ongoing exigencies of the group. Imagery provides a medium in which many dimensions can be represented simultaneously in one, or a series of clear pictures (Ettin, 1984, 1985a, 1989b). These word-pictures convey existent feeling states and unfolding scenarios with precision and perceptual acuity.

For example, when a member says, "I am depressed," a general affective category and class of experience is conveyed with which others might freely identify. However, few clues and little specificity is offered as to the exact nature of the subject's experience. To say, on the other hand, as one participant did, "I feel as if I'm tied to a pole with birds picking away at me" conjures a more immediate and particularized vision of immobility, disintegration, helplessness, and incessant torture at the hands of others. The group members can readily see and directly respond to this potent image and its impassioned plea for release.

Ahsen (1977), working with a fixed series of images, talks of the "staggering number" and "geometric progression" of images possible in a group setting. A flexible and creative visual language is invaluable when working with such a dynamic and complex process as created when people come together to express their feelings, pool their reactions, and share their therapy. By carefully allowing for portending images, members are helped to personalize meanings, participants can clarify interchanges, while the group itself can both analyze its current trends and make necessary adjustments to its progress (Ettin, 1985a). Winnicott (1971) elaborates on the value of imaginary productions as necessary transitional objects that close the gap between inside and outside, self and other, patient and psychotherapist, and individual and group. Thus, through imagery work, experiences in the group can be represented, symbolized, compared, transformed, and worked through.

Image Evocation

Metaphoric mental pictures can make an appearance within the psychotherapy group as: (1) deliberately structured interventions; (2) spontaneous therapeutic communications provided to the group as a clarification or interpretation; and (3) members' unbidden, visualizable, and subsequently amplified figures of speech. Group leaders differ in how they view their role and in what manner they choose to comment on or affect the group process—whether suggesting a specific image to the group for guided visualization or rather waiting for images to occur more naturally to members and/or the leader within the ongoing context of the session.

The free flow and often dream-like quality of the therapeutic session may be enough to call forth metaphoric images. At other times, group leaders may induce a hypnogogic-like state of consciousness. They may encourage the production of mental pictures by instructing clients to close their eyes, relax, and visualize with the mind's eye. Hypnosis, meditation, and relaxation techniques represent such a concentrated effort at quieting external stimuli and maximizing the imaginative flow.

Structured Images

Directed daydreams (Desoille, 1965), guided affective imagery (Leuner, 1969; 1981), and imaginary scenarios (Shorr, 1978, 1983) may be introduced at any point in the group process. The utility of such exercises depends on how well the constructed imagery matches the stage of the group, or the particular focal conflict, impasse, or shared conflict presently operating. Thus, a blocked or resistant group can be asked to imagine journeying up a stream to plumb obstructions to a free flow of material (Leuner, 1981). A group exploring mastery issues can be asked to visualize interactions and challenges as members cooperate or compete around an imaginary task or quest. A group stuck in a punitive, nonproductive struggle can be instructed to imagine that they are in prison together and asked to elaborate both their offense and plan of escape (Shorr, 1983).

Imaginative activities may alternately be initiated by simply providing a starting image and instructing the group members to explore the motif either singly or collectively (Leuner, 1990). In guided fantasy (Leuner, 1969), the group might start with the structured image of entering a cave. Members then develop the scenario according to their own spatial and temporal prerogatives, which usually clearly correspond to internal structures and outward styles. In a more directed fantasy approach, the group is guided on the mental journey with the therapist describing the particular opportunities and obstacles to be encountered along the way. Here, the group might be escorted into the cave mouth, directed down a rope leading to a series of subterranean channels, introduced to a great room of stalagmites and stalactites, before being ushered to the surface by a prescribed route. Symbolically rich starting images and imaginary scenarios are usually preselected for their evocative power and ability to capture and transform universally relevant human experiences.

Once the journey, whether free flowing or guided, is complete, members are encouraged to compare and contrast the particulars of their excursions, looking also toward parallels from in and out of group. A wide variety of projections and dynamic interactions become available.

Provided Images

In more traditional approaches to group therapy, it is generally agreed that interventions should be "short and sweet"—highlighting, punctuating, and furthering the ongoing flow of the session without artificially affecting the spontaneous quality of the material. Single, summary, affect-laden images can be provided by way of clarification, elaboration, and interpretation (Hammer, 1967; Sledge, 1977; Gans, 1991). For example, when a group member fired questions at others, he got some insight into his style of interaction when told that he acted "like a basketball player always applying full-court pressure." The pressing member immediately saw the connection to the nature of his strained relationship with his wife. The other participants could now explore the strengths and weaknesses of this style, for him and for themselves, both in and out of the group setting.

The emergent image is not inherently threatening, nor is it an accusation requiring justification or defense. Rather, it is a creative picture for which the imaginer claims full responsibility. The image appears to its imaginer as a concrete depiction of his or her experience that is neither right nor wrong. It is merely a product of introspection made present for oneself and made available for the viewing of others.

By assuming a "passive receptive mood" and listening with a "free-floating" and "evenly-focused attention" (Reik, 1948), the group leader is able to free his own creative capacities for the production of integrative gestalts (Wertheimer, 1912; Koffka, 1947; Kohler, 1947). By sharing his images, the therapist lends meaning and context to the collective endeavor, whether addressing individuals, dyads, or the group-as-a-whole. Lothane (1981) describes the process. The analyst, or in this context the group leader,

> arrives at his deepest insights neither by searching for a conclusion nor by jumping to one. The best way is for him to wait until a conclusion jumps to him. He often prefaces the various instances of emergence by the characteristic remarks: "I suddenly recalled . . . the mental picture was vivid but fleeting." And then suddenly the visual images occurred to me. The pictures occurred to me when I listened to my patients. (p. 495)

By such a method, the therapist is able to arrive at preconscious insights about the central themes, quality of relationships, and particular meanings of the groupwide events. The amount of data and observation available at any one time in the group often makes a more logical, ordered approach too pedestrian. Rather, the group leader needs his or her own experience and creative capacities to follow and organize the collective experience. By such a method, silent and latent meanings become capable of conscious and foreseeable representations.

Amplified Images

Often the group will spontaneously develop images that depict problems and preoccupations. A member may describe an inside or outside event or feeling with colorful evocative language. Many turns of phrase can be readily visualized and elaborated. An anxious member may talk of "crawling out of his skin." The therapist might wonder aloud what in the group is making the member so touchy? Which internal processes are so hard to contain? How has his or her envelope of protection been compromised and to where would he or she like to crawl off? A suspicious participant may decry the dangers "lurking in shadow." The shadow image can be amplified as a visage of hidden, split-off personal qualities. Hearing the predominance of a shut door in a member's report, the leader might ask the member to imagine himself as the door and consider what is closed off. What is passing through him, and who in the group is he keeping in or out?

The therapist thus highlights, clarifies, and amplifies these naturally occurring images, focusing on the themes being described and enacted. Using the full potential of the group, members are encouraged to elaborate and associate actively to their own and each others' images. To do so means completing the picture from varied perceptual vantage points, thus providing the group-as-a-whole with a multirepresentational perspective.

Several imagery techniques derive from Jung's (1976) work in "active imagination" and "symbol amplification." This method is intended to do more than merely reduce or translate an image to a set referential base and thus specify latent meanings. Rather, the emergent image is playfully expanded in meaning and utility by considering its directionality, mobility, implication, and connotation. Jung explains, "When you concentrate on a mental picture, it begins to stir, the images become enriched by details, it moves and develops . . . and so when we concentrate on a mental picture and we are careful not to interrupt the natural flow of events, our consciousness will produce a series of images that makes a complete story" (p. 172). Psychotherapy groups can work with just these pictorial collages that represent the varied or common perceptions of its members.

Goals of Imagery Intervention

Attending to naturally arising or carefully crafted transformative images and other metaphoric messages can clarify dynamics and foster therapeutic movement at the three levels of group organization: the individual, the interpersonal, and the group-as-a-whole. The overall goal at each level of group organization is specified here, along with representative subgoals. For each successive subgoal, an intervention involving structured, therapist-provided, or member-amplified imagery is respectively described. Neither the subgoal listings nor the type and progression of intervention is meant to be exhaustive. There are other subgoals that can be identified, and certainly every method of image evocation can be fruitfully used to work within any subgoal. The various aims and practices described here serve as exemplars of ways in which imagery can be called upon in working with the psychotherapy group to practice and enhance the art of depiction.

Goals	*Subgoals*
A. Clarify individual dynamics, self-perceptions, object relations, and behavior potentials.	1. Solicit self-disclosure and diagnostic information and point the way to structural change.
	2. Enhance the range, power, and openness to therapeutic interpretations.
	3. Clarify and highlight transferential and countertransferential reactions.
B. Enliven and depict the quality of interpersonal interactions, relational potentials, and self-object perceptions.	4. Highlight and focus on members' strengths and weaknesses, and clarify the nature of interactions and relational patterns.
	5. Encourage feedback, constructive criticism, and positive confrontation.
	6. Foster intimacy and cohesion, while considering fears of enmeshment and engulfment.
C. Capture and symbolize complex group-level themes, universal processes and conflicts—including perceptions about the essential nature of the shared experience and group life cycle—while fostering indi-	7. Create and work through fantasy experiences that imaginatively stand in for groupwide themes, conflicts, or normal developmental issues, while considering individual variations of experience.

Continued

Goals	*Subgoals*
vidual transformations amidst the group-as-a-whole's movements.	8. Underscore the structure and movement of the group by providing lively metaphoric vehicles. 9. Recognize, amplify, and provide transformative symbols in a collectively homeostatic process that takes the group-as-a-whole from disorganization and chaos to specificity and conflict resolution.

Subgoal 1: Solicit Self-Disclosure and Personal Description

Early in the group, the client's task of sharing begins. Members tell their stories by providing factual information about their lives. This initial information is often couched in descriptions of external circumstances and life events. As is often the case, impulses to disclose are counterbalanced by desires to conceal. While the group members should be encouraged to discuss these conflicting motivations openly, more than mere hesitation often prevents such free exchange. Members are often unsure of how to communicate their essence or clarify their purpose for being in the group.

Here, the therapist may suggest a structured imagery exercise wherein members depict themselves as an inanimate object. Through the mechanism of projection, internal states and essential relationships are openly displayed. Through the emergent imagery, a more introspective accounting is encouraged. Resultant images often predict the nature of future interactions with other group members, while serving as a nodal focus around which therapy goals might be structured. Such a personal, initial orienting image also provides a reference point against which progress can be measured—the first exposure of a before-and-after picture.

One rather pleasant young woman came to group feeling out of control and directionless. She pictured herself as in an "overstuffed chair"— immobile and nicely furbelowed and upholstered. People enjoyed sitting on her because she was comfortable and conformed to their various shapes. She enjoyed the feeling of supporting others. However, as the image progressed the sensation of being weighed down emerged. She was struck by a sense of immobility and lack of her own supports.

Another member pictured himself as a "shiny brass trumpet" capable of wondrous melodious tones. However, he, as instrument, lay untouched in the corner of his room. Feelings of nonproductiveness, resentment, and loneliness emerged. He suddenly realized that he was unable to function without attracting a musician to free the notes trapped inside.

A third member viewed herself as an "old-fashioned, high-necked Victorian dress." She was displayed in the corner of a dress shop. Many people admired her but always from afar. Others were afraid to touch the material lest it crumble in their hands.

Groupwide, these images were experienced as powerful and enlightening. A mere verbal insight into the members' self-concepts and styles of relating could not have resounded with such clarity. Members were encouraged to react to their own and each other's images. This exercise fostered interaction, dialogue, feedback, and creative risktaking.

The first woman described (as an overstuffed chair) proceeded to define her role in the group as the therapist's helper. She was responsible for making other members glad to be in the group. The trumpet passively waited to be approached before launching into an articulate oration of opinions and feelings. The antique dress sexually attracted the male group members. However, she fled in fear when approached, while angrily denying her seductiveness. Thus, the images vividly predicted members' interpersonal styles with their inherent rewards and shortfalls.

Images have the advantage of mobility. If one is able to picture effectively a change in representation, one can correspondingly change the reality represented. A reconjuring of the overstuffed chair image allowed that member to, in time, restructure her relationship to others in the group. The chair, while not losing its comfort, became less flexible and accommodating. It was able to sit unoccupied without anxious discomfort. Behaviorally, the client worked on developing her personal interests, learning to be less solicitous and better able to tolerate unstructured situations. Being overweight, she worked to contain her feelings of aloneness and to fulfill herself without overstuffing.

In another group, Mike, a young man who had vaguely spoken of low self-esteem and lack of assertiveness, described himself as a "beach chair, capable of reclining and supporting others, but having no spine." As the image progressed, the beach chair talked of feeling inferior and less substantial than other chairs. Mike conjured up a big mahogany throne as an ideal perch. Yet he saw the throne as unapproachable and indifferent to his existence. The "beach chair" proceeded to make a casual and sloppy appearance in group, which led to feedback and insight on how he sabotages his desire to appear important. The image also predicted an authority clash with the "throned" leader, who Mike did not believe valued his opinion. Transference phenomena were then explored, as were the roots of Mike's self-description of "spinelessness."

Subgoal 2: Enhance Range and Power of Therapeutic Interventions

The group can be a difficult arena for making interpretations since members are socially exposed and vulnerable to shame. Therapeutic assessments, seemingly thrust at clients, are often quickly parried, resulting more in resistant defensiveness than in insight. Interpretations couched in metaphoric pictures can enhance constructive criticism by encompassing both positive and negative elements, thus softening the blow to a member's self-image and preventing unnecessary narcissistic injuries. The therapist's vision, in the form of a provided image, is presented to the group as a photographic amalgam of important dynamics. The targeted individual, with the group's help, can then refine the image by extrapolating its implication.

In a long-standing therapy group, it became clear that Dirk was having difficulty remembering the content of the sessions from week to week. He was also beginning to solidify a pattern of nonparticipation. Members tended to leave him out of their interactions and forget him in their own review of the group process. The therapist initially adopted the tactic of inviting Dirk to join the conversation at points during which he might have been expected to relate to the material being discussed. These interventions were largely unsuccessful, with Dirk saying a few words and then fading back into the periphery. Yet he came faithfully every week and seemed to be intently watching other members interact.

During a session marked by this pattern, the therapist conjured the image of Dirk "sitting alone on a screened-in porch watching the outside world while intently wishing he could join in." To others outside the porch, Dirk was invisible through the heavy meshing of the screen. The screening also prevented a clear view or understanding of the world outside. The therapist shared this image with the group, and Dirk readily identified with this metaphorically removed position. He talked sadly about his feeling separate from others and not knowing how to make contact. In this first extended self-disclosure, Dirk described to the group his long-standing pattern of separation. The oldest in his family of eight siblings, he was often left to his own devices, never quite feeling within the flow of his nuclear group. Dirk was, in fact, quite used to not being noticed or taken into account.

As a result of his revelations, the group felt a bit closer to Dirk, approaching the porch but still not quite getting inside. Nor could Dirk yet get out. The therapist believed that Dirk might be encouraged if he could develop a relationship with at least one other group member. He was told that, for now, it was okay for him to sit on the porch and watch the group. However, he was asked whom in the group he might like to invite through the screen to sit with him for a time. He readily chose Diana, a relatively new member. The image was amplified with Dirk and Diana invited to imagine their time on the porch together.

Not coincidentally, Diana shared Dirk's concerns and welcomed the opportunity to make contact with another member. The porch image became a lookout point from which Dirk's efforts in the group and his progress might be measured. Dirk began to work concertedly toward letting people in and not "screening off" quite as much of the group material. The group, instead of isolating Dirk, started to include him more and to take pride in his small yet steady steps toward making contact.

Subgoal 3: Clarify Transference and Countertransference

Clients in group therapy can also be encouraged to dip below consciousness and draw upon their imagery to depict and project feelings about the therapist and the therapeutic process. Resultant images usually combine realistic visions with more transferential projections.

After two new members joined an ongoing group, the discussion turned to formulating goals. One new member expressed doubts that the group would be of much help to her. Provocatively, she asked questions about the process while challenging the leader and members to justify and explain the purpose of "group" to her. With this gauntlet thrown, old members examined their own progress and speculated about the essential nature of participating in a shared treatment format. Some confusion and concern arose about how to formulate and reach various personal goals while in group. The therapist became very active in pointing out specific paths for several members. This unusually directive therapeutic behavior stirred fantasies about the leader and led two members to independently visualize the image of the therapist-as-wizard.

The wizard is a time-honored symbol suggesting wisdom, mystery, and magic. As such, it is capable of receiving many powerful transference projections. The group was invited to amplify the wizard image as a way of tapping expectations of powerful others and of eliciting current reactions to the therapist's seemingly omniscient behavior. One member focused on the group facilitator's role as a "psychopomp" or spiritual guide, objectively leading him through the labyrinth of his inner turmoil. Another member, not so satisfied, frankly wished more of the therapist. She wanted the wizard to wave his wand, thereby more fully defining the group's direction while simultaneously binding the disturbing energies stirred up for her in the process. A third member anxiously wondered, as with the *Wizard of Oz*, if there was any substance behind the therapist's seemingly powerful demeanor.

By highlighting the reactions of various group members to the therapist, the wizard image vividly depicted personal concerns and idiosyncratic reactions to authority. When the group focused on the wizard image and particularized its meaning for the various members, a valuable consideration of trust and dependency issues was spurred. Who was in charge of the group's direction? Where in the group does wisdom and power reside? By elaborating on the emergent image, the group was encouraged to confront its own working principles, formulate its own goals, and delineate the realistic role of the therapist in the process. Prompted by the image, the genetic "roots" of the various transferential reactions could be explored. Meanwhile, the therapist could examine the realistic components of the projection by looking to his own need to be so authoritatively helpful.

Subgoal 4: Depict Strengths, Weaknesses, and Relational Patterns

In an anthropological summary, Firth (1973) has pointed a finger toward the use of body parts as one of man's earliest and most natural symbolic forms. Bodily action can serve as communication, as when bowing to another's opinions. The body has also been used symbolically to stand for the social unit, with its interrelationship of parts. Thus, a person's unique position relative to the whole can be expressed in metaphors such as "head of the family," "backbone of the team," or "weak limb." Various body parts have evolved natural and stable symbolic meanings, as when the heart is equated with warmth and feeling. Such meanings may be further particularized by developing mental pictures associated with these symbolic forms and by combining organic symbols with inorganic modifiers. Thus, "heart of gold" would symbolize generosity and kindness, whereas "heart of stone" would imply a cold and hard affective stance.

Anzieu (1984, p. 118) suggests that "the metaphor of the body plays an extraordinary role in the history of ideas." The inside of the body itself comes to stand for the enclosed, dark, unseen, and unconscious elemental and transformative space—differentiated by functional organs such as the heart, spleen, kidney, liver, and womb, as well as by viable processes such as circulation, digestion, and elimination. For example, the womb, heart, spleen, and belly can signify, respectively, birthing, caring, venting of gall, and containing. Various bodily openings and mediating organs (eyes, ears, nose, mouth, navel, rectum, genitals, skin) can represent the exchange point between inner and outer, subjective and objective processes. Anzieu (1984) suggests,

> *A group is born when a number of individuals bound together by, and anxious over, the omnipresent image of the dismembered body, manages to overcome this anxiety, to reassure themselves and see and feel themselves as human beings, to feel pleasant, common and positive experiences. . . . When they come to feel themselves as "us," when a unit superior to each individual, but in which each has a part, comes into being, then group is born, like a living "body." (p. 123)*

Imagery techniques can be fashioned utilizing ongoing body symbolism to "organize" the unique interrelationships among group members. In one therapy group, the members were asked specifically to imagine the group as a body and then to differentiate the various parts. The group freely associated to the resultant images, coming to consensus about the meaning of various body-part attributions and part-whole relations.

Sherry, a repressed member, was seen as the skin (protective, keeping toxins in or out, and at times thick and impermeable).

Fred, a bright and overintellectualized member, was viewed as the brain, able to express complex thoughts but often putting up a barrier with his ideas. He stayed encased in a hard and protective shell with so many complex processes and intricate firings going on under the surface that he remained isolated from more visceral experience.

Steve, a rather obsessive man with distinct paranoid tendencies, was depicted as the eyes of the group, always intently looking out at others. When voyeuristically viewing the world, he often neglected more direct participation, leaving himself isolated, lonely, and immobile. The group saw his steely gaze as penetrating and frightening and often avoided his presence along with his scrutiny.

Kate, an effervescent and somewhat hysterical young woman, was seen as the blood—essential to life, ever-coursing below the surface, but most evident during an injury to herself or to others that required immediate attention.

Sue, a warm, passive, and recently divorced woman, was called the heart of the group, adding warmth, sentimentality, dwelling in the past, working harder for others than for herself, and appearing brokenheartedly depressed. In the image, as in life, she was throbbing, trapped, and without arteries connecting to the outside world.

Ted, a direct and confrontively aggressive member, was described as the conscience (keeping the group honest) and the penis (excitable, standing out, and penetrating).

The therapist was seen as the digestive tract—taking things in and distributing nutrients throughout the whole of the body.

These various images provoked lively discussion and provided a corpus of experience and knowledge from which to identify individual strengths and weaknesses. The relationship of individual members to the whole of the group as body politic pointed out the structural changes necessary for each organ or part-process to most adaptively carry out its function. The "skin" could work toward letting the group massagingly soften her complexion on life, while allowing toxic removal through catharsis. The "brain" could realize the importance of checking with the heart and more sensually engaging the body. The "blood" might come to see how others appreciated her life force without the compulsion to swell matters out of their normal proportion.

Subgoal 5: Encourage Feedback and Constructive Confrontation

The therapist can provide "images of connection" that call attention to the nature of member-to-member relationships within the group. Complex experiences, patterns of attraction, and prototypical interactional anomalies can be captured in succinct images. The group setting provides a perfect forum in which individuals gain awareness of how others actually see and respond to them. The chosen member can then compare such reflections with those images carried on since childhood and with those pictures currently depicting critical outside relations.

An ongoing group was having difficulty largely due to the "changed" feelings and "bellicose" behavior of one of its male members. The whole group atmosphere was tense and unproductive. To directly confront the group member as "hostile" would surely evoke defensiveness or more of the same. Conjuring the picture of "a frustrated bull intent on charging the first object that moves" was a more descriptive and effective intervention. Working within the image, various group members added precision to the picture by coloring in their own particular perspectives on, preparations for, and reactions to the imminent attack. Within the image, the angry member also explored perceived provocations, including invasions of his personal space. What red flags were being waved at him? Did he, in fact, know how to defend or assert himself in a less belligerent manner? He might also ponder how his group stance was reminiscent of other provocative outside occasions.

Subgoal 6: Foster Intimacy and Cohesiveness While Considering Fears of Enmeshment

At various points in the group process, images arise that serve to emphasize and reinforce the cohesive ties between the members. Other images may express the difficulties inherent in just this joining together. Some ambivalent images stimulate a consideration of paired opposite reactions, individuation and merger or attraction and repulsion, clearly depicted within one picture. The group itself simultaneously provides psychological strength in the "hermetic protection" of the closed circle, while constantly representing the danger of dissolution of individuality within a web of entrapment. In fact, group psychotherapy stimulates a continuous ebb and flow between protecting the needs of the individual while accommodating to collective concerns.

An ongoing group was struggling with intimacy issues. Desires to be close to each other were counterbalanced by fears of losing freedom, individuality, and personal integrity. The group wondered aloud: How was it possible to enter into intimate and cohesive unions without inevitably giving away precious parts of the self? Sharon, a new member, expressed her attraction to the group's ability to provide feedback and support, while fearing that amidst such close confines her own opinions would be summarily swept away. In this session, she hungrily sought the opinions of others and then hurtfully accused the group of undue influence, of always telling her what to do.

Paul's solution to the merger/separation problem was to seek out "horizontal rather than vertical relationships." He meant to develop a cadre of associations and affiliations without the pressure of going deeper or remaining constant with any one individual. This interpersonal stance was well demonstrated in his even-handed yet distant group behavior. Paul was given feedback by one of the female group members that his inconsistent availability and refusal to go any further was infuriating and ultimately unsatisfying to her.

Doris, a newly married member, talked of how during her honeymoon she used irritation and pickiness to push her new husband away. The group explored how fears of engulfment often led to such distancing maneuvers. Spontaneously, Doris prefaced her next remark with the phrase, "Both part and parcel of my response to my husband . . . ." This dual-faced image of simultaneous separateness and to-getherness became the transformative focal motif for many sessions to follow. How was it possible to be oneself when with others? How was it possible to be both "a part and a parcel"?

Subgoal 7: Work Through Imagery Scenarios that Represent Shared Themes and Groupwide Developments

Leuner (1984) presents a core series of five symbolic motifs that can be adapted to a group context. Each imaginary scenario engenders different psychic contents and world views. For example, the image of entering a meadow introduces projective concerns about the hospitality of inner and outer environments. Following a brook to its source symbolizes the course, blockage, and free access of psychic energy. The exploration of a house provides a self-symbol whose various rooms and overall condition can be carefully inspected. A character emerging from the edge of the woods stands in for the hidden yet surface qualities of unconscious identifications and introjects. The act of climbing a mountain represents ascending into the world of paternal strivings and calls forth issues of task mastery, ego ideals and constrictions, and relations to authority (Ettin, 1988c).

A group of male adolescents on probation were considering mastery issues. After a brief relaxation exercise, each boy was asked to imagine standing in a field of tall, flowing grasses. In his possession was a sword and a basket. On the edge of the field was a mountain. His task was to reach the top of the mountain in any fashion he chose. After completing the exercise, each member was asked to relate the manner of his epic journey. The other group members then shared their interpretations and reactions to each other's experiences. Spirited discussion and gestalt techniques were utilized to work with the specific emergent images.

Mark saw himself climbing the mountain and using his sword as a cane. He came across a huge boulder in his path. Not knowing how to get around it, he sat and leaned his chin on the sword. He soon fell asleep. When he awoke, the boulder was gone. Ken started climbing up the sheer rock by using his sword to wedge his way. He climbed trees and surmounted every obstacle in his path. Tom started climbing and soon found the terrain rough. The wind blew him down into the mud where he struggled to release himself, to no avail. The wind finally blew him up to the top where he felt free and exhilarated.

These images certainly depicted the active, passive, perseverant, or wishful styles of the various members. For these boys, obstacles were often met by loss of hope or impulsive or magical solutions. Not one of the boys expressed a well thought out, sequenced plan for traversing the difficulties that faced them.

An example of how the images might be worked with is demonstrated in the cases of Jeff and Tony. Jeff, in climbing, came across weeds about waist high. He started to cut them with his sword. There were so many to cut, he wondered if he would get through. The group reenacted this scene by becoming the weeds. They called back to Jeff that he must cut harder. The therapist asked the soft-spoken Jeff to use his voice as a sword. To cut the weeds, he must become more assertive and demand that they fall. Jeff became more vocal, but still appeared overcontrolled and constrained. The weeds, unconvinced, refused to yield, and Jeff, ever frustrated, yelled that he would burn them down. This reaction made his probation offense of setting fire to an outhouse more understandable as an act of impotent rage. Jeff received empathy and support from the group. In this and subsequent sessions, he was helped to express himself more directly, to recognize the source of his anger and frustrations, and to develop alternate coping mechanisms.

Tony climbed to the top of the mountain and found an ancient city with trunks of jewels and riches. He loaded his bucket up, but the mountain soon disappeared before he had his fill. Tony was left disappointed, confused, and unfulfilled. The group explored with Tony his materialism and impulse control. They related this "stolen treasures" image to his offense of pilfering a snowmobile.

Subgoal 8: Provide Transformative Images to Depict the Essence of the Groupwide Process

Various symbolic motifs may be used metaphorically to underscore the group's dynamic progress and emergent conflicts. By holding these images and symbol sets in mind, the therapist may better understand the group and more confidently decide when or how to intervene. Canetti (1984) has written of crowd symbols as "collective units" that "shed natural light" and stand for the crowd in "myth, dream, speech, and songs." Such symbols as fire, sea, rain, forest, and wind all provide natural metaphors for certain properties and processes of a group.

The image of fire, for example, might be conjured by the therapist to depict and elaborate the panic and emotional contagion of a group in crisis and unbounded emotionality. As with a natural conflagration, the dissolution of the group may seem contagious, insatiable, and inevitable, devouring of the life remaining, as a sudden and mysterious flame of discontent is lit. Each group member may be careful to provide no other combustible material to further inflame the discussion. With the fire image as guide, the group therapist could recognize member concerns and subtly work to contain the blaze, while encouraging nonincendiary participation, and thus protecting what remained of the group. The cleaning and purifying aspects of fire could also be tended so that the heat generated from within could rid the group of empty, anachronistic structures, while creating new space for needed changes and formative developments.

Similarly, a prevalent and particularly malleable group-level image is that of a container, womb, or transformative vessel. Whitmont (1964) has associated the therapy group with the formative fires and life-sustaining powers of the archetypal great mother. The intrinsic connection between the group and the principle of containment yields transformative group symbols—such as caves, tombs, ovens, shelters, vessels—that emerge spontaneously or can be called up by the therapist to highlight aspects of the group experience.

A long-term, open-ended group was dealing with the imminent termination of a key member. Dan had made substantial progress during his five years in group. His initial depression had lifted long ago and his passive-suspicious stance had given way to more confident and assertive footing. As a direct result of these personal changes, his work situation and his marriage had improved. In group, Dan had become an emotional leader. He was well liked and connected with all the other members, and he demonstrated the perseverance to courageously pursue hot and heavy issues.

With about six weeks remaining in Dan's group stay, the other members appropriately began to query him about his progress and confidence about "being on his own." Dan answered questions evenhandedly, while openly talking of both his readiness and his remaining problems. Although everything in his life was not resolved, he expressed confidence that "whatever comes up, I'll handle it."

Rather than being satisfied with Dan's responses, the group escalated its concerns and presented test case after test case for Dan's consideration. What if you have a fight with your wife? What if your supervisor at work treats you unfairly? What if you get depressed again? What if . . . what if . . . ad infinitum. The group seemed in a frenzy around issues of strength versus weakness, and self-sufficiency versus reliance on others. The therapist had a sense that more was involved for the group than Dan's readiness to leave. The remaining members seemed afraid of Dan's departure and anxious about their own cohesiveness and abilities to hold together without him. Various prosaic interventions failed to calm the assault on Dan or focus the group on self-doubts about its own resiliency.

The therapist tried to imagine what the group was up to. What was really going on here? Suddenly, and with great conviction, he saw in his mind's eye, and shared with the members, an image of the group "testing its metal—by turning up the temperature in escalating degrees, as if in an industrialized furnace." In such an enclosure, any resolve might melt. The group effort, led by Mike (not coincidentally from Pittsburgh), was seen as actively stoking the fires of uncertainty. The therapist suggested that the group was concerned about whether or not it could withstand the heat of its own unresolved conflicts. Missing Dan's mediation, the group would have to forge its own solutions, despite sinking to a critical membership low of four participants.

Focusing on this "testing the metal" image allowed the group-as-a-whole to consider its own tinsel strength and fears of unraveling or melting away. Of those left, several troubled dyads existed. The two women, Constance and June, burned with unresolved jealousies and competitive feelings. The two men, Mike and Jack, had great difficulty melding. Mike was very direct and action oriented. Jack was more tangential and cerebral. Dan had provided necessary linkages between many of the members, holding the group together. The next month was spent recasting relationships, solidifying the shape of the group-as-it-was-to-become, while taking the heat off Dan so that he could leave intact. The group now actively considered what new vessel could be forged in and salvaged from the group-as-kiln.

Subgoal 9: Highlight Transformative Images of Groupwide Conflicts and Impasses

Hobson (1959) and Willeford (1967) lyrically adapted some of Jung's ideas about symbolic transformation to a group setting. They practiced a special use of "active imagination" and "symbol amplification" to depict and work through conflicts. Willeford considered the role of group members as "contingent parts of a dynamic whole." Group therapy is viewed as a homeostatic process. The therapy group undulatingly moves through a series of chaotic disintegrations and reintegrations, in which imagery plays an important role in cohesively binding energy and meaning, while ushering in transformative changes.

Willeford (1967) gives a history-bound example of a group in which patients' anxiety mounted as a result of cutoffs from each other, their communities, and intrapsychic splits. Here, a member spontaneously fashioned the picture of the Berlin Wall. This image served as a container and transformer of the energy, concretely empowering patients to explore their "walls" and "separations." (Time and current circumstances have now turned the Berlin Wall into a symbol of healed splits.)

Willeford elaborates that the normal free flow and "scattered contents" of the group discussion often breed anxiety among members and guilt in the therapist, as any "constraining totality [seems] so far away." He coaches that the therapist who can respect the chaos, bear the tension, and hold up under the anxiety and guilt "holds open the possibility that there may be spontaneous movement within the whole constellation."

Using a metaphor from jazz improvisation, someone in the group will have the "dominant ear of the moment," hear what the group spirit is straining to say, and provide a content (image or symbol) that moves the group from cacophony to a consideration of a recurrent and present melodic pattern. In a *peripetria,* or decisive moment of turning, personal relevance will be found, and a *lysis,* or group resolution, will be crystallized with the emergence of a transformative symbol. The member most immediately affected by the underlying theme often serves the needs of the larger group by spontaneously providing the symbolic image necessary to integrate seemingly disparate material. That member surely functions as the group spokesperson, voice, or, in this case, instrument (Agazarian & Peters, 1981). With the production and utilization of the emergent image, anxiety is reduced and the group moves toward harmonious understanding and resolution of pertinent themes, issues, or conflicts.

A group was struggling with intimacy needs and trust issues. Attempts at approaching others were being mediated by each member's personal boundaries and defenses. The subsequent interactions were becoming confusingly intricate and obtuse. Words of explication served to add to the muddle. One member spontaneously began to speak of "the wall" she erected, as a metaphor for her defensive operations. It was apparent that other members identified with the image of the wall as both a protection and a barrier. The therapist helped each member describe his or her personal wall. The nature of the interactions and defenses began to come clear.

Joe depicted an acrylic shield that completely encased him. The shield had one small door that could be opened only from the inside. Inside the shield was room for one person besides himself. As he moved, the shield moved with him. He saw it cutting down people, even those to whom he wished to get close. Joe could now explore the contour of his barrier, the circumstances leading to its erection, and his criteria for opening up and letting another in. The group could investigate its attempts to reach Joe and the feelings aroused as he sliced through them.

Eva pictured a wall fluctuating between being a picket fence through which she could extend her hand and a thick concrete barrier. Her inconsistent interactions and her personal sense of confusion could be explored within the context of her changing barriers and invitations.

Ann pictured a wall like the Great Wall of China. It was long and straight and she wasn't sure who was in back and who was in front. Her emergent imagery conjured feelings of vulnerability and panic. Ann pictured herself running to where the wall was sturdiest and tallest. Fright and confusion over alliances could now be explored. Who, in reality, was on her side?

These diverse images represented variations on the common theme of barriers, protections, and defenses. Interestingly, an absent member, upon returning the following week, spontaneously talked about missing the session as representative of the wall she builds to keep others away. This seeming coincidence bespoke the power of images in reflecting current and preconscious group focal issues (Whitaker & Lieberman, 1964).

Metaphors for the Group-as-a-Whole

All in all, the group itself can be depicted in metaphoric language. Various superordinate conceptions such as group mind (Le Bon, 1977), group-level consciousness (Colman, 1975; Wells, 1985), group illusion (Anzieu, 1984; Pines, 1985), or group fantasy (Boris, Zinberg, & Boris, 1975) have been formulated to explain the collusive level of experience. Jung (1969) believed in the existence of a collective unconscious, a content-related repository containing the shared history of the race—encoded as organizing patterns or archaic types through which more modern individuals and their groupings act out commonly held existential proclivities. These archetypes manifest as collectively inspired images, actions, and symbolic reproductions. Usandivaras (1986) suggests that the group itself may represent an archetypal formation, yielding up primordial images, that reflect on the essential collective nature of human aggregates. The group, taken together, becomes a body of people in like relation (Prodgers, 1990). When any group becomes a singular body, of one mind, or under the influence of a particular vision, it must be reckoned with as a whole.

Previous epistemological reckonings have built the notion of the group-as-a-whole from inductive processes or have derived a sense of holistic phenomena through deductive reasoning. A third way of understanding group-level configurations can be formulated.

- Process 3: *Both the idea and experience of the group-as-a-whole can be reached through intuitive, holistic, depictive processes as expressed in analogies, metaphoric images, and symbolic representations.*

Following a depictive paradigm, reasoning proceeds by way of analogy, metaphor, and symbolic relation. The particular or the general nature of group relations can be depicted by forming pictures and symbolic transformations of the shared experience. What is the shared experience like?

What does the group's context, content, consequence, and part-processes most nearly resemble?

In a symbolic paradigm, a metaphoric vehicle comes to stand in for, represent, and carry meaning about a more fundamental, abstract, or hidden aspect of the overall group dynamics. Here, the group is perceived by way of analogy. Its intangible qualities are compared to the more tangible properties and transpositional relations of the metaphoric vehicle, which, in reality, composes an altogether different class of object or event (Glucksberg & Keysar, 1990). The group can then be comparatively understood and literally changed by holding in mind the descriptive and transformative possibilities of the metaphoric vehicle "as if" it were coincident or identical with the group itself or with the collective's various intrinsic elements, properties, and dynamics.

By producing pictures of reality, depictive processes combine elements of inductive and deductive reasoning with more classical gestalt notions of primary sensory perception, intuition, insight formation, and creativity. Here, the notion of the whole is neither contrived (bottom-up) nor derived (top-down). Rather, the organized entity, the group-as-a-whole, is directly perceived in the form of structured, organized, complete, and stable gestalts (Meissner, 1978). The puzzle that is the whole of the group experience can be grasped, in toto, by directly forming holistic perceptions that attribute meaning to the otherwise scattered proceedings. Arcaya (1985) suggests that group psychotherapy is essentially a hermeneutic process of meaning construal.

Hermeneutics typically relies on the technique of internal self-validation, involving the repeated contrast of parts of the text with the whole. . . . The patient's verbalizations can be treated as text, using the patient's metaphors as the unifying elements in the unfolding narrative. (p. 20) The metaphor plays a vital role in permitting thoughts and realizations to be formed. It allows the human mind to bridge seemingly discrepant categories, to perceive unities where dualities formerly existed. Thus metaphorical speech rearranges or dissolves boundaries between domains of thought. Notions that were previously split-off from one another become rearranged through the act of metaphorical communication, and new symbols of understanding result. . . . From the hermeneutical perspective, working-through becomes a process of familiarizing the patient as well as the group with those common themes uniting their metaphorical constructions. (pp. 22–23) A kind of secret language is thus brought into existence which coalesces the participants into an authentic dialoguing, therapeutic community. (p. 26)

The metacognitive assumption underlying depictive procedures is that human groups are capable of forming a shared level of experience where heterogeneity is lessened and where homogeneity manifests as a unity of perception, vision, and representation. Working with symbolic depictions allows for the externalizing and projecting of common experiences into a public arena (Ettin, 1985a), making shared realities more available for visualization, metaphoric analysis, and psychotherapeutic transformation. Members can literally see each other's pictures and therefore relate within shared visions of current reality. Meaning is derived from understanding and operating within this deeper, and often preconscious contextual setting.

The validity of depictive procedures follows from the esthetic and existential veracity of the comparative relations. Both general and particular analogies, metaphors, and symbols are apt as they foresee, capture, evoke, or amplify the nuances, essences, and implications of the shared group experience. Depictive relations are circular, encompassing events that succinctly capture self-images, world views, relational pictures, and group-as-a-whole pictorials in the form of clear metaphoric and/or symbol systems. The act of making a picture from the collection of experiences is a boundarying event (Durkin, 1989)—a framing of the unknown by way of more knowable experience. It is as if to say, "We can look at the group essence and movement, which we all share, as if it were analogous to...."

Many mutable symbols and metaphors can stand in for the group or its part-processes, as experiences together suggest every manner of natural, geometric, and synthetic comparison (Canetti, 1984; Ettin, 1985a, 1986, 1989b, 1989c). There is an infinite store of available metaphoric vehicles that can be shared or just kept in mind as general guiding contexts. For example, it is possible to visualize the group as a finely tuned instrument able to sound out the rhythmic and melodic strains of its various players, thus turning cacophony into harmonic relation. Working within a similar metaphor, the British School of Group Analysis (Foulkes, 1965) casts the facilitator as a conductor, bringing to mind the group-as-orchestra, while equating the leadership task with fully orchestrating the proceedings.

Various symbolic motifs may also be used metaphorically to underscore the group's dynamic progress. A group whose violent winds are quickly rising might be compared to an approaching tornado capable of sucking up within it all the energies and objects in its path. A group with members missing might be talked of as a broken circle whose contact and safe enclosure have been threatened. A group expending a perfusion of energy while moving nowhere fast might be seen as similar to a car revving its engine and spinning its wheels but never leaving the drive.

As metaphor and symbol, these configurations of experience are capable of ready visualization and evident transformation, thus helping the depicted group to change its course, shape, or motive force. By holding these images and symbol sets in mind, the therapist may better understand the group and more confidently decide when or how to intervene.

Mother Group: The Containing and Transformative Nature of the Collective Process

Neumann (1963), in his classic treatise on the Great Mother, suggests a universal symbolic formula for the feminine aspects of reality: Woman = body = vessel = world (or group). "As elementary character we designate the aspect of the Feminine that as the Great Round, the Great Container, tends to hold fast to everything that springs from it and to surround it like an eternal substance" (p. 25). The transformative character of the feminine is rather characterized by "the wheel which rolls onto itself," most nearly represented by the feminine mystery of childbirth. This formula for the feminine suggests derivative body symbolism that can stand in for the mother, mother functions, or mother parts. The intrinsic symbolic connection between mother, body, and container, as developed by Neumann (1963), yields transformative symbols such as ovens, kettles, and pots. Here, once something is put inside, it can be expected to change its form.

Symbols of nourishment derived directly from symbolism of the breast include bowls, goblets, cups, and chalices. Good vessels can serve quenching liquids, whereas bad vessels proffer poison. Symbols of containment proper include many types of man-made enclosures, such as chests, sacks, jars, boxes, pockets, or troughs, as well as natural formations such as chasms, caves, abysses, valleys, depths, and holes in the earth. The quality of the crevice is determined both by what it envelopes and how well it encloses. Symbols of protection may include nests, beds, pouches, cradles, and, in some cases, even coffins, as imagined shelters from the pain of life. Boundary symbols include walls, doors, gates, fences, and motes.

Images taken from the natural world or "Mother Earth" include flora, fauna, and geological forms. The ocean is considered a potent derivative of feminine mystery and represents the underlying power of less-than-conscious, intuitive processes. Creatures emerging from the sea represent specific unconscious contents. Symbolic equivalents of fecundity are represented by pods, cows, cornucopia, or springs of water, suggestive of offspring. Worldly goods can also stand in for the mother, in body and in spirit. Ships, planes, and cars are often christened as female, thereby implying maternal containing and transporting properties. Any of these metaphoric figures may spontaneously emerge from within the normal speech and associations of the group members. All of these symbolic vehicles may be called upon intentionally by the therapist to artfully render the parts or the whole of the group process.

Leuner (1990) describes a group imagery technique useful for working directly within symbol systems. In preparation for an imaginary journey, the members discuss a means of transportation and a scenic direction to explore.

One particular training group decided to travel together by ship to the ocean. Once the vehicle and itinerary were set, the members turned their chairs around, facing outside the center of the circle as if ready to go off, closed their eyes, and engaged in a dialogue beginning from the starting image. Just as in a psychotherapy group, anyone might speak and influence the process by describing what they saw for themselves as the group proceeded.

Here, the sailing vessel, as a derivative mother-symbol, allowed each member to reestablish contact with his or her own maternal issues, while guiding the group-as-a-whole on its alternatively free flowing or constrained way. Tim quickly assumed the captain's role. He suggested that in order for the ship to move, the membership-turned-crew needed to hoist a sail. A young woman, Alicia, saw herself volunteering to be the captain's mate and helping out by climbing the mast. Ethel, a woman in her mid-forties, argued that a sail was too slow a means of propulsion, and that the group boat needed a motor.

A compromise was reached in dialogue. The clipper ship remained intact, but moved precipitously from the harbor to the open sea. There, it set anchor, while Ethel and some others swam in the cool ocean amidst dolphins, waves, and sea breezes. Anthony did not join in the frivolities. He found himself at the back of the boat, becoming increasingly seasick as the vessel rocked on the waves. Anthony derived no comfort from what others experienced as gentle and soothing rocking. Margaret and Jim imagined themselves coming back to look after Anthony. They saw themselves holding and reassuring him and Margaret even brought him a cup of hot milk. Tim, after completing his leadership tasks, became anxious to move on, feeling increasingly constrained by the boat's anchored position, with so much still out there to do or see. In the fantasy, he became annoyed with Anthony, who he teased about being a baby, and with Ethel, who he ordered back on board.

After some debate, the group vessel moved on, with the understanding that they would set a course for a deserted island some nautical miles away. There, they would once again set anchor and allow each crew member to work or play as he or she wished. Once the spot of land was reached, Anthony felt better to be on solid ground and proceeded to raid the galley. Sarah found more dolphins in a protected cove and frolicked in interaction with these emergent sea creatures. Tim and Alicia set off on reconnaissance. They climbed cliffs, gazed from precipices, and finally located a cave large enough to provide the crew with shelter from the night. Together, and in private, Tim and Alicia explored the crevice before alerting the other members of their find. Soon the others did arrive, Ethel with a bottle of wine, Margaret and Anthony with marshmallows, as the group-as-a-whole came back together. Tim made a fire and the crew settled down for the night.

This jointly conceived imagery exercise continued until the group had success-fully made its return voyage. Members then rejoined the real world by opening their eyes, turning their chairs face in, and talking about the nature of their experi-ence. The members considered the individual and collective dynamics amplified by the trip—how particular members responded and interacted with each other, and how the whole formation proceeded aboard the shared vessel, which was, after all, the group itself.

Many were surprised by their roles and behaviors. Anthony was particularly disturbed by his inability to adjust aboard ship and spoke of his concomitant fears of the outside world. As a child, he had been overprotected by his mother, and he felt ill-equipped for life's journeys, transferring his own familial relations to other less constraining life vehicles. Ethel revealed that her own children had recently moved out, and that she was wanting to proceed quickly past the maternal role by inviting less constraints and having more fun. She wasn't sure, however, just how to get into the swim of things.

Tim received feedback from the group that his self-initiated leadership was both helpful and annoying. His restlessness around any inactivity and feelings of anxious constraint when the ship was still related to his own reaction formation against being held back in his family-of-origin. In this context, he considered his anger at Anthony. He also acknowledged that women on the outside, like those aboard ship, sometimes experienced him as bossy and controlling. Sarah looked at the emergence of her dolphins, which in this voyage only came up to lead her on when she was close to the island and within the safe confines of the cove. An artist, Sarah reported being creatively blocked since leaving a long-standing relationship four months ago. This breakthrough was exhilarating for her and perhaps pene-trated the surface of her cut-off resources.

Other members considered their experience until the group completed their journey by a conscious processing of the experience. Leuner (1990) advises against interpreting or translating symbols to the point where they lose their fluid, trans-forming potentials. Here, working with the mother-symbol of the shared vessel, the group was able to reexperience and reexplore current and prototypical difficulties with containment and mobility, enroute. Certainly male allusions also arose within the feminine motif of the ship. Alicia became quickly attached to a strong and older man in Tim, perhaps as a father transference. In her excitement, she impulsively scaled the mast.

It is difficult to avoid criticisms of sexism when describing symbol systems that invoke such powerful feminine and/or masculine images. However, the supporting archaeological evidence of graphic phalluses and fecund mother figurines dates to upper Paleolithic Europe, some 30,000 years B.C. (Leroi-Gourhan, 1967; McCully, 1977; White, 1986; Ettin, 1987). Leroi-Gourhan (1986), studying the cave art at Lascaux and other Dor-dogne sites that originate about 15,000 B.C., concludes that "mythograms" of complimentary masculine and feminine animals and signs decorate the walls in meaningful configuration. Brown (1978) describes the distinctive symbolism of the matriarchy that preceded the signs of patriarchal rule in many primitive settings.

When describing the mother-group, reference is made to just this "mothering principle," evident in nature and marked in time. As a major symbol system, mother transferences are capable of structuring much of human understanding. Later, when describing how dependency and revolt arise as a natural phase in the group development, as derivative of father transferences, the same nonjudgmental ascription is intended. In neither case are real flesh-and-blood women or men, mothers or fathers described, though we all more or less partake, in the Platonic sense, in various aspects, both masculine and feminine, of these ideals or human prototypes.

Brown (1965), in a social psychology context, suggests that generalizations from individual instances to group data are often warranted, whereas stereotypes that move from group generalizations to attributions about particular individuals are not scientifically acceptable. Mothering and fathering, by definition, denote and connote various attributes. Particular "mothers" and "fathers" have the power to act anywhere within these general parameters, as does the group and its leadership in symbolic transference.

The Metaphor of the Mother-Group in Theory and Practice

The theory of the mother-group proper proffers a representative depictive paradigm for the group-as-a-whole. Schindler (1966) suggested that the therapy group, in the natural course of its development, forms multiple transferences—father transferences to the facilitator, whether male or female; sibling transferences to the other members; and mother transferences to the group-as-a-whole. Similarly, Slavson (1964) believed that the power of the psychotherapeutic grouping came from its serving "in loco maternis." Foulkes (1964), following Bion and Klein, identified the group with the insides of the mother, the womb, or the "matrix"—that "common shared ground which ultimately determines the meaning and significance of all events" (as quoted in Ahlin, 1988, p. 212).

Reviewing speculations about this "mother-group," Scheidlinger (1955, 1974), following Anna Freud's concept of "need satisfying relationship," suggested that "the group-as-a-whole represented a covert wish to restore an earlier state of unconflicted well-being inherent in the child's exclusive union with the mother" (p. 48). Identifying with such an encompassing group entity meant "ascribing to the group an emotional meaning—as an instrument of need satisfaction—on a genetic level a mother symbol . . . [characterized by] self involvement in the group—a giving up of an aspect of personal identity—I to We" (p. 420). Durkin (1989) identifies the "to-and-fro" exchange between the members and the group as reminiscent of the infant's symbiotic give and take with its mother.

Roberts (1982), as cited by Prodgers (1990), concurs that the group's matrix or shared therapeutic space is a seemingly feminine, oft maternal background or interstitial substance in which the members are contained, supported, and ultimately reformed. Metaphorically, the members may experience the group as "womb-like," a "collective cradle of fresh offsprings" characteristic of the "good mother" image (Roberts, 1982, p. 118). The group can also be experienced as the "tomb-like" coffin of hidden dangers characteristic of the "bad mother" analogy.

How, then, might the fullness of the group's varied mother-like qualities be described? The archetypal or essential positive attributes of mothering include life giving, holding, containing, warming, accepting, loving, nurturing, protecting, sheltering, talking to, comforting, and allowing for differentiation and separation while supporting maturation. More negative aspects of mothering might include smothering, dropping, withholding, abandoning, freezing out, ensnaring, rejecting, depriving of love, devouring, destroying, remaining silent, disquieting, fusing, and prematurely pushing away so as to wean too soon. Positive mothering can lead to feelings of security, safety, growth, independence, self-soothing, confidence, contentment, fullness, togetherness, wholeness, hopefulness, joy, and competence. Negative mothering can engender feelings of insecurity, danger, stagnation, dependence, dysphoria, self-doubt, despair, emptiness, loneliness, disintegration, hopelessness, pain, and incompetence (Neumann, 1963; Raphael-Liff, 1984; Glenn, 1987; Prodgers, 1990).

It must be remembered that these descriptions entail more than the actual essence of the group-as-mother, but also reflect how the collective is experienced by its various members. Amelioration includes helping participants change their misguided perceptions and transferential ascriptions, as well as in extreme instances, working through the adverse qualities of the group-as-a-whole.

The psychotherapy group is an essentially amorphous structure capable of being represented by either or both positive and negative maternal analogies—a ready transformation of "womb-tomb" symbology. Equated with the Great Mother (Prodgers, 1990; Usandivaras, 1986; Neumann, 1963), many basic dualities are held simultaneously within the body of possible group experiences: activity/passivity, integration/disintegration, affirmation/negation, and death/rebirth. The group matrix takes on different forms, feeling tones, and dynamic meanings throughout its life course.

The long-standing group described in the "testing the metal" vignette was down to four members after Dan's departure. The group, as so composed, felt barren and empty to its members, as if it were missing necessary ingredients, while notably short of available energy and novel material. After a period of consolidating remaining alliances, four new members were simultaneously added into the mix. During a hopeful initial session, many images of rebirth spontaneously arose, including visions of a new start, the shared view that the change in group composition was clearly in the service of revitalization, as well as parallel talk concerning new job opportunities or recent changes in living arrangement. The old members described the group to their new compatriots as a life-sustaining and positive climate. Further generative metaphors portrayed the group, and its therapist, as supportive and helping members out. Veterans informed newcomers, that after spending sufficient time in the group, departing members usually went on to better cope with the outside world.

Right before the next session, one of the new members unexpectedly called to say that he would not be coming back to group. When this message was relayed in the meeting, images quickly changed to those of stillbirth, death, loss, and murder. Some members wondered if they had killed off or scared the neophyte away. Others were enraged that he dropped out before learning to live with his initial anxiety and without giving the group-as-a-whole a chance to thrive. Pictures emerged and histories were suddenly shared of miscarriage, divorce, parental abandonment, suicidal ideation, and the precipitant unavailability of those most dearly needed. The therapist was expressly questioned about his foreknowledge and responsibility for the premature termination. The members could no longer maintain the naive fantasy that the newly composed group would always and forever be a containing, growth-enhancing, safe, and conflict-free environment.

Taking into account its changing characteristics, Gibbard and Hartman (1973) equate the small group with the ambivalent Oedipal mother, capable of simultaneously loving and hating its charge. Likened to the Goddess Kali, the group can be at once a source and a rival for love and life (Hearst, 1981, p. 25). Similarly, Slater (1966) suggests that the mother-group is sometimes "perceived as . . . a source of succorance and comfort, even a refuge. At other times, this mother image is a frightening one involving primitive fantasies of being swallowed and enveloped" (p. 189). Ganzarain (1989) suggests that certain group situations, such as therapist absences, canceled sessions, or the arrival of new patients foster "bad mother-group transferences" (p. 72). Similarly, Hawkins (1986) writes of the group in times of flux as being experienced as if it were an unstable environmental mother.

Progress as Calling Forth the Positive Aspects of the Mother-Group

Progress in psychotherapy groups might be equated with the abilities of the collective to form into a life-sustaining and growth-enhancing matrix. A positive group space would be equated with an adequate place within which to play (Winnicott, 1971) and work (Bion, 1961). Hearst (1981), elaborated by Ganzarain (1989), equates the positive aspects of the group-as-good-mother with its ready abilities to be

> *(1) life-giving (a group member becomes someone, 'belongs' only within the context of the group's existence); (2) confirming (being worthy for the narcissistic group self); (3) sustaining (within the group setting); and (4) accepting (everything can be expressed in and will be received by the group). (p. 71)*

Rothberg (1984) uses a "Mother Nature" analogy to suggest that an open, congruent, and essentially positive group environment is necessary to support individual maturational efforts. "The intrinsic assumption is that people, like plants, want to grow and will do so if the environment is hospitable and enhancing" (p. 4). These essentially positive groupwide characteristics correspond with Yalom's (1970) curative factors, most notably belonging, cohesion, and instillation of hope.

Progress as Coming to Terms and Transcending the Negative Aspects of the Mother-Group

Schindler (1966) believes that members often project bad-mother images onto the group. Here, the progressive task becomes to reduce the negative and terrifying aspects of joining together. Durkin (1964) argues that the group as a mother symbol is harsh, like the pre-Oedipal mother. Usandivaras (1986. p. 117) describes the group-induced image of the "choking mother" or "spinning woman" who binds her children to her, wrapping them in a swaddling of constraint and greed. Ganzarain (1989) suggests that the group-as-bad-mother can be characterized as

> *(1) over demanding—it imposes group values on the individual, 'leaving no freedom to be oneself' (Bion, 1961); (2) devouring—it threatens its member with a "loss of individuality" (Freud, 1921), taking away member's credits and possessions; (3) lacking in reciprocity—just as mother does not need her infant in order to survive biologically, while the infant requires maternal care to survive, so can the group survive socially without any given member . . . ; (4) intrusive— the group inquires with hostile curiosity about secret, private affairs, attempting to influence them and ruthlessly make them public. (p. 68)*

The negative aspects of the grouping process are often represented by the derivative images of the labyrinth, the spider web, and the witch's cauldron, where members become lost, captured, or cooked (Roberts, 1982). The process of working out negative mother-group images corresponds most closely to Yalom's (1970) curative task of corrective recapitulation of the primary family.

The same symbol set that stands in for the mother-group can also depict the mothering experiences of individual members, past and present. Those maternal visions may cleave to nuclear family dynamics or heed subsequent self-parenting efforts. The art of representation, at whatever level of abstraction, is meaning making. The act of contributing to the making of a holistic image is a formative experience. When one takes perspective from the whole of the group configuration, one engages in an act of personal revision. If members can flourish and grow within the womb and at the bosom of the psychotherapy group, then transferentially they can overcome blockages, inhibitions, and failures to thrive in other formative settings, including work situations, peer groups, reconstituted families, and even families of origin.

Ted's formative dynamics could be traced back at least as far as the birth of his sister, when he was 4 1/2 years old. Until that time, he had his mother's undivided attention. Although the birth of a second child represented a normal stimulus for familial change, Ted's experience was one of sudden abandonment. Not understanding why love and care were less available to him, he became angry, suspicious, and withdrawn. Afraid of his father, who he experienced as either distantly silent or as too close and yelling, Ted seemingly had no one to whom to turn.

When he was 8 years old and his sister was 3 1/2, Ted began exposing himself to her, as a sexually charged attention-getting device. This behavior shocked his conservative and religious family and was met with severe punishment and shame induction. Ted developed a series of obsessional rituals and excessive intellectualizations to rid himself of the guilt and to protect himself from acting on his impulses. He entered psychotherapy as a young adult, reporting anxiety attacks, potency problems with women, and fears of homosexuality. After a course of individual treatment, his overt anxiety subdued and Ted gained some insight into his distrust of women and his search for viable male models. Ted was then referred to group, at first concurrent with individual therapy and later as sole treatment.

Ted was now in his last group session after a 6-year stay. He was encouraged by newer members to reminisce about both his group history and the progress of his outside life. Ted related how, for the first few years in group, he was very quiet, not trusting either his own reactions or the group's response. Wanting to be close and involved, he just couldn't bring himself to interact. He would often think of things to say, ruminate excessively about how his contribution might be received, and thereby miss every opportunity for dialogue or contact. Ted described how, little by little, he learned to open up and become more trusting that his instinctive responses would not be met with scorn or derision. He in fact became an active member, using his intellectual proclivities to the benefit of others. For himself, Ted was able to acknowledge and allow his feelings in a way not possible for so many years. Ted proudly talked about his success at work and how he was now teaching business courses at a night school. He reiterated that he was now very close to his family, mother, father, and siblings, who respected him as a competent adult. "They've changed and I've changed." Ted also described his current relationship with Sally, an older women, who he has found increasingly intriguing.

In his group experience Ted was able to rework many of his personal difficulties, consolidated over the years into distinctive characterological traits and styles. The original trauma of maternal separation was replayed in many missed and cutoff relationships and much paralyzing immobility inside and outside of group. In the mother-group, Ted was able to reconnect with his affect and his libidinal impulses and work through his anger and distrust, thereby refinding his lost sense of safety while regaining his viability as a man. His connection to Sally, remaining mother-transference and all, was his healthiest heterosexual relationship to date. This intimacy may provide a transitional female relationship to carry Ted away from the group and toward women his own age.

Building the Group by Reforming Common Bounds

Durkin (1989) underscores the concept of the mother-group as an intervening variable that brings individual and groupwide events together within a common boundary. "The basis of this important bridging is the connection between the object relations focus on the vicissitudes of the mother/infant dyad in the separation individuation process and the idea of mother-group formation" (p. 199). He further explains how the group-as-a-whole serves as both a hypothetical construct and a realizable transitional object:

> *Mothergroup-as-a-whole . . . is neither fantasy or reality, but a new class of entity formed through a new class of events. . . . Drawing a self boundary is a circular event which causes itself to occur. When members of a group say to each other: "We are here now!" the participating members have called forth a hierarchy shift in which a number of individual defining boundaries have opened up to each other and joined to form a boundary defining the group-as-a-whole. (pp. 209–219)*

Group as the Formative Context
for Individual Relations

Whatever the specific emotional connotations of this maternal motif, the group-as-whole becomes equated with the medium, context, climate, or meaning-laden environment that prepares, prefigures, and predominates the interactive potentials of its members. The group-as-a-mother symbol leads to derivative notions of the group as a formative container (Bion, 1970) or holding environment (Foulkes,1964; James,1984; Winnicott, 1986), with womb-like transformative potential (Bion, 1970). The group also becomes a vessel for the projections of its members, wherein images of reality are held, transformed, and eventually returned in order to promote individual development (Durkin, 1989). Visualizations about the nature of the container and the contained are stimulated, as are images of the protective and destructive qualities of the matrix. The symbolic mother-group paradigm specifically encourages working within the holistic aspects of the group climate, atmosphere, and bounded, formative enclosure. The group, as such, becomes the object of analysis. To secure a working matrix is to allow and cultivate a natural and sacred space (Schlachet, 1986) where individuals can mature as the group culture progressively moves along in complexity, potency, and empathic resonance.

As the group transitions through its various stages of development, the container image changes in function and in form. The therapist may use the understanding of containment as a guide to shaping and maintaining the group's experience. In the early group, the circle serves as the congealing image of commonality and unity that brings and holds disparate individuals together in purposeful community. As the group begins to formulate norms and catalytically questions its aims and operations, the container must become a flexible and malleable crucible, allowing and restraining the diverse and bubbling energies within. In the working phase of group, the container must be a mortar in which grinds the pestle of change. In the final stages of group, the container can no longer greedily hold the mead of the group mix, but rather, as a pitcher, must pour energies and substance back into the diversity of life's various holds.

Applications: Psychoeducation

The study of both how we learn in groups and how we might construct a group as a viable learning environment requires that we turn to training and psychoeducation. An ancillary question is how groups, when faced with nondirective leadership, naturally structure themselves. This second half of the book begins with a look at a collective format, the training group, which was developed subsequent to World War II as a psychoeducational setting for introducing participants, often practitioners or managers, to collective dynamics through direct participation as group members. In these training endeavors, often facilitated in the nondirective Tavistock tradition, the group's formative processes and developmental progressions become apparent in the form of shared fantasies, myths, and rituals. Such creative composites of imagination and enactment, while the product of massive projection and surmise, provide the group with structural hypotheses concerning its own workings (Chapter Eight).

It is a challenge to integrate these naturally evolving group processes and symbolizations with predetermined tasks. Here, the group facilitator introduces a structured format while recognizing and managing preemptive unformatted processes as they arise and lubricate the proceedings. To ignore the emergent group process is to detract from the very potentials of the collective medium. Suggestions are made and examples are given for blending the planned with the spontaneous when leading targeted, theme-centered, or content-oriented groups in order to enhance the adoption of psychoeducational perspectives (Chapter Nine).

Time-limited and theme-centered group protocols can be built by relying on just those standard notions of group development that came out of the training and study group tradition. Members of homogeneous groups can thereby enhance their affective learning about a wide range of topical concerns. The leader becomes a content expert and task organizer by developing a psychoeducational blueprint that makes specific use of the group's phase-specific proclivities. By introducing a blend of didactics, structured exercises, and open discussions, the facilitator helps the group move from anticipatory anxiety and formative maneuvering, through resistive trends, before entering a productive working mode, in prelude to ending in summary and termination (Chapter Ten).

Issues introduced for study in this section include:

- What forms of imagination can be used to comprehend the relevance of the emergent group culture, especially in unstructured group settings?

- *What is the intimate relationship between task and process, and how does structuring or not structuring a group affect its evident dynamics and appreciable outcomes?*
- *How can attuning to group dynamics and process management specifically enhance the work of theme-centered or symptom-focused groups?*
- *How might an appreciation of the normative structure and phases of group development be directly applied to the organization and facilitation of psychoeducational groups so that time boundaries can be used for the group's progressive benefit?*

CHAPTER EIGHT

Myth, Metaphor, and Miracle in the Moment of Making:

Leadership and Residence in Unstructured Process Groups

The role, training, and person of the leader is a crucial determinant in realizing a group's inherent potentials. Leadership stance is overdetermined by character, intuition, skill, philosophy, values, and training, as well as by overt and covert goals. By virtue of personality or position, the group facilitator can assume the stance of collective power broker by maintaining a fixed, centralized, charismatic, dominant, opinionated, or intrusive stance. Paradoxically, the same leader while less forthcoming may appear impassively controlling when silently sustaining projections of mystery and enigma. The structure and flow of the collective endeavor is largely defined by where the leader can be located on this continuum of interventional extremes.

Urdang (1972) defines the act of intervening as that of "interceding or occurring between two events or periods." Group facilitators must constantly choose when, where, and how to come between the members—whether, for example, at notable moments of confusion or at times of overwhelming emotion. Such interventions serve to close gaps and lend connective coherency to the shared proceedings. Facilitations, large and small, aim to create an integrated and pragmatically recognizable conjunction through which participants can see themselves and each other.

Interventional styles and strategies strongly influence what kind of working space is created and perpetuated. Groups can be "leader centered," with all interactions coming through the central authority. In contrast, groups can be "member centered," with the facilitator assuming a more peripheral position. In member-centered groups, the facilitator acts like a frontier guard, always vigilant but usually silent—until the collective faces a danger or opportunity where his or her special skills at clarification, interpretation, problem-solving, conflict management, or process elaboration are required.

The challenge of working with unstructured collectives, as in a training or process setting, is to understand how, provided little formal direction, the group organizes and moves on informally. Once the skeletal ground rules of the journey and fixed boundaries of the shared territory are identified by way of rough mapping, a vacuous hush commences as the leader sits in silent sentience and the members commiserate on the enormity of the task. Participants worry: "What now? How do we really go about studying ourselves in process? Where are we all headed anyway?" Unlike the directive leader, who provides the group with ongoing, overt structures in the form of exercises or didactics, the nondirective leader rather lets the group struggle within an authoritative void so that they can eventually discover and create personal leadership potentials and collective meanings on their own.

The ambiguity and scope of the task are noteworthy. To cope with the unknown, members recast the proceedings in an amalgamation of real and imagined relations. Having limited guidance, the group and its representative members set up guidance systems that often involve creative elaborations, sometimes in the form of fantastic, bizarre construals, and at other times as surprisingly coherent accounts. Bolman and Deal (1984) suggest that, in fact, all "organizations are full of questions that cannot be answered, problems that cannot be solved, and events that cannot be understood or managed. Whenever that is so, humans create and use symbols to bring meaning out of chaos, clarity out of confusion, and predictability out of mystery" (p. 152). The group facilitator may then respond to the group's imaginative efforts with clarification, interpretation, and amplification.

The Parameters of Group Structure

Structure, in a group context, denotes a nonrandom configuration or arrangement of elemental parts into an organized whole; some sense of innate, evolving, or patterned construction is implied. A group can be lightly or tightly structured. Beck (1981a) equates a group's structure with its skeletal frame. That framework can be either external, visible, and specifically prescribed, or internal, invisible, and inherently programmatic. In both cases, some order is found, as the collective takes on a consistency of form and a coherence of meaning. The directive group leader provides ready-made forms for the group to take up in turn, usually in ordered, rational, linear progression. The nondirective leader, by his or her silence or seemingly unpredictable, quixotic, punctuating remarks, often stimulates form-less anxiety, infighting, and a mad dash toward any semblance of order or consensus, however irrational.

Every facilitator, as task leader, must function with whatever degree of subtlety to orient members concerning the nature of the collective me-dium, both in preparation and as ongoing circumstances require (Beck, Eng, & Brusa, 1989). Practicing a managerial function, the formal leader is responsible for setting up and maintaining the logistical boundaries of meeting time, place, and group composition. He or she must also establish a basic agenda, while shaping effective procedures and tapping available resources, so that the collective can proceed with its primary aim, whether training, psychoeducation, or psychotherapy. Members can easily lose sight of the group's goals when caught up in personal reactivities stimulated by the affect of the moment. To exercise structural or administrative authority (Patterson, 1966), one must keep the group on task by apprising the mem-bers of where the essence of the work is located, specifying what needs to be done to stay on course, clarifying collective agendas as they come to the forefront, and fostering ongoing constructive relations among members. Whatever style or interventional mode is chosen, the group leader must ultimately work to establish and maintain a viable facilitative environment while simultaneously protecting individuals from irreparable harm.

How directive the leader is when fulfilling various task and manage-rial functions affects the participants' sense of safety and security. Intro-ducing overt structure into a group usually leads to less anxiety for the members. That which is required of the members is clearly specified. The leader is observable, active, ever-present, and predictably involved. This generalization holds true unless, of course, the suggested structure involves highly confrontive or self-disclosing exercises—turning up the heat by put-ting people under the spotlight. Then it may be safer for the members to hide within the silent anonymity of an unstructured group process. In set-tings where little overt structure is provided, the leader and the group be-come shadowy presences and projective screens for expectations, fantasies, judgments, and other manifestations of internal processes.

At one extreme are psychoeducational leaders who design highly structured group protocols that rely on a series of predetermined lesson plans and preformatted exercises. At the other extreme, Tavistock leaders severely limit both their interactions and their structuring efforts. While clearly specifying general boundaries and carefully preparing a framework for the group interaction, facilitators in the British tradition quickly recede into the unspoken milieu that characterizes the group dynamic. Once the group proper begins, Tavistock leaders never tell the group what to do. They rarely even address individual group members, going so far as to avoid direct eye contact by looking at the ground, intervening infrequently, and then usually coming alive to address the regressive trends of the group-as-a-whole.

This verbally inactive consultative stance lends considerable anxiety to the proceedings, since consensual reality is neither provided nor reiterated. Members must, at least initially, rely on their own interpretations of events, persons, and tasks. Participants come face to face with the proclivities of their own and each other's unconscious structuring attempts. Members make what they will of matters by knowingly or unknowingly attempting to reassume some familiar structural relationship with the leader, with each other, and with the group-as-a-whole. The collective itself takes on surplus symbolic significance and instrumental powers as members are propelled together by uncertainty (Bion, 1961). When the leader fails to intervene, fantasy comes in to bridge the gaps in experience.

Taking Up Residence at a Group Process Conference

In order to gain the distance necessary for viewing collective dynamics more clearly, process groups often meet in extremity, away from the regular confines of human commerce. Staff and management groups may go off together to some lakeshore or mountain hideaway, where, in a relaxed atmosphere, participants try to come closer, so as to interface better when returning to the office or institution. Other training groups bring together participants who have no formal relationship outside the current group context. Often gathering together in some bucolic setting, these newly convened organizations are specifically created for the purpose of learning about groups in general and, as a result, enhancing interactive understandings and communicative skills in vitro. Members get to observe and contribute to the many cultural transformations and distinct phases of development through which the group-as-a-whole passes.

Process-oriented training groups (T-groups) can be convened in conference, student-study, practitioner-training, workshop, or laboratory formats. Prototypical training models include the National Training Laboratories begun in 1947 and typically held in yearly, two-week residential meetings in Bethel, Maine. Similarly, A. K. Rice Conferences, begun in the United States in 1965, range from weekends to two-week trainings. They are patterned after the protocols begun in England, in 1957, under the auspices of the Tavistock Clinic and the University of Leicester. Also, ongoing courses in group dynamics may combine didactic instruction with free processing, as separate components of a normal semester sequence offered in the Harvard Social Relations tradition (Shaffer & Galinsky, 1974; Rioch,

1975b; Slater, 1966). Goffman (1967), highlighting the prodigious opportunities for learning about face-to-face encounters in extended residential placements, has deemed such conferences and workshops as "interactional mastodons that push to the limit what can be called a social occasion" (p. 1). Residential group-training experiences are now widely available in a variety of locations and forms.

A review of the development of shared beliefs arising on the cultural island created by a typical human relations conference helps us to understand the meaning-making process as it occurs. Within a structure of fixed meetings and a variety of different types of groupings, participants try to understand the interaction between the evolving group process and their own work as members and leaders. Two interacting collectives are often built into the structure of the experience—staff/consultant and membership-at-large groups. Initially, the membership seeks to define itself in relation and in contrast to the authority, the staff group. In fact, these conferences are loosely organized around the themes of authority, leadership, interdependence, and the place of the individual in society and organizational life. Yet the staff group eschews the normal expectations placed on leaders, whether parents, teachers, or bosses.

In a Tavistock primer, Banet and Hayden (1977) warn that "the consultant does not engage in social amenities, advice-giving, parental nurturance, or direction" (p. 161)—so much for the active cultivation of a benign, security-enhancing "mother-group." Rather, the consultant's role is restricted to primarily interpreting the group dynamics while addressing unattended tasks, transgressed boundaries, abused structures, and cultures in evident dysfunctional consortium.

Members' individual dependency needs remain largely unrequited. Group relations conferences focus specific attention on the group-as-a-whole level of experience by attending to collective dynamics to the virtual exclusion of individual processes. Members become known for their contributions to the life of the collective and the evolution of subgrouping tendencies that either further or impede overall group aims. Covert processes, including imaginative formulations normally present only as background noise, are thrust to the foreground as the group specifically examines bubblings from within the collective cauldron.

The conference itself is thereby transposed into an experiential laboratory—a kind of crucible in which holistic configurations and the dynamics of their part-processes are precipitated in unusually graphic and salient forms. The assumption is made that these same emergent processes typically catalyze in other kinds of groups as well, including psychotherapy groups where ameliorative structures and clinical purposes make the expression of such underlying issues and projective devices less immediately obvious. In psychotherapy groups, for example, members' reasons for participation are perhaps more homogeneous and compelling, their perceptions and expectations of the leader more uniform, and the therapist less likely to be quite as dispassionate and "oracular" as the standard Tavistock "consultant."

The Tavistock situation, as such, is more likely to foster acute feelings of uncertainty, rage at authority, a reactive turning to peers for security and affirmation, and the emergence of fantasy material in the absence of more concrete rhymes or reasons. Again, these same relational dynamics and formative tendencies also exist and ultimately require processing in ordinary therapy groups. However, the underlying forces often manifest more subtly and therefore become more difficult to sort out from the clinical problems and purposes that the members, as "patients," bring to group.

The conference itself is open to receive and process whatever transpires, with no set learnings, themes, or clinical guidance provided or anticipated, except as generally related to the primary task of learning about the exercise of authority. Banet and Hayden (1977) explain,

> *The design of the conference is such that a number of aspects of authority can be examined in a variety of contexts. Throughout the conference, the staff encourages examination of all aspects of its behavior as well as the behavior of the members. Thus the accountability of those individuals exercising delegated, sanctioned, and personal authority is a significant aspect of the conference experience, just as it is a critical aspect of the exercise of authority in all institutional and organizational settings. (p. 159)*

Forms of Imagination

Access to otherwise invisible group processes, including those dynamics related to the identification and assertion of authority, often come in the form of figurative, primary-process, intuitive elaborations. In fact, it might be argued that the group-qua-group comes to life exactly as a consequence of members' shared fantasies and projections (Bion, 1961; Dunphy, 1974; Gibbard, Hartman, & Mann, 1974; Ashbach & Schermer,1987). Vignettes from a typical Tavistock conference are used to explore these varied forms of imagination.

Fantasy

There are very few facts in group life—only apt narrative descriptions arrived at by fantasy constructions. As meaningful integrations and/or communications, such emergent fantasies are intended to be internally coherent and correspond more or less to the sensual and phenomenological data of the group. Fantasies come about through preconscious, sometimes playful and constructive, and sometimes demeaning and destructive processes. Their content can reflect accurately and helpfully or inaccurately and misleadingly on real people, relations, and events.

With a minimum of overt guidance from the consultants, conference members attempt to derive shared understandings within an ongoing context that proceeds and unravels rather quickly. To make sense of the experience and to contain anxiety, participants initially look toward the consultant staff with a mixture of observation, intuition, projection, fear, and wish. As an initial structuring effort, rumors fly and flourish in an ether of uncertainty and surmise. "Rumors tend to develop when there is a strong need to know what is going on, but for various reasons information and communication are limited" (Luft, 1970). Insinuation is an attempt at allaying anxiety by piecing together available data points to imaginatively fill in the wider gaps of the unknown—an attempt at intervention through a distinctive act of confabulation.

Persons and situations of high import and high mystery often attract such speculative attentions. Here, the group consultants become the target of wishful and fearful fantasies. Whether an intuitively accurate account, a misnomer, or a poorly articulated hypothesis, various privately formed and publicly shared beliefs shape the evolving group culture. These whispered impressions provide a loose suit to conceptually cover otherwise naked reality—the barely true protecting against the truly unbearable.

A rumor circulated when a participant reported to a few other compatriots that on the first afternoon, before the initial formal meeting, the ceiling above her hotel room began shaking. She "heard" strains and groans coming from directly above her. The member, and a newly formed group of accomplices, secured a floor plan and traced the room to the youngest and most attractive female staff member. The rumor passed through the membership that two consultants were having vigorous afternoon intercourse. The news was met by the larger society with both titillating curiosity and righteous indignation at such a speculative surmise and violation of privacy.

Considerable wish fulfillment was involved on a personal level for the avid reporter, who later revealed her own loneliness and wish for sexual liaison. However, to understand adequately the passing of a rumor, one must also explain the function it serves for the community-at-large. Occurring early in the conference life, this raucous cultural product expressed for the group both a desire for intimate contact and a fear of public exposure. The whole of the uncertain atmosphere and lack of task clarity within the conference milieu engendered vigilance, suspicion, and innuendo. Members assumed a relationship to the staff akin to what Klein

(1946) referred to as the "paranoid-schizoid" position. Individuals defended against their own sexual and aggressive impulses by projections onto authoritative others. The voyeurism of the rumor bespoke the dark side of the curiosity about the consultant staff that permeated the membership early on in the life of the conference.

The membership worried that in this intense collective format there could be no privacy or inviolable, impenetrable personal boundaries. Participants initially struggled with whether or not they could or would remain in their "rooms" (self-symbol) or, if not, how they might expose themselves without being too open, obvious, easy, or vulnerable. For the group-as-a-whole, the reality of the sexual liaison was less important than the emotive forces spurring, capturing, and spreading the fantasied occurrence.

Negative configurations of social fantasy, such as rumor and its hand-maiden gossip, involve projections that are thrust out at others through projectiles, whether sharp tongue, piercing glance, or penetrating innuendo. Whatever their social significance, wounds can result from impinging another's boundaries with the imposition of one's own conflicts and fantasied distortions (Von Franz, 1980). Yet Ashbach and Schermer (1987, p. 219) normalize the process by suggesting that "phantasy elements located in members must be put somewhere and available locations are the psyches of the other members" and the container of the group-as-a-whole. Insight and healing over often comes with the subsequent withdrawal of projections, thereby incisively calling one's shadow qualities and disowned needs back into personal orbit.

Myth

Group myths provide a normative social structure that defines possible roles, interactions, and outcomes within an evolving culture. The myth can provide helpful allusion to the collective process, thus allowing members to open up to current realities and age-old possibilities with a sense of awe and an intuition of underlying forces. To be caught up in a constraining myth is to act out a collusive, scripted, fantasied scenario. To identify and challenge a prevalent, entrapping myth is to engender other possibilities and overcome prescribed collective relations.

Sometimes speculations and rumors more accurately and symbolically stand in for the subtleties inherent in relationships before any elucidating data become explicitly available.

Shortly after the conference began, the senior female consultant fell on the stairs and had to be rushed to the hospital. The myth of powerful contesting forces was perpetuated by surmising that the male director, her former protégé, had violently pushed her down. It took the rest of the week to learn that, in fact, a volatile verbal confrontation had actually occurred between these two staff members just prior to the accident. Arriving on site, the experienced female staffer was told, in what was later labeled a paternalistic belligerent manner, that she had been relieved of her primary conference duty. A fiery verbal altercation ensued with the male director. Shortly after, distracted and distraught, she fell down the stairs, bloodying her lip and biting her tongue. Metaphorically, the director did "push her downstairs," unbeknownst to the member from whose imagination the mythic formulation sprung.

Within such mythic narratives, the play of powerful and often contesting forces struggle to reconcile a range of human polarities such as safety and risk, impulse and restraint, activity and passivity, weakness and strength, male and female. Slater (1966) suggests that groups construct myths to deny or ward off feelings of aloneness and attributions of nonsignificance. Myths assume some overall plan or greater meaning as antidote to the powerlessness of the individual in isolation, or the confusion of the society in anomie. In times of distress, the body of myth may symbolically substitute for "the soothing song, word, or touch of the missing group-Mother" (Dunphy, 1974, p. 316)—in this case literally as well as figuratively.

Following the protean struggles of these would-be Olympians, the members-at-large subscribed to a myth around the exercise of power and influence among men and the women. A pairing of male authority and sadism with female masochism and withdrawal in injury was reenacted in many instances. Eventually, women literally gave way for fear of being pushed down. Myths, however distressing, attempt to creatively contain, explain, and illuminate elements of the reference group's shared concerns, including inevitable and emergent fears, catastrophes, frustrations, sufferings and "falls from grace" (Eliade, 1960).

Mental Imagery

Seeing is believing. Depictions, phenomenological descriptions, clarifications, and interpretations offered as mental images make information available in a readily communicable form. Unlike complicated logical expositions of collective events, members can immediately see the images suggested by their peers or by the facilitator. Such mental images provide direct access to preconscious processes, bringing up for the group's consideration all manner of figurative expression while touching deep emotions and underlying meanings. Visually encoded experiences tend to be remembered.

Images appearing as day or night dreams often carry intuitive force and social significance.

In charged group settings much information, seemingly available to be breathed in from the unspoken airs of the collective atmosphere, can be forseen, often in inspiring ways. These preconscious perceptions have a magical quality, with the receiver feeling as if he or she somehow knows the "yet to be revealed." One facet of the conference is participation in a traditional Tavistock small study group composed of eight members and a leader.

In the first session of one such meeting, a readily observable transference/counter-transference reaction between a male member and the group's female consultant was quite apparent to all. He seemed particularly uninterested in his peers, rather fixedly probing the consultant in an evident attempt to seduce her into more active interaction with him. While trying to maintain the traditional unperturbable Tavistock stance, she noticeably reddened and blanched at the member's intimate and frequent solicitations. The evident affective connection between the two was striking, but the basis of the bond was as yet unknown to either the couple or to the group.

Prior to the next day's meeting, a different male member had a dream that a female friend was pregnant with twins and that he was asked to watch them—a distinct transpersonal "pairing" image. In the dream, the babies were fetus-like, fragile stick figures, precious, vulnerable, and hard to handle. The dream, shared in the next small-group session, had personal significance for the dreamer and also seemed to symbolize the nascent stage of this group's precarious development. The message in the night accurately depicted the dreamer's feeling and position when awake and watching the charged pairing of member and leader. However, these idiosyncratic, personal associations and generalized groupwide interpretations proved unsatisfying and incomplete.

Later, it was revealed that the consultant (the same one as was accused of having a sexual escapade) was barely two months pregnant. In real life she worked as a banker, as did the persistent member's wife, coincidentally two months pregnant. The evident affinity between member and consultant, later acknowledged in the group, was well elucidated by the dream image of fetal twins. The dream's prescient occurrence, prior to the conscious presentation of confirming information about the pregnant connection, proved startling to the dreamer and to the group alike.

Perhaps these kinds of synchronicities (Jung, 1973), or meaningful pairings, are frequently present in many settings but typically go unnoticed or remain unremarkable. In intensive process group experiences, people are more apt to attune to information provided by their preconscious and unconscious imageries, whether originating in day or night dreams or primary process thinking. Within the mental and emotional pooling possible in the intense, supersensitive group experience, thresholds for attending and responding to prescient images, mythic themes, and organizing fantasies are lowered. Thus various emergent phenomena or seemingly hidden data—those facts and extrapolations that might ordinarily go unnoticed—are assimilated in prototypical schemas and complexes, as in the dream image of fetal twinship.

Metaphor

To figure out what is really going on in the group, one needs to listen to the figures of speech being spontaneously developed by the members. The facilitator can also allow his or her own creative capacities free reign to fashion metaphors. These metaphors serve as an internal mapping or as an external communication to describe and advance the essence of the current state of affairs. Various metaphors arise that also prefigure future motifs and themes.

Some conference experiences, hard to explain except by vague notions or meaningful coincidence (Jung, 1973), serve to connect the microcosm of the group with the macrocosm of the outside world by way of living metaphor.

Between two meetings, a male member went jogging. Uncharacteristically, this well-oriented participant got lost and wound up in an off-site residential neighborhood. There, he literally ran into the reformed rabbi who married him and his wife some seven years earlier and 3,000 miles away. Thrilled by the encounter and still somewhat disoriented, the member continued his run, only to pass an old orthodox Temple. The wandering Jew then came directly to the next meeting of the large group. Just prior to the session, he privately told one other person about his experience. During that meeting, the membership was again struggling with the authoritarian stance of the male director. Suddenly an uninformed member said to the Jewish director in seeming benediction, "Your devil's advocacy doesn't bother me anymore. You remind me of my old rabbi." Coincidence or not, this startling comparative recapitulation proved an inspiring event in the organizational experience for the jogger, for his confidant, and upon later revelation, for the whole group—a numinous, symbolic, and almost dream-like linking of the outside world with the inside experience.

Religious lore can be built out of just these foreshadowing, temporal contiguities, as meaningful concurrences that intimately relate metaphor with reality. The word *miracle* signifies such an imposition of the sacred onto the profane (Eliade, 1959).

Symbol

During the course of any particular group's development, general and universal images appear as guide and waystation. These "collective representations" arise from within the linguistic and cultural heritage of the members. Symbols coming out of the shared experience suggest time-worn relations, themes, patterns, and motifs with which every group must work and through whose meaningful semantic context every collective must pass.

The boundaries between the various group events and the community life at large became more and more permeable as the conference proceeded. A particularly distressing real-life event pointed up the thin veneer separating psychical and physical reality. Halfway through the conference, as racial tension mounted, a male minority member, upon emerging from the communal shower, found feces smeared on his shaving kit. The residue of the experience was soon discovered by others in the community. Although the desecration might have been perpetrated by someone outside the registered conference group, the working assumption was that this unscheduled event represented a group dynamic, an acting out of inherent tensions or prejudices.

The first meeting following the incident involved the whole of the membership. The victim angrily reported the incident and openly testified to his own feelings of terror. Others responded with outrage and a show of support for the soiled member. The consultants, staying in role, essentially interpreted the groupwide regressive aspects of the action. "This group is having difficulty containing its shit." This intervention settled some and infuriated others, who demanded a break in set and an acknowledgment of the difference between symbolic expressions and messy realities.

Tension mounted as members turned detective, trying to flush out the culprit into a confession of guilt. No one "confessed," and the silence and paranoia became excruciatingly tangible until one member softly spoke. A young Indonesian man who had said very little to date now entered the group. His confession, while not resolving the objective mystery, somehow took the edge off the danger and put the incident into its proper psychological perspective. He admitted, "I don't speak English very well. I only understand about half of what is said here. I do understand well enough to know that outside this room it wasn't me. Inside this room I could have done it."

Here, symbol and symbolized certainly converged more completely than is ordinarily expected. In times of heightened group affect, members are subject to regression, decompensation, and panic. Symbolic acts can result, in which thought, impulse, and behavior merge in episodes that are not fully differentiated (Ashbach & Schermer, 1987). Segal (1957) writes of the "symbolic equation" as those calculated instances when the symbol as

representation and symbol as object (or action) are confused and inter-
changed inappropriately.

Ritual and Rite of Passage

Significant events in the course of a group take on ritual importance.
Events that serve to act out and resolve group dilemmas or impasses are
remembered and imbued with special significance. Aspects of the experience, when retold, relived, or remembered, guide the group by giving it
direction and faith in the process, as well as providing an established basis
of historical precedent.

In some instances, groupwide enactments and cultural symbols of
lasting importance can be recognized as they are forged within the ongoing
experience.

In a large group setting of 44 participants and 3 leaders, a highly respected and
impeccably qualified female consultant was having difficulty pulling her thoughts
together and finding her voice. As a minority member, she was entreated and be-
sieged by the Black and Hispanic members, as well as by the women in the room,
to act as their sole, unique spokesperson, however biased a representative. Rarely
at a loss for words, the consultant, like the minorities, found herself the object
of projection, and, like the women, found herself tongue-tied, fragmented, and
withdrawn.

Following a particularly stressful meeting, two male members, in heated exchange and ventilation, wandered far from the meeting site. They came late to the
next session. This breach of the time boundary brought all the attention toward the
two as they entered the room and conspicuously took up the exposed seats left for
dawdlers at the center of the cyclone. During their walk on campus, one of the
two had found a gold earring. Upon reentering the room to apprehensive stares,
he nervously asked if anyone was missing this piece of jewelry. So saying, he lost
his grasp and the earring tumbled to the ground, only to be picked up and passed
from row to row and member to member. A sudden gasp came from the female
consultant as she touched her ear and recognized that the earring was hers.

Von Franz (1980) outlines three purposes of ritual: (1) exorcism—
casting out; (2) protection—keeping safely within; and (3) reconciliation —
bringing back together. The illustrious earpiece, given back ceremoniously
by the members to the leader, became a ready ritual of returned parts—the
re-creation of an unbroken circle (a golden ring).

Readorned, the consultant wore a ready reminder of her commitment
to listen to all of the membership. Seemingly empowered by this spontaneous rite of passage, she could now hear the group more fully. Finding her

lost voice, she responded to the whole of the membership, including the women and the minorities, with an enhanced sense of personal integrity. The legendary return of the ring, now in the possession of the whole community, was remembered at many sittings as a relic of adulation and an event to emulate.

Imaginary Scenario

The meaning behind various ongoing actions and reactions can be told in story form. As moving pictures are developed in active imagination, fears, wishes, defenses, motive forces, adaptational stances, skills, difficulties, and interactive patterns become clearly foretold in fantasy as prelude to being comprehended more clearly in reality. The story in the act of being told is often precursor to the parallel reality in the process of being lived. As the telling approaches the tale, compelling scenarios can take on mythic importance.

As the conference proceeded, many shared experiences became magical and myth-like reminders of the meaning and richness of the group process. In time, more accurate and complex perceptions took form, as vague speculations gave rise to more schooled understandings. The group culture continued to evolve as members proposed and tested various hypotheses about the shared experience, comparing fantasies and conceptual reckonings with the data that spawned and supported them. Various hypotheses provided the group with a feedback loop, whereby adjustments and enrichments to the process could be made. In the Tavistock model, the ultimate aim is to find self-understanding, personal integrity, and authorization by first freely contributing to the evolution of the group-as-a-whole. Only then, by realizing and taking back personal distortions, individual projections, and misinformed and misguided conclusions, can real growth take place for the individual and for the group.

At the conference end, a reigning hypothesis in the form of an imaginary scenario was arrived at in a group brainstorming session. The derived story held that the conference "happened to be just like" the director's Bar Mitzvah. The Black female consultant (golden earring recipient, seen as his peer and wife) was to have been associate director. Instead, the director invited both of his Tavistock parents to participate, and, out of respect, named the older male consultant as his associate. The elder female consultant (pushed downstairs) was also invited and assigned major responsibilities, only to be later demoted.

In a generational scenario with distinct Oedipal components, the director struggled both to honor and overcome his consultative parents—escaping from the influence of his metaphoric mother by giving her less importance, while seeking to identify, incorporate, and supersede his sacred father by reversing authority roles. The whole conference could be viewed as a distinctive rite of passage, symbolically enacting a generational succession. This unconsciously motivated playlet, involving considerable energies and enactments, proved both influential and confusing to the community-at-large. Despite having little overt knowledge about these behind-the-scenes dynamic configurations, the membership viewed the older associate director as the real power behind the throne. Wisdom is often projected into age, and the "wise old man" remains a prevalent archetype often evoked in self-exploratory and educational settings.

With the early, unscheduled departure of the senior female, the women in the membership reported feeling especially displaced. No wonder the conference, to date, had seemed so patriarchal and without semblance of nurture. Then the feisty older female consultant made a reappearance, very much alive and still the good queen mother. The collective matrix was again stirred and mixed. The women, as if resurrected, became more evidently involved by actively exploring their participatory hesitations. In the process, the consultant's broken lip and chipped teeth were invoked as ready symbols for female castration.

In this mythic scenario, the other consultants readily took their places in the Olympian family. The male contemporary of the director acted out the part of the brilliant but prodigal son, a hero to the members but often depreciated by the consultant staff. The membership readily sought to win him over as a Promethean linkage between consultant-gods and member-mortals. He often stole the fire by outshining his organizational superiors. He also fueled the fantasy of rebellion against authority by refusing to enter the large group room in advance of the members, as instructed, thereby splitting the consultant staff. When he was courted, however, members' seductive overtures were returned as brilliant interpretations. The wished-for identification with this so-seen "individuated genius"—as a rekindling of vicarious fantasies of merger with a folk hero—was paradoxically reinforced and unrequited.

The other male consultant, Black and outspoken, was pushed to the periphery, simultaneously a shepherd and black sheep. He was given the official role as "consultant to the boundary" between staff and membership, interpreting the relations between the consultant group and the member group. It was often unclear to which group he actually belonged, as he reflected on and struggled with both. His special position did provide privileged access from which he formulated glorious and prophetic insights about the staff, member group, and their interface. No wonder seers are relegated to the fringes of society where they are able to see within and without with equal facility. Campbell (1988) suggests that the shaman's power and authority comes out of just this psychological experience of being between worlds.

The place of minorities within the conference was also symbolized by this consultant's place at the borderland of the power hierarchy. The conference scuttlebutt was that this was the position from which the director could best control his outspoken and potent staff member. The consultant himself later wondered aloud about the meaning of his position on the outskirts of the organization. Bion (1977, 1985), in "Container and Contained," writes of the complementary roles and inevitable struggles between the mystic and his society. The "group and mystic are essential to each other; it is therefore important to consider how or why the group can destroy the mystic on whom its future depends and how or why the mystic may destroy the group" (p. 130).

The two younger female consultants were readily typecast in the roles of promiscuous and backward daughter, further assuring the impossibility of a legitimate or effective female succession. Thus, consciously or unconsciously, the consultant group came to be viewed by the membership as a dysfunctional patriarchal family whose squabbles and jealousies played out in the conference-as-a-whole. Surely parental and familial transferences served the group as metaphoric milestones from which members could assess and adjust their own positions in the organization-as-a-family.

This formulation points up the role of imaginary scenarios in helping to bring order and meaning to the group experience. Such storied narratives are an organization's way of specifying and communicating central themes and events to both insiders and outsiders. Imaginary scenarios can be reworked by narrative retelling. As the story comes to light, it can be edited and replotted. In fact, the director was deeply touched and partially freed from the restrictive bonds of tradition when the generational scenario was presented to him by the members.

Cultural Transference

In an individual psychological sense, transference refers to the shift or conveyance of emotions and/or perceptions—especially those experienced from childhood—from one person to another, as in the transfer of feelings about a parent to a therapist. In cultural transference, a group's conflicts and triumphs cycle through an organization passing from one level of a system to another, with affects and interactions carried across a permeable boundary. Most often, the directionality of the conveyance follows the structure of authority relations, spatially represented as from above to below. Struggles in an organization's hierarchy can play out in subordinate audiences, fostering repetitions that filter down within a system, whether from management to labor, government to populace, faculty to student body, or conference staff to members-at-large.

In this conference, the succession and the authority themes being played out in the consultant group were vividly reenacted within the membership group with the appointment and dethroning of a peer leader.

The whole of the membership met, without consultants, for the purpose of breaking up into smaller self-selected contingencies to study particular aspects of group or authority relations. In this particular exercise, the membership was having difficulty organizing itself. One member, with hands-on, business-world experience, suggested that the membership- as-a-whole elect a chairperson and vice chairperson whose roles would be managerial and secretarial—helping the larger gathering identify, select, record, and coordinate its inherent interests and subsequent task group choices.

After some discussion, the person making the suggestion was nominated and elected to "the chair," apparently unopposed. He, with a self-chosen assistant, threw himself avidly into the task for which, in reality, minimal authority and little cooperation was given. His leadership quickly dissolved as members ignored proposed structures and procedures, caucused in unsanctioned contingents, and ultimately walked out of the meeting, at first piecemeal and then en masse. Small groups were formed according to a chaotic, idiosyncratic, and unspecified selection process based largely on unspoken affinities.

At first, the chairman vocally fought this trend. Parodying the conference director, he belligerently shouted out commands and seemingly unalterable instructions. As this strategy failed, he appeared more and more distraught—unable to have an impact yet unwilling to give up the guise of governance. He remained so personally invested and identified with his bogus leadership role that as the job deteriorated so did his psychological integrity. He became shaky, tangential, emotional, and panic stricken. The vice chairperson, less invested and accurately reading the larger group's consensus, easily rejoined the membership. The chairman more and more assumed the role of martyred leader—an effigy to the failed attempt at structure and loyalty played out in the whole of the conference. He broke down into an embittered, tentative, hesitant, and displaced personage looking to recover his lost authority by literally wandering the halls in search of a constituency.

In the course of this exercise, a small group did eventually form around him. This group, which named themselves the "rules committee," tried with often obsessive energy to hold out for some level of conscious control and social order. However, they were clearly an unruly bunch, outside the mainstream of the group sentience. They expended considerable malcontent and futile energy in going headstrong against established, if unspoken, membership norms. The chairman received some holding within this subgroup, as they took up his cause in puppet regime. However, he remained noticeably tenuous for the remainder of the conference, a frightening specter representing the possibility of disintegration at the hands of the group.

For better or for worse, subordinate activities mirror higher order relations. Identified patients, whether subgroups or individuals, often serve as displacements for the superordinate unit's tensions when they act unconsciously in an attempt to mirror and/or heal the parent group. By repetition compulsion, a group's constituency often identifies with and imitates dysfunctional authority patterns, proliferating structural problems throughout the system. This cultural transference applies whether speaking of children in families, workers in organizations, or members in therapy or training groups. By casting its reflection, the group-as-a-whole projects formative proclivities, while leaders can recognize what they do, as displayed by members' words and deeds.

Transitional Phenomena

The movement of a group or society is recognizable as a series of transitions that serve to bridge from an organization's past to its future, while holding within its structure elements of both. Too drastic a move away from the establishment leads to separation anxiety, acting out of normal channels, and cutoffs from the main body of the work. Too sacred an institutionalization of power leads to entrapment fears, fixation, staid interaction, and a stifling of innovation. For an organization to change face, it must take heed of its stabilizing conventions while transforming antiquated facades.

Transition, as such, implies a movement, passage, or change from one position, state, stage, or subject to another. A disequilibrium and release of energy ushers in an impending phase shift. It is instructive to look within the group for the forces and carriers of change. What trends serve as intermediate phenomena and what persons act as transitional objects?

Amidst the conference membership was a vocal and influential subgroup of would-be consultants. This cliquish cadre became the "infant-terribles" of the conference. Close in sentiment and aspiration to the consultant group, they acted out for the membership the tensions around presumed and authorized leadership. Members of this subgroup expressed both envy and contempt for the consultants through rumor (intercourse story) and in the guise of honestly "doing the work." For example, using truth as a lethal weapon, one of this group praised, exposed, and undermined a consultant as a "brilliant, crazy, and unpredictable alcoholic." Another member of the clique went on a diatribe against the tactics of the director, while publicly declaring his desire to be accepted into the consultant group. Nowhere was the ambivalent wish to kill off and take up the powers of authority so clearly demonstrated.

During the whole of the conference, members, in imitation and in contrast, tried to define their loyalties, roles, and places in the community. Rules of engagement were hard fought. Distinctions had to be made between exposing oneself and setting up others. Toward the climax of the conference, some reconciliation occurred as a representative group composed of would-be consultants and seasoned group facilitators proposed the "Bar Mitzvah hypothesis." They properly took up the role of family mediators and earned the position of consultants in their own right, a distinct and real advance in personal and shared authority, and a move toward legitimate succession and generational shift.

Motif

The focal conflicts and recurrent themes evident in any group represent variations on the vast array of basic human concerns around social living. A pooling and reorganization of individual motives results in the configuration of groupwide motifs as prominent collective figures. Overriding organizational themes, or leitmotifs, represent issues of high cultural importance. Prevailing motifs surface in the form of preoccupations, juxtapositions, or persistent questions and recurrent organizational difficulties.

In any culture, boundaries are fluid and permeable as overriding group issues effect the whole of the evolving process.

It was learned that one of the key sponsoring agencies of the conference was itself undergoing extreme chaotic disintegration. A key leader at the central location stood accused of wrongdoing. There, too, rumors and innuendoes flew, and the Board of the larger organization was, as yet, unable to reorganize, hold firm, and move on with its primary task of providing for training and trainers. Consequently, many experienced consultants, some of whom were at this conference, were threatening to quit or retire. The boundaries of this conference were breached by the problems of the outside society, which shaped and adversely effected the here-and-now working atmosphere. Certainly any group's working conditions must be understood in relation to its foundation matrix (Foulkes, 1965)—the larger society of which it is a part. Thus, evolving issues of group maintenance and succession took on further contextual and transferential meaning in leitmotif, as the many-tiered organizational process unfolded.

Problems similar to those evident in the conference organization are likely to occur in many ordinary everyday institutional settings, even those replete with prestructured tasks, preordained working roles, and clearly defined procedures. There, however, disruptive events are likely to be considered peripheral nuisance phenomena and soon forgotten—even if their actual implications are serious and connect with central issues. This is not so in experiential process "conferences," where reactivity to such phenomena properly becomes the central focus of attention.

Group Events as Cultural Milestones

Although many interactions and experiences made up the whole of the conference, these and like events stand out as cultural milestones—those shared perceptions or charged events that give touchstone significance to the whole of the process. Bolman and Deal (1984) remind us that "what is most important about an event is not what is happening but what it means" (p. 149). The descriptions and interpretations reported here make up only some of the available viewpoints. Other eyes necessarily see alternate realities, fashion competing and coincident fantasies, and cull out synchronous points of contact for consideration and meaning attribution. There are a million stories in the big city.

Much of the group interaction, at least initially, is carried on unconsciously. Psychic contents are collected, passed around, and amplified (Rogers, 1987) in the form of specific rumors, beliefs, themes, images, and other cultural manifestations. The whole of the overt process takes shape as a collection of private events is made public business. Taken together, ever-present themes, processes, developments, and symbolic reckonings provide for the collective representations (Durkheim, 1974; Levy-Bruhl, 1985) by which the group-as-a-whole organizes and further fashions its experience. When the leader doesn't intervene, fantasy comes in to bridge gaps. By creating concrete cultural byproducts, such as myths, symbols, and enactments, and by discovering apt metaphors, scenarios, and motifs, the group simultaneously energizes, expresses, evaluates, and adjusts its own functioning. Imagine the conference group as a tribe, where fresh, naive experience prototypically defines the meaning of life within the natural confines of the collective setting. Here, history is in the process, and myth, metaphor, and miracle are in the making.

Advance and Decline

The conference group-as-a-whole and the members therein obviously progressed and regressed, undergoing groupwide and personal integrations and disintegrations. Loss of self often preceded reconstitution. Confusion descended before clarity emerged. Rumor antedated fact. Throughout, mystical participations fostered and foreshadowed the quest for objective truths. Two ways of knowing, mythos and logos, were never far apart, mingling together through the whole of the ongoing process in a mixture of fantasy and reality (Bion, 1961; Rioch, 1975c).

Members first sought to define themselves by understanding and identifying with the prescribed leadership. Similar to forming legends and myths around a pantheon of heroes and gods, the member group projected, intuited, and introjected the conference staff. Only human, the consultant group also worked out their own issues in interactions with each other and with the membership-at-large.

The group wellspring fed from below as well as from above. The members found or placed in the leaders those particles of truth and consequence that they brought to the conference in search of consideration and resolve. It is often easier to struggle with the parts of oneself as reflected in others. The impetus to change the stranger often leads to discovering an all too familiar face in the revealing mirror of the group. Packed in with their preconference garb, members brought along their own foibles, frailties, and forebodings. Issues around mourning, loneliness, sexual dysfunction, handicap, commitment, assertion, and prejudice were progressively unpacked and redressed. Luckily, potentials, talents, strengths, and integrities were also brought along. The variety of evident transferences were in prelude to members reclaiming their own preoccupations and finding their unique positions in relation to both the authority and the larger society of their peers.

Given the levels of distress and disorder often present, one might ask why the consultants would let matters get so convoluted and conspiratorial. Many times the tenets of sound organizational and dynamic group management went seemingly unrecognized or planfully ignored. Training groups are ultimately more concerned with learning than with amelioration. Rioch (1975b) suggests that T-groups are committed to "a ruthless honesty about one's self and one's group without any assumption that such honesty will necessarily lead to resolution of conflict" (p. 8). In this context, both advance and retreat are condoned as legitimate tools of learning, akin to experimentation involving trial and error. The full experience then consists of coming in touch with the profundities of the group in all its various configurations.

Personal growth is incidental to this process. Slater (1966) suggests that "members may actually benefit in inverse proportion to their therapeutic need" (p. 252). He goes on to differentiate how the aims of consultants working in educational confines differ from the role of therapists working in clinical settings. In training groups, little attention is given to members' formative pasts or personal outside experiences. Psychoanalysis of the group-as-a-whole is taken as the proper object of study and intervention. Therefore, the focus is not on interpreting individual behavior but rather on clarifying shared dynamics. Intellectualizing is encouraged as it relates to the accurate depiction of immediate group events and as it fosters sociological insight. The goal of such training endeavors becomes understanding and "innovation at the cultural level." The essential difference between training and clinical groupings may be the distinction between "understanding what is happening in a group of which one is a member and modifying one's personality structure" through participation as a member of a group (Slater, 1966, p. 255).

True insight or psychotherapeutic gain, although not an overt goal, can occur as members apply the lessons learned to their own human relations. Members can also deteriorate. In the course of the experience, many narcissistic injuries were suffered, owing to the lack of structure and individual attention inherent in the groupwide focus. Regression and psychotic sequelae resulted. In "application groups," the last formal activity of the conference, members were encouraged to generalize and ground themselves by debriefing. A reinstituted sense of reality was sought, as conference learning was generalized and related to "back-home" applications.

An experiential human relations conference is an excellent medium in which to study a group's developmental issues and the creative meaning-making through which these issues gain expression. As such, therapists can certainly benefit from participation in Tavistock laboratory experiences as part of their own educational background and "sensitivity" training. Clinicians can learn about, witness, and become caught up in the midst of operative group dynamics. The conference experience is less amenable, however, to the needs of patients who are unlikely to receive the targeted care and holding required where the intent of grouping needs be expressly therapeutic.

A group facilitator's choice of leadership style and intervention strategy needs to fit the primary task of the group, which is matched with the personal goals and ego strengths of the participants. Where the aim is discovering intrapersonal, interpersonal, and group dynamics, less overt structure is often better than more. Shaffer and Galinsky (1974) suggest that in training groups "one of the roles of the 'leader' is to create a vacuum which the participants must fill with their own behavior" (p. 193). Generally, the more intact the members, the less central and directly facilitating the leadership need be. Members can provide for themselves many of the ongoing structures and leadership postures needed for the group to progress. The formal facilitator is left to pick and choose when and how to intervene. Where specific needs dictate concrete actions, more overt structure and preparatory guidance will need to be provided. The less intact or mature the members, the more the leader must directly provide for the care and management of his or her charges. Here, insufficient attention and unspecified organizational procedures would only make for disorganization and dysfunction, both personal and collective.

CHAPTER NINE

Managing Group Process in Nonprocess Groups:

Working with Structured Theme-Centered Tasks

Most specifically formed groups have a planned task in mind. A select membership, formal structure and format, and panoply of resources are brought to bear on the successful completion of a shared activity, joint venture, or mutual production. The group-as-an-enterprise finds internal cohesion and public persona by identifying with this fully specified aim as its raison d'etre. Miller and Rice (1975, p. 62) define a group's primary task as "the task that it must perform to survive"—the overriding goal that lends meaning and substance to the very acts of joining in and carrying on. Members become assimilated by avowing set purposes and accepting available roles as offered within the organizational structure.

If the primary task is time bound or short lived, a group may be formed as a *task force,* convened to address a particular concern and disbanded once the set aim is completed. Juries, for example, are task forces formed for the express purpose of deciding a case. Once the foreman reads the verdict and the judgment is proclaimed, the jury is dismissed. Likewise, psychoeducational and theme-centered groups usually form for the short-term purpose of learning about and effecting more person trials. Should a group lose sight of its primary task, become embroiled in conflicts between members, or get distracted with alternate agendas, whether private or public, then confusion, ineffectiveness, disintegration, and/or wholesale structural or personnel changes are likely to ensue.

An earlier version of this chapter, coauthored with Eleanor Vaughan and Nancy Fiedler, appeared in *Group, 2*(3), 178–192, copyright 1987. Reprinted with permission of Brunner/Mazel, Inc. Also incorporated is material from a previous article in *Small Group Behavior, 20*(2), 279–186, copyright © 1989. It is reprinted with permission of Sage Publications.

233

Task groups can ultimately be defined by *what* it is they are meant to accomplish. These same groups can be judged by how well they carry out a set of functions and subtasks in the service of their primary aim. An ongoing group that manages to stay "on task" is often referred to as maintaining its *"work-group* function" (Bion, 1961). By contrast, *process groups* meet specifically to explore the dynamics and interactions occurring naturally in intimate, collective settings. The group itself is studied as it forms, evolves, progresses, and disbands. The primary task of process groups is to utilize the experience together to explore self-contained and self-perpetuating behaviors (Redlich & Astrachan, 1975). Such a group literally turns back upon itself in order to discover those regularities and irregularities that effect collective functioning and influence the accomplishment of stated objectives. Such experiential learning serves multiple purposes by providing individual enlightenment and fostering social awareness, while practicing cooperative endeavor.

Although, in a process group, any set task, other than exploring the self-other-group interface, is secondary, ready applications and generalizations can be taken back to one's primary groupings—whether vocational, familial, or interpersonal (Rioch, 1975b). Often the pinnacle of discovery is finding out just how difficult, yet exciting, it is to work as a unit whose aim is simply to define a goal and stay on task. An ongoing group that strays off course is said to be engaged in a *"collusive culture"* (Bion, 1961).

The Twinship of Task and Process

Distinctions between task and process groups, once made, are not steadfast nor mutually exclusive, as significant leakage and overlap blurs actual differences. Even when clothed differently, these twin offspring of different mothers are often hard to tell apart—showing up together and sharing much. Simply put, process groups have tasks and task groups have processes. Process groups carry a primary task of self-observation, accomplished through various subtasks that support their work-group function. Task groups, on the other hand, must at least manage evident processes, such as distracting member behaviors, ineffective interactions, and impaired teamwork, to sufficiently assure the progressive carrying out of appropriate, goal-directed endeavors.

No one is left untouched by the group experience. Feelings, moods, and affective reactions are inevitably stimulated and vulnerabilities are inexorably exposed as work on the formal task proceeds. Whenever instruction is given by the leader or information is introduced by another member, feelings are stimulated. Members greet each other's views, attitudes, beliefs, and work products with emotions. Such affects, in turn, spur judgments.

So often, members say that they want information or clarification about the task but really seek support, acknowledgment, ventilation, conciliation, or affective confirmation. How many times have you sat in a meeting and annoyingly wondered what in the world this or that person was going on about? In addition to whatever publicly agreed upon and fully acknowledged agendas group participants may hold in common, their needs to be important, liked, safe, and intimate are all acted out in collective settings. Familiar inveterate problems are displayed with characteristic style in the hopes of resolution or at least a fair hearing for overreaching concerns. The task itself can become a projective vehicle for members' intrapsychic and interpersonal needs, a container imbued with surplus significance and latent meanings (Bion, 1985).

The life, structure, formal leadership, composition, and shaping environment of the group itself creates problems of its own making, both stated and unstated, recognized and unrecognized. Dysfunctional dynamics can be engendered by structural anomalies, bureaucratic rigmarole, or rigid power hierarchies. Resultant problems may manifest as confused or mixed messages, troublesome relations, fixations, resistances, tangents, regressions, differential aims, or diversions from work. How many times have meetings gotten so confusing that you lose track of why everyone is gathered together? Task groups are always subject to being interfered with by hidden agendas—those pressing member or groupwide conflicts that are not nearly amenable to specification, fluid rendering, or targeted resolution. Besides the formal agenda, members have much on their minds and the group-as-a-whole has many preoccupations that affect the working process.

In the course of any group much goes on beyond the words spoken. Verbal tones may suggest strong feelings where seemingly neutral positions are evinced. Noisy nonverbal behaviors may indicate participatory reactions where quiet otherwise prevails. An active and apparently productive discussion may be initiated in response, reaction, or resistance to considering a more threatening and current topic of concern. Thus, for example, a theme-centered group can discuss male and female role expectations in such an abstract manner as actually to preclude the men and women talking directly to one another—with gender tensions resulting in the men sitting on one side of the room and the women on the other. Much more goes on in the group than is normally understood or acknowledged.

When a group and/or its members are working on unacknowledged, private, or covert agendas, public and overt tasks usually suffer. Yet hidden agendas are a natural outgrowth of the grouping process. Bradford (1978) suggests,

> *The main reason for people's coming together and forming a group is that there is a publicly stated, agreed-on task to be accomplished.*

This is the surface, or public, agenda. . . . But below the surface there
are quite apt to be hidden agendas which the group probably does not
openly recognize. . . . Before our judgment of groups becomes too
severe, however, we need to realize that groups are working simulta-
neously and continuously on two levels. (p. 84)

Every group, then, can be followed by using a dual tracking system—
assessing behaviors that are "on task" and "off task," thereby reflecting
both overt/stated and covert/unstated agendas.

The leader and the group must find ways to deal with its inevitable
quirks and quagmires. For instance, every teacher must figure ways to cope
with students whose tangential questions seem more an attempt to join the
leader than to learn from him or her. Every group facilitator must have a
strategic response for the provocateur, who, through persistent interruption, breaks the flow of the session and contravenes normal leader-follower
relations (Rioch, 1975a). How well a group, whatever its context, manages
the monopolist, showoff, bore, helpful Hannah, complainer, self-righteous
moralist, teacher's pet, femme fatale, machismo aggressor, narcissist, histrionic performer, silent party, paranoid participant, or consensus buster
goes a long way toward determining its efficiency and ultimate success
(Bogdanoff & Elbaum, 1978; Yalom, 1970, 1985).

Similarly, how well a group encourages and favorably utilizes its more
progressive forces—whether these be members' attention spans, participants' skills, leadership potentials or; varied interactions, available feedbacks, diverse opinions, constructive confrontations and criticisms, conformity pressures, or brainstorming (Kissen, 1976a; Janis, 1982)—also
contributes substantially to the collective's effectiveness. The whole of the
group process needs access to its full range of part-processes, its ideas, emotions, and member contributions, in order to be fully represented. Just as
importantly, it is essential that the group harness its affective powers, using
collective passions and motive forces in service of shared aims.

Group Protocols and Participatory Practices

Every group must evoke a method of operation and participatory practice,
whether Robert's Rules, the whimsy of an autocratic leader, a casebook of
procedures, roles, and rituals, or the free speech that accompanies democratic precepts. Who can talk, about what, and when must be clearly specified, tacitly understood, or continually renegotiated. The evident progression through the course of the meeting can follow a formal protocol marked
by structured interventions, depend on the minute-to-minute management
decisions of an acknowledged leader, or more loosely flow in open forum.

Although differing in operational mode, task groups' structured agenda setting and process groups' unstructured turn taking are equivalent phenomena. In the former, relevant points of business are identified and prioritized in advance of the meeting and then successively taken up, in turn, during the session. Successful task performance requires more or less moving through the group's agenda in a satisfactory fashion marked by closing old business, handling current concerns, and introducing new issues for active consideration and synergistic problem solving.

Unstructured groups may seem to have no set, overt agenda or preordained talking order. However, on closer examination, each member can be seen as providing his or her own informal person-oriented program, identifiable as idiosyncratic viewpoints and pressing needs to speak or be heard. For an unstructured group to be successful, all the members must be at least minimally involved in taking up their own agendas, thus lending regularity and definition to group-as-a-whole's exploration of common themes, recurrent motifs, and focal concerns.

The group process can move in a formalized "go-around" or more resemble the popping of corn as each kernel of self-interest rises and expands within the heat of the moment. Some participants, by style, need, or skill, command more of the group's attention and time, but protracted silence or withdrawal by any member or subgroup threatens the very viability of the collective format. Participation will never be equal, as all other variables are nonequal. However, the chance to express oneself and the right to gain access to the group, the leader, and the current topic must be fairly evenly spread. Every group needs to move through its agenda in unison, whether that agenda is task or person oriented, structured or unstructured. With everyone having a voice, no one is disenfranchised, and the group-as-a-whole most fully takes up its relevant tasks.

The Use and Abuse of Structure and Exercises

A more active and central leader is required when the group is organized specifically for problem solving. Psychoeducational, theme-centered, and behavioral group leaders, working with more observable, tangible focal material, tend to provide overt direction in the form of planned activities, didactic instruction, and structured exercises—all carefully mapped out within sequenced protocols. A format that relies directly on skills training requires a leader in the expert-trainer-guide-advisor role.

It is, of course, virtually impossible for facilitators not to exercise an effect on the process and workings of their groups. They do so with every move. When leaders inquire after particular information, highlight a theme, or make connections between individuals, they provide structure and overtly influence the direction of the group process. More subtly, a leader's attitudes, personas, countertransferences, and nonverbal stirrings shape the experiences possible in the group room.

When introducing didactic material or specific exercises within the ongoing context, the therapist most directly controls the course of events (Shapiro, 1978; Yalom, 1985). A didactic presentation introduces new material that will inevitably stimulate feelings and reactions. Similarly, an exercise takes time and attention while formalizing, freezing, or introducing a new group process. The facilitator most directly influences the proceedings by giving directions about how to explore a topic and by specifying the behavior necessary to carry out a task.

The use of structured presentation or exercise also affects the members' perceptions and expectations of the leader and of the group. Introducing an exercise is a direct and powerful intervention. In many exercises, the leader becomes the center of the group world. The excessive use of exercises and instructions can lead to dependency on the facilitator, as members expect and wait to be led and directed. Such gratification can foster a belief in reified wisdom and magical or pat solutions to life's diversity of problems: "If only I was as wise as the leader, I could understand and handle my problems so much better," "If only the leader would tell us how to think and what to do, we would move so much faster and proceed with so much more certainty."

Such grand expectations can create inordinate pressure on the facilitator to have all the answers, to work faster, and to be right there with the perfect advice or technique for all occasions. One is reminded of the old Mighty Mouse cartoons: "Here I come to save the day!" Such grandiosity, either assumed or attributed, may prevent the group from finding and valuing its own resources and creative solutions to varied personal or shared problems. The marks of a good exercise may be that it quickly turns the responsibility over to the members and modestly serves to foster ongoing exploration of the focal issue. The utility of a didactic presentation may be that it provides a conceptual/linguistic model within which members can more intelligibly address their common concerns.

Whitaker and Lieberman (1964) suggest that the critical aspects of any group intervention are its timing and its referent, that is, the aspect of the group task or process chosen for special attention. Schutz (1967), a pioneer in the encounter movement and the inventor of many nonverbal and interpersonal exercises, suggests tailoring what one does to what is actually going on in the group. Yalom (1985) concurs, "Group workers agree that proper timing is essential in the use of . . . exercises; a poorly timed exercise will 'bomb out,' be puzzling or harmful to the group. Such exercises are best used to clarify some shared, but dimly conscious group concern or problem" (p. 334).

The aim is never to take away the group's opportunities for free exchange by moving past awkward situations and difficult impasses. Exercises are not recommended when they divert the group from an important ongoing dynamic. This is true if the action at hand is heated discussion or cold resistance. Nor is it enough merely to stimulate affect or generate more information. In theme-centered groups, exercises are most effective when they work along the cutting edge of the central focus, allowing members to recognize and elaborate the various subthemes, subtleties, and implications of the major identified concern. Like a song in a theatrical musical production, a well-crafted exercise heightens the action, amplifies the feeling, and moves the drama from one point to another, hopefully at a greater level of composition, integrity, and focal specificity.

The Process and Phases in Utilizing Structured Exercises

Assuming proper choice and timing of an exercise, what is the process by which it is carried out most successfully (Pfeiffer & Jones, 1975)? Here are five steps associated with the use of exercises in the ongoing group.

1. *Preparing.* Any exercise should be introduced to the group before proceeding. A brief rationale should be provided for why the exercise is being suggested at this time, what it hopes to accomplish, and what is expected of the members. The group works into the exercise by handling resistances, fears, or concerns, and by securing initial compliance. The exercise can be introduced as an experiment with the members encouraged to participate fully, but with assurances that they ultimately control their level of participation.

2. *Exercising.* The facilitator now creates whatever atmospere is necessary to most fully to carry out the exercise, whether a state of relaxation, a new focus of attention, a postural shift, or an imagined scenario. The leader sets the stage and creates a mood conducive to active participation. Members are encouraged to be spontaneous, creative, and open to the experience. Within the limits of the particular structure, control should be turned over to the members to project their uniqueness into the exercise. The leader provides the form and the members supply the content.

3. *Processing.* Once the exercise is completed, the group dialogue begins anew, hopefully at a richer and more informed level than was possible before. A free play of sharing and interpretation is encouraged. The brainstorming capacity of the group is engaged to extract the meaning and applicability of the exercise. Most likely the procedure was attuned to affective, behavioral, or imaginative processes. The time has come to reintroduce cog-

nitive consideration to anchor the experiential work: "What was the experience like? Were there difficult points and how did you get through them? What emotions, memories, or images were elicited? What do you make of what happened? What did you learn? What questions were raised? How does the exercise connect with what we've been doing in group and with the issues you have been personally considering? What directions are provided for further work? How does your experience compare and contrast with those of the other group members?"

4. *Generalizing*. With any intervention, and most especially a structured exercise, an important part of the process is to generalize awareness and behavior potentials to the patient's real inside-the-group and outside-the-group experiences. Thus, an exercise can be worked back into the member's life by considering, for instance: How does your experience here connect or reflect on the problems and concerns that brought you to group and/or experiences you've had while here? What of the emerging material is familiar to you? "Have you heard any of this feedback before?" Once connections between the group exercise and real-life experiences are made overt, then the member can be helped in converting insights into skills, coping strategies, and new behavioral and emotional possibilities.

5. *Remembering*. Any memorable experience, whether spontaneous or induced, becomes part of the history of the group and the heritage of each member. The experiences accrued in the exercise can serve as nodal reference points, mnemonic aids, and navigational tools for the member in negotiating inside and outside the group. Members may spontaneously refer back to these charged and symbolic moments to contrast or to clarify a current impasse or to highlight a significant change. The therapist can knowingly refer members back to their own experiences to remind them of various insights, trouble spots, vulnerabilities, repetitive patterns, or to make an interpretative link between current and past behaviors. By referring back to the group's nodal workings, the facilitator helps build the richness of context and continuity of culture so necessary to th process of change.

Exercises can be borrowed or built. The literature is rich with possibilities drawn from encounter, gestalt, transactional analysis, psychosynthesis, psychodrama, T-groups, guided imagery, and improvisational theater (Spolin, 1963; Zweben & Hammann, 1970; Mintz, 1971, 1974; Saretsky, 1977; Goulding & Goulding, 1979; Buchanan, 1980). In a psychoeducational context, exercises can be constructed by roleplaying or creating practice actions, by using imagination to break mental sets and construe alternate possibilities, or by creating new habits through behavior modifications and the evocation of constructive rituals and symbolic enactments. While the variety of and possibility for providing exercises abound, to be effective, structured interventions must be incorporated within the bounds of the ongoing group. Finding or inventing an exercise is easier than learning when and how to use it effectively.

Working with Theme-Centered Psychoeducational Groups

Psychoeducational, theme-centered, social skills and life skills, or nonprocess groups are currently enjoying a renaissance (Cohn, 1969, 1972; Druck, 1978; Drum & Knott, 1977; Shaffer & Galinsky, 1974). Such groups are a staple in mental health clinics and hospitals and are an increasingly popular model for organizational and private sector consultations. Such psychoeducational approaches lend themselves to efficient, targeted, and time-limited interventions. Groups may be organized around any of a variety of symptoms (depression, anxiety), problems (assertiveness, self-esteem, stress), developmental milestones (adolescence, parenting), management issues (morale, productivity) or topical concerns (fostering positive male-female relations, overcoming the generation gap). Such theme-centered work often relies heavily on focused attentions, a structured format, didactic presentations, and experiential exercises (Poey, 1985).

The contrast between training or psychotherapeutic and psychoeducational groups centers largely around the role and use of the group process. Yalom (1985) argues for the primacy of a process orientation in group psychotherapy, in which *content* (informational and topical material) mainly serves to carry the group to the next analyzable *process*. In the psychoeducational group, the primacy is reversed. Content is of major importance. Specific material is often preselected as the skeletal frame that holds the group together and gives a particular shape to the proceedings. Each session may have various tasks to accomplish and specific material to cover. Subsequent sessions often depend on the assimilation of the previous material, as the group flushes out a fuller understanding of the theme in question. In the psychoeducational group, little attention is specifically focused on the group process as "an object of study" and intervention. However, "sophisticated use [can be] made of the various processes" to lubricate, support, and move the content along to the next informational point (R. Klein, 1985, p. 322).

Unfortunately, all too often, group process is actually ignored and/or viewed as an interruption to the didactic presentation. The psychoeducational leader may become anxious, frustrated, or even hostile when group processes emerge and disrupt the more ordered educational format. With an eye toward completeness, sessions are often packed with material or prescribed tasks, leaving little time for reaction, discussion, or the more subjective aspects of the learning process. Yet, group processes will not unobtrusively step aside. "Process characteristics . . . are an intrinsic and inevitable aspect of all groups no matter what their size or function" (Whitaker & Lieberman, 1964, p. 3).

For example, blind adherence to format and content in a heart attack prevention group actually served to impede the group task. In the first session, the leader was enthusiastically describing various books and handouts on stress reduction that were organized neatly on a table in front of the five group members. As the leader talked, one member distanced himself from the material by leaning back in his chair and disdainfully looking in the other direction. Another member fidgeted nervously, while a third bubbled over with irrelevant questions and comments. It was apparent that the very nature of the task, as well as the material content of the session, coincident with the leader's presentational style, were having a strong and immediate effect on the members. Personal reactions of the members were obviously affecting their availability for learning, while directly reflecting strong feelings about being identified as at "high risk" for a heart attack. How much more relevant, constructive, and "on target" might the psychoeducational experience have been if such dynamic processes were recognized, allowed for, and incorporated into the structural flow of the session.

No group of breathing souls stands still to be educated and "psychologized." Learning is an active and interactional process. To use the group medium effectively and to maximize learning opportunities, the psychoeducational leader must be attuned to the movement and stirring within the group. Certainly, the leader can have an outline of prepared didactic material and a ready store of experiential exercises in mind. The group can even be structured in a lecture discussion format, allowing time to teach and time to talk. However, ongoing attention to group processes allows for proper presentational timing, selection of relevant informational points, and a sensitivity as to when it is advisable or even necessary to interrupt and punctuate the lesson plan in the service of ventilation, integration, and assimilation.

In the theme-centered psychoeducational group, the leader becomes a technical expert who mediates and balances between the topics, tasks, and member reactions (R. Klein, 1985), while aiming for optimal rather than maximal theme centeredness. This is true "particularly if the discussion up until then has been so theme focused as to have excluded . . . more personal reactions to the theme or task, to the leader, to one another, and to what occurred during the session thus far" (Shaffer & Galinsky, 1974, p. 242).

Many group processes can be predicted, given the structural and time-determined constraints and opportunities provided by normal group development (Bennis & Shepard, 1956; Lacoursiere, 1980; Tuckman, 1965). Every group, regardless of the stated task or focus, can be characterized by its boundary integrity, cohesiveness, normative structure, evolving culture, and place on an existential continuum from formation through termination. Other ongoing group processes or hidden agendas arise more spontaneously, owing to the idiosyncratic character or circumstances of the members, the eliciting quality of the didactic material, evolving interactions among participants, and reactions (realistic and transferential) to the manner and sensitivity of the group leader's presentational style.

Therefore, group process must, and can, find a necessary place in any psychoeducational model. The theme-centered psychoeducational leader would attend to group development, maintenance, culture building, and facilitation of enabling norms by fostering a working atmosphere while ministering to the more effervescent and idiosyncratic aspects of the evolving group processes. Some built-in feedback is necessary to create a working dialogue between the presented content and the reaction that comes out of the group to greet it. No amount of careful planning or captivatingly colorful presentation can prevent dynamic group processes from arising. Nor should they. The leader's only real choice is how and when to use the group process to support psychoeducational aims. By constantly monitoring the group and blending content, teaching formats, and preselected exercises with the evolving process, the psychoeducational group leader provides a lively opportunity to enhance the content and go beyond general learning to a more engaged, affectively resonant, and personally meaningful experience.

An Experience in Process Consultation

Although there has been a recent proliferation of groups for consultative and psychoeducational purposes, little has been written about attending to the group process in these same structured nonprocess groups. The following model investigates the management of various dynamic forces in a group contracted to work on stress-management skills with upper-level executives from a busy and high-profile organization. The stress-management training was part of a larger organizational intervention run successfully for approximately a year and a half. Similar groups, following a cognitive behavioral format (Murphy, 1984; Schwartz, 1980; Sime & Tharp, 1982), were already being conducted with lower-level personnel by the female psychologist who designed the program.

The stress-management model uses a 10-week, 2-hour per session protocol that can accommodate up to 8 participants. The group experience is summarized over the full course of its short-term contract in order to demonstrate the blended interspersal of task and process management. Special attention is drawn to the boundary between psychoeducational and psychotherapeutic intervention.

Male cofacilitation and process consultation was specifically sought for this largely male executive group in anticipation of problems with boundaries, authority, competition, and hierarchy. A secondary aim of the consultation was to gain feedback on the group process aspects of the program so that revisions of design could be implemented. This group consultation actually began after the members were already selected and oriented. Commitment and attendance became a major problem and ongoing dynamic for this group, largely due to insufficient groundwork and contracting. Subsequent design efforts have bolstered the pregroup aspect of the program.

Session 1: Evaluation

Subtask and Content
Baseline measures of stress are taken, and some brief explanation of the Stress Management Program is given by a technician not directly involved in the groupwork. Subsequently, detailed written results of the evaluation are mailed to each participant.

Group Process
The stress evaluation represents the only intervention accomplished with the prospective members prior to the group's convening as a body in Session 2. Given that the facilitators are not involved in the evaluation or the feedback, the pregroup process is cut off from the whole of the group proper. Members' reactions to their psychological and physiological stress measures are not discussed and channeled toward the aims of the primary task or the possibilities of the collective intervention. Rather, whatever reactions would-be participants do have to the test results remain as private processes likely converted into hidden agendas—whether the initiation of denial, the stimulation of irrepressible anxiety, a budding dependency on the leader-as-helper, the impulse to fight or flee, or the penchant for an active participatory merger.

Process Management
Pregroup work is a critical part of any group's development. Attention to this *"preparation" phase* facilitates later member participation and the creation of an optimal learning atmosphere. Specific goals of the pregroup work include: (1) evaluating prospective members; (2) building initial rapport, trust, and alliance; (3) processing relevant prior experiences and calming initial anxieties; (4) making selection decisions and securing firm

participatory contracts; and (5) orienting the matriculating members to the group format while instilling normative expectations about the nature of the upcoming collective endeavor.

In this stress-management group, lack of such a usable pregroup process prevented the identification of two members who were insufficiently motivated and less than fully available. These two subsequently dropped out, reducing the group membership to five. With foreknowledge, additional participants might have been recruited. The smaller group was certainly viable. However, the reduced size created undue pressures on members and on leaders, as attendance and involved participation now became critical to the very existence of the group.

The issue of attendance remained a recurrent management issue throughout this group's course. With a short-term, information-oriented approach, new members cannot easily be added once the protocol is underway. For the group to maintain momentum, an inductive, bottom-up, building process is assumed, as each new session relies on prior learnings and accrual of earlier experiences, thus lending itself to a closed contract. Unfortunately, in theme-centered groups, the ethics of consistent participation often are not emphasized as they would be in a psychotherapy group. Participants may believe that missing sessions will not adversely affect the ongoing dynamics of the lesson plan. The leader needs to communicate a more active and involved psychoeducational etiquette, one that views each participant as a responsible and intimate partner in the informational exchange. Members need to be reeducated so that "cutting group" is not equated with the impersonal gesture of "cutting class."

Another pregroup issue not satisfactorily addressed concerned several members who worked together either as parallel department heads or, in two cases, as supervisor/supervisee. Feelings and norms concerning safety, confidentiality, power and role, and the interplay of existing subgroups should have been worked out prior to the first group meeting. The failure to anticipate or uncover important pregroup dynamics was in the misguided service of technical advance. This tactic of quickly moving ahead with the structured program, led to many repercussions that ultimately surfaced and interfered with subsequent success of the otherwise well thought-out psychoeducational paradigm.

Session 2: What Is Stress and How Do You Respond?

Subtask and Content
The concept of stress is specified so that participants and leaders have a common language and shared understanding of its physical and psychological impact.

Group Process

Upon entering the group room, the participants (Barry, Don, Gary, Curt) show many signs of initial anxiety. They awkwardly joke about which color "Participant's Manual" to select. Obviously, beginning the group, becoming vulnerable around coworkers, while being "scrutinized by two psychologists," was proving stressful. One member is late (Bill), and two members are missing (Susan and Jim).

Process Management

The first spontaneous group discussions in this *"orientation" phase* are trend-setting events. The leaders initially outline important group rules and boundaries, including confidentiality, attendance, punctuality, and active participation. As the session progresses, the leaders work to cultivate a supportive, cohesive, and task-enhancing group climate. Process norms of open discussion, relevant self-disclosure, and attention to pressing here-and-now reactions to the didactic material are suggested and specifically reinforced.

In a focused psychoeducational, theme-centered effort, the explicit aim is to use the emerging group process to support and personalize exploration of the contracted focus. That is, the leaders constantly ask themselves: "How does this emergent process relate to the task of stress management?" Facilitators then link emergent dynamics directly to the prescribed didactic material. In distinction to psychotherapy, the leaders respond to the participants' personal expressions and emotional needs by directly relating them to the group's thematic focus (Shaffer & Galinsky, 1974), rather than to more personal, etiologically inspired, characterological problems of the individual members.

High hopes and anticipatory fears are a normal part of this first stage of any group experience. In this group, the leaders' choice is whether to address the initial anxiety or attempt to channel or bypass it and go directly to the psychoeducational material. Given the group task of teaching stress management, the emerging stress reactions precipitated by coming together as a group are directly explored as a lead-in to the psychoeducational content. Thus, in an initial "group go-around," members are invited to comment on what stresses brought them to the group, and on how they are experiencing and coping with "this new and stressful experience."

In this orientation phase, it is important to point out concurrences, similarities, and universalities in member experiences so that the group can coalesce around common concerns. Thus, the leaders listen to member responses and generalize about stress inducers and stress reactions, all the time facilitating discussion, questioning, and involvement. The built-in homogeneity in this group is the prevalence of Type-A behaviors. When the particular manifestatons of the stress response are outlined in detail in prepared presentations, the leaders act in consultancy to the membership. Following a dual-intervention strategy, "live material" generated within the session is also used as a springboard and source of example and amplification. Such an approach creates and maintains involved and curious learners while using the abstract didactic material as cognitive binding for real and emergent feelings.

Session 3: Building Stress Awareness— Coping Strategies

Subtask and Content
Participants' awareness of the internal and external events that cause them stress are explored. Individuals' physical, emotional, and behavioral responses to these stressful events are identified.

Group Process
The two members (Jim and Susan) who were absent last meeting arrive 45 minutes late. They report that the Chief Administrator has called a weekly meeting which usually runs over in time, just prior to the stress group. The late members begin to monopolize the session, with Jim appearing hostile and Susan seeming agitated and frantic. The group's boundaries, leadership, and very existence are challenged as members talk about other responsibilities impinging on this time together.

Process Management
Here is a group process that cannot be easily ignored. The planned subtask and content elaboration are interrupted with the entry of the new members. Boundary challenges have to be resolved in order to reestablish the viability and integrity of the group. Such "storming," doubt, and turbulent questioning is normal for the *"dissatisfaction/resolution" phase* of a group's development. It is critical that the leader be prepared for this normative crisis point, nondefensively allowing the boundary challenge to stretch group possibilities, while providing enough adhesion to hold the group together when solidifying participatory commitments.

Initially, when the new members arrive, confusion ensues. None of the already engaged participants knows how or whether to proceed with the format underway. The coleaders assume control by welcoming the latecomers and gently pointing out that their arrival is stress inducing for all involved. The group is given the new and immediate task of resolving the issues of continuity, punctuality, and attendance. The leaders reframe the present conflict in stress-management language, and move to facilitate problem solving and conflict resolution. Specifically, the leaders acknowledge the interruption and invite the group to "consider how to handle the stress of the new members' arrival as an example of the myriad of times when the flow of their work is interrupted by a new and pressing crisis."

Jim initially responds by saying how impossible it is to make it to the group. Without demonstrating any emotional connection or investment in the proceedings, his assessments are pessimistic and his suggestions are destructive to the group's vitality and purpose. Jim suggests that the group meet for half its allotted time, starting later and ending earlier. After some discussion, the group leaders hold the boundaries firm by saying that "the group's primary task of teaching stress management cannot be accomplished in such a reduced time period."

This strong leader intervention begins to shift the flow of the crisis toward the dynamics underlying the interruption and uncertainty. The group begins to talk about the stress of having a new administrator. They are all "on their toes." Some feel insecure about their jobs, while others believe that they have to prove themselves anew. Jim's job is specifically in jeopardy, a fact he does not reveal, but rather acts out by missing a session, coming late, and ultimately rejecting the group (intrapsychic/interpersonal process). In a parallel process, the members are also working on their dependence and anxiety about pleasing their new and present authority figures—the group leaders. Performance anxieties and pressure around authority are pinpointed and discussed as an example of a generalized stress inducer.

Here, the anger at the chief administrator, or "identification against the aggressor," helps to consolidate the group's energies and commitments to each other and to the collective as a body. It should be pointed out that "resistance from above" is a common difficulty in organizational groups. It is a consultative maxim that the facilitator's point of entry usually defines the level of possible accomplishment. Cohn (1969) strongly recommends that "the group therapist-leader must know the hierarchy of staff functions before he intervenes. . . . A positive working relationship with top management must take priority before working with other staff groups" (p. 261). Similarly, Agazarian and Peters (1981) point out that every system is multilayered. The superordinate system, in this case the organization itself, makes up the cultural milieu within which this particular task group operates. In deductive paradigm, the stress-management group provides information about the stresses evident in the larger context, while in turn being influenced from on high.

In this session, the leaders allay and normalize fears and help the group realistically define the challenge to its mission and existence. Enabling solutions (Whitaker & Lieberman, 1964) are sought, which allow the group to manage successfully its first turbulence. During this dissatisfaction phase, norms are established concerning conflict management, leadership is solidified, and critical boundaries are redefined and reaffirmed. Various members begin to demonstrate their level of commitment to the group and to formalize the nature of their group participation. Are they in or out, up or down (dominant or submissive)? The group's being able to move successfully from dissatisfaction to resolution models optimum stress management. Thus, the psychoeducational group becomes a workshop as well as a classroom.

Session 4: Cognitive Stress Intervention—The Art of Using Your Head

Subtask and Content
Participants are educated about how their cognitions affect their stress responses. An A-B-C (Antecedent-Belief-Consequence) model of stress is introduced (Ellis & Harper, 1975).

Group Process
As the meeting begins (Barry, Don, Gary, and Curt present), obvious tension is apparent between Barry and Curt (emerging interpersonal process). During the week, they exchanged angry memos about a mix up in interoffice responsibilities.

Process Management
The leaders are faced with another immediate decision of whether to push on with the didactic material, especially since the group is already behind schedule due to last week's boundary negotiations, or whether to acknowledge and work with the present conflict between Curt and Barry. It is quickly decided that Curt and Barry, now comprising 50 percent of the available membership, have to be addressed. They are invited to air their misunderstanding within the context of the group task. "Would you be willing to tell us about what 'stress' has arisen between you two, so that we can both help out and use your real situation to learn about how thoughts affect our stress reactions?" Some of the work in conflict resolution the previous week makes it safer and more inviting to do so.

Psychoeducation, in part, consists of generalized learning arising from particular instances. Here, the leaders move the group from the issue of memos to the challenge of direct and effective communication, trying in the process to help each member identify his own effective and ineffective communication styles. In the service of the content requirements of the session, both Barry and Curt are encouraged to identify their "automatic thoughts," or subvocal reactions concerning the memo incident. The discussion is then translated into the A-B-C model for generalization and teaching purposes.

The nature and timing of this emerging group conflict is not random or necessarily interruptive. Members often serve the larger group needs as spokespersons (group-as-a-whole process), moving the group along its developmental course by presenting issues in line with the agreed upon focal theme. Thus, boundary issues arose in "dissatisfaction/resolution," and the "memo conflict" marks the beginning of the *"working/production" phase*. The material arising introduces the group's necessary work of identifying how cognitions (automatic thoughts) affect stress responses, foreshadowing a formal consideration of how to develop more effective coping strategies. To ignore or circumvent this group process would be to miss its timely communicative and symbolic value. The leader moves in the right direction when he or she can find "a direct point of contact between the workshop's theme and the immediate event in the group that highlighted and illuminated it" (Shaffer & Galinsky, 1974, p. 243).

Before the session ends, the missing member issues are readdressed. Bill is expected back in two weeks. The group leader indicates her intention to call Jim and propose that he come to all the remaining sessions if he is to continue in the group. Since attendance and punctuality remain a problem for this group of busy and overcommitted executives, the norms of continuity and commitment are again reinforced with those present.

Session 5: Automatic Thoughts/Self-Talk

Subtask and Content

Members are taught to identify automatic thoughts through different stages of the life cycle by recalling stressful events from their childhood, adolescence, and adulthood. Once these events are identified, then recurrent patterns, resultant stress reactions, and evident coping strategies are noted and explored.

Group Process

Two members are present (Don and Curt). Susan does not show up. Bill and Gary are away on business. Barry is on vacation. After a call from one of the group leaders, Jim has decided to drop out. Initially, the two members are hesitant about participating.

Process Management

Having only two members present certainly affects the available group process. Cohen and Rice (1985) advise that group leaders recognize the bonding potential and therapeutic value of the small groups and project a confidence in the "group enough" group. Moreno (1953) reports experiences with groups as small as two. Most therapists have had experience in individual and couples therapy and so can adjust their model to fit the group size. Basic principles of group interaction and member-to-member communication can and should be preserved.

Here, realities and feelings about the "small group" are processed. The group leaders take an encouraging stance. "While it would be good to have everyone here, what might we accomplish in this more intimate setting?" With the leaders' support, the group, as so composed, agrees that two members are the minimum required for holding a session and decide to move ahead with the agenda. With morale preserved, participation available, and a quorum norm established, the preplanned work begins. This session allows for some focus on personal history and intrapsychic dynamics, and turns out to be quite moving as both Curt and Don remember touching and telling stories about their pasts.

Material from the past and the conflictual roots of current stress reactions are explicitly solicited. However in contrast to psychoanalytic psychotherapy, the leaders guard against any overt regression, working instead at the members' highest level of achievement, maturity, and self-control (Cohn, 1969). In fact, members self-select poignant rather than traumatic events to report. The leaders encourage progressive use of the historical material, hearkening forward to current stress reactions. Early memories and affective reminiscences are given current cognitive context, as they are converted to lessons and generalizations about the stress response. Primitive affects are avoided or, if arising, are quickly rechanneled into the service of ego enhancement and problem solving. For example, on hearing about a childhood trauma, the leader might say, "That must have been painful back then. How would you handle a similar stressful situation now, as an adult?"

Session 6: Changing Automatic Thoughts— Thinking Differently

Subtask and Content
Participants are given an opportunity to practice changing their automatic thoughts. Various distorted automatic thought patterns are highlighted, including blaming (placing responsibility for your actions on someone else), filtering (picking out the negative aspects of an event and magnifying them, while disregarding the positive aspects), and mind reading (making snap judgments about what people are thinking, feeling, or doing, while attributing motivational causes to their actions).

Group Process

Four members are present (Gary, Don, Barry, and Bill). Curt is out sick. One of the leaders relates that Susan was called, and it was decided that, because of her many absences and inability to commit firmly to the remaining sessions, she would formally withdraw from group.

Process Management

In the service of continuity, Don is encouraged to tell last week's absent members what went on in the previous session. Some discussion of attendance follows, and the previously absent members maintain that problems attending the group mirror problems they generally have in controlling their own schedules and time commitments. The stress-inducing aspects of overcommitted scheduling are briefly discussed.

The leaders now present didactic material on distorted automatic thought patterns. Bill takes exception to the "filtering" concept and argues that successful people need to focus in a one dimensional manner, as an instance of troubleshooting. He cites many examples of successful athletes whose distorted onesidedness fostered dedication and excellence, while conceding that other areas of their lives suffered. The rest of the group rallies to this theme. At no other time is the Type-A orientation of this group of highly stressed executives more evident.

The group leaders now face an important choice point. Should they encourage and facilitate further discussion of success-driven behavior, or steer back to the prepared didactic material? Much energy is invested in the current discussion, and the leaders decide to allow the evolving process to flow freely. What follows very much resembles a psychotherapy session. Members tell of their underlying beliefs and reveal their personal struggles for success and fears of failure. The leaders encourage such self-disclosure and interaction, and gently point out consequences of this driven approach to life in an attempt to dent the ego-syntonic, Type-A stance. Concepts of balance, task boundaries, and prioritizing are introduced as new mediating variables for coping with overcommitment, onesidedness, and stressful living.

Both leaders experience strong countertransferential reactions during this session. Both come in touch with the "success-driven" parts of their own lives. Such a reactive identification helps the leaders understand the group members' entrenched Type-A positions by way of their own susceptibility to overwork in response to increasing professional responsibilities. Since this theme-centered group operates more within a normative than an overtly pathological field, the leaders have an extra degree of freedom for self-disclosure. Without getting too ego involved or using the group to work out their own conflicts, the leaders' reactions to the "drive for success" might be shared as a lead-in, model, or counterbalance to the group members' proclivity toward stress-enhancing behaviors. Leader self-disclosure should be used only in cases where actively joining the resistance will more clearly focus, normalize, and work through the theme. Here, the facilitators' revealing their own relation to the "success issue" humanizes the work and fosters a more intimate sharing about the ambivalence inherent in these difficult life choices.

Session 7: Changing Automatic Thoughts (continued)

Subtask and Content
Participants are given further practice at recognizing and changing their automatic thoughts by becoming more familiar with a great variety of cognitive distortions generative of stress reactions.

Group Process
Two members, Curt and Barry, are present. Bill, Don and Gary are absent. Curt needs to leave early for a business meeting.

Process Management
With two members present and Curt having to leave early, it is decided to do a general review during this session and to wait until next week to move ahead. Barry, who has some administrative responsibility for this group, is upset by the ongoing lack of attendance. The leaders suggest that we use the A-B-C model to explore Barry's feelings and thoughts.

Curt is supportive of Barry's concerns, and subtle relationship repair continues (memo altercation). Much work can be accomplished within the healing process of the group interaction, regardless of the content being considered. In line with the previous norm of two members needed for a quorum, the group is ended early when Curt leaves.

The group leaders subsequently discuss amongst themselves how to reaffirm participation and "finish strong." After this session, three meetings remain. The group is now one session behind in its planned format. The leaders decide that next session they will directly address the work that remains, offer an additional session, and solicit a renewed commitment from the participants.

Normally, extending the therapeutic contract is contraindicated since such an action violates agreed upon temporal boundaries and fosters the fantasy of unlimited time to work out problems. Certainly, extending the number of sessions of a group in its termination phase would be a regressive move and an acting out of dependency issues. In this group, however, the decision is to make up the abbreviated session, to extend the working phase, and to intervene actively in order to prevent premature termination. The leaders are guided by an intuitive sense of what is needed for closure and successful completion with this particular group. It is important, however, to present the additional session as a group option, with unanimous consent needed to change the group boundary. The leader always guards against sacrificing the sanctity of the circle in the service of enlarging or enriching it.

Session 8: Internal-External Locus of Control— How to Change

Subtask and Content
A measure of internal/external control (the subjective sense of how much one's destiny is controlled by oneself and how much by external forces) is explained and administered as another example of a cognitive distortion leading to stress. Participants are given the opportunity to identify and practice shifting their locus of control so that their perceived influence will be closer to their actual/real impact.

Group Process
Four of five members are present (Don, Bill, Barry, and Curt). The issue of the remaining work and time is raised, and group decisions are fostered. A discussion spontaneously begins, spurred by the internal/external control measure.

Process Management
The leaders begin the group by raising the issue of the time and work remaining. The group is formally offered an additional session in the service of completion and a strong finish. After a brief discussion, members agree to extend the contract. The integrity of the group is thereby consolidated.

The locus of control measure is administered and members begin predicting the scores of mutual acquaintances. To bring the discussion "into the room," it is suggested that they predict their own and each other's scores. These predictions are recorded and a lively interchange follows. Allowing some exploration of the amount of internal control exerted by mutual acquaintances helps anchor the scale. The leaders believe, however, that predicting each other's scores will increase feedback and interaction, as well as personalize the learning. The working phase of any group is normally marked by direct member-to-member interaction and confrontation. Joint mastery, skills acquisition, insight, consensual validation, and mutual cooperation are invoked. Team work, very much in evidence here, is of the essence.

Session 9: "Shoulds, Oughts, and Musts"

Subtask and Content

Participants are familiarized with various "shoulds, oughts, and musts" (inflexible rules, values, and codes of conduct for oneself and others) in order to enhance awareness of the constraining aspects of their automatic thoughts, and to encourage members to "think differently." A "Shoulds Test" is administered, scored, and discussed.

Group Process

All members are present. A playfulness ensues as an extension of the intimacy and sharing of the preceding session. Gary appears somewhat confused and left out, since he missed the last two sessions.

Process Management

The spirit of the work atmosphere is reinforced by the group leaders. Gary, who seems surprised by the camaraderie, is specifically reinvolved. The participants' predictions and actual scores on the "Shoulds Test" are charted. Members note their own scores and compare them to each others', with much involvement and relating to previous group history. This continuation of the comparative process, begun last session, allows for additional reality testing and consensual validation around stress-related matters.

The comparisons spur further self-disclosure and exploration. The group leaders facilitate the discussion and explore how various beliefs, such as perfectionism, lead to stress. The group points out to Gary the extreme nature of his scores. He acknowledges yet rationalizes their significance. The consultant supportively confronts Gary about his disavowal and takes the opportunity to point out that he consistently minimizes the effects of his stress. Gary has bragged about how much aggravation and abuse he accepts from his superiors without showing any "outside" reaction. Previous testing has shown that he holds much "inside," to the point of somatization. It is suggested to Gary that his disavowal of distress is quite convincing to others who are then likely to place more demands on him, thereby exponentially increasing his inner turmoil. Gary is coached to let others know when he has had enough so they will back off.

In a psychotherapy group, the motivation and etiology behind Gary's inability to admit his vulnerabilities would be explored. Likewise, his ready supply of "shoulds, oughts, and musts" would be analyzed with respect to his need to appear competent and unassailable. In a short-term psychoeducational group, the leader relies more on direct interventions like clarification of stress-inducing behaviors, teaching new coping skills, and coaching the members on how to respond innovatively. Dynamic issues are guided back toward the theme (Cohn, 1969), as members are encouraged to use the healthy parts of their ego to integrate suggestions in the spirit of relearning and reacting with novel adaptation.

It is not coincidental that Gary became the center of attention and target of intervention. Because he missed the previous sessions, he was outside the group's cohesive circle. Focusing on an outsider requires a tricky balance between inviting reentry without spurring further exclusion through scapegoating. Here, other members are encouraged by the facilitators to respond to Gary, as exemplar rather than as martyr. While specifically analyzing his dysfunctional relations to authority, the other members are also invited to relate their own versions of his story.

Session 10: Problem Solving—Coping More Effectively

Subtask and Content

Participants are taught a simple, structured, six-step problem-solving approach for dealing with life's hassles, and are encouraged to generate flexibility and innovation in their response modes.

Group Process

The consultant is absent for medical reasons. Under the tutelage of the coleader, the group follows a more structured approach. A theoretical example of a problem arising between a male boss and a female secretary is presented as a working example. There is some sexist kidding between the all-male group of executives and the female facilitator.

Process Management

Sexuality, along with competition, is an important issue worked on in the "production/working" phase of a group's development. In a psychotherapy context, evident Oedipal fantasies stimulated by the male coleader's absence and the sudden exclusive possession of the female authority, might be explored. In this psychoeducational context, the leader uses the sexual tension and transference to foster a consideration of the stressful aspects of male/female and female/male supervisory relationships. Gary talks of his relief that Susan, his supervisor, left the group.

Curt then raises questions about the biofeedback stage of stress management training, a separate part of the overall consultative package. His inquiries have a genuine information-gathering component, while also expressing feelings about the upcoming end of this group experience, thereby marking entry into the *"termination/graduation" phase*. The group now officially acknowledges that next week is the last session and speaks about bringing in coffee and doughnuts.

Ritualization of endings is a common cultural phenomenon. Funerals formalize the mourning process and symbolize a passing on. Graduation ceremonies celebrate the commencement process and mark a passing along. It is critical that a "breaking bread" ritual does not replace a verbal summing up and emotional closing of the group experience. Any such rite of passage should punctuate the ending process, not merely cater it (Rutan, 1985).

Session 11: Additional Practice Problem Solving— Facilitating Understanding and Generalization

Subtask and Content

Participants are given further practice in using the problem-solving model introduced in the previous session. Understanding and generalization of the various procedures is facilitated.

Group Process

The group begins the session by talking and kidding among themselves. They seem resistant to coming up with an additional problem to work on.

Process Management

Many times, in the beginnings of a group session, it seems like time is being wasted in small talk. While the group may in fact be resisting work, at other times a conflict-free warm-up period is a necessary prerequisite to beginning the work at hand. Members need to reconnect before the more intimate and anxiety-provoking group tasks can be approached directly. In this case, the group is in fact warming down. This is the last session and the members need to end the group experience and take leave from the leaders and from one another. Thus, they initially prefer easy relating and joking to a serious rededication to the psychoeducational task. The light manner actually belies many closing processes being accomplished in the warm-down.

This particular group consists of coworkers who will likely remain in some contact within the vocational setting. Some will even continue in the next stage of treatment, though not necessarily together. Yet, this collective is ending and the work of the stress management group proper must be brought to conclusion.

Curt serves as group spokesperson when, out of the social banter, he produces a summary symbol of the shared experience. Curt asks members if they saw the recent Disney movie about a "bionic husband." He describes how the protagonist left job after job due to stress. The hero then has an accident and is given bionic parts. Now he can "handle anything."

Often, out of apparent tangential randomness of group talk, one member will bring the group together by suggesting an image or symbol that coalesces the energy and meaning in the room (Hobson, 1959; Ettin, 1986). The bionic husband image represents the fantasied wishes and prevalent fears of these Type-A male executives. "To handle the many challenges and stresses in life, one needs to be superhuman." A similar theme underlies many sessions, most especially the free-floating discussion of success and failure. The multidetermined bionic image also signifies the place of the stress-management training in providing members with some concrete help and added strength (bionic parts) when facing up to the multitudes of life's demands.

Gary now circulates a newspaper article on how people make their own stress—a testimony to the impact of the work on internal/external locus of control accomplished in the previous session. This literature also serves, instead of coffee and cake, a thematic motto that summarizes the joint psychoeducational effort, as if to say, "Stress can be controlled."

With the leaders' prompting, the group does move to some final didactic practice in problem solving. Two potential problems are chosen for consideration: enforcing nonsmoking regulations and encouraging a dress code that would increase the public's respect for the organization. These issues metaphorically reflect members' desire to move on from here in a more healthful and self-respecting manner. Throughout the discussion, the participants use terminology and concepts learned in the group, thus demonstrating that a meaningful framework has been communicated and adopted.

The leaders now turn the group's attention to the imminent termination. The consultant models self-disclosure by sharing his reactions to the group's ending. It is suggested that members address the nature of their own group experiences, including "what has been accomplished and what has been left undone."

The leaders accept and support members' disclosures and critiques. Keeping within the agreed upon thematic focus, the facilitators reframe the participants' comments by encouraging realistic assessments of the group experience uncontaminated by automatic idealistic or perfectionist strivings. In the service of generalization, members are encouraged to purposefully call to mind and actively practice what they have learned. The group ends with handshakes and well wishes.

Termination is a very important group phase and one that often receives insufficient time and attention. The last session is not generally a good time to introduce new material. The pull inside the room is toward ending what is unfinished. New material that cannot be monitored, worked through, or assimilated should not be introduced. In this last phase, the group needs to come to terms with the accomplishments and limitations of their shared experience. The conclusion of the contracted work makes a terminus—a threshold that signals both an ending and a moving on.

Feedback Between Task and Process

As a result of this consultation and group experience, the stress-management program has revised its pregroup procedures. A feedback/orientation/contracting session has been added to the intervention package. In this session, reactions to the stress evaluations are discussed and other pregroup tasks are accomplished with the group facilitator. Specific steps are also being taken to secure firmer initial participatory contracts. Additionally, the amount of information to be covered in each session is under consideration, as greater priority is being given to working with predictable and spontaneous group processes in the service of task enhancement.

Cohn (1969) eloquently summarizes the ebb and flow of task and process in theme-centered, psychoeducational groups.

> *The method leans heavily on dualism. Freud advised us to lead the patient to the past if he stays too long in the present and into the present if he ponders about the past. Similarly, the theme-centered group is guided back and forth between intellectual considerations and emotional experiences; between intrapsychic and interpersonal involvement; between intergroup and outside world phenomena; between strict adherence to the theme and free associations and interactions. The leader functions within this model in the duality of being a participant group member who thinks, feels, and reveals himself, and as a leader who uses his background knowledge to steer away from group pathology, regressive movement, and fixation to either side of the chosen theme. (p. 266)*

Thus, the theme-centered, psychoeducational group requires an ongoing balancing of *task* and *process,* as well as a blending of structured intervention with unstructured discussion. Members are never passive recipients of information. Participants have a built-in need to react, speak to, and personalize the material presented to them. As members move through the group together, individual dynamics are inevitably stimulated and acted out, interpersonal styles and communication patterns emerge and provoke reactions, and natural group-level concerns arise at each successive stage of involvement. Such collective processes can either impede or enhance the nature and applicability of the psychoeducational content. It is strongly suggested that group process be viewed as an opportunity for assimilation, rather than an interruption to the didactic presentation. Then, each encounter between the material presented and what presently materializes becomes a most precious learning opportunity.

CHAPTER TEN

Group Development:
Building Protocols for Psychoeducational Groups

Groups are made, not born. An unsupervised, chaotic horde characterized by raw excitation, regression, contagion, and poor judgment (LeBon, 1977) can be transformed into a progressive psychological grouping of high purpose and character. By introducing ongoing organizational structures, continuity of membership, specialization and differentiation of individual function within the group, and the development of norms, customs, traditions, habits, rituals, and interactive rules, the collective can become a civilized working enterprise (McDougall, 1973).

Constructive use of the group format is especially relevant when people are brought together for a short term for the express purpose of psychoeducation. Here, the focus and intent of making a group is most clearly delineated. Tight time constraints and set purposes demand the efficient use of various naturally occurring group processes while working within the inherent structure of the developing group. Ideally, group dynamics will be channeled toward the mastery of various symptoms (depression, anxiety), habits (smoking, overeating, drug use), developmental milestones (latency, adolescence, young adulthood, menopause, old age), organizational problems (morale, productivity, problem solving), or normative (relocating, parenting) and traumatic (divorce, sexual abuse) life crises. The list of possible group foci and subsequent collective clinical intervention strategies is limited only by the varied approaches possible to the many common experiences engendered by growth, life, and relationship.

Psychoeducational (Budman, Bennet, & Wisnewski, 1981; Druck, 1978; Drum & Knot, 1977), theme-centered (Cohn, 1969, 1972; Shaffer &

An earlier version of this chapter coauthored with Marsha Heiman and Steven Kopel, appeared in *Group, 12* (4), 205–225, copyright 1988. Reprinted with permission of Brunner/Mazel, Inc.

Galinsky, 1974), and focused short-term groups (R. Klein, 1985; Poey, 1985) are highly visible and efficient treatment modalities popular in hospitals, clinics, counseling centers, and industry. The impetus for the formation of a particular group can result from a pressing organizational dilemma, such as a clinic waiting list, or can arise out of a predictable and recurrent organizational snafu, such as underlying unrest or undue stress in the workplace. In the former case, initial contacts and existing caseloads may reveal a homogeneity of complaints that intuitively suggests the possibility of a combined treatment approach. In the latter case, since the problems are environmentally or collectively induced, group treatment becomes the logical intervention alternative.

In other instances, the idea and energy behind forming a psychoeducational group may come from the specialized interest and expertise of a particular practitioner. A studied curiosity about panic disorder, for example, may spur a clinician to seek out select treatment cases. The group format provides a particularly apt setting for the therapist to disseminate knowledge while working along a shared focus and simultaneously learning from the phenomenological experiences of the members.

Whatever the impetus for the formation of a psychoeducational group, the prospective leader often approaches the thematic focus (whether panic disorder or organizational stress) with certain dynamic formulations, clinical observations and experiences, and various programmatic and treatment notions. As practitioners consolidate their experiences and expertise, a model may seemingly call out for ordered and structured presentation. Assuming the availability of a willing and homogeneous population, the theme-focused psychoeducational group is formed. For such a group to succeed, its purpose, process, and design must quickly congeal, with the group's growth and development planfully built, shaped, monitored, and managed.

What we know about the natural evolution of small-group processes and dynamics must be wedded with an expertise in the phenomenology and psychodynamics of the particular theme, issue, topic, or pathology chosen as the psychoeducational focus. A knowledge of group dynamics and group process becomes the critical, although often ignored, determinant of the ultimate maturation and fruition of the psychoeducational conception. To enhance and personalize the psychoeducational experience, the choice, order, and method of presenting didactic material should be masterfully matched with the dynamic realities of the evolving group processes and tightly linked to the readily developing receptivities of participants.

This chapter will present a general model of group development that can serve as a template onto which to build, organize, and order any particular content or group focus. To demonstrate the utility of the model, two populations with extremely diverse thematic foci, smoking cessation and

latency incest, will be used to illustrate the ordering of the group protocol
and the building of appropriate didactic structures.

Defining Characteristics of Psychoeducational Groups

The Leader as Content Expert and Task Organizer

Any consideration of the basic characteristics of psychoeducational
groups begins with the expertise of the leader in the subject matter that is
to make up the group's central focus. Even in the classroom, however, the
most knowledgeable professor is not necessarily the best teacher. Considerable skill and sensitivity is necessary to create a learning environment and
to handle the multiple flow of communication necessary for assimilation of
the presented material. When psychotherapeutics becomes an added aim,
the give and take of action and reaction in the group becomes even more
technically complex and crucial to the meaningful adoption of the material.
Here, focusing on a targeted issue with a select clientele will elicit personalized responses and evoke groupwide reactions. Such predictable occurrence
needs to be actively anticipated, acknowledged, and prefigured into the resultant group protocol.

Developing a group protocol, much like a traditional lesson plan,
allows material to be ordered and structured according to sound group dynamic principles and made consistent with the members' evolving ability to
take up and take in the material. It is suggested that prior to the group's
convening, the leader develop a session-by-session outline to serve as the
skeletal frame around which to build structures and to plan didactics, discussions, and other psychoeducational exercises and activities. After the
thematic flow of the sessions is sketched, within-session planning, including
the use of specific didactics and experiential components, can be added in
and fleshed out in detail. The actualities of the group experience will require
modifications of pace and substance, but the initial framing can guide and
organize the experience.

Determining the Optimum Group Size

The size of psychoeducational groups varies from the large audience
to the small interactive group. As the size of the the group decreases, the
initiation of interactions shifts from the podium to the circle. Even in the
large-audience format, learning can be enhanced and personalized by subsequent small-group processing, akin to the lecture/lab format. The size of

the small interactive psychoeducational group depends on how many members the structure can accommodate and how many members can accommodate to the structure. A *small work group* might be defined as the optimum number of members who can interact intimately in one setting. This number will vary according to population and task. A small interactive adult group may be able to accommodate from 5 to 10 members, whereas a children's activity group will function best with 4 to 6 participants.

Given the progressive nature of the presented material, it is very difficult to add new members once a short-term psychoeducational group is underway. Some dropout (15 to 35 percent) is normal. Consequently, it is practical to begin with a group at the upper matriculation limit, and it is critical to conscientiously screen and select members who demonstrate the best chance of staying the course.

Selecting a Homogeneous Focus and Finding a Heterogeneous Member Mix

Psychoeducational groups are inherently homogeneous. Members are selected and a group is formed around a common theme. Such a built-in focus makes for ready cohesion and clearly defined goals. However, just because members share a common problem does not necessarily guarantee that they can work together. Selection considerations must also include individual appropriateness for group, situational and motivational availability, and the compositional compatibility of the group mix.

Predetermining the thematic focus does not save the group leader from conducting evaluations and making thoughtful selection decisions. A common mistake made in the name of expediency is to begin the group sight-unseen with self-selected or other-referred patients. Such streamlining is not recommended since the tasks of the pregroup (evaluation, selection, preparation, contracting, and establishing a working alliance) are critical to the ultimate success of this joint endeavor. Consequently, the leader should meet with each prospective member individually for assessment and to clarify and secure agreement on the participatory contract before convening the group.

Although prospective members may be homogeneous for psychoeducational focus (e.g. smoking, sexual abuse), there can be wide differences in demographics, life experiences, character, and coping styles, as well as in motivations for participating. Normal exclusion criteria for short-term treatment (Malan, 1976), short-term groups (Poey, 1985), and group participation in general (Grunebaum & Kates, 1977; Yalom, 1970) must be followed. Once individual appropriateness is decided, the selection goal becomes to match members who are similar enough to relate and work together and different enough to present a wide continuum of possible perspectives, feelings, and coping strategies around the common concern. Such a heterogeneous mix within a homogeneous focus creates a potentially rich interpersonal learning environment.

Using Didactic Instruction and Structured Exercises

The active use of didactics and structured exercises to teach and work along the central focus differentiates psychoeducational from traditional process groups (Buchanan, 1980; Lazell, 1930; Marsh, 1933; Mintz, 1971,1974; Pfeiffer & Jones, 1975; Saretsky, 1977; Zweben & Hammann, 1970). Following a psychoeducational format, a range of information is purposefully disseminated and a variety of experiences specifically encouraged. The mark of a valuable lesson is that it most succinctly addresses common concerns—those shared elements that are intricately and intrinsically subsumed by the chosen focus. Members move from recognition through self-understanding to self-acceptance and the active assimilation of new perspectives. Timely and targeted exercises foster awareness and amplify affects along the shared focus.

Members move from heightened experiencing, through increased risk taking, to the enhanced accommodation and the adaptation of expanded behavioral repertoires. When choosing pointed or poignant structures to further psychoeducation, it is critical to select material and to build exercises specific to the needs of the members, appropriate to the overall goals of the group, sensitive to the ready availability of the participants, and consistent with the various phases of the treatment process (Ettin, 1989d; Saretsky, 1977). With each progressive group phase comes inherent dynamics that can be harnessed in the service of knowledge acquisition and skill enhancement.

Contracting for a Specific Time Limit

Time-limited psychoeducational groups usually range from 6 to 20 sessions, with the normative mean between 8 and 12 meetings. As the lower session limit is approached, the group more resembles crisis intervention, with the leader in the authoritative role of expert/provider and the members in the dependent role of novice/receiver. As the upper session limit is approached, the group more resembles a traditional open-ended therapy/discussion group, with the leader's role shifting to educator/facilitator or interactive participant/observer, and the members' complementary roles approaching learner/discussant or initiator/respondent. As the number of sessions increases, members' latent dynamics invariably come to the fore, as affect-laden material is increasingly stimulated. As the embedded and the underlying arise, it becomes more difficult to stay strictly within the chosen focus and to adhere to a directed, task-focused approach.

The number of sessions planned is, in part, related to the requisite specificity, complexity, and chronicity of the chosen theme, the amount of material to be presented, the diversity of subthemes to be covered, and the goals set out to be accomplished. Particular psychoeducational foci will require a conscripted body of material, based on inherent phenomenology, dynamics, and treatment requirements. Thus, a smoking cessation group with a tight symptomatic focus may be amenable to a 6- or 8-session contract, whereas a sexual abuse group reflecting a variety of intersecting issues may require additional sessions to adequately handle symptomatic and situational sequelae. In either case, it is critical to preestablish and hold to the agreed upon session count. By adhering to the numerical structure of the experience, the various phase-specific dynamics are stimulated to occur in proper sequence with their full instructive and transformative potentials intact.

Group Development and Phase-Specific Dynamics

A model of group development is adapted for psychoeducational purposes from Lacoursiere (1980), as derived from the earlier work of, among others, Bennis and Shepard (1956) and Tuckman (1965). This section, summarized in Table 10-1, provides a rationale and a format for group building that takes into account progressive group phases, leadership roles, and psychoeducational tasks, as well as inherent member decisions, morale issues, group dynamics (Bradford, 1978; Cartwright & Lippitt, 1978; Day 1981; Durkin, 1964, 1976; Kissen, 1976a, 1976b), and curative variables (Yalom, 1970). This model also suggests guidelines for breaking down the number of available group sessions by percentage of the whole contract, according to relative phase-specific temporal requirements.

Pregroup Phase

The pregroup phase begins before the group proper is convened. Working with the targeted population, the leader evaluates each prospective member individually according to the criteria set up in the planning stages, assessing homogeneity, group fit, specificity of symptoms, and availability for treatment. Appropriate members are selected and prepared for the upcoming experience by imparting information about the goals, rules, procedures, and common focus of the group. Initial queries and resistances are worked through, and expectations and relevant prior experiences (including

TABLE 10-1 • Format for Group Building

	Pregroup I	Phase II	Phase IIIa	Phase IIIb	Phase IV	Phase V
Group Phase	Preparation	Orientation	Dissatisfaction	Resolution	Working/Production	Termination/Graduation
Group Task	"Borning"	"Forming"	"Storming"	"Norming"	"Performing"	"Adjourning"
Phase of Human Development	Birth	Infancy/Latency	Adolescence	Young Adulthood	Maturity	Old Age
Member Decisions	Interest-Disinterest	In-Out	Up-Down		More-Less	Before-After
Morale Issues	Questions Prior experience Expectations Needs	High hopes Anticipatory fears Heavy reliance on leader	Questioning Doubt Frustration Crisis of confidence	Acceptance Leap of faith	Positive feelings of involvment Interdependence Mastery Confidence Skills acquisition	Coming to terms with loss Preparing for future Moving on
Leader Role	Evaluation Selection Preparation Contracting Working alliance	Orientation Define tasks Set stage Create working atmosphere	Allay & normalize fears Foster enabling norms Protect the group boundary Help realistically define possibilities Begin to develop plans & skills to succeed		Facilitate work & maximize learning Foster didactic & skills training Encourage insight & feedback	Process ending Review Learn from experience Plan & generalize

Continued

Psychoeducational Tasks	Assess homogeneity & fit Understand individual variation on theme	Establish focus Teach basic terminology & concepts Probe dynamics & phenomology of theme Highlight similarities & common dynamics	Allow & contain affective component of theme	Promote mutuality, identification, cohesion Channel resistance into alliance against the dysfunctional aspects of the central focus	Present major didactic thrust Foster comparative activities & interactions Foster risk taking & change Support uniqueness & individuality	Review Generalize Close Move on
Group Psychodynamic Issues	Working alliance	Positive transference & expectations Identification Common group fantasies Urge to share & pressure to self-disclose Dependency on leader	Negative transference Resistance Acting out Acting in Counterdependence Contagion Ambivalence Fight-flight	Ventilation Norm setting Boundary consolidation Containment of affect	Reality testing Imitation Insight Sublimation Working through Interdependence Consensual validation Identification Vicarious learning Confrontation Knowledge acquisition Modeling Competition Cooperation Multiple transferences	Termination Independence Loss Disappointment Group history Resolution of cutoffs Working through of curtain calls

TABLE 10-1 • Continued

	Pregroup I	Phase II	Phase IIIa	Phase IIIb	Phase IV	Phase V
Curative Factors	Instillation of hope Universality	Curative fantasies Belonging	Catharsis Ventilation	Cohesiveness Containment	Imitative behavior Altruism Interpersonal learning Development of socializing techniques Recapitulation of primary family experiences	Existential impact of participating and completing group experience
			◀—— Imparting information ——▶			
% Session by Phase	10%	10%	15%	15%	50%	15%
Number of Sessions by Phase						

Total	Pregroup I	Phase II	Phase IIIa	Phase IIIb	Phase IV	Phase V
8	1	1	1	1	4	1
10	1	1	1	1	5	2
12	1	1	2	2	6	2
14	1	1	2	2	7	3
16	2	1	2	2	8	3
18	2	2	2	2	8	4
20	2	2	3	3	9	4

268

group experiences) are processed and channeled toward effective current group participation. By coming together in the pregroup for initial preparatory work, the leader and member are helped to establish a working alliance and begin to foster hope and a sense of universality, common purpose, and mutual concern. It is recommended that the pregroup make up 10 percent of the total group experience.

During the pregroup phase, the leader assumes the role of expert/organizer in order to:

1. Use topical and diagnostic skills

   a. To evaluate prospective members
   b. By assessing specificity of symptoms, availability for treatment, and ruling out the presence of exclusion criteria for short-term, theme-focused group treatment

2. Use the role of group composer

   a. To assess homogeneity of client concerns and establish good group fit and mix
   b. By assessing potential members and deciding if working along the chosen focus will meet various clients' needs and if a working relationship can be established with other prospective participants

3. Use initial working alliance and clinical authority

   a. To clear away impediments to effective group participation
   b. By processing and working through prior relevant experiences as well as current concerns, hesitations, unrealistic expectations, and resistances

4. Use positive transference inherent in the benevolent authority position

   a. To invite membership and solicit active and knowledgeable participation in upcoming group
   b. By clarifying ground rules, establishing individual goals, setting forth the common purpose, and agreeing on a firm participatory contract

Orientation Phase

The group proper comes together in the orientation phase. Most groups begin on a positive note. Members matriculate with expectant hopes as well as anticipatory fears. The first session is rarely as awkward as members or the leader might imagine. Survival of the initial meeting often engenders relief and sense of "so this is what it's going to be like."

Appropriately, in the orientation phase a heavy reliance is placed on the facilitator to lead the group in defining the common task, to help establish the ground rules, norms, and boundaries, and to set the stage for the substantive work to follow by shaping a viable working atmosphere. The leader can proceed directly from the preparatory work accomplished in the pregroup. Here, the psychoeducational aims include clearly delineating the common focus, teaching basic terminology and concepts, and encouraging members to share and compare experiences along the phenomenological boundary of the chosen theme. The leader highlights similarities and common dynamics by constantly exploring: How are we the same? What experiences do people here share? What similarities underlie seemingly idiosyncratic orientations and personalized adaptations around the common focus?

As the group begins its work together, prominent group dynamics and processes arise, including the establishment of positive transferences, a developing dependency on the leader as expert, individual sharing of experience, member-to-member identifications, the availability of groupwide curative fantasies, and a shared sense of belonging, purpose, and fit. It is recommended that the orientation phase make up 10 percent of the total group experience.

During the orientation phase, the leader aims to provide didactic experiences and build structures that:

1. Use initial group dynamics of dependency and positive transference

    a. To imprint enabling ground rules and orient members to the ongoing and upcoming group processes
    b. By didactically outlining or facilitating exploration of group goals, expectations, norms, and operating procedures

2. Use attributions of expertise and role of imparter of information

    a. To clearly define the central focus and teach basic psychoeducational concepts
    b. By didactically or experientially expanding awareness and enhancing curiosity around the central focus

3. Use the proclivity toward universality and member identification

    a. To spur a recognition of present similarities and to establish a common working ground
    b. By structuring the relating of experience specific to the psychoeducational focus

4. Use the desire for belonging

    a. To extend the working alliance to the interpersonal field

    b. By encouraging, engaging, and reinforcing interactions, self-disclosures, and comparative exposures designed to enhance the group's initial cohesive sense of "we-ness"

Dissatisfaction/Resolution Phase

The next group phase, composed of two distinct subphases, dissatisfaction and resolution, is often the most difficult for the novice as well as the experienced group leader. Most groups usually begin with some modicum of success, but they may quickly reach a point where questioning, doubts, and a crisis of confidence ensue: "Can we really affect this problem in this group?" "Why isn't the leader doing more?" It is important for the facilitator to recognize, contain, and channel these normal process concerns in the service of the psychoeducational focus and for the purpose of establishing the power and viability of the group forum. The "storming" of this initial insurgence is affectively fueled by the dysphoria and panic inherent in facing the intransigence of the focal problem, as well as the pressures and exposure of being in the group.

It is possible to anticipate the crisis of confidence and build into the protocol some space and time to allow, drain off, neutralize, and channel these disturbing, sabotaging, and chaotic feelings and doubts. As protests arise, the leader works to allay and normalize fears. He or she helps members share their common concerns around the difficulties and intransigence inherent in the symptom or topic, and around the potential pressures and contagion of the group setting. The leader helps the group define what is expected and what is possible, and begins to teach and develop the requisite skills for realistic goal attainment. The ready power of the resistance is channeled toward a rebellion and alliance against the symptom, as the leader works toward helping members challenge the problem rather than challenge the group by acting out or dropping out. Consequently, the psychoeducational goal, at this stage, becomes containing and redirecting the affective components of the theme, while promoting mutuality, identification, and cohesion.

When making a successful transition from "dissatisfaction" to "resolution," the group moves on with a larger repertoire of responsivity and a truer sense of shared purpose, in contrast to the unrealistic pseudomutuality of the orientation phase. Prominent group dynamics arising in the dissatisfaction subphase, which need to be worked into the protocol, include negative transference, resistance, acting out and acting in, counterdependence, contagion, and fight-flight. The group dynamics inherent in the resolution subphase include catharsis, cohesion, boundary consolidation, and norm setting. It is suggested that dissatisfaction/resolution compose 15 percent of the total group time.

During the dissatisfaction/resolution phase, the leader aims to:

1. Use tendencies toward counterdependence

   a. To encourage the expression of fears, resistances, and leader challenges
   b. By allowing or structuring the free expression of frustration, doubt, concern, and crisis of confidence

2. Use the leader's steady and consistent presence to fashion and fortify a group container

   a. To hold in the various negative reactions and prevent contagion and dropout
   b. By providing a ready space and steady presence for ventilation, catharsis, empathic resonance, and acceptance within the group

3. Use the emerging negative affective components of the central focus (anger, sadness, fear)

   a. To encourage ventilation, catharsis, and breaking of the symptom cycle of paralysis, shame, secrecy, and isolation
   b. By shaping exercises and discussions that allow the free expression of affect and experience and that purge, normalize, and neutralize dyphoric feelings and self-imposed isolation

4. Use individual member's tendencies to act out

   a. To encourage the group's acting in of fears and concerns
   b. By interpreting members' negativity as spokesperson reactions amplifying groupwide concerns essential in coming to terms with the negative aspects of the central focus

5. Use the commonalities in the negative and spirited reactions

   a. To harness, direct, reframe, or channel the group's emotional energy in the service of building cohesiveness and fostering an identification against the symptom
   b. By encouraging exploration of how the group can use the available energy and shared commitment in the service of goal attainment and change

Working/Production Phase

Once the group has been consolidated and initial challenges to its existence have been met and resolved, the working or production phase proper begins. The bulk of the group life occurs here, as psychoeducational tasks now most directly approach the stated group goals and major program areas. The leader addresses essential elements of the central focus, with the general aim of increasing competence and mastery while decreasing dysphoria and dysfunction. Didactic material is presented, structured skills training is facilitated, and discussion is encouraged. The group works toward increased understanding, insight, risk taking, practice action, skill acquisition, and effecting basic changes in orientation and reaction to the issues and implications inherent in the central theme.

With the group established as a valuable ameliorative forum and with member interactions available as a ready resource, active involvement and interdependence are encouraged. At this stage, members are most able to help and influence each other. Dependence on the leader is increasingly supplemented by an active reliance on one another. An important leader function becomes the facilitation of interactions, enhancing and enriching the learning by fostering open sharing, feedback, and other comparative activities. Such mutual exploration allows for the unique needs and skills of the individual members to be expressed and addressed. The major dynamics of the working phase include reality testing and consensual validation, imitation/modeling/identification, insight, sublimation, working through, skills acquisition, deconditioning, competition, cooperation, and confrontation. Major curative factors include altruism, interpersonal learning, development of socializing techniques, and the recapitulation of primary family experiences. It is suggested that the working phase comprise 50 percent of the group time.

During the working phase the leader aims to:

1. Use the newly consolidated cohesion and renewed sense of shared purpose
   a. To build an effective forum for interpersonal learning and skills acquisition
   b. By fashioning didactic lessons and experiences that most directly engage the members in knowledge acquisition, insight, and practice action around the major program areas of the thematic focus

2. Use the group's potential for consensual validation, reality testing, and feedback
   a. To foster comparative activities, encourage a diversity of perspectives, and encounter distortions and projections
   b. By building exercises and structures where members directly compare and contrast their experiences and understandings around the issues inherent in the central focus

3. Use the group's proclivity for identification, modeling, and altruism

   a. To encourage members' helping, teaching, and learning from one another
   b. By structuring discussions or exercises where members demonstrate mastery and assume leadership functions in the service of adopting new skills and cognitive structures

4. Use emerging cooperation, competition, and confrontation

   a. To understand and unlearn dysfunctional behaviors, challenge dysfunctional adaptations, and sublimate primitive urges and needs
   b. By structuring experiences that foster habit disruption, deconditioning, and encourage subsequent rechanneling, reconditioning, and the development of alternative coping mechanisms

5. Use the intimacy, deep emotional resonances, multiple transferences, and ready recapitulation of primary family dynamics naturally arising in the group

   a. To indirectly foster the clarification of early and recurring family issues while exploring points of impasse and vulnerability
   b. By fashioning experiences that isomorphically work through early issues while directly expanding current behavioral repertoires and increasing the individual's capacity for adaptation, spontaneity, creativity and novel responsivity

Termination/Graduation Phase

Seemingly, just as the group is working well on the main business of exploring and challenging elements of the chosen focus, all too soon the end of the psychoeducational contract comes in sight. In time-limited groups, somewhere after the midpoint session the members who are most sensitive to loss may begin prematurely to close-up and close-off by becoming resistive, pessimistic, or actually withdrawing. It is crucial for the leader to work toward preventing premature termination by assuring group participants that they still have ample time together to continue working within the psychoeducational frame.

As the last sessions actually approach, the ending of the experience must be faced. The group emphasis turns from the consideration of new material and skill acquisition to cognitive and emotional closure. It is important not to raise parting issues that cannot be processed within the treatment. Now members must come to terms with the impending loss and prepare to graduate and move on. The leader aids the group by processing the ending, reviewing the whole of the experience, retouching meaningful elements of the major program areas, and helping members say goodbye and plan for the future. The psychoeducational tasks in this stage include review, generalization, and the active assimilation of newly gained perspectives. Relevant dynamics that naturally arise in this termination phase include desires for and fears of independence and subjective feelings of loss.

If additional treatment or intervention is mandated, decisions should be discussed in individual followup sessions. It is not usually helpful to extend the contract as a last-minute strategy aimed at covering more material. Most experiences in life are more or less complete, and part of the subtle lesson of endings is to deal with what has been accomplished and what has been left undone. Whatever the individual dispositions at termination, the group per se is ending, and participants must close with each other and with the group-as-a-whole. It is recommended that the termination/ graduation phase comprise 15 percent of the total group time.

During the termination phase, the leader aims to:

1. Use the fear of loss of group support

   a. To prevent premature termination and encourage the development of outside supports and reinforcements
   b. By structuring a consideration of continuity of care, troubleshooting, outside sharing, and encouraging the resolution of cutoffs with important available others

2. Use upcoming termination

   a. To spur a review of the psychoeducational content and emotional learning
   b. By having members go around and identify and generalize from the most important lessons of the group experience

3. Use lingering disappointments

   a. To pinpoint what has been left undone and what is yet incomplete
   b. By encouraging disclosure and discussion of disappointment, sadness, and the working through of previous losses

4. Use desire for independence

   a. To come to terms with the ending of the group and to plan for the future
   b. By facilitating leave taking, graduation, moving on, continued progress outside the group, letting go of symptoms, maintenance, and relapse prevention

5. Use available group history

   a. To review critical group events and turning points, and foster contrasts of before and after
   b. By structuring consideration of and interactions about changes, growth, and what can be carried on after the group proper ends

Steps in Building Psychoeducational Protocols

Once the defining characteristics of psychoeducational groups are taken into account and the phase-specific dynamics of the group are understood, it is time to build the group protocol. A four-step process is suggested: (1) developing a blueprint for the group, with the identification of major program areas that differentiate and amplify the central focus; (2) ordering the major program areas coincident with the tasks and dynamics inherent in the group's developmental processes, and then using the time requirements of each group phase to shape the major program areas into a session by session plan; (3) building or adopting didactic structures and experiential exercises that specifically make use of the group dynamics and curative potentials inherent in progressive group phases; and (4) developing within-session lesson plans for exploring elements of the central focus, while building in a participatory process that fosters assimilation of the material content.

Developing a Group Blueprint

Before the group actually begins, the leader preplans by setting up a blueprint for the group's construction. The following list of general questions can help establish the unique focus of any particular psychoeducational group. The answers, by way of example, are drawn from the smoking cessation group.

- What is the target population? *Smokers*
- What are the psychoeducational goals? *Quitting smoking and remaining abstinent*
- What assessments are necessary to define the parameters of the central focus? *Motivations for smoking and particulars of the smoking pattern and habit, and motivations and supports for quitting*
- What are the relevant didactic points, major program areas, and skills acquisition breakdown necessary to effect a meaningful change? What do the group members need to know, experience, and master

concerning the central focus? What does the leader wish to cover and build into the group contract?

Assessing motivations, patterns, and cues for smoking

Teaching habit awareness through self-monitoring

Invoking behavioral techniques to disrupt and modify the smoking habit

Introducing cognitive behavior modification to address recurrent needs and urges

Fostering problem solving and developing alternate coping strategies, thereby reducing psychological reliance on cigarettes

Breaking addiction by progressively lowering the intake dosage of nicotine

Preventing relapse by fostering a nonsmoking lifestyle and adaptational resilience

Similar framing questions and answers are reported for the sexual abuse group of latency age girls.

- Target population: *Latency age girls who were sexually abused*
- Psychoeducational goals: *Crisis intervention, reduce the trauma and long-term consequences of the abuse*
- Assessments: *Nature of abuse, traumatic impact, possibilities of recurrence, available support systems*
- Major program areas and didactic points:

Breaking secrecy

Breaking isolation and helplessness

Validating feelings of betrayal and victimization

Ventilating feelings, including the expression of rage

Working through guilt, confusion, responsibility

Dealing with others' reactions to the abuse

Reestablishing age-appropriate sexual behaviors

Developing assertiveness skills, including the ability to say "no"

Promoting a positive self-image

Letting go of the trauma and moving on with normal childhood development

Ordering the Major Program Areas in Accordance with Normal Group Phases

A progressive consideration of the identified major program areas can be overlaid on the template of normal group development, so that the content and the process that naturally arise in response to the group experience can mirror, match, and magnify those affects and issues inherent to the central problem focus. Most generally, major program areas are arranged according to the evolving ability of the group members to work together and to handle heightened emotions and the increasing specificity of the central focus at deepening levels of trust, intimacy, and work ethic. Examples of ordering major program areas into a sequenced group protocol will be taken from the smoking cessation group, outlined in Table 10–2.

The smoking cessation group was planned for eight sessions in accordance with the content and process requirements of the major program areas. Actual quitting was arranged for session 6 in the working phase, after assessments and initial commitments were made (pregroup), the group brought together with its common purpose clarified and avowed (orientation), resistances in the form of habitual smoking attitudes and patterns disrupted (dissatisfaction), the group's cohesive power for persuasive psychoeducation established (resolution), and alternative coping skills taught (working). Since smoking is a two-part problem, quitting and remaining abstinent, the last two sessions (termination) were dedicated to relapse prevention.

An assessment package was prepared, to be administered in a one-session pregroup held with individual members prior to matriculation. The

TABLE 10–2 • *Smoking Cessation Group (8-Session Model)*

Phase	*% and Number of Sessions*	*Major Program Areas*	*Session Breakdown*
Pregroup	10% (1)	Assessment	S1 Individual Assessment
Orientation	10% (1)	Group formation	S2 Group Building & Orientation
Dissatisfaction/ Resolution	15% (1)	Habit disruption	S3 Strategy/Feedback
Production/ Working	50% (3)	Skills acquisition Addiction breaking	S4 Mind Power: Cognitive Behavior Modification S5 Problem Solving: Coping Strategies S6 Smoke Holding: Quit Day
Termination	15% (2)	Relapse prevention	S7 Maintenance S8 Relapse Prevention

aim of this evaluation and contracting session was to monitor smoking patterns and to tie individual goals to the shared group purposes of habit disruption, quitting, and abstinence. To enhance the group-building requirements of session 2's orientation phase, an initial go-around was structured to allow members to share and compare just these smoking histories and habits. Didactic material was prepared on the universal aspects of the habitual behaviors, including research findings about conditioning, reinforcement, habit strength, addiction, and dependence. Last, a charting system was devised for use in collecting group data about cigarette consumption and nicotine dosage, as the group-as-a-whole would be encouraged to consider the question: What kind of group are we?

Based on phase theory, it was predicted that the group would move from a period of initial optimism and positive expectation about quitting to a time of difficulty and doubt. Addressing these normal resistances was to be the work of session 3 and the dissatisfaction/resolution phase. The leaders anticipated that, at this stage, members might be asking themselves a variety of regressive questions such as: Can I really give up smoking? Do I really want to forsake such a pleasurable experience? What if these other people see how addicted I am? Maybe the leader will humiliate me in front of the others, especially if I fail in my attempts to quit.

Impulses to rebel against the leader's inherently optimistic efforts and to resist the group's anticipated coercive pressure for change are a natural occurrence in the dissatisfaction subphase of every group. The reactive power of intransigence, or resolutely holding to the status quo however dysfunctional or painful, was expected even in smoking cessation groups where many members had dire medical reasons for giving up cigarettes. Consequently, a time and a process for members to directly express their fears and doubts was built into the protocol. Members were encouraged to express the angry affect inherent in being enslaved to smoking, thus motivating a fight against the entrenched habit rather than against the progressive efforts of the group.

In order to provide more concrete assistance, didactic material was readied concerning commonly experienced difficulties in giving up smoking, matched with specific habit-disruption strategies and dosage-reduction procedures for combating a habit strength accumulated over many years. The aim of this resolution subphase was to foster members' understandings of their particular smoking patterns and to provide working tools for beginning to overcome these overlearned behaviors. Such targeted interventions would seek to reduce demoralization by directly combating perceived helplessness.

In sessions 4, 5, and 6 of the working stage, the group's psychoeducational efforts would address more expressly the major program areas of skills acquisition and addiction breaking. The aim was to use the interactive and consensual dynamics of the work group to instill alternatives to smoking and to teach strategies for dealing with the antecedent situations that invoke it. Didactics, discussions, and exercises were planned to convey and to practice a variety of theme-focused perspectives and skills, including cognitive behavior modification (mind power, rationalizations, urges, and traps); problem solving (alternative behaviors and combating high-risk situations); and urge-resistance training (differentiating needs, wants, and urges).

Thus, by the end of session 5, members were to have an intricate awareness of their smoking patterns, to have actively encountered resistances to giving up the habit, and to have taken steps to disrupt their smoking patterns while reducing their dosage of nicotine. They would also have learned alternative skills and options to substitute for and to resist smoking. The actual quit day was arranged for the last session of the working phase, where a specific aversive deconditioning technique (smoke holding) was planned to extinguish the remaining positive associations and sensations of smoking.

The last two sessions, 7 and 8, were to make up the termination phase and focus on the major program areas of maintenance and relapse prevention. Review and generalization procedures were planned to help members adapt to the loss of habit and to consider moving on in new and healthful ways. Transient withdrawal symptoms and the continued presence of high-risk situations were to be discussed and worked through in guided exercises. The group dynamic of consensual validation and the behavior-sustaining powers of cognitive dissonance would be invoked to reinforce the negative aspects of smoking and the positive aspects of having quit. Members with needs for additional help would be addressed in individual followup and booster sessions.

Using Phase-Specific Group Dynamics to Build Exercises and Structures

Once the basic group protocol is developed, the specific intervention strategies, structures, and exercises can be planned in more detail. Examples of building exercises based on phase-specific group dynamics will be taken from the sexual abuse group for latency age girls, outlined in Table 10-3. With a population of girls between 8 and 10 years old, the use of play activities is more appropriate than straight didactic presentation. Pregroup work was accomplished in a last individual session (Session 1), where each girl was prepared for moving from an individual to a group format, and where contracts were established for participation.

As part of the first group session (Session 2), the leader presented an

TABLE 10-3 • *Latency Girls' Sexual Abuse Group (12-Session Model)*

Phase	% and Number of Sessions	Major Program Areas	Session Breakdown	Phase-Specific Dynamics
Pregroup	10%	Assessment of readiness for group	S1 Members prepared in last individual session	Working alliance Positive transference
Orientation	10% (2)	Share secrets Validate feelings of betrayal & victimization Breaking isolation & helplessness	S2 Orientation & Group Building: Rules, Norms & Puppets S3 Naming Group Storytelling & Sharing	Universality Affective expression Belonging Unconscious expression
Dissatisfaction/ Resolution	15% (2)	Ventilation of feelings Expression of rage	S4 Additional Storytelling Board game, SASA S5 Unstructured Discussion	Sharing Catharsis Regression Negative transference
Production/ Working	50% (5)	Working through of guilt, confusion, responsibility, other's reactions Establishing age-appropriate sexual behavior Development of assertiveness skills Development of positive self-image	S6 Coloring Books I S7 Coloring Books II/Discussion S8 Age-Appropriate Collage S9 Collage II/ Roleplay S10 Letting Go Exercises Letters to Abusers	Reality testing Consensual validation Modeling/ imitation, identification Insight Establishing age-appropriate norms Socializing skills
Termination	15% (2)	Building outside supports Letting go	S11 Letting Go Ritual S12 Party	Reinforcing strengths, new skills, & independence Mourning loss Termination Moving on

exercise formulated to create a safe environment, while building on the group dynamics of working alliance and positive transference. The girls were helped to make puppets to serve as transitional objects, alter egos, and trusted companions. This playful and constructive activity calmed many initial fears, made the group a fun and safe place, and began the process of working together. After the children completed their puppets, they used them to introduce themselves and give some minimal information about the circumstances of their abuse.

In session 3 of this orientation phase, the leader wished to consolidate the group-as-a-whole by stimulating the dynamics and curative factors of universality, belonging, and cohesion. This work was in the service of breaking the isolation that victims often experience as they maintain the secret of their abuse. Therefore, the session began with a discussion about naming the group. The girls suggested three names, representing a range of feelings about the abuse and the abusers. The most neutral suggestion was "The Girls' Club," whereas the most affected choices were "The Killers" and "The Unicorns." With the eventual choice of "The Unicorns" at the next meeting, membership cards bearing the totem picture and name of the group were provided to solidify further the group's affiliative ties.

After naming the group, a structured exercise involving a storytelling fantasy was presented. Here, the leader wished to validate feelings of betrayal, while providing a safe space and structure from which members could ventilate, contain emerging rage, and continue to counteract the disabling norm of secrecy. A story was begun about a mean giant coming to a village where a young girl lived with her family. The girls were encouraged to add to the story, in turn, developing a plot, denouement, and fashioning an eventual resolution to the conflict. Within the emerging narrative, dynamic resistance was channeled toward thwarting the abuser, rather than rebelling against or holding back the group. Stories that began with powerlessness and helplessness evolved to include asking heroes (adults) for help (breaking the secrecy), and taking out aggression against the giant, who was eventually exposed, contained, and punished.

In session 4, a playful cooperative board game, designed specifically for sexually abused children, Play it Safe with Sasa (SASA), was used to structure discussion and allow the girls to begin more directly the personal sharing process. As the girls exposed the particulars of their own experience and began comparisons and contrasts with others in the group, they came to realize that many of the feelings they thought were unique, isolating, and shameful were shared by others. Many powerful emotions were evoked in this dissatisfaction/resolution phase. The sadness and rage about their abuse came fully to the surface in session 5. The intensity of these primary feelings threatened the integrity of the group, as girls wished to retreat and withdraw as a defense against their emotions and in the service of repressing their trauma. Thus, no new exercise or material was introduced while the leader helped the girls to express and to resolve more directly their emerging ambivalence about the group. A go-around was facilitated in which each member expressed dissatisfaction as well as positive feelings about being a member of The Unicorns. At session's end, a commitment to continue was secured from each participant.

The next five sessions, composing the working phase, were devoted to helping the girls work through issues of guilt, blame, rage, and responsibility. They were also taught assertiveness skills and provided corrective positive messages about their bodies. For example, in session 8, the targeted major program area was establishing age-appropriate sexual behaviors in this population of precocious and overstimulated girls. The leader harnessed the collective dynamics and curative factors of reality testing, consensual validation, establishing norms, cooperation, and the development of socializing techniques, as the group created a collage of pictures of girls at various ages. The group actively discussed, debated, and voted on which pictures accurately portrayed girls of various ages, and analyzed and enacted age-appropriate behaviors. Developmental norms for behaviors, such as the ages for kissing, wearing make-up, and dating, were established.

In session 11, the beginning of the termination phase, a ritualized event was constructed to symbolize letting go of the abuse trauma. The girls wrote or drew on a piece of paper the feelings, thoughts, and/or events they wished to leave behind. As the circle came around, each girl verbally shared a painful memory, then crumpled the piece of paper that held the memory, placing it in a pile in the middle of the group. Following the ritual, the girls requested that the leader take all of the crumpled papers home and burn them. The girls ended their group experience with a party, which included reminiscent play and the recitation of a collective group motto containing positive messages about themselves and about moving beyond their trauma.

Developing Within-Session Organization

Structures, exercises, and didactics, however well conceived, must be embedded within the group session to provide proper antecedent, context, and closure for the procedures. The phase model of group development can also be used to organize and plan the flow within each group session. Most group meetings begin with an introduction or *warm-up* (orientation phase). Here, the leader helps bring the members together, clarifies the goals for the day, and highlights those aspects of the psychoeducational focus that will receive attention. Next, a brief time for considering *old business—* whether homework, problems during the preceding week, or questions about or reactions to the material presented earlier—is fielded and resolved (dissatisfaction/resolution). Once the group is brought up to date and immediate impediments to moving on are cleared up, the session turns its major attention to the new material, whether didactically or experientially presented. Some processing or practicing with the psychoeducational content rounds out the *new business* phase of the session (working/production).

The last task is to *warm-down* by briefly reviewing what has been accomplished, setting the stage for future sessions and closing off, at least temporarily, any loose ends (termination/graduation). The object of such structuring is to foster completeness. While the psychoeducational group builds on itself from week to week, each session can be presented as a complete unit.

Potentials and Possibilities for the Psychoeducational Group

The time-limited psychoeducational group is not a substitute for long-term reconstructive psychotherapy or the ongoing holding environment necessary to ameliorate or contain severe psychopathology. However, the short-term group may very well be a viable intervention where there is a homogeneity of population, a specificity of problem focus, and where targeted difficulties are circumscribed enough so as not to have fully infiltrated the client's wider adaptations.

When the central focus is symptomatic or habitual behavior, such a group may go a long way toward deconditioning dysfunctional patterns and reconditioning a more healthful responsivity. When the presenting problem is a common life stage or milestone, the group experience can normalize, inform, and move members through various maturational processes. When the issue at hand is environmentally related, the group can identify, ventilate, and air out the toxic situation. When the focus is a traumatic life event, the psychoeducational group can provide timely support, crisis intervention, and enhanced coping strategies for moving through the trauma.

For such a group to be effective, it cannot be haphazardly organized. Since time is at a premium, the group meetings must be effectively arranged in the service of teaching and working with the relevant collective foci. The various group dynamic processes that inevitably arise can provide a hindrance or a help in the construction and evolution of the group. Only by blending process with protocol, can timely and targeted psychoeducational groups be developed.

PART FIVE

Applications:
Psychotherapy

Added care and expertise are required when individuals are treated in a long-term context along the fault line of their most troublesome and hurtful sensitivities. The group itself must transform into a multiservice medium and the group's dynamic processes must be harnessed with specific ameliorative intent. There are three major ameliorative tasks in group psychotherapy: (1) holding *members together while* containing *feelings and problems;* (2) analyzing *and* working through *dysfunctional patterns; and (3)* attributing *meaning and* transforming *experience. Each chapter in this section will present a model for addressing one of these ameliorative tasks.*

- Amelioration 1. *Group processes can be contained and individual members held within the matrix of the healing circle.*

The group itself becomes a protective and enveloping matrix, wherein analysis can proceed, metaphoric images can arise, and hurts can be cushioned. In this, the title chapter, the metaphoric symbol of the circle, or enclosed "sphere of influence," calls special attention to a group's ability to bring members together, thereby reducing remoteness while fostering empathy. The geometrical properties of the sphere are directly invoked to grasp the peripheral boundaries, the internal matrix of structures and relationships, the common topics, shared space and available content, and the containing potentials of the group-as-a-healing circle (Chapter Eleven).

- Amelioration 2. *Group processes and individual dynamics are worked through by fully explaining their shape, force, direction, and genesis.*

The group can be analyzed and the members treated by looking to individual and collective motives, those causes and reasons that ultimately propel and shape the grouping process. After a period of free interaction, an impasse or powerful dynamic may arise that requires focused attention in order to understand, work through, and move past its compelling or fixating influence. This impasse is often isomorphically related to the group's formative history and/or the members' nuclear issues. An analysis of the ongoing proceedings can be based on Aristotle's notions of providing full explanations or causes to account for the nature of objects, actions, or events. A logical, working-through sequence would explore what is going on, how events have been initiated and affectively maintained, where interactions are headed or avoiding, and why ingrained patterns are emerging just so (Chapter Twelve).

People in Motion by Ulrich A. Frank (1968) (fiberglass, 6' 10" × 12' × 12"). Reproduced by permission of Dr. Ruth E. Frank. Location: Coastal Medical Center, Hardeeville, South Carolina. Dr. Peter Frank, photographer.

- *Amelioration 3. Group processes take on meaning, and individual dynamics can be transformed within the group culture by discovering and developing apt images, metaphors, and symbols of the shared experience.*

Understanding the logic of the proceedings is rarely enough. As the group progresses, its changing dimensions reflect the deep levels of meaning that underlie logical and structural parameters. The group itself can be recognized as a cultural phenomena. Shaping circumstances, from inside and outside the group domain, influence collective dynamics. Shared images and mutually transformative symbols are evoked as conveyors of meaning and vehicles of change. When expressing common concerns by way of spontaneously arising collective representations, the group and its members are able to creatively reconfigure themselves and their interpersonal environment. The therapeutic culture thus enriches and enlivens the experience of its participant members (Chapter Thirteen).

Framing questions in this section include:

- *How can collective dynamics be encapsulated within the group's own boundaries in order to create a safe transitional space and holding environment, reducing estrangement while fostering intimacy?*
- *When should the leader allow and encourage free interaction and when and how might he or she facilitate an analysis of the ongoing process?*
- *In what ways can the group objectify and resolve its impasses by way of metaphoric maneuvers and symbolic transformations, bringing order and harmony out of chaos and disillusion?*
- *How does the progressive collection of group norms, images, and projective processes conform into a discrete and resilient therapeutic culture?*

CHAPTER ELEVEN

Sphere of Influence:
Holding Together in Remote Groups

Every psychotherapist who works with groups has experienced hauntingly disjointed times in the treatment process when real contact seems impossibly far away. Every psychotherapy group, no matter how well formed or fine functioning, goes through periods of stretched connection and strained commitment. Such remoteness inevitably spurs fantasies of total group disintegration. These periods of distance can disturb the leader's waking thoughts and spur dreams about specs out of alignment, lone voices in the wilderness, or strangers in a strange land.

Those psychotherapists who do not work with groups may be seeking to avoid just this sense of lonely remoteness. They may fear that their potential groups will never jell or that, if they do, the connections will be so precarious that the group will fragment and ultimately fall apart. Being alone or coming apart in the midst of others adds elements of ostracism, shame, and noticeable nonrecognition to an otherwise private and removed stance.

Psychotherapeutic treatment always straddles the thin edge of its own extinction. When working with an individual patient, remoteness of character or of therapeutic sequence can forge a frustrating fissure between the two principals in the dialogue. When dynamics get too close, feelings may get out of hand, and the client may move out of reach. In dyadic therapy, an individual client whose participation is becoming slight or faint may follow a path of remoteness, leading to a point of departure. When working with a remote group, the distance between members, and from members to the leader, multiplies in the intervening space, which then invariably echoes

An earlier version of this chapter appeared in *The Psychotherapy Patient, 6* (1 & 2), 229-261, copyright 1989. Rreprinted with permission of Howarth Press. Various citations throughout this chapter from Pines (1985) are reprinted with permission from *Group 9* (1), pp. 60-73. Copyright 1985 by Brunner/Mazel, Inc.

with silence, solitude, and separation. In this collective therapy, when an individual member publicly moves out of proximity, the group, by seemingly contagious and centrifugal forces, may be pushed and pulled toward some magnetic and distant black hole of nonparticipation and nonexistence.

Each group manifests a differing shape, shade, and shadow of remoteness. Every group evolves a distinct personality made up of the combined history of the members, the working norms of the common culture, and the interventional forays of the therapist. Thus, patterns of remoteness or resistance differ according to the specific character of the individuals and of the conglomerate. The overintellectualized and verbose group may create distance by becoming remotely relevant in utterance while simultaneously removed from feelings. The depressed group may recapitulate its aura of loss by dying a thousand deaths. The therapist's initial task is to understand the impetus, unique character, and meaning of the remoteness, its foundations, and its functions in the history and current experience of the group. Interventions can then be specifically fashioned to interpret, work through, and repair the distance by fostering connections and by bringing matters and members back together.

Periods of remoteness may result from actual breaks in the treatment process, such as canceled groups, leader or member absences, or other events that stretch or cut into the group's continuity or peripheral integrity. Members may move out of proximity as interactions and communications become limited, stilted, or superficial, and as connections become risky, tentative, or truncated. Feelings of distance may also reflect a paucity in the contributions so necessary to fill the group with meaning. Similarly, a loss of containment may result from a fissure in the group's ability to hold its members within a shared envelope of belonging and curative fantasy (Stone, 1985).

The Group and the Circle

Group psychotherapy is a spatial endeavor, joining together and taking shape over time. Heretofore unrelated participants are encircled with the intention of creating a combined, stable, and meaningful working whole. Individual and group psychotherapy can, in fact, be differentiated by the diverse images of "the couch and the circle" (Spotnitz, 1961). The motion of going around the psychotherapeutic enclave brings dynamic issues into existence. As group time rolls on, this transformative movement revolves around in a recurrence of dysfunction patterns and through cycles of conformity and differentiation. On its normal rounds, therapy groups convolute their shape, at times becoming elliptical and confusing, hyperbolic and self-important, or parabolic and obtuse in symbol and meaning (Russell, 1983).

Human gatherings have long been associated with the geometry and mythopoesis of the circle and its related transformational forms. Our progenitors came together around a ring of the fire for warmth, protection, nourishment, and communion. In prehistoric encampments, the hearth served as the organizational center of primitive community (White,1986)— a circle of humanity around a circle of fire and light. Circular motion itself was believed to mimic the sweeping, spinning, and stirring process of creation. Dancing a "round" was thought to animate the still forces of nature. Roundness became a sacred shape, and the perfect sphere evolved into a universal symbol of totality, wholeness, and perfection (Cirlot, 1971; Cooper, 1978). The circle also became associated with healing, given its inherent potentials for mixing, arranging, and enveloping disordered and polarized multiplicities. Pointed edges could be smoothed, centrality and relation might be circumscribed, with splits conjoined and chaos contained (Jung, 1969). Bachelard (1964), writing on the poetics of space, describes how "images of full roundness help us collect ourselves, permit us to center an initial constitution of ourselves, and confirm our being intimately, inside" (p. 234).

Equating the psychotherapy group with the circle allows the therapist, by analogy, to understand the intactness, movement, viability, and enclosure of the group, at any point in time. Every circle can be defined by four structural properties: (1) its bounded circumference; (2) the connectivity and cohesion of its internal elements; (3) the quality, density, and arrangement of the space inside the periphery; and (4) its wholeness and capacity for containment. Similarly, the sphere of mutual influence, that is the psychotherapy group, can be understood by its (1) boundary integrity, (2) the closeness of its members and the cohesion of the group matrix, (3) the admixture and topical arrangement of issues and emotions contributed to its lifespace, and (4) the holding and protective power of the conglomerate. A remote group is a group out of bounds, out of touch, out of shape, and inside out.

It is argued that all of the group's abrasions and geometric permutations can be recognized, the forces within and without analyzed, and the circle reformed and reinforced with specific psychotherapeutic intent. Examining and solidifying this shared enclave is exactly the task of group psychotherapy. Investigations and therapeutic interventions engage members around the integrity, interactional potentials, assumed shapes, and inherent safety of the group. By implication and direct application, similar personal issues are delimited and worked through.

During periods of distended remoteness, the overall group process, with its inherent individual contributions, can be examined for dysfunctional forms and repatterned to reassume its spherical integrity. The group is then freed to move along more smoothly, until the next period of remoteness and configural transformation. In like analogy, Pines (1981) has suggested, "All members of the group, including the therapist, share the same space, the powerful universal symbol of the circle, and I do not think we have yet fully appreciated the psychic significance of that fact—the circle as a symbol of unity" (p. 279).

This chapter will present a model for understanding and working with the remote psychotherapy group, based on a spherical analogy and the symbology of the circle. Table 11-1 presents an analysis of the geometric properties of the psychotherapy group as a circle, with its inherent patterns of remoteness, concommitant phenomenology, along with prescriptions for corrective psychotherapeutic reformulations. By way of example, a clinical vignette of an ongoing group will be followed to demonstrate how the properties of the circle might be invoked psychotherapeutically.

- Amelioration 1. *Group processes can be contained and individual members held withing the matrix of the healing circle.*

Going Around in Remote Circles

A long-term group of severely depressed and schizoidal patients reached a period of painful impasse. During this remote sequence, two participants threatened to drop out, while the other members often sat in deadly and protracted silence. In their outside orbits, many of the members lived with tragic loss and traumatic circumstance. Their history of premature cutoffs and the failures of the holding environment contributed etiological context to the current atmosphere of disillusion and lost hope.

Both of Patty's parents died when she was a child, and she was placed in a series of foster homes. Subsequently she lost a marriage and a teenage son to drugs and homicide. When Ellen was an infant, her mother abruptly left the family to be hospitalized for psychosis. When her alcoholic father could not care for her, she was sent across country to live with an aunt. As a young adolescent, Ellen, suddenly and without her consent, was returned to her still troubled father and his new overcontrolling wife. Don, a product of sexually confused and nonaffectionate parents, recently went through the breakup of his marriage. He struggles with containing his sexual impulses, which historically are acted out in bouts of hopelessness and exhibitionism. Joe, a young adult with a history of dyslexia and school failure, is currently trying to complete a master's degree in the health sciences. With rage and suspicion, he predicts disaster, periodically withdraws, and sabotages his own efforts in a manner that may ultimately get him kicked out of school and may also play out in his prematurely leaving the group.

TABLE 11–1 • *Description of the Group's Spherical Properties and Patterns of Remoteness*

	Boundary	Matrix	Space	Container
Structural Component of Group	Circumference Border	Internal cohesion	Inside area	Receptacle
Functional Form	Environmental barrier	Linkages & connections	Shape Topical configuration Composition	Holdings
Level of Group Description	Periphery Perimeter Ambit Enclosure Membrane Frame Epidermis	Milieu Force field Web Patternings Pathways Admixture	Shared space Common space Life space Arena Transitional space Intermediate area	Envelope Womb Domain Sanctuary Vessel Urn Haven
Function of the Structure	Keeping in/ Keeping out	Touching/Being out of touch	Filling/ Emptying	Holding/ Letting go
Main Property	Permeability/ Impermeability	Accessibility/ Inaccessibility	Open/Closed	Security/ Insecurity
Member Decisions	Staying in/Staying out	Moving close/ Moving away	Putting in/Leaving out	Holding in/ Holding out
Group-Related Issues	Selection Matriculation Boundaries Continuity Confidentiality Attendance Punctuality Outside contact	Composition Heterogeneity/ Homogeneity Promixity Mutality Intimacy Mobility Interaction Bonding Cohesion Merging Identification Reciprocity Connectedness Bridging Feedback	Sharing Participation Self-Disclosure Secrecy Association Topicality Hierarchy Territoriality Density of meaning Receptivity Active listening Group focus	Safety Empathy Acceptance Belonging Reliability Stability Containment Limitation Protection
Patterns of Remoteness	Being out Acting out Staying out Keeping out	Ruling out Cutting out Having it out Butting out Fizzling out Missing out	Leaving out Spacing out Screening out Filtering out Censoring out	Holding out Withholding Staying out Being unholdable

Continued

TABLE 11–1 • *Continued*

	Boundary	*Matrix*	*Space*	*Container*
Therapy Tasks	Boundary regulation Maintaining frame & structural norms	Connecting up members & material	Expanding group contributions to topical space	Securing & holding safe environment
Therapist Functions	Managing group's integrity	Facilitating interactions Connecting & interpreting material	Encouring varied & rich participation Enlarging norms around themes, contents, emotions	Maintaining benevolent group climate Dealing with failures of empathy & narcissistic injury

These members experience the effects of premature extrusions and failures of formative circles to maintain boundaries, provide proper and enriching connection, or otherwise hold together in security and support. These members continually struggle with feelings of disconnection and perceptions of being left in limbo.

Other members of this group struggle with the effects of overprotection and inordinate and inappropriate encircling within their families. Steve, a 26-year-old doctoral candidate in physics, shuffles between home and dormitory, serving as substitute husband for his oft-traveling executive father, and as confidant and ready companion to his ill-satisfied mother. His dissertation is stalled, as he is not at all sure he can graduate and move away from home. Deborah, a conforming parental child, left her familial confines for the first time at age 35 when her mother died. She is now living through a deferred adolescence, replete with authority battles that include impulsively quitting jobs whenever progressive expectations are put to her. Jill, a bright, active, and inappropriately cheerful young adult, comes from a neurotic family with an intensely opinionated father whose tirades and intrusions know little bounds. As a bulemic teenager, she hid in her room obsessively depressed. Having now come out, Jill struggles with closeness with men, prematurely letting down barriers by quickly becoming sexual and engaging, and then just as quickly panicking, erecting walls, and cordoning herself off. Darlene, the youngest member of the group, is a graphic artist with an active fantasy life but little skill or confidence in putting her thoughts into words. Her difficulties exacerbated when she was 12 years old, and the family abruptly moved away from the old neighborhood and friends, an event precipitated by the revelation of her father's long-term affair with her mother's best friend. Darlene now demonstrates a twin-like bonding with her mother, a ready pool of unrecognized anger at men, and a repressive style from which she often vaguely threatens to walk out of group. These later members

live with the effects of inordinate and restrictive enclosure. Cloistered within parental confines, their individual developments have been forestalled.

All of these formative issues contribute to the group's recurrent struggles between closeness and distance. As in all dynamically oriented psychotherapy, the work takes place within this ambiance of ready ambivalence
and around cycles of meaningful repetition. Pines (1985) aptly encapsulates
this process.

> *An analytic group seems to follow a spiral course, returning again and
> again to some of the same eternal human issues of love, hate, of hopes
> and disappointments, of dependency and interrelatedness, of individ-
> uation and togetherness, of the relationships of the self and other in
> childhood and in the present. As these issues return in the evolution-
> ary spiral there will often be a better grasp by the members of the
> meanings of these issues, based on their common history and under-
> standing—though spirals can be regressive as well as progressive. The
> analytic work of the group can lead to the recognition and acceptance
> of patterns of relationship both in the present and from the past. An
> appreciation can be garnered of the organization of personality from
> its childhood origins in the family setting through the transference
> and transpositions within the group setting by which these formative
> configurations reappear, repeat and recycle. The evolving context of
> the group provides its members with an opportunity to transcend and
> to transform these powerfully laid-down early patterns. (p. 63)*

The Group Boundary

The *group boundary* is defined as that functional shell whose encasing
properties regulates the ins and outs of the group process. The group's basic
integrity can be realized by an inspection of its boundary. The periphery of
the therapeutic circle serves as environmental barrier mediating between
what is within and what remains without. Thus, the function of the group
boundary is *keeping in* and *keeping out,* and its main functional property
is its *permeability* or *impermeability.* How easy is it to get in and out? How
protected are the material contents, objects, or persons contained within?
The circumference of the circle provides the definitive form and structurally
limits the frame for the shared experiences of the group.

The group boundary can be visualized as a wall or membrane that
encompasses the whole of the group experience. At any point in time, the
group therapist can imagine the concrete and confining properties of this
enclosure. Of what material is the group perimeter constructed (i.e., paper

mache, brick, or barbed wire)? Is the group's encasing wall high and imposing, fully bounded, or are its surroundings easily avoided and evaded? Is the enclosing barrier porous or solid, translucent or opaque, penetrable or impenetrable, strong or fragile? Picture something trying to pierce the periphery. What happens? Is it admitted or expunged? Imagine something trying to leave the circle. Is it impeded, bound up, or merely extruded?

The group barrier is a two-way symbol, a threshold giving rise to comings and goings. Bachelard (1964) reminds us that "every circumstance of life that is raised out of the sphere of indifference and commonplace, forms its own ring of existence, a walled-off zone separated from its surroundings by fixed limits. All movement into and out of the ring is governed by sacral regulation, 'rites of passage'" (p. 103). Here, outside and inside form a geometric opposition, a dialectic of yes or no, in or out. Bachelard suggests that this basic opposition becomes "tinged with aggressivity. . . . Formal opposition is incapable of remaining calm. . . . You feel the full significance of outside and inside in the alienation which is founded on these two terms" (pp. 211–213)—as an intimate transposition between inclusion or exclusion.

Various therapeutic issues can be ascribed to the boundary properties of the group. Members must decide whether to enter and whether to remain within the circle. Group-related issues of selection, matriculation, continuity, confidentiality, attendance, punctuality, and keeping relationships within the therapy room arise and need to be progressively resolved for the group to remain intact. Various patterns of remoteness, such as keeping out, staying out, acting out, or dropping out, challenge the group's structural limits. Without defining inclusion criteria, and without closing gaps, cracks, and breaches in the fabric of the experience, the group cannot hold together and will ultimately fragment and disperse. Consequently, norms must be set and salvaged around appropriate and inappropriate traversing of the peripheral barrier. What are the therapeutic criteria for entering and remaining a group member? When breaks in the structure invariably arise, how will they be patched? When members miss sessions or get together outside the constraints of the meeting time, how will this material be used and how will the group boundaries be reiterated? The therapist's main task around the periphery of the group is boundary regulation—managing and maintaining the group's structural norms and integrity.

The individual correlates of the group boundary are ego continuity and ego strength. Can the members contain themselves, or do they spill out in borderline episodes or in bouts of anxiety or psychosis? The protective skin of the group also effectively corresponds with the patients' current availability and history of predictable and encompassing formative ties, their experiences with reliable and safe inclusions. What is the ready history of cutoffs and binds? How much can members rely on important others to keep themselves together? Clients with diagnosed problems in containing and defining their own ego boundaries, and those with truncated or intractable closeness, often struggle with consistently remaining within the confines of the group. Much psychotherapy takes place along the group boundary—a reality not to be avoided but to be recognized and utilized. The therapist, realizing that members' struggles for personal integration can be worked through transferentially and symbolically around the group perimeter, can contain and utilize his or her own anxiety in periods of dispersion and remoteness.

Weiner (1983) suggests that group impasse can result from insufficient attention to therapeutic contracts and the insufficient enforcement of group rules. Boundary violations, such as repeated absences, prolonged disruption, outside contacts, and betrayals of confidence, can mire the group in periods of estrangement and nonproductivity. Weiner suggests that to break these circumferential impasses, the facilitator must encourage enclosure, disclosure, and the investigation and interpretation of boundary and norm anomalies.

Hawkins (1986), writing about group instability and following the work of Winnicott (1986), likens the group to the "good enough environmental mother." He suggests that the group must hold firm to its boundary integrity even as members seek to distance or defeat the process. Similarly, "if the mother abandons her job in providing the holding environment when faced with the child's struggles, and becomes too intrusive or too unavailable, the child losses its sense of intactness and feels overwhelmed by her intrusion or by its own process and feelings of absence" (p. 243).

Hawkins also suggests that when the group is intact with "regular meetings, good attendance, and relatively predictable behavior," members can maintain their own sense of personal stability. In times of instability, he prescribes stabilizing the environmental mother by analyzing member responses to this instability, and by active measures such as reaching out, firming up, and reestablishing the group's enabling boundaries and norms.

Working along the group perimeter is not an easy task, as boundary disputes flair. Outside and inside are always ready to be reversed, "to exchange their hostility. If there exists a borderline surface between such an inside and an outside, this surface is painful on both sides" (Bachelard, 1964, pp. 217–218). Members may alternatively run for protection toward the center of the enclosure or seek escape through the peripheral threshold, a seeming juxtaposition between agoraphobia and claustrophobia.

Collectively, and within the therapeutic process, this group continually struggles with the appropriate boundaries of participation. They periodically debate, with transferential vigor, the merits and demerits of participating within set limits, and heatedly act out their ambivalences about remaining in group-as-a-family. In times of group disruption and instability, members become shaky, angry, or disturbed. In one particular session, Jill, the most active member, is away on a two-week vacation. Joe, whose attendance and participation had been sporadic, is absent unannounced. The therapist is back after a week's vacation. In his absence, the group met with a substitute leader. In an individual session just preceding the group meeting, Patty strongly responded to the therapist's "abandoning her." In the intervening week, Darlene, who has been inactive in the group, contacted Patty and they lunched outside.

During the current session, Patty and Darlene are withdrawn, in seeming conspiratorial silence. Ellen is noticeably depressed. Don is working hard to reach out to others in affectionate display and social conversation, with minimal group reaction. Only Deborah is responsive in a happy and superficial way. Steve furtively glances at the therapist, smiling knowingly but not sharing his thoughts or fantasies, and not engaging with the other members. The feeling in the room is of great remoteness and distance.

The therapist's initial attempts to reach across the abyss, by directly stimulating interaction and connection, largely fail. After much resounding silence and some aborted attempts at awkward interchange, the therapist directly addresses the feelings of remoteness in the room. He ties the current impasse to the recent gaps in the group boundary. With care and gentleness, he describes how given various members' personal histories of loss, extrusion, or inappropriate confinement, this group's current silence feels particularly dysphoric and deadly. Ellen then volunteers that her sister-in-law, one of the few people to whom she has felt close, has suddenly died. Ellen attributes her own withdrawal to that sudden loss of connection and alliance. As an aside, she relates that on the way to this session, her husband offhandedly commented that she is getting no better and that she doesn't need "group."

The anger and shock inherent in "sudden loss" becomes the working theme for this group's recent break in continuity. Ellen's revelation awakens the group from its malaise and, in response to her immediate and resounding crisis, the members come back together. The group-as-a-whole once again encircles and bands together as the distance and solitude slowly dissolves. Members work with Ellen to ventilate and talk about her sudden loss, just as the therapist actively encourages other members to deal with their own cutoffs, extrusions, and stifling envelopments.

Toward the end of the session, the therapist reminds the group that they have yet to consider the meaning of Patty and Darlene's out-of-group contact, mentioned earlier in passing. Calling specific attention to this boundary violation directly evokes Patty's participation, as if the unspeakableness around having acted out has been lifted. Darlene responds with anger to the therapist's challenge. "What's the big deal anyway?" In so doing, she rejoins the group process. This issue of between-session subgrouping is highlighted for consideration in the next session. The therapist ends this meeting by redefining and reinforcing the circumference of the therapeutic circle, inviting the group to "go around" and "have a last word." Ellen ends the session by saying that she does, in fact, need the group. "At least here I'm connected, where elsewhere in my life I'm so removed."

The Group Matrix

The *group matrix* is defined as "the potential web of communication and relationship within any group" (Foulkes, 1964, p. 292). "The shared history of interpersonal relationships in the group and . . . the shared work in deriving meaning . . . together lays down this dynamic group matrix" (Pines, 1985, p. 63). The group's connectivity, mutuality, and mobility can be recognized by an examination of its network of connections. This copula of interaction serves to align and configure the intimate relations that lend the group its organizational and fiber strength. The purpose of the group network is to put and to keep its members in touch, and the main functional property of the matrix is the *accessibility* or *inaccessibility* of its constituent parts (Ahlin, 1988). How easy is it to come together or to stay apart? How intertwined and interdependent are the various participants? These patterns of interaction within the therapeutic circle account for the group's unique structural and interpersonal design.

The group matrix can initially be visualized as a series of discrete entities along the circumference of the circle. How do these self-contained units proceed toward each other, and how do they connect? At any point in time, the therapist can imagine pathways of intersecting lines, a latticework comprising the group weave. Are connections intact or broken? Are the pathways fluid or impeded? Do individual members remain separate and discrete, become enmeshed, or assume a comfortable interpersonal distance? Picture two members trying to connect. Do both parties come an equal way, or does one participant move the greater distance? Are the movements within the group space random, fixed, metered, or spontaneously interactive?

The symbolic value of the group matrix is as a transducer of interpersonal interchange and a crucible for personal change. Here, both similar and dissimilar parts are brought together in creative union, an attraction to the familiar and a play of opposites. Edinger (1982) quotes Jung: "For two personalities to meet is like mixing two different chemical substances: if there is any combination at all both are transformed" (p. 20). The group, as the collecting, meeting, and mixing place, becomes the ready vessel for individual and collective transformations. The admixture of individuals creates a wider field of perception and experience, and the group-as-a-whole becomes a cultural milieu, capable of exerting an influence on its constituent parts.

Pines (1985) describes the unique and alchemical properties of the group matrix as a setting for human development, a force field and forum for socialization, participation, exchange, mirroring, and shared resonances. He also describes how the group takes on its meaning and evolves its task. "Personal maturity (social, emotional, and intellectual), as a member of an analytic group, develops in the context of the maturation of the group as a social system. . . . Gradually [members'] symptoms, their reasons for coming to the group, become disentangled and their relationship problems become located in the group process" (p. 67).

Various therapeutic issues can, in fact, be identified within the matrix of the group. Members must decide how close and active to be, how often to move in and out of the ongoing group process. Similarly, how open and available to group influence and input will participants be? Group-related issues of proximity, transference, interaction, and intimacy arise and need to be worked through to establish a proper balance between individuation and merging, between introversion and extroversion, and between aloneness and togetherness. Various patterns of remoteness, such as staying out, ruling out, fizzling out, butting out, and having it out challenge the group's interconnections. Without effectively working with cutoffs, buffer zones, screens, barriers, hurdles, knots, strands, embattlements, distillations, and other impediments to contact and admixture, members will remain unattached and unincorporated.

Consequently, identifications, empathic resonances, similarities in style and substance, and other areas of homogeneous attractions must be discovered and consolidated. What do members have in common? How might each participant relate to the content and feelings being expressed in the room? The therapist's main task around the group's networking is the fostering of connections, interpersonal mobility, exchange, and meaningful interaction. It is also important to encourage a communication and reciprocity within the wider field of heterogeneity. Members who might tend to move apart or lessen their participation can be brought back together in synthesis, as an intimate coalescing of differences and a purposeful bridging of splits and fissures.

The individual correlates of group networking efforts are social and communication skills, as well as the desire and ability to establish and maintain affiliative ties. What are the social histories of the various group members? How able are members to seek out and hook up with others? How willing are participants to join and contribute to the larger whole (Ormont, 1990)? Clients with recognized problems in relating will have difficulty appropriately embedding themselves within the social and participatory fabric of the group. The thrust of the therapy for such clients will take the form of continual adjustments and accommodations to the group matrix. The therapist seeks to enhance members' abilities to function fully within the psychosocial context of normal peer relations. Consequently, the leader works to help members be open to the shared experience, thus finding themselves within the group.

Kron and Yungman (1987), following Buber, specifically identify group therapy as an interplay between intimacy and distance. This "betweeness" can be vacuous, isolating, alienating, and anxious, with communications taking the form of self-involved monologues. Alternately, true "dialogues" can be initiated wherein identifications, empathies, closeness, and intimacies are exchanged. The characteristics of such "we-ness" includes reacting existentially to a common center, demonstrating openness to each other, interacting with immediacy of communication and ready contribution, and displaying a mutuality conducive to genuine "speech-with-meaning." Kron and Yungman argue that, for members, such dialogic participation is not an artifact or epiphenomenon but "a therapeutic objective of the highest order, certainly to no less a degree than the analysis of their experiences and feelings, for only we can make a significant breach in their isolation possible" (p. 534). Likewise, group members often equate such full participation with having a good session.

Such togetherness and cohesion pervades the group literature as a precursor and curative variable that underlies and sustains the collective working environment (Kellerman, 1981). Yalom (1970) defines *group cohesion* as the attraction of the group to its members (Yalom, 1970), that invisible bonding that makes comrades out of strangers. He believes that "cohesiveness in group therapy is the analogue of 'relationship' in individual therapy" (Yalom, 1985, p. 48). In addition to interpersonal attraction, Stokes (1983) identifies several additional components necessary to sustain the group's cohesion, including the instrumental value and perceived helpfulness of the group for its members, the degree of risk taking and self-disclosure, and the amount of feedback regularly given and received.

Firth (1973), from an anthropological perspective, further specifies *reciprocity* as the basis of social organization. Members of any group have an obligation to give and an equal obligation to receive. The tokens of exchange in group psychotherapy are disclosures and feedbacks, affections and disaffections. Firth suggests that some equivalence of exchange is necessary to maintain the social equilibrium. If the balance gets too disturbed, there may be a show of aggression or a move toward disintegration. Balanced and reciprocal action and reaction provide the adhesion (the glue, gum, or resin) for holding the group matrix together (Edinger, 1982).

The encouragement of such full participation and genuine availability within the group matrix requires sensitivity to the vulnerabilities and suggestibility of particular members. More is not always better, and aggression can be easily disguised as simple honesty. Some members tend to become prematurely trusting and intimate, thus exposing themselves to hurt and disappointment when the group responds with less than total acceptance. Other members may be overly susceptible to influence and emotional flooding. Intense interactions and confrontations can then elicit countertherapeutic reactions such as unmanageable anxiety, narcissistic injury, or solidified defensivenesss. Donors of feedback usually offer up a contaminated mixture of reality and transference. The group leader must help titrate various contributions by separating out the perceptive from the projective. By fostering such discrimination, the therapist models social discretion and facilitates safe and genuine interpersonal explorations. By so doing, the leader ensures that the group is protected from interpersonal extremism, including alternating bouts of contagion and conflagration.

The next session of the group begins with an active consideration of the out-of-group contact between Darlene and Patty. These members are invited to explore their mutual attractions and to uncover the precipitant for getting together at this time. The revelation emerges of a lightly veiled attempt at parent-child alliance in the therapist's absence. Reaction to recent member and therapist absences are now manifestly considered by the whole of the group. Fears of disaffiliation, lack of support, and group disengagement are openly discussed. These fears are contrasted with the evident strength of affective ties within the group.

Members are generally supportive of Darlene's attempts at engagement, given her developmental need to establish peer relationships and socialize outside her home. Various members also express jealousy at not having been chosen for such special attention and subgrouping. Using this symbolic pairing as a jumping-off point, the therapist asks members who in the group they would like to ask out, to whom do they feel particularly close. Both Patty and Ellen pick Joe, representing the group's need to bring him back into the fold. Ellen adds Patty to her list, suggesting that their histories of loss bind them in affiliation and identification. Don gives a noncommittal response, as any direct gesture of affection appears too threatening for him. Joe picks everyone, further demonstrating his reluctance and inability to identify ready supports. Steve chooses the therapist as a model of attraction, a parental substitute, and as a defense against peer contact. Insightfully, he speaks for the group when saying that he is afraid of both being left out and of being included. The members continue to directly explore their attractions and their feelings of exclusion. The out-of-group socializing, which originally threatened the group integrity, is brought back into the group as a "common center" and a basis for constructive dialogue.

Joe, who continually cuts off, is confronted about the difficulties encountered in trying to make contact with him. Patty and Ellen relate how much help he's been to them, with hugs and encouragement, after particularly difficult sessions. They both, in their own ways, tell Joe, "You won't let us return the favor." Jill and Don talk about how exhausting it is to try to draw Joe out, lamenting that "nothing comes back." In a show of support and understanding, Deborah identifies with

Joe's nonavailability, while glancing at Darlene. She recalls being withdrawn and depressed earlier in her therapeutic experience. "I had so much trouble talking and I felt so angry inside. It was like I had a brick wall around me. Everytime I couldn't respond, it was like putting another brick in the wall." Throughout this feedback, the therapist monitors Joe's reactions and actively works to help him stay connected and available, while safeguarding that he not be overwhelmed by the encounters. The therapist also attempts to help Darlene see how the current discussion is relevant for her. She remains reticent and disavows the possibility of any meaningful import or connection.

The group ends with the therapist directly reinforcing the group boundaries and intimacies. He comments that this session has been valuable in directly addressing the group's mutual affections, and in beginning to bridge their difficulties and misunderstandings. The leader reiterates the value to members of talking out the feelings between them, rather than acting them out between meetings and outside the confines of the group.

The Group Space

The *group space* is defined as that life arena or "sphere of between" that the members construct and configure progressively or regressively with each passing session. Within this transitional area of the psychotherapy group, it is possible for members to bring together their intrapsychic and interpersonal worlds (Schlachlet, 1986). The group's basic openness, participatory availability, and richness of process and content can be realized by an examination of this shared space. The common or intermediate area of the therapeutic circle serves as the arena for what is put in and what is left out. The particular usage and contributions to the group's life space creates its distinctive shape. The function of the group space is to be *filled* or *emptied,* and its main functional property is its *opening up* or *closing off* to new material and to the wide variety of member contributions. The transitional space within the circle provides for its density of meaning, its diversity of concern, and the concentricity of the group's focus.

The group space can be visualized as a hollow, filling or emptying with the whole of the shared experience. The group therapist can imagine the shape, configuration, and composition of the group space at any point in time. What relevant issues, ideas, and feelings are contributed and collected within the group? What is put in and what is left out? What happens when new material is introduced or new elements added to the space? Does additional material and context fill in around, or do verbalizations float within lonely confines? Are free associations, relevant current events, and poignant interchanges readily provided? Or does the group sit in empty silence, waiting for each other and for the leader to add something meaningful?

Symbolically, the group space provides for the fluid and nutrient mixture of issues, concerns, and contextual provisions so necessary for sustaining the group life by feeding and nourishing its interactions. What range of material is readily available for the members to share? How does such material arise, arrange itself, and become assimilated within the space? What issues surface and assume the forefront, and what matters remain submerged or are relegated to the background? In the hierarchy of group priorities, what comes out on top or bottom? What material winds up central or peripheral, right or left of the group's overt concerns?

In pointing out specific perspectives, the group squares the circle by orienting itself in the direction of specific polarities of opinion and feeling (Cassirer, 1955). Crisscrossing the space with alternative viewpoints provides the referential tracking and mapping of this shared terrain. Ulanov (1985), from a Jungian perspective, writes of the numinous potentials of such shared space—"that space between us all where we bump into each other and figure out issues of work and love, with whatever degree of success" (p. 72). Following a cultural imperative, the group space can become a place of exciting, albeit precarious, play, a time of "sacred moments of communication" (p. 72).

Various therapeutic issues can be attributed to the spatial qualities of the group. Members must decide whether to be open and receptive, or whether to remain closed and blocked off. Group issues relating to trust, sharing, secrecy, active listening, verbal and nonverbal participation, and assumed levels of association and self-disclosure arise and need to be negotiated for the group to be meaningful, current, and active. Various patterns of remoteness, such as staying out, leaving out, spacing out, screening out, blocking out, and censoring out challenge the group's relevance and vivacity. Without breaking down the barriers that preclude material contributions from all its members, the group will become barren and unresponsive. Norms must be encouraged and continually reinforced around appropriate and inappropriate additions and deletions to the group space. What is expected of the members verbally, factually, and emotionally? What do others need to know about each other to feel informed and involved? Are there unspeakable topical areas in the group, and if so how can these spaces of taboo be breached? When empty, dull, or silent spots arise, how might they be filled? When is a group silence meaningful, and when is it resistive?

Here, the therapist's main task is expanding what can be brought in, thereby keeping the group space enriched, receptive, and fluid. The therapist widens the range of shared experiences by encouraging members to talk about currently relevant in- and out-of-group experiences, to reveal pertinent relational and intrapsychic histories, and to give free expression

to fantasies, fears, hopes, beliefs, images, memories, and group-related reactions. Additionally, secrets, shames, and impulses can be revealed, as hidden places are opened up and private material is poured out into the public
space. The group becomes a place of shared intimacies and insecurities,
sequenced narratives, and consensual comparisons. With more and varied
material offered up, configural and topical norms continually expand, thus
freeing up additional themes, concerns, and emotional resonances for
group consideration.

The individual correlate of these spatial issues is the members' capacity for genuine communion. How easy is it for participants to say truly
what's on their minds and in their hearts? How well can they operate within
a social context? What are their capacities for empathy and responsive rep-
artee? Do members have enough confidence and sufficient range of experience to make ready contributions to the combined space of the group?
Those with diagnosed problems in sharing, talking, playing, and working
together often have difficulty adding significance to the group. Here, the
thrust of the therapy becomes helping such patients break down barriers to
participation, and facilitating confidence in the worth of what they can add
to relationships and social interchanges. The therapist's hermeneutic role
is to find the common meaning in even the most obscure and seemingly
idiosyncratic contributions, so that members' utterances are brought back
within the scope of the group discussion. In moments of true sharing,
"members get to reveal what they can contribute to the gaps between us,
and discover what is common and worth living for" (Ulanov, 1985, p. 75).
Members construct a full and shared life, "creatively living it and thus filling it" (Ulanov, p. 75), as a partnership in the mysteries, joys, and traumas
of life is encouraged.

Initially, the common space provides a place for solitary or parallel
play, a stage on which to view each other's lonely and "walled off sanctuar-
ies" (Schlachlet, 1986, p. 34). Schlachlet suggests encouraging a more cooperative enterprise.

*Effective group interaction can be enhanced if the mutual construc-
tion of a transitional space is fostered, and the participation in the
group spaces is encouraged. . . . As the group members permit themselves to enter the shared space, and they are encouraged by the therapist to do so, their ability to respond to others in a trusting way is
enhanced. Further, in circular fashion, as they learn to do so, their
ability to relate more freely and more creatively is also increased.
. . . As this occurs both their behavior and their feelings about the
group change. They tend less frequently to withdraw by being silent
or absent. (pp. 47–49)*

The group space can be intentionally defined and configured by identifying the central foci emerging from within its process (Whitaker & Lieberman, 1964). These common themes serve as attentional centers. With the eye of the storm so delineated, members can ground themselves by filling in with their own perceptions and experiences, however tempestuous. By defining what is common to all the members, the therapist accelerates internal spirals of introspection and reminiscence. Such associations and memories can then be shared and put back into the group space for further empathic resonance and consensual comparison. In this way, the circle fills out in perspective, and members realign themselves in reference to the common center.

The group's shared space actually goes through alternating cycles of fullness and emptiness. The space can resound with the voices of active and common concerns. The space can also close off very suddenly, with its life constricted by paranoid suspicions, splittings, repetitive or stereotypical contributions, or scared and depressed withholdings and silences (Ulanov, 1985). Work within the group space stimulates many issues of dominance, submission, dependence, and independence, as members jockey for position and struggle over how much space they can legitimately claim or take up. Within the traditional time limits of the group, there is only so much that can be said and done. Members may alternate between adding too much or adding too little, a juxtaposition between narcissistic and hysterical overflows and schizoidal and obsessional constrictions.

Don begins the next session by making the rounds and checking in with various members, acting on his need to be recognized and on the group's need to have everyone contribute. Jill takes up the task and asks Joe if he is doing any better this week. Joe replies, "About the same," and then uncharacteristically volunteers that he still isn't sure if group is an appropriate treatment setting for him. His additional comment leaves the door cracked for exploration. The therapist suggests that the last group session had an impact on Joe, and prescribes that "we continue to directly explore the benefits and liabilities of participating in the group, rather than leaving matters vague, undetermined, and outside our purview." The group is also reminded that Darlene made a similar parting statement at the end of the last session, disavowing that the group could be helpful and doubting that she had anything worthwhile to contribute.

Members now directly try to involve Joe and Darlene, while making testimonial statements about their own experiences. Patty speaks about how difficult it has been for her to open up and talk in the group. She reminisces about how she would censor and leave things out because all her interactions were fueled by anger. "I don't know how it happened, but I'm not so angry anymore. And when I am, I catch myself. That makes it easier to talk here." Jill flirtingly jokes with Joe about how "if its hard it must be working. That's why I know that its important for me to discuss here what's going on in my life." She goes on to say how the group helped her some weeks ago figure out how she was contributing to her work problems. Members had pointed out to Jill a recurrent dysfunctional pattern of asking for help she doesn't need, thus portraying herself as less than competent. What she really seeks is approval and praise.

With some prompting from the therapist, Darlene reiterates how she feels similar to Joe. She explains that she originally came to group to hear how others thought, but doesn't know why she's currently here. Darlene adds that she's having difficulty sleeping, and that if she wasn't here tonight she could be home in bed. Bringing these outside symptoms into the group, Don asks Darlene what's been disturbing her sleep. She answers that she doesn't know. Patty suggests, "It might be better if you used group to get clear about what's bothering you, so you could sleep better." Don concurs, and says that last night he didn't sleep well either, but he knows why. He goes on to describe an incident with his mother where she accusingly demanded that he bring his children to see her. Don initially stood up for himself and then angrily capitulated. His mother was understandably unresponsive and ungrateful when Don and his three children showed up unannounced at 10 o'clock that night. The group explores this interaction and encourages Don to be more direct with his feelings, talking rather than acting them out angrily in indirect ways. Don acknowledges the meaning of his behavior and expresses the bind of both wanting to give up on his trying relationship with his mother yet simultaneously wanting to be closer to his family. The group debates the better course and winds up encouraging Don to find a way to stay connected.

The therapist suggests that "the same dilemma is playing out in this family." Should the group give up on Joe and Darlene, or should they continue to try and get closer by encouraging them to express themselves directly? Jill reiterates that although she wants these distant members to stay and participate more freely, it is self-destructive for her to work so hard to keep them involved. "To get something out of the group, you have to put something in." It is true that Joe and Darlene have the most difficulty contributing to the group space; consequently, of all the members, they feel the most remote and unattached. It is assumed that if the barriers to participation could be understood and worked through, they would have less need to distance from the group.

The discussion now directly turns to a consideration of the impediments to Joe's and Darlene's more freely contributing to the group space. Patty gently suggests to Darlene that she never volunteers anything. "You only talk when asked, and then you say very little." Darlene feigns confusion about how much she contributes, and receives feedback and clarification that "maybe you think you say more than you do." The therapist supports Darlene by saying that he believes that she has benefited a great deal from being in the group, by listening to and learning about the others. He coaches, "The next step would be for you to say how you feel about people's concerns. Your voice is important here." Quite suddenly Darlene becomes tearful and blurts out, "No one listens to me." This is a statement that

Darlene has uttered before, albeit less emotionally, when talking about how her parents don't take her seriously, especially when she talks of moving away from home. This interaction reveals a central dynamic that interferes in many of Darlene's interactions, whether with family, peers, work relationships, or in group. On a deep level, Darlene is angry and hurt, believing that her opinion doesn't really matter. She couldn't, in fact, keep her father interested in her and in the family. By bringing this issue directly into the confines of the group, Darlene is allowed to be an important part of the proceedings, and her continued threats to leave, or more precisely to move away, make sense.

Joe spontaneously joins in at this point to say that one thing that has held him back is that he isn't sure what is appropriate to talk about in group. In exposing his thinking process, Joe demonstrates how he constructs exclusionary spaces and mind sets that preclude participation and sharing. "Others won't understand the specifics of what I'm talking about." The group supports this exploration and suggests to Joe that maybe the details aren't as important as he thinks. "We can certainly understand your feelings." Joe now experiments by sharing his frustration with his ambulance squad, which "is more interested in selling hot dogs at the Fourth of July fireworks than in coming up with emergency contingency plans." Deborah rewards Joe by saying, "I'm interested and can relate, as a potential crowd member, to your concern." Jill now identifies her own conscientiousness and overresponsibility in various settings, and wonders how everything gets to be her problem.

For most of the session, Ellen is quiet and removed. In an attempt to bring her into the shared space, the therapist asks Ellen how she is feeling as Joe and Darlene are being confronted and encouraged. Ellen replies that she is struggling with her own tendency to feel their pain. She doesn't want to say anything because "I can't be constructive or objective. I can only be sympathetic. But what people are saying to them is very important. That's my problem—I get too involved."

The Group Container

The *group container* refers to the basic capacity of the therapeutic aggregate to receive and sustain nascent and kindred life within it. The group's holding function (Winnicott,1971, 1986) can be recognized by an investigation of its ability to accommodate its membership in a chrysalis of protection, security, and transformation. The enveloping properties of the therapeutic circle determine what can be accepted and what cannot be tolerated within its bounds. Thus, the function of the group-as-a-container is *holding within* and *pouring without,* and its main functional property is its inherent capacity to provide *adequate and stable social sanctuary.* The container of the group also provides a receptacle for gathering and accepting the group members' otherwise disparate and untenable attributes (Bion, 1961; James, 1984).

The group container can be visualized as a vessel or urn. Being encompassed implies both a protection from the vagaries of the outside world and a defense against the torments of the inner self. The group, as container, provides definition and acceptable confinement for those elements of the human experience that need proper management and guidance. At any point in time, the therapist can imagine the content, shape, and tinsel strength of the group vessel. How binding are the collective conformations and encapsulations? What personal attributes, worries, or fears can be so enveloped and becalmed? What bubbling or volatile substances are contained? What experiences resist such restraint and composure? Are the group's inner processes straining turbulently against confining walls, or accommodating adequately to shared limitations. How strong is the group container? What internal and what external pressures can it withstand?

Scheidlinger (1974) reviews studies that identify the psychotherapy group as a mother symbol, an archetype representing the holder of life, the giver of forms, and the crucible of change. At the most primitive and positive level, the group, in loco maternis, stimulates fantasies of utopian protection, along with those concommitant oceanic feelings inherent in "need satisfying relationships" (p. 421). Kosseff (1975) further equates the group's felt presence with an internally held comforting mother image that "serves the affective function of calming, soothing, and reassuring" (p. 74). Here, the group is distinguished as a protective ring and womb-like enclave.

The group as mother can, in actuality, be an ambivalent figure, providing such succorance, comfort, and sanctuary but also conjuring up an engulfing, swallowing, frightening, or abandoning presence. The constrictive "mother-group" must ultimately be escaped in the service of individual autonomy (Neumann, 1963). Members must find their ultimate balance between being held onto with care and understanding, and being held back by overcontrol. Psychotherapy groups do not truly mature into a safe haven until at least one member successfully terminates, thus demonstrating the possibility of appropriately escaping the group's grasp.

Various therapeutic issues can be identified with the containing properties of the group. Members must decide whether to be held in or whether to hold out. Group-related issues of safety, acceptance, and belonging need to be explored and maximally encouraged for the group to function as an inviting and freely accepting domain. Various patterns of remoteness such as holding out, withholding, failure to hold, and inability to be held challenge the group's empathic and containing powers. With holes, cracks, or leaks in the structure of the therapeutic vessel, the group cannot protect its members and will prematurely release them and their dysfunctions, dysphorias, and insecurities back into the outside world, unchanged or worsened for having had an unsuccessful group experience. To risk remaining, members must be protected from the projections of critical others and safeguarded from their own punishing introjects.

Consequently, norms of empathy, acceptance, positive regard, and mutual respect need to be fostered and supported. What is expected from and what is allowed of the members? In what ways do members appear judgmental or distantly disapproving? To what extent can participants be their unbridled and primitive selves, and in what ways must they sublimate their more voyeuristic and sadistic impulses in the direction of constructive curiosity and dynamic investigation? How can participants be a comfort and a support to each other, while still maintaining the necessary capacity for confrontation and feedback? Here, the therapist's main task is maintaining a benevolent group climate amidst ready opportunities for honesty and challenge. Curative fantasies (Stone, 1985) are nurtured, including, "the hope that the group contains all that is necessary" (Boris, Zinberg, & Boris, 1975, p. 35).

The individual correlates of group container issues are self-acceptance and the ability to reconcile loss, failure, imperfection, and traumatic history. What have members gone through in their lives that has pained and scarred them? What have they come to expect from others and to demand of themselves? Similarly, what can they countenance in others, and what can they tolerate in themselves? To which interpersonal affronts are the various participants most susceptible?

Clients recognized as self-demeaning will have difficulties letting the group sooth, hold, and matter. Those who are rigid, nonaccepting, or opinionated will find it hard to provide enveloping protection for others. The work here is to create a holding and protective environment conducive to fostering "corrective emotional experiences" (Alexander, 1948). Within such a cultural canon, formative hurts can be recognized, addressed, and to whatever extent ameliorated by the transmuting transferences of the group. As such, the psychotherapy group can become both a current refuge and a transitional space representative of and generalizable to the outside world. Members pour themselves into the group experience. Through accepting, sharing, and exchanging, and with continual feedback, and consensual validation, the group helps the individual differentiate reality from fantasy, wish from truth, and functional from dysfunctional interaction.

This group process, however, is not always smooth nor totally benign. The individual bubblings up within the group container can be jarring and pressured. Prior hurts and failures in the patients' holding environments may surface, and members may become vulnerable and upset. Ulanov (1985) suggests that "the analyst must hold the situation securely enough to allow the patient to regress back into periods of gap (and narcissistic injury) when the person was dropped or discarded because [they were] not seen or cherished'' (p. 73). Healing actions must play out in a "good-enough" environment. Ulanov quotes Winnicott's edifying parable about the "good-enough mother": "This is the mother who may find herself hating her child when she sings the lullaby, 'Rock-a-Bye-Baby', with its concluding disaster. But hers is a hate she can hold and not take out on the child too crudely, at too great a distance from her love" (p. 72).

Ulanov (1985) argues that feelings of being alive and real cannot be reached unless all parts of the self are gathered into the shared experience, "the mad and the sane, the fragmented and the whole" (p. 74). "Our task is to house all the pieces and spaces of the psyche, not to get rid of any of them" (p. 75). In the psychotherapy group, various parts of the self and various social roles get configured, transferred, played out, and, in some cases, refined or transformed. But not everything changes. Some basic level of reconciliation must be built into the constraining arms of the group for its holding to be soft and comforting enough. The group experience ultimately becomes that container, open and readily available to house those recalcitrant and unacceptable parts of the self, "a place for wounds that do not heal and bits of madness that do not yield" (p. 74). As such, the group container can be a vehicle for hope and striving, or a vessel of resolve and acceptance.

In a subsequent session, Ellen is again noticeably upset, yet unwilling to talk about what's bothering her. She looks down in her lap and remains silent. With the group's persistent prompting, Ellen finally reveals that she has been "overreacting and tearful" about her 11-year-old son's difficulty in making friends and being part of his peer group. Ellen then attempts, in an embarrassed fashion, to retract her feelings by saying, "I know its stupid." She expresses a fear that if her children, or the group, witness her emotional reactions, "it will only make things worse." In reacting so, Ellen again reports being "crazy like my mother." Other group members try to soothe Ellen. Don, with tenderness and longing, relates how he wishes his parents cared enough about him when growing up to get upset about his social difficulties. Steve talks abstractly about the importance of closeness between parents and children. Jill remembers the saving grace of her mother's comforting involvement with her in times of social confusion and ostracism.

The group goes on to explore more directly Ellen's intense feelings and self-assessments of overinvolvement. We examine her difficulties, finding the proper balance between holding on and holding out. To do so, the therapist gets Ellen's permission to recount a pertinent piece of pregroup history. Ellen is reminded of a dream she had just prior to joining the group. In the dream, she goes to a new job and finds the people there behind bars and suffering. In an act of compassion, she feeds them raw meat. In an act of self-defense, she grabs a young girl and escapes by climbing a restraining wall. She and the girl then swing through the trees, feeling safe when outside and above. This dream reflects Ellen's anticipatory fears about group and her childhood defense of psychologically flying away (also a recurrent childhood dream motif). She wants both to belong and to flee, fearing that whenever she tries to become involved with others, she winds up in a crazy place, confined within the walls of her own history and pain.

Ellen feels overly responsible for every group silence and misstep, believing that the conglomerate functions better when she is not present. In her outside life, Ellen often works double shifts so that her overwrought presence won't "screw up the kids." In a mixed gesture of support and aggression, Patty, who feels protective of the group as a surrogate family, now challenges Ellen. "What makes you think you are so important that you can ruin this group?" This confrontation fosters an instantaneous narcissistic injury, as Ellen returns affectively to the site of her prior hurts and noninclusions. Having been moved from home to home, Ellen is not sure where she belongs and what impact her presence actually evokes. She usually assumes the worst, as on a deeply ingrained level she blames herself for her mother's psychosis and her father's alcoholism. Ellen expects to be abandoned, rejected, or treated as an unwanted intruder. If somehow incorporated, she fears being the carrier of pain and ruin.

With the group's encouragement, Ellen begins to recognize and explore more directly her sensitivities and uncertainties. She reports current experiences of being unappreciated or misunderstood by her husband and by her boss. When her feelings are hurt, Ellen immediately believes that she is no longer wanted and no longer belongs. Her impulse is to flee. In light of these disclosures, Patty softens toward Ellen. She reveals how she identifies with Ellen's sudden reactivity, often feeling insecure about her own position in the world, as well as in the group. Ellen and Patty compare histories, and empathic repair begins.

The therapist now connects Ellen's fears about her son with her unbridled empathy and difficulties separating herself from Joe's and Darlene's hurts. Transferentially, these young people represent that hurt child with no friends who is never really accepted and incorporated, a self-image, and a projection onto her own children and onto the remote group members. Ellen responds by reiterating how inappropriate her behavior is and how different she is from others. Patty, this time with an empathic force drawn from their therapeutic alliance, challenges Ellen's removal from the container of the group experience. She unequivocally states, "We all have differences. We're all a little crazy. But don't you dare remove yourself. We're all part of this group."

Coming Full Circle

Having parsed the psychotherapeutic circle, in closing it is time to bring matters back together. The image of eternal recurrence, the uroborus or snake eating its own tail (Eliade, 1988, Neumann, 1973), symbolizes the group's task of firmly grasping its slippery and segmented edge, while making an end to useless and compulsive repetitions. The circle as a symbol of wholeness and continuity allows disparate parts to be brought together under the sign of common concern. The protection of the geometric and symbolic properties of the psychotherapeutic sphere allows group boundaries to be maintained, an interactive matrix to be spun, group space to be meaningfully filled, and individual members to be safely received and held.

The centripetal and centrifugal forces within the vortex of the group help untangle and separate out life's complexities and Gordian knots. The group's hermetic band of protection provides shelter from heretofore vicious circles and the undulations of self-reflective Mobius rings. The group's capacity for viewing matters from the inside-out ultimately helps its members become more self-contained, as if securely encased in personalized versions of Klein's bottle (Levi-Strauss, 1988). When participants turn their attention to the tasks shared within the therapeutic circle, by necessity they become less estranged and decreasingly remote. In so doing, their experiences in group, and isomorphically in life, come full circle.

CHAPTER TWELVE

Group Analysis:

A Causal Paradigm for Working Through Impasse

Psychotherapy is concerned with the cause, management, and resolution of psychological problems. This simple exposition makes for a complex task. Working at psychotherapy en masse further complicates the ameliorative journey as various group processes, observable at many different levels of understanding, create multifarious paths for possible analysis.

What is the best route to human understanding and change? How do we track the seemingly random meanderings of thought, action, and feeling occurring in the psychotherapy group? Do we travel the well-lit road of lucid avowals, hunt amidst the murky swamp of quixotic purpose, descent into the subterranean currents of deepest meaning, or merely swim in a sea of human interactions? To explain the behavior demonstrated in groups, do we go back to journey's origin or project forward to decipher destination? Do we painstakingly study paths trodden, or closely monitor the mechanics of the shared journey?

Watching the therapeutic experience unfold in all its capricious irrationality and mystery, one often wonders if, in reality, it is really possible to render group events intelligible with anything approaching logical, rational exposition. The movement of the psychotherapy group, as advanced by member contributions, soon develops a shape, force, direction, and overdetermined significance that might be rendered comprehensible by expressly considering the ways and means of the emergent process.

At times, the flow of a group session proceeds unimpeded, as members simply interact and discuss their problems. At other junctures, the free flow becomes blocked or stifled. It is precisely at these points that a logical

An earlier version of this chapter appeared in the *International Journal of Group Psychotherapy, 38* (1), pp. 81–99, copyright 1988. Reprinted with permission of the American Group Psychotherapy Association.

perspective is helpful to make sense and work through impediments. But the goal is not simply to overcome an emergent problem; rather, it is to analyze difficulties in style, communication, character, and problem solving as they emerge. In a paradigm based on insight, change becomes possible when the course of the group's overall behavior is fully understood, with the members' contributions specified and thus made amenable to conscious control.

Group psychotherapy, approached from a logical perspective, is akin to theory building (Ettin, 1984). The therapist's initial task is semantic. The members' words serve as minitheories or summary processes connoting the participants' phenomenological experiences. The therapist first works with the group members to describe more adequately the data of their experiences and the stories of their lives. The descriptive process itself is ameliorative since, like the scientist, the members gain predictive and aesthetic control by developing a more adequate and exact depiction.

The next task of the group therapist, working within a logical mode, is to look for patterns behind empirical observations that recur in some predictable fashion. Hospers (1957), a philosopher of science, remarks that "knowledge in sciences begins with noticing regularities in the course of events. . . . Events occur over and over again in the same way" (p. 315). He goes on to talk about the pragmatic function of formulating explanations of these events. "Amidst the constant diversity in our daily experience. . . . We trace the thin red vein of order through the flux of experience . . . we trace regularities so we can predict future occurrences and take precautions" (p. 316).

Many group theorists (Laplanche & Pontalis, 1973; Haskell, 1978; Rutan & Stone, 1984) equate a full working through of problems with just such a discovery process. The therapist helps the group find and follow the affective threads that bind recurrent psychodynamics together in various contexts and at multiple levels of meaning. Fromm-Reichmann (1950) recommends "tying together . . . seemingly disconnected pieces of information [and] guiding patients in repeatedly working through in various and sundry connections the emotional experiences which have come to their awareness" (pp. 69–70). Laplanche and Pontalis (1973) explicate the group facilitator's role: "Working through is expedited by interpretations from the therapist which consist chiefly in showing how certain meanings in question can be recognized in different contexts" (quoted in Ganzarain, 1983, p. 282). Group analysis implies a connecting of predictable, often-repeated patterns over time and across diverse circumstance, thereby rendering a consistent series of groupwide events understandable and amenable to change.

The wisdom of Aristotle can be directly invoked here as an explanatory framework within which to approach the complex task of group analysis. Certainly Aristotle's concept of man as a social animal gives a philosophical rationale for an interpersonal treatment forum. In fact, Aristotle's metaphysics and Freud's metapsychology have a great deal in common. As early as 360 B.C., the practical physician, philosopher, and scientist began a life-long consideration of the issues of identity and change (Sahakian & Sahakian, 1966). He speculated about the shaping forces or impulses that mold matter into particular forms and outlined a linear theory of growth and development—a theory of potentials realized and maturity lost or found. As summarized by Durant (1954), Aristotle believed that "the mistakes and futilities of nature are due to the inertia of matter resisting the forming force of purpose" (p. 70). How similar these ideas are to the modern psychological concepts of fixation and psychic inertia (Freud, 1915; Parkin, 1981), resistance (Fenichel & Flapan, 1985), and impasse (Weiner, 1983).

Aristotle also appreciated that people sought answers to causal questions as a prerequisite for familiarity, understanding, and changing nature—human included (Sorabji, 1980). To grasp the logos of an object or event means that one must find an adequate explanation for its evolving form and timely occurrence. Allen (1966) paraphrases Aristotle's view: "It is clear that we must obtain knowledge of primary causes because it is when we think we understand its primary cause that we claim to know each particular thing" (p. 286). *Cause* is defined as "any of the things necessary for the movement or coming into being of a thing" (Random House, 1972). *Analysis,* from its Greek root, means "to loosen, dissolve, lay out" or resolve (Random House, 1972). Thus, in a group psychotherapy context, a causal analysis would imply a process by which the nature and dynamic processes underlying dysfunctional individual and collective behaviors are laid out, loosened, and dissolved.

Aristotle formulated a fourfold theory of descriptive causality in an attempt at a full rendering of the nature of objects and their inherent properties of stability and change. He posited four questions, which, when answered, supply a necessary and sufficient causal explanation.

1. *What* makes a thing what it is: What is its essence, or defining characteristics? (material cause)
2. *How* does a thing change: How do external events or internal stimuli set change in motion? (efficient cause)
3. *Where* are various changes aimed or headed: Where will matters end up? (final cause)
4. *Why* does something change or develop in a particular manner or fashion: Why does the present representational form of a thing look like it does? (formal cause)

Aristotle believed that every object or event was amenable to understanding by invoking interlacing descriptors. A full accounting necessitated explanation within each causal quadrant in order to create the full-ranging observational perspective necessary to effect change. "We might say that the doctrine is intended to have both heuristic and therapeutic value" (Charlton, 1983, p. 99). Table 12-1 gives a comparative description of the four causal foci.

Yalom (1970) operationalizes the call for an encompassing model by proposing four levels of insight attainable in the psychotherapeutic group. His levels, which include interpersonal, characterological, motivational, and genetic insight, are loosely based on Aristotle's causal principles. Yalom champions the view that the "concept of causality . . . has considerable explanatory potency for human behavior" (1970, p. 182). He does not, however, provide guidance as to how these levels of insight might be systematically explored, combined, and sequenced so as to provide a basis for a comprehensive intervention strategy.

Criteria for Initiating a Process Illumination

To work with a psychotherapy group means more than to investigate the fourfold causes of human behavior. First, the group must simply interact, openly and honestly; only then can the leader call the collective's attention to the nature of operative interactions and dynamic processes. Yalom (1976) differentiates two steps in working with the present-centered group: "*here-and-now activation*" and "*process illumination.*" In the former, the group merely interacts in a free-flowing fashion, taking up topics and talking about problems and relations as they become relevant for the members. In the latter step, a "self-reflective loop" is initiated, wherein the group members go back over notable interactions, identifying prevalent feelings, dynamics, distortions, and themes. Yalom warns that pure activation leads to an affect-dominated group with little understanding, whereas too much illumination dries up and overintellectualizes the process. Optimally, a balancing and shifting focus between free process and guided metaprocessing is sought.

Process illumination is never purely an intellectual experience. Such an explorative method furthers the group experience by stimulating affects and interactions, as well as by fostering associations, memories, and insights. However, any analytic process, in essence, stops the action in the service of understanding and integration. How does the therapist know when to interrupt the free flow with the aim of understanding and in the hopes of influencing what is transpiring?

Kernberg (1975) suggests that

TABLE 12-1 • Working Through Causal Foci

Cause	Material	Efficient	Final	Formal
Analytic question	What	How	Where	Why
Aristotle's definition	"Out of which a thing is made"	"Source of change or staying unchanged"	"That for the sake of which"	"What is the why for so and so to be"
Dictionary definition	"That of which a thing is made"	"The agent or force that produces a change or result"	"That end, design, or object for which anything is done"	"The elements of a conception that make the thing what it is; or the idea as a formative principle"
Explanatory focus	Personality Attitudes Beliefs Object relations Ego states Defensive structure Character Communication & interpersonal patterns Therapeutic content Themes Focal conflicts Groups norms	Stimuli Cues Triggers Impulses Drives Instincts Emotional states Meaning attributions Sensitivities Vulnerablities Conflicts Group atmosphere Group culture	Purposes Goals Designs Reinforcements Rewards Object of behavior Agendas Gains Secondary gains Ends Reasons Motives Hidden agendas	Essences Genesis Roots Primary experiences History Conditioning Imprinting Transferences Repetition compulsions Derivatives
Reached by	Process analysis Cognitive elaboration Exploring material content of issues, processes, & structures to assess patterns & general character of individual or event	Behavioral analysis Emotional elaboration Identifying the impetus & emotional antecedents of events and reactions	Motivational analysis Design elaboration Exploring wishes, fears, expectations, & secondary gains Clarifying aims and hidden agendas	Genetic analysis Etiological elaboration Uncovering, interpreting, exploring genetic roots; following associative flow and transference connections

Temporal frame	Recent past	Present	Future	Distant past
Type of insight	Characterological insight	Behaviorial & emotional insight	Motivational insight	Genetic insight
Goals of analysis	Configural realignment	Reactive retuning	Ends-means reassessment	Transformational adaptation
Change mechanisms	Awareness of behavior patterns Character work Increased impulse control Self-understanding, reeducation Generalization Understanding unconscious trends Ego building Universality	Catharsis, abreaction Raise sensitivity thresholds Overcome overlearned responsivity Become aware of vulnerabilities and emotional triggers Modeling Increased impulse control Increased evocative potential (spontaneity) (immediacy) (enactment) Changing agency & impetus of actions Increasing intimacy Skills enhancement Reduced isolation from own problems Emotional Bonding Empathy	Discover more functional means to goals Challenge & rechannel primitive needs Identification Establish new reinforcement patterns Working through normal stages of development Increased planning ability Encourging positive interaction Changing aim & function of behavior Reality testing Uncovering disparate parts of self Improving judgment Strategizing Clarifying aims Expand available choices Problem solving	Lift repression Encourage regression in the service of the ego Awareness of genesis of current reactions Work through to more adaptive and less overdetermined positions Corrective emotional experience Decathect habitual patterns Cathexis to new objects Insight Fostering new solutions to old problems Working through transferences Sorting out projections & distortions Redirect pathology Sublimation Build new psychic structures

technical skills [are] involved in the group therapist's decision-making as to when "experience" should be encouraged and when "thinking" should be encouraged. . . . The observing ego of the group therapist stands at the boundary between cognitive analysis of the meaning of what is going on and experiential unfolding of the emotional realities of individuals within the group and the group at large. (p. 262)

More specifically, Rutan and Alonso (1978) suggest enhancing the meaning of the group process by punctuating sessions with summary statements: "The leader decides that the meeting has produced some profitable data that bears further exploration. . . . The result . . . is to cause a 'pause' in the process" (p. 13). In a similar vein, Tauber (1978) proposes a choice point analysis where the group therapist "spots the point in the therapy flow that has a demand quality. Then he chooses an intervention to deal with that choice point" (p. 168). Tauber suggests that such choice points often occur at those moments of group impasse or resistance that seemingly demand a working through of the issues or dynamics causing blockages.

Stein (1976) further clarifies the technique and timing of moving from experiencing to processing.

The therapist . . . maintains a group centered and interactional fostering approach until the rise in the intergroup tension produces the intense member to member interaction. . . . This is permitted to go on until the nature of the interaction and the character traits each member contributes to the interaction have become clear—that is when it has served the therapeutic purpose of demonstrating interaction. At this point, unless a member of the group does it, the therapist intervenes . . . in a group centered fashion by asking the group, that is all the members of the group, what is occurring in the group. This serves to halt the interaction and the therapeutic work of describing and discussing and interpreting it [the process] begins. (p. 45)

Similarly, many group-centered leaders, as reviewed by Horwitz (1977), begin process illumination with the emergence of a "common group theme" or "unifying factor" that influences all group behavior at any one moment (p. 425). Bion (1961), for example, analyzes the group's "basic assumptions." Whitaker and Lieberman (1964) work with "focal conflicts," and Ezriel (1980) interpretively addresses the "common group tension." Ezriel's sense of transition from process to processing is evident as he advises, "When the therapist has been able to diagnose the common group tension as well as the idiosyncratic responses of each individual to the group theme, he offers a comprehensive interpretation of the 'group structure' at that time" (cited in Horwitz, 1977, p. 425). Horwitz (1977) suggests reversing the sequence of the interventions, moving from the individual to the group level. Whatever the order of the sequencing, it is advisable to analyze both the general and the particular manifestations of a given dynamic, theme, or impasse—that is, the significance for the group-as-a-whole and the meaning for particular members.

Causal Analysis and Working Through

The choice point for initiating a process illumination, or, in this case, a causal analysis, is the emergence of a strong specifiable trend: whether a transference, resistance, or impasse; the stimulation of a poignant interchange, projective identification, or evident parataxic distortion; or the consolidation of a resounding, common groupwide theme. In all these cases, "material" has arisen out of the ongoing free associative process and consolidated sufficiently to be identifiable and analyzable. No matter what level of material organization emerges (individual, interactional, group-as-a-whole), or what the order of therapeutic exploration, such regularities benefit from a full-ranging causal analysis (Rice,1969; Borriello, 1979).

- Amelioration 2. *Group processes and individual dynamics can be analyzed and worked through by fully explaining their shape, force, direction, and genesis.*

The timing and systematic movement between causal foci can be sequentially mapped. The suggested flow of the causal analysis follows a what → how → where → why sequence. Such a flow imitates both standard therapeutic practice and the natural logic of causative inquiry by first considering present dynamics and later moving toward a fuller understanding of implications and antecedents.

Thus, a set of questions, reflecting a fully descriptive therapeutic mapping, can be formulated that moves the group toward more encompassing understandings and toward a full-ranging working through of dynamic issues.

1. *What* is now going on in the group?
2. How was the group process initiated and sustained and how do members feel about what's going on?
3. *Where* are these group processes leading and where are they avoiding going?
4. *Why* have the group processes evolved as they have and why are they so ingrained, persistent, and hard to change?

The following clinical vignette will be tracked through the various steps of the causal analysis. The example begins with a description of an impasse in an ongoing group that initiated a "pause for cause." This working through sequence, which played out over many sessions, is offered as a prototypical process illumination in the causal mode. It was repeated many times in a variety of forms and across myriad content areas during the group's lifetime.

A group that had been meeting for approximately one year became mired in a stilted, turn-taking, advice-giving mode, despite many attempts by the therapist to foster more open-ended and spontaneous interchange. For several weeks, members complained that their needs were not being met in the group.

During one session, Lisa, an attractive and dramatic 26-year-old, begins a long narrative about her ambivalence in deciding whether to stay with her job. She reports getting "no direction" from her boss who "isn't taking her seriously." Lisa works for a large company of which her father is president. She recently moved out of her parents' home amidst similar concerns and worries about personal authority. The group was instrumental in helping her carry out the decision to move and in dissuading her from taking up residence in a townhouse owned by her father. Lisa presents her current job concerns in histrionic fashion, saying that she wants advice from the group, while looking directly at the therapist. The group is restless and inattentive. At this "choice point," the therapist calls a halt to the ongoing proceedings for the purpose of process illumination, or, in this case, for initiating a causal analysis.

Material Cause:
What Is Now Going on in the Group?

Material causality reflects the *what* of an experience or "that of which a thing is made." In the psychotherapy group, the *what* refers to those stable configurations of character, pattern, structure, or process that have arisen, solidified, and given a specifiable shape to the proceedings. To explore the *what* of the group is to assess and elaborate generalizable characteristics of individuals, interactions, and events. To arrive at such an understanding, the therapist might ask himself or herself, "What matters here?"

The material that an individual brings to group and his or her manner of presentation provides the substance for a causal analysis of conscious attitudes, beliefs, and behaviors, as well as for exploring less than conscious intrapsychic dynamics, personality trends, ego states, complexes, defensive structures, and configurations of character. Interpersonal interactions result in feedback, encounters, and direct experience, which highlight members' styles, object relations, transferences, roles, communication, and relational patterns. An analysis of the *what,* at the group level, yields persistent themes, norms, trends, conflicts, and group phase phenomena, as well as revealing the more symbolic, universal, and collective nature of the group-wide experience. Groupwide trends may also manifest as defensive maneuvers, such as impasses or resistances. Exploring the *what* of the group requires bringing together seemingly diverse elements into a meaningful summary exposition that expresses the essence of the ongoing process.

Material cause operates within the temporal mode of the recent past. Right on the heels of the active process taking place in the present, a narrative restatement of salient aspects is intended. Such a summary may be fashioned by the leader or may more spontaneously arise as a member catches the group voice and becomes the spokesperson of a common concern. This may immediately spur additional here-and-now reactions, clarifications, and amplifications, until the group, by *"cognitive elaboration,"* comes to some consensus about *what* is transpiring.

To know what one does in reference to oneself, others, and the group-as-a-whole is curative in and of itself (Yalom, 1970). An analysis of the material cause makes sense out of the proceedings. Patterns become less habitual and more recognizable, and some dynamic trends can be brought under conscious control. Increased awareness, interpersonal sensitivity, and reeducation can help hone the rough edges of character into a finer profile. Comparing styles, identifying, and modeling can lead to discovering new ways of being and developing more effective social skills. Recognition of groupwide and universal trends can break patterns of isolation and help put problems into a wider and more acceptable context. The goal of a material cause analysis is *"thematic clarification"* and eventual *"configural realignment."*

As an intellectual exercise, identifying what is going on in group is the least threatening of the causal steps. Specifying trends often stimulates a curiosity to delve behind regularities to uncover motivational, directional, and shaping forces of behaviors, interactions, and group-level processes.

The steps of the material analysis are as follows:

1. Groupwide processes (themes, trends, impasses) are identified and elaborated on. *"What is going on, right now, in this group?"*
2. Key interactions relating to these specifiable trends are identified and explored. *"What is going on between members that relates and contributes to this noticeable pattern?"*
3. Individual contributions to the process are specified. *"What has each individual contributed to the group process?"*
4. Group patterns are now reiterated, with a fuller understanding of their individual and interpersonal elements. *"It seems that what is really going on now is. . . ."*

5. Next, the group will be encouraged to look at how these trends evolved and were maintained.

The therapist acknowledges Lisa's complaints and concurs with her assessment about the group's inattention (interpersonal process). He suggests that, in addition to the personal significance and meaning of Lisa's reactions (transferential process), she is also acting as spokesperson for the group by bringing up feelings of dissatisfaction with authority, confusion resulting from nondirection (or perhaps misdirection), and impulses to quit the group. It is pointed out that lately, the group has appeared consistently disgruntled, restless, and inattentive. The group members are now invited to respond to the leader's observations. A causal analysis begins with a focus on "What is going on here?"

Various group members avow vague dissatisfaction and confusion with the turn-taking process. Dottie (a persistent storyteller) and Lisa express specific anger at the therapist and at the group for not being interested in their accounts, which are most important tales to them. Other members clarify their response to the various stories and comment on their actual level of interest or disinterest. Members directly address each other and the therapist as a consensus about what has been going on is sought.

Each member's contribution to the turn-taking process is clarified. Doug describes how he feels conflicted and somewhat restless during the turn taking. He admits, however, that his incessant questioning of others keeps the focus on the storyteller and away from him. Tom, the youngest member of the group, is given feedback by the group that he also supports the pattern by acting as junior therapist, making objective comments and rarely relating the material to himself. Dottie talks of how she attempts to make herself interested in the various narrations as a felt obligation to others in the group. Lisa complains of trying to engage others in more emotional interactions but of being rebuffed, often being told that she is "too emotional." Lisa reports that her feelings then build up. In a rush to express herself, she talks quickly and often loses the thread of her argument. The group concurs with Lisa's assessment and adds that at these times they can't follow her and become inattentive. Ward relates that many of the group situations described "touch home" and that his silent assent to the storied turn taking is not a sign of disinterest but rather of "morbid introspection." Jane tells of "not wanting to interrupt people" and so she stays quiet. She is not sure how important her comments might be anyway. Jane then leaves group sessions frustrated and with her own needs unmet.

Thus, the material configuration is described in a "cognitive elaboration." The therapist compliments the group members on being willing to share their life stories. He acknowledges that good advice is often forthcoming. It is suggested, however, that the process of monologue and problem solving has inherent frustrations built in, given realistic time constraints and needs to share the therapist. Concurring with the group's own observations, it is pointed out that the turn-taking impasse is not accidental but, in fact, reflects the particular needs and fears of the various members. A further analysis is suggested to arrive at a fuller meaning of the process in question.

At this point, the group is in agreement as to *what* has transpired and has delineated *what* each member has contributed. It is time to explore *how* the group process was initiated and sustained.

Efficient Cause: How Was This Group Process Initiated and Sustained? How Do Group Members Feel About What's Going On?

Efficient causality describes *how* an action or reaction arises, or "the agents and forces that produce a change or result." In the psychotherapy group, the *how* refers to the impetus that generates the group process and leads to consolidation of specific material configurations. To explore the *how* of the group is to assess and elaborate the eliciting mechanisms and affective meanings of various individual, relational, and groupwide processes. To arrive at such an understanding, the group therapist might ask himself or herself: "How efficiently are the members working together?"

The psychotherapy group is an ideal forum in which to search out the efficient causes of behavior. Specific emotions, sensitivities, vulnerabilities, impulses, and drives are released in response to a variety of cues, triggers, meaning attributions, and confrontations. Invariably, the varied group personalities and the group's developmental sequence will stimulate and mimic key formative experiences. Strong feelings will be evoked and patterns of reactivity will be cued. These feelings and patterns can be analyzed, as individual reactions receive therapeutic attention and as interactions are subsequently played back and explored. Additionally, groupwide moods, tones, climatic, and atmospheric conditions that accompany the more cognitive characteristics of the group can be identified.

Consistent behavioral and affective patterns that are left unanalyzed frequently result in the repetition of dysfunctional cycles, often with an accompanying dysphoria, stultified group climate, and the consolidation of a groupwide impasses or resistances. Thus, it becomes increasingly important to analyze how the group got to this position. Knowledge of mechanisms of action and of personalized affective meanings is reached by linking antecedent events with current reactions, by exploring empowering feelings, and by deciphering the symbolic and the personal meanings of various group instances, actions, and circumstances.

Efficient cause is as close to present-centered analysis as any retroactive consideration can be, for it seeks to specify the ongoing meanings and mechanics of the process. Aristotle considered efficient cause contemporaneous with that for which it is responsible (Charlton, 1983, p. 101). How are members feeling and reacting within themselves, toward each other, and in reference to the group-as-a-whole? Such an elucidation of cues, triggers, and sensitivities can be initiated by encouraging the most currently affected member to be directly expressive, or alternately by the therapist labeling the overall group mood. Turning specifically to the affective realm may spur various members to be actively expressive of feelings until, by *"behavioral analysis"* and *"emotional elaboration"* the group becomes aware and attuned to *how* it is acting and feeling.

Understanding the *how* of experience is evolutionarily crucial for adaptational learning. Emotional elaboration of recurrent themes allows for catharsis, abreaction, and empathic bonding between the group members, as well as reducing isolation from one's own feelings. Knowing the efficient cause of our human motion allows for more impulse and emotional control, as sensitivities and vulnerabilities are accurately perceived and anticipated. Group members can better learn to predict trouble spots and then adopt prophylactic measures and alternative strategies to prevent overlearned reactivity. In other instances, a member, in the face of continuing emotional stimulation, can decide to act differently. Thus, the goal of an efficient cause analysis is to understand automatic behaviors and affective patternings, and eventually raise sensitivity thresholds as an instance of *"reactive retuning."*

The steps in an efficient causality analysis are as follows.

1. The prevalent group mood, atmosphere, or climate is identified. *"How does it feel to be in this room, right now?"*
2. A behavioral analysis of various cues and triggers present in the interactions is explored. *"How were these feelings set off amongst us?"*
3. Individual variants and contributors to the group mood are specified in an emotional elaboration. *"How are each of you feeling and reacting to what is going on?"*
4. The group history is now searched for similar triggers, emotions, and meanings that have contributed to the current mood and shaped the overall group culture. *"How the group got to this point is now understandable given. . . ."*
5. Next, the group will be encouraged to seek out the directionality and motivating forces leading to various emotional and reactive patterns.

The therapist now asks the group "how" this particular turn-taking/problem-solving process was triggered and how they actually feel about it. The group takes a turn toward the affective realm as members share their previously unspoken reactions. The emotional feel of the proceeding process is elaborated. In a more free-flowing discussion, various sensitivities, assumptions, and projections surface for consideration. First, the prevalent group mood is identified. Various members talk about their confusion, frustration, boredom, and anger. Such unspoken feelings fester and infect the group process. As members come to agree on the prevalent group mood, a shared sense of responsibility emerges, as does the impetus to move through this group impasse.

Dottie reveals how other people's plights create a sense of panic and urgency in her. She is propelled by "compulsive internal pressure" to help, moving quickly to "solve a pressing problem that, if not immediately resolved, is only likely to get worse." Other members talk about their own reasons for perpetuating surface talk and quick solution. Doug explains that he harbors many underlying judgments about "people's situations," but is wary about exposing them. He is not sure how others will react and does not want to hear the criticisms that others might have of him. Doug is given feedback by the members that despite his attempts to hide his feelings, judgments come through "loud and clear." The women in the group are especially uncomfortable with the strength and chauvinism of Doug's opinions. Ward now reveals that he, too, is consciously worried over the strength of his own reactions. Ward reports often feeling "psychotically distressed and agitated." He fears that the group can't handle his emotions and so he bottles up his affective reactions, leaving himself charged-up, removed, and overintellectualized.

Lisa admits to being intimidated by the intelligence of the various group members, like Ward. She describes the "pressure to be on their level." Lisa now expresses direct annoyance at Ward and Dottie for "their big words" and chastises them for avoiding feelings and intentionally "talking down" to her. Tom reveals that he feels more immature than others in the group. Tom's shame and reluctance to share his "child-like concerns" in part explains his attempted identification with the "grown-up" therapist, as well as his tacit support of the emotionally distant fact-finding process. Jane remains silent during the emotional elaboration. When invited to talk, she expresses a pessimistic view of the prospects of getting one's needs met in this or any other group.

Next, the various group members' responses are compared and contrasted with previous reactions, behaviors, and perceptions from the group history. An attempt is made first to isolate and then provide context for recurrent emotions, reactions, themes, and affective patterns. With the material and emotions now elaborated, the causal analysis turns to the more motivational aspects of various patterns, dynamics, and resistances, by considering their final cause.

Final Cause:
Where Are the Group Processes Leading?
Where Are the Group Processes Avoiding Going?

Final causality represents the *where* or end of any behavior or attitude, or "the end, design or object for which anything is done." In the psychotherapy group, the *where* specifies the end to which the group trend is invariably leading. To explore the *where* of the group is to assess the directionality and motive forces behind individual, interpersonal, and groupwide trends and patterns. An axiom of psychology is that behavior is purposeful. Yet group members' behaviors are not always direct, consciously intended, or immediately specifiable. Beier (1966) writes of the individual's disguised affective requests, which can be easily denied if "wished-for" consequences do not follow. Similarly, Ezriel (1980) writes of "avoided" and "calamitous" relationships, and Whitaker and Lieberman (1964) work with "disturbing" and "reactive" motives. Thus, when focal conflicts arise in the group-as-a-whole, compromise solutions are sought between the collective wishes and fears of the members. To arrive at an understanding of a group's directionality, the therapist might ask himself or herself: "If unchecked, where in the final analysis will all of these turns of event wind up?"

A group member's communication may present both a wish and a defense. Even apparently dysfunctional behaviors may seek out "secondary gains" or disguised wishes. Such hidden agendas often eventually result in confusingly obtuse communications and unsatisfactory and distorted interactions. Self-fulfilling prophesies may result, as disguised communications directly elicit feared consequences. For example, the wallowing behavior of a depressed patient wishing for caretaking and sympathy may actually elicit anger and rejection from other members. The recipients of the dysphoric affects may feel threatened, while having difficulty calmly countenancing their own resultant feelings of impotence and frustration. To work toward understanding the final cause of behavior means decoding both the wishes and the fears inherent in the individual, interpersonal, and groupwide interactions. Similarly, aims and expectations are clarified, secondary gains and hidden agendas are exposed, and the expression of heretofore excommunicated issues, affects, and impulses are encouraged (Goodman, 1986).

Final cause logically and intuitively jumps to the future where the outcomes of behaviors, interactions, and group negotiations can be previewed. By investigating the teleology of interaction, the direction and misdirection of behavior can be specified in a *"motivational analysis."* The work of *"resistance analysis"* specifically traces the fear component hampering free and clear action and interaction.

To know where one is headed is to allow foresight to guide us; blind alleys can be avoided and dysfunctional patterns can be short-circuited. Once aims are specified, alternative and often more effective means toward goals can be explored. In cases where aims are unrealistic or reflect primitive impulses, these motives may be challenged, rechanneled, or sublimated, as higher levels of maturity are cultivated. Patterns of reinforcement can be clarified and changed; successful attainments can be identified and rewarded. By encouraging more direct and honest communication within the safety of the group, the therapist diminishes the need for personal disguise. Secrets can be told, and guilt can be worked through. More issues can be faced more directly.

In the group, a sense of universality and belonging often results as members with diverse backgrounds, histories, and characterological styles discover strikingly similar aims, needs, and fears. Working toward common goals, the members can take a more active and constructive role in meeting their own needs and in determining the group's direction. Thus, the goal of the final cause analysis is an understanding of the motives and directionality of behavior, culminating in an *"ends-means reassessment."*

The steps of formal analysis are as follows:

1. The direction and outcome of the group process, agenda, or aim is identified. *"Where is this group culture leading us and where is it preventing us from going?"*
2. Concomitant interpersonal defensive maneuvers and security operations are identified. Self-fulfilling prophesies, dysfunctional interpersonal patterns, and projective identifications are specified. *"Where are members going with each other and where is it dangerous to go? Are members getting what they want and expect from others in the group, and if not, where have interactions gone wrong?"*
3. Individual wishes, needs, impulses, hidden agendas, and secondary gains are made overt. Fears and anticipated negative consequences are elaborated. *"Where is each member trying to move and where are they stuck? Where are the hidden agendas that are being acted out in the group?"*
4. Groupwide conflicts are now respecified in light of both the wishes and fears of the individuals and the aggregate. Previously excommunicated issues are brought within the bounds of the group's consideration. *"It is now clearer where the group is going in light of . . . and that to change this direction we must. . . . "*
5. Next, the group will be encouraged to uncover and explore the generative experiences that have led to such habitual and dysfunctional behavioral and motivational patterns.

The group is now invited to look at the expected directions and predictable outcomes of their behavioral and emotional stances. Where are interactions leading and where do they avoid going? It is suggested that the group "fact-finding mission" presents anew, for various members, an attempt to meet interpersonal needs yet avoid feared consequences. The strategy of turning the group analysis to final cause fleshes out many covert, overlearned, and unconscious strategies.

First, felt needs and conscious wishes and expectations are considered. Dottie speaks of wanting to be close to other people, believing that demonstrating her interest and willingness to problem solve will get her there. She is confused and hurt when such a "factual stance" leads group members to experience her as aloof, judgmental, and nonfeeling. Doug talks of "just accepting" the group process. He likes to "jump on the band wagon" as a way of being involved without the risk of taking initiative. Lisa genuinely hopes that the group problem solving will provide her with answers to life's dilemmas, feeling ill-equipped to resolve them herself. She sadly reveals her ambivalence about this tactic, realizing that such a strategy infantilizes her and prevents her from being "taken seriously."

Tom realizes that keeping the discussion content oriented serves his purpose of personal disguise, protecting him from others getting to know and possibly dislike him. Ward reports using "intellectualization" his whole life as a way to "ward off" painful emotions. With prompting, Jane reveals that she wishes that "someone" (mostly the therapist) would invite her to talk. Being recognized and invited would serve as a measure of her worth.

As the group considers *where* their interactions actually lead, many underlying and motivating processes become conscious. Tom realizes that a factual discussion keeps him away from disruptive feelings that often engender stuttering and subsequent ridicule. He projects his fear of a critical audience onto the group. Doug is afraid to show his sensitive side to the women in the group lest they "dismiss or cut him down." Thus, he portrays a cavalier macho image, while fearing that his real feelings will irrupt in angry foray, a pattern in evidence in his marriage.

Lisa seeks emotional involvement but she also fears the demands of close relationships. She has developed a pattern of attracting attention, encouraging intense interaction, and then withdrawing. Dottie's "mad rush to solution" often disregards more subtle aspects of experience and precludes possibilities that provide the excitement, richness, and soul of attachments. Hence, she feels, and often is, disconnected and left out. Fear of strong emotions leads Ward to underdifferentiate his feelings and to overidentify with objective problems, automatically withdrawing into an introspective stupor. As a result, he feels dissociated from the group and lost in "an intellectual fog." These diverse members' motivational patterns clarify the group impasse of isolation, inattention, and intellectualization.

Jane's situation exemplifies the nature of the self-fulfilling prophesies that underlie many of the group behaviors. When Jane is called upon to talk, she "pours out" her troubles, jumping from issue to issue while rarely pausing to take a breath. The group's initial interest and tolerance quickly disintegrates. Jane, very sensitive to nonverbal cues, believes this only proves that others don't really care and that, in fact, she is insignificant and worthless. Her disappointment and hurt transform into impotent rage. She then withdraws, emanating an aura of nihilistic, castrating pessimism, which others, in fact, spurn.

In this group, Jane's projection of other's noncaring is questioned, as members are invited to address the nature of their reactions to her monologues and self-absorbed behaviors. Ward tells Jane that he is initially concerned with her problems, but that she soon becomes hard to follow, while not allowing room for others to comment, respond, or relate similar feelings or circumstances. Dottie says that Jane seems so fragile and vulnerable to hurt that any response or interaction feels unsafe. Doug admits that sensing underlying hostility makes him afraid that his feedback will be taken the wrong way and that Jane will "bite his head off."

In this and subsequent sessions, the nature of Jane's needs, fears, and interactions are explored further. The self-fulfilling aspect of her behavior is analyzed. Wanting others to validate her, Jane holds back. Fashioning a test of her value, she waits to be "asked to dance." During this wallflower period, disappointment mounts and her need state builds. Jane really wants others to see through her silence and anticipate her needs. When she is finally chosen, her desire to empty herself is so great that she uses the group as a bottomless container, thereby overwhelming others in the process. They then turn off or turn away, and she feels empty again. Jane accurately perceives the members' restlessness and uses this data to validate her original feelings of low self-esteem and diminished faith in other people. Here, and in many other instances, this teleological and dysfunctional pattern is pointed out in its various manifestations.

Jane is encouraged to recognize this prosaic interpersonal proclivity and learn to behave differently—to be more direct about her needs and not let them build up and fill her so completely. She is asked to maintain a more steady connection with the other group members and to monitor the results of this change. The group invites Jane to satisfy her social hunger in bits and bites, not in binges and purges. Using Jane as a model, other members also explore their own self-defeating styles of interaction. As long-standing patterns are clarified, attention naturally turns to the past and a consideration of formal cause. *"Why did these patterns arise in the first place, and why are they so prevalent and hard to change?"*

Formal Cause:
Why Have the Group Processes Evolved as They Have?
Why Are These Emergent Patterns So Pervasive?

Formal causality depicts the *why* of an experience, or "the elements of a conception that make the thing what it is." In the psychotherapy group, the *why* refers to those formative experiences that serve to generate stable configurations, reactive and affective patterns, and motive forces. To discover the *why* is to go back, uncover, and explore genetic experiences, looking for essences, roots, imprints, derivatives, and repetitions of prior primary experience. To arrive at an understanding of the genesis of various individual and groupwide behaviors, the group therapist might ask himself or herself: "Why do members consistently conform to the group process the way they do?"

This last step in a causal analysis looks to the formative creation of symptoms, patterns, and pathologies, and specifically aims at lifting repressive defenses, encouraging regression in the service of the ego, and fostering adaptive reconstruction reflective of more current realities. Early memories and feelings may become available for conscious consideration, as realization is fostered that the group interactions occur in response to both current realities and the transferential influence of previously crucial relationships and experiences. Projections, identifications, and projective identifications arise and are analyzed.

The collective itself also evolves a rich formative history, influential in shaping in-group behaviors. When attempting to account for group dynamics, various antecedent and primary group experiences can be referred back to as seed causes. Each participant traces how various powerful group events interface with his or her characterological stance and how they influence more immediate group decisions, norms, and cultural dynamics. Disabling solutions to former group dilemmas may have contributed to shaping the present group resistances and impasses. Early formative experiences of members or of the group-as-a-whole may be reached by following the free associative flow, or by purposefully traveling an affect bridge back to the root of the multiple and varied transferential reactions. It may be asked: "Why are these feelings or experiences so powerful? When else in your life have you felt just this way? What of the whole of your life is reanimated and represented through these particular part-processes?"

Formal cause fosters a now-to-then focus, linking the present to the past by means of compelling memories, emotional and behavioral similarities, and historical reconstruction. The present is seen as a derivative or isomorphic representation of primary formative experiences. The genesis of current dynamic patterns may be spontaneously reported by a member in a moment of insight or reflection. At other times, the therapist connects the past to the present by way of specifically formulated interpretive linkings. Considering genetic or formal cause may elicit further remembrances and comparisons of experience until, by *"genetic analysis,"* the members and the group come to a fuller understanding of why they react the way they do. Members come to know and appreciate the generative forces behind present behaviors.

To know why one responds as one does provides insight, richness, and depth to human understanding. By becoming aware of the genesis of current reactions, group members can avow their early necessity and trace the incorporation of earlier influences in later personality and character structure. The appropriateness and utility of carrying on patterns conditioned in childhood can be considered. Working through can aim toward deconditioning dysfunctional patterns and adopting less troublesome and more freely chosen ways of reacting and interacting. Pathology can be redirected, distortions and projections sorted out, novel attitudes and alternative objects cathected, and new psychic structures built. Strong affect may be tied up in these early experiences. Exploring the formal cause can engender catharsis and abreaction. Thus, the aims of a formal causal analysis are *"genetic reconstruction"* and eventual *"transformational adaptation."*

The steps of a causal analysis are as follows:

1. Formative group historical events are recalled as they reflect on current processes, trends, themes, or impasses. *"Why has the group gotten to this point?"*
2. Functional and dysfunctional interactions are recalled, and transferential and countertransferential reactions uncovered. *"Why have members reacted to each other as they have? Why are these particular interactions so meaningful?"*
3. Individual genetic interpretations and revelations are made, corrective emotional experiences fostered, new adaptations encouraged, and sublimations are wrought. *"Why does this happen to you and why is it so hard to change?"*
4. A more comprehensive understanding of the group theme and/or adaptive solution to the group impasse is fostered. *"It is, now, much clearer why the group has arrived at this point and why we've been stuck here. Let's look at how this situation is different from. . . . "*
5. Next, the group will be encouraged to move on to more integrated "process activations" reflective of a more actively and freely chosen responsivity.

Now the group, under the therapist's direction, speculates about and interprets the "root causes and emotional antecedents" of the various dysfunctional and self-perpetuating intrapsychic patterns and interactive styles that underlie the group impasse. It is assumed that the urgent necessity of various group behaviors is overdetermined by both current group realities and past proclivities. Thus, an exploration of both individual and group histories follows earlier considerations of more current causes of the dysfunctional group process.

The "formative group experiences" that might have generated, conditioned, or necessitated the intellectualized group approach are initially considered. What is the group's historical context for the turn-taking/problem-solving tact? What group incidents encouraged this norm? What group problems arose that suggested this particular solution?

It is now recalled how Ward had "overreacted" and "attacked" Jane's style of interaction during one of the few times that she had volunteered information about herself. The group cited this incident as contributing to a "we better stick to the facts" attitude. Lisa's absences after particularly "hot sessions" were also pointed out as having a diffusing effect on the group's emotions. These events seemingly demonstrated that members couldn't withstand confrontation and, that faced with charged feelings, will attack, flee, or fall to pieces. These and other group events tended to lead to a group avoidance of strong feelings and expressive dialogue.

The group now looks to the history of individual members that contributes to the less than interactive process. The therapist interprets various formative life experiences of particular members as root causes of current reactions. Members are invited to examine, clarify, and elaborate on relevant past history. An emotional rendering is sought, as participants compare notes and empathically relate to one another's formative experiences. The early necessity and utility of particular psychodynamic patterns is considered, along with the self-limiting side effects of just these internal complexes and external configurations.

When exploring his strong reactions in group, Ward reveals his direct descent from Armenian holocaust survivors. His father lost many close relatives and had his own life disrupted by fleeing to America to escape persecution. Stories of atrocities permeated the family atmosphere. To prevent a recurrence of such devastation, Ward's father held a tight reign on his son, wishing him to become a powerful doctor, immune to political instabilities. He pushed Ward unrelentingly in his studies, prescribing a curriculum to be accomplished after and in addition to the normal school day. Ward became a very serious and overwrought child and adolescent, fearing a vague and impending doom while failing to differentiate between the drastic and the mundane. His intellectual skills and his overintellectualized stance led to exaggerations and morbid preoccupations. In the group, Ward worked toward relabeling his experiences more accurately so that he wasn't frightened by his own internal dialogues and so others weren't overwhelmed by his devastatingly powerful rhetoric. The group's ability to provide affective anchoring and consensual reality became most helpful to Ward in this regard.

Tom now reveals his own localized version of being terrorized by his brothers. They teased him unmercifully, often with sadistic vehemence. He learned to be overly accommodating and to seek out "safer" adults so as not to incur the wrath of his siblings. Tom feared expressing his real feelings lest his words be used against him. His hesitancies in interaction and in speech transferred to the group setting. Here, Tom was encouraged to see himself differently and to assess if these others, his current peers and transferential siblings, still related to him with such malice and shame induction.

Dottie explores, in some depth, her early family situation, which engendered proclivities for getting the facts and relying on reason and immediate, practical action. She was born with a congenital heart defect, which as a child greatly limited her mobility. She was often quite ill, with high temperatures and "scary symptoms." No action was taken to correct the defect since her father "did not believe in doctors." At age 12, Dottie needed emergency surgery. She was terrified and unprepared. No wonder it seems unsafe to "leave matters alone and unsettled." Fast fact finding, immediate diagnosis, and a reasoned approach to problem solving are needed to quickly resolve heart-wrenching difficulties. Otherwise, drastic consequeunces may ensue. Additionally, Dottie shares how her father became "increasingly irrational'' and subject to ''primitive emotional outbursts'' as a result of his own untreated medical condition. It was important for Dottie to cultivate her rationality in contrast and in defense of her father's destructive irrational attitudes. She developed a deep fear and distrust of emotionality and of any mental processes that were less than consciously mediated.

These formative events influence Dottie's current difficulty in forming warm and in-depth personal relationships in and out of the group. Her friendships tend to dry, reality bound, and consultative in nature. Derivatively, Dottie also relates how her professional writing endeavors are overly factual and suffer from a lack of emotional involvement and imaginative elaboration. It is suggested that Dottie slowly learn to trust the messages and contextual richness of her less organized reactions, emotions, imaginings, and introspections. In the group, she can experiment with loosening her control without actually risking the chaotic disorganization of her father's world of irrationality, distrust, and unconsciously inspired acting out.

Doug, in considering his reluctance to disclose his feelings and vulnerabilities, describes his troubled and enmeshed relationship with his mother. In his matriarchal Jewish family, mother wielded the emotional clout. Doug experienced her as needy, manipulative, and castrating. He sadly reports that ''she never accepted my feelings or the way I went about doing things.'' Consequently, Doug developed a style of limiting self-initiative, withdrawing at crucial moments, and closing up to routine emotional expressions. He fully expects to ''get put down'' for his beliefs, actions, and feelings. His long-standing anger, suspicion, and vigilance crystallize in his taking defensively superior postures toward women. Jane's judgments and castrating stance make her a ready target for Doug's transferred mother feelings.

In a subsequent session, Jane shares the essence of a phone call she received from her father. She was surprised as he woefully admitted his inadequacies as a parent. Jane relates how, in fact, he had ''shut himself off in a room'' while she was growing up. She reports experiencing no warmth, support, or encouragement from her dad. Jane's hiding within the group becomes more understandable as an angry identification with her father, as do her motives from wanting others to seek her out. Her rage and disappointment when men ''don't meet her expectations'' also becomes understandable. The group works with Jane to be more inviting of contact, and thereby interrupt the self-fulfilling pattern of silent expectations, disappointment/neglect, withdrawal, rage, and the assuming of a cold uninviting stance.

Doug and Jane begin to realize why their personal histories predispose them to get embroiled in miscommunications and ill feelings, as the nature of their mutual transference is clarified. Their relationship is explored in some detail in the context of these formative experiences. Doug is able to see how his withdrawal and demeaning attitudes toward women initiate Jane's hostile and retaliative response. Jane is able to explore the scope and impact of her hurt at feeling abandoned, which eventuates in distrust and a subsequent retaliatively castrating stance.

Life and its mirror, the group, interact and inform each other. The past can be indirectly relived through animated transferences, parataxic distortions, and individual idiosyncratic reactions to groupwide themes and conflicts. However, group therapy does not occur in a vacuum. Real life goes on and members bring their current circumstances into the therapy room. Often, members may be struggling with just those powerful figures who stimulated and inspired the various transferences, dysfunctions, and distortions. In an active interplay between inside and outside, relationships and reactions to real-life figures make up part of the group's content, while within-group processes also influence out-of-group adaptations. Causal insights and subsequent changes in perception and interaction can help reshape outside as well as inside relations.

Prior to the next session, Doug's parents have come for a visit. His enmeshed relationship with his mother flares and engenders problems with his wife. Doug reports, "I cannot seem to please either woman." He expresses his great distress to the group. Much to his surprise, Doug receives support and empathy from the female as well as the male group members. He comes away feeling legitimized and less powerless and ashamed. Doug also receives some gentle challenge and feedback concerning his own self-defeating attitudes. Dottie relates how Doug's group behavior is reminiscent of her father's confusing demeanor. Even when her father reacted out of worry, love, or concern, his actual expression was one of angry accusatory outburst. This left Dottie confused, hurt, and reticent to engage him. Through her transference to Doug, Dottie is able to see that more lay beneath the monster that was her father. She is able to experience vicariously some of the warm feelings and personal anguish of her father's experience.

As a direct result of the group session, Doug is able to go home and share his feelings with his wife, thus beginning to take assertive steps to disengage from the triangle created by his mother's proximity. Through sharing feelings and vulnerabilities in group, Doug actually gains a new and respected standing in the group community, thus in some ways countering his fears of being devalued and emasculated. In later sessions, he goes on to consider his "view of women" and his self-imposed constraints in initiative. Hopefully, Doug will appear increasingly less opinionated and judgmental as he learns to share both frustrations and tenderness more directly, and as he establishes an internal sense of parity with women.

The prior group confrontation between Ward and Jane is now reexamined. Ward personalized and reacted to Jane's underlying rage and cold assessment of men as "wimps," like her father. Ward responded by the astronomical hyperbolic assessment of Jane as a "black hole sucking up any warmth or chance at closeness." Once the genetic roots of Jane's actions and Ward's reactions are specified, they are both free to react in a less predetermined manner. In subsequent sessions, a new found warmth emerges and Ward and Jane begin to discuss their mutual attraction.

Lisa misses one of the next sessions. She returns to group sullen and withdrawn. With time running out in the session thematically marked by the discussion of

Jane's father, Lisa complains about the therapist's lack of reaction toward her. She reiterates that he doesn't take her seriously and that she no longer knows where to go with her problems. The therapist encourages this disclosure and, in an attempt at creating a genetic context, talks about the difficulties of being a father. A father has to support the growth of his child and yet create an atmosphere conducive to independence. Lisa is encouraged to talk about her own father's difficulties in striking a balance between care and caretaking. She describes how her dad withheld counsel while she was growing up, tending instead to provide for her materially. Thus, Lisa gained the accouterments of success but not the confidence achieved by steady guidance in support of self-initiative. Her anger and feelings of abandonment when the therapist is not a "helpful and accessible daddy" become more understandable.

Lisa's assessment of the therapist's turning away from her is like most clients' judgments, a combination of projection and accurate perception. Here, the therapist reveals how he has not wanted to reinforce Lisa's anxiety attacks or her exaggerated self-absorption. In fact, advice given to her at these times of such personal intensity has often been swept away in a tornado of escalating worry. The therapist confesses to turning Lisa off at these times. A "cry wolf" scenario has evolved. Usually, as Lisa calms down, she spontaneously deflates her own concerns, thus negating the need for the other person's assurances. However, the perception of an insufficient response leads to narcissistic injury similar to when as a child she felt her father withhold active attention and guidance. Feeling abandoned, Lisa then acts out by withdrawing from the group. This pattern leads to uneven relationships marked by periods of high intensity and subsequent disconnections.

Lisa relates the similarity of this pattern to her early childhood temper tantrums and to her current histrionic heterosexual relationships. Lisa and the therapist work toward a new pattern of interaction that does not recapitulate dysfunctional formative dynamics. Lisa works to clarify her needs, and the therapist seeks to find ways to intervene that support her ego, foster maturation and autonomy, calm her frenzy, and put Lisa back in touch with the other group members.

Thus, corrective emotional experiences are sought. Subsequent sessions explore the fathering of the group from the dynamic viewpoint of the other group members.

Technical Parameters and Limits of Causal Analyses

The progression of causative exploration may not proceed as completely, smoothly, or evenly as the steps outlined above. There may be sessions between descriptive sequences, as time elapses and timing prevails. When other pressing issues emerge, the process illumination may need to be postponed in the service of further process activation. Group time, like unconscious time, is linked by emotionally tinged themes. Significant moments, although temporally discrete, string together in seemingly uninterrupted chains of experience. Thus, in proper time, various group experiences are rekindled or reconjured in their full moment. Curtailed analyses can be continued as "suspended animations" come back into the group's life. If group shifts are resistant by nature, these trends can be brought back within the analysis. It might be asked, for example, "How does this new material relate to the issue we have been considering?" Many distractions turn out to be elaborations of the operative theme. As such, the new material adds depth, feeling, and additional context to the ongoing work.

Not every here-and-now interaction demands such detailed investigation, and some causal sequences may be more important for particular members than for others. The depth of personal meaning depends on the extent to which the individual and group processes under consideration stimulate and reflect any particular member's core issues and formative dynamics. Similarly, not every group member will garner or require the same attention or attain a similar degree of insight during each sequence of the inquiry. However, each member invariably gains from understanding their peers in greater depth, as vicarious learning is always possible. The most effective causal analyses are those that touch the greatest sample of the membership and reflect on universal and group-as-a-whole themes.

Certainly, various issues or dynamics may spontaneously arise that necessarily alter the order of the inquiry. Reminiscences or associations may lead directly back to the formal causes of behavior, whereas hidden agendas may demand the immediate decoding of their final aim. As with any model of behavior, guidelines for intervention cannot be applied in rote fashion. Rather, clinical judgments must mediate usage within the general framework and suggested causal mapping sequence. This model does provide a comprehensive way of viewing group analysis and lends directionality to the psychotherapeutic quest, especially when working through impasse. Such an approach takes into account that behavior is describable and overdetermined by a conditioning sequence of shaping experiences from the providential past (why = formal cause); subsequent conscious and unconscious intentions, designs, and resistances (where = final cause); more immediately evoked behavioral patterns and affective reactions (how = efficient cause); and resultant structural regularities, characterological configurations, and evident symbolic or symptomatic manifestations (what = material cause).

The ideal flow of the causal inquiry would reverse this conditioning process by working through in a what → how → where → why, or deconditioning direction. Such a flow follows standard psychotherapeutic lore by moving from the present to the past, from the manifest to the latent, from the controllable to the habitual, from the defensive to the impulsive, from the conscious to the unconscious, and from horizontal to vertical analysis.

While each step in the causal inquiry stands on its own merits, the understandings accumulated are also progressive and an increased potential for change is gained with each successive step in the analysis. Each cause, once uncovered, stimulates curiosity, and each cause, once worked through, reduces resistance and launches the next relevant phase of inquiry. Thus, the knowledge of what has transpired stimulates a curiosity to know how this particular configuration arose. Unfortunately, aside from fictional versions of psychotherapy, an understanding of the genesis of behavior and an emotional rending of corresponding feelings do not automatically change ingrained patterns. A more pedestrian, repetitious, and less dramatic working through and structural rebuilding at each causal level are necessary to initiate and sustain change. Since no one level of causal inquiry can provide sufficient insight to lay out and loosen the bonds of dysfunctional behavior, Aristotle's fourfold conceptualization is offered as an encompassing analytic and fully descriptive contextual model.

The act of working out causal sequences in a group setting adds synergy and back-and-forth interplay to an otherwise straightforward process. As one member changes within the system of the group, other participants must, in accommodation, shift their own positions. Challenging a key dynamic causes a chain reaction, as other parts of the system conform by coming up with new arrangements. For example, the identification of a resistive trend makes it hard for members to maintain an impasse just so. When the mechanisms supporting dysfunctional interactions are discovered, an impetus to adjust behaviors accordingly is created. The discovery of real intent or hic den agenda brings an end to the possibility and need of further disguise. The exposure of the root causes of various overdetermined responses goes a long way toward grasping their essence and "giving up the ghost" of trauma past.

Such complex and interactive possibilities may sometimes overwhelm the group psychotherapist. One might be tempted to throw up one's hands in a frustrated gesture of, "It's all Greek to me." The demands on the facilitator are indeed great. Without a template for proceeding, the reasonable management of the group process may appear an untenable task. Interventions can become haphazard and directionless as members become distant and unconnected, while evolving material is viewed as confusing or irrelevant. To track the groups' multiplicity effectively, the therapist needs all of his or her conceptual tools—relying on causal as well as noncausal understandings.

This chapter presents a manner of working with the therapy group that allows the activated process to unfold, while encouraging a nearsighted and far-reaching process illumination. Armed with the wisdom of antiquity, the modern group psychotherapist is encouraged to logically stalk the lost cause. For when a therapist convenes a psychotherapy group, he or she joins Aristotle in the complex exploration of "things which have in themselves the source of their changing or staying unchanged" (Aristotle, translated in Charlton, 1983, p. ix).

CHAPTER THIRTEEN

The Group as a Cultural Phenomenon:

Transforming Experience Through Collective Imagery

Conducting psychotherapy groups involves more than working within safe confines and unraveling lost causes. The impulse to find meaning in chaos (Gleick, 1987) leads the members of a group to formulate compelling analogies about their joint endeavor. Pictorial metaphors representative of particular parts or the affective whole of the process emerge spontaneously within the free flow of the group dialogue. These images represent a comparative language of perceptual acuity, as they look to the twists and turns of interaction and foresee sequences of meaningful exploration. Such symbolic word-pictures serve to depict individual and interpersonal dynamics, while aptly characterizing the collective's thematic patterns, resistances, and impasses (Ettin, 1986).

Unlike the fixed motifs of Desoille (1965) and Leuner (1969, 1984), or the standard situations of Shorr (1978, 1983, 1986) and Ahsen (1981), these creative configurations often arise unbidden (Horowitz, 1970; Ettin, 1982). Suddenly, a mental picture comes to mind in direct response to the group's timely need for concrete representations of its more abstract processes. Migliorati (1989) asserts that "sessions are highlighted at more or less regular intervals by the appearance of meaningful 'relational images'" (p. 198). Srivastra and Barrett (1988) reiterate that, "as a self-regulating organism, the group provides itself a generative metaphor when difficult topics are being considered and when radically new knowledge needs to

Portions of this chapter were adapted from material included in earlier publications in *Small Group Behavior, 17* (4), 407–426, copyright 1986, published by permission of Sage Publications; and *Imagery: Current Perspectives,* published with permission of Plenum Press and Joseph Shorr et al. (Eds).

happen" (p. 54). Ganzarain (1989) adds that "the group as an entity is often represented by emotionally laden mental images manifested in the patients' dreams, fantasies, or responses to group meetings" (p. 3).

By carefully attending to such portending metaphoric messages, members are helped to personalize meanings and clarify interchanges, while the group itself can both analyze its current trends and make necessary adjustments to its progress (Ettin, 1985a). The quest for overall visions and underlying meanings is universal, a desperate call to Panacea, the ancient Greek goddess of healing, for a cure to existential uncertainty.

The purpose, then, of constructing symbolic relations, and the impetus for attuning to images that spontaneously arise from within the flux of the group experience, is the need to impose grammatical order on a mass of seemingly unconnected utterances or occasions. The occurrence of an organizing image creates a framework, an appearance of coherence in a form that has both structure and direction implied within. It is as if to say, by seeing our experience in this way, we can make sense of our goings on together, today and possibly tomorrow. Srivastva and Barrett (1988) recommend the identification of "central or root metaphors" (p. 37) as the "basic unit of group analysis" (p. 62). Migliorati (1989) considers these symbolic missives "analogous to other concepts used in group theories [such as] the basic assumptions of W. R. Bion and to S. H. Foulkes' matrix concept" (p.196). The group-as-a-whole and its part-processes come to be transformed by way of such configural metaphors, imageries, and "over-arching symbol system[s]" (Hartman & Gibbard, 1974b, p. 316). Collective representations (Durkheim, 1974) predictibly arise to express what is particular and what is shared within the evolving group culture.

Individual and Collective Meanings

The group facilitator can initiate or reinforce the therapeutic process by working within the linguistic and perceptual frame set up by the emergent image form. Attention is given to both the common understandings and the particular meanings of transformative images. Ultimately, it is the individuals in the group who must be treated. It becomes critical to work alternately between the general and the specific and from universal to particular levels of imagistic elaboration and decoding.

Simon, a new member in a young-adult group, presents a problem of adjustment and a problem of assertion in the form of a story with symbolic implications. While doing his laundry in the house he shares with three others, including his landlady, Simon's favorite shirts got "caught in the washer housing" and "frayed under the collar." Quite distraught, Simon wonders whether he should demand that his landlady reimburse him for the shirts, even though the damage is negligible. He questions his own need to be perfect and wonders if anyone else would even notice the disrepair.

This dilemma spurs others in the group to consider practical issues around letting matters slide or coming to grips with what's bothering them. More basically, participants allude to defending, protecting, or hiding their own self-perceived flaws—tactics that actually foment fear and exacerbate fragmentation. Maria spins out worries about whether men notice her slim body type, which she underplays in self-critical fantasies reminiscent of her father's persistent fault finding. Lilly demurely explains that when self-conscious or angry, she shows little on the outside while going to pieces on the inside. To do otherwise in her family was to risk being caught in the rift between her divorced and feuding parents. Nick is readily reminded of how he assumes a preemptive belligerence, presenting his rough edge by becoming hot under the collar as a way of holding himself together while fending off others. He fears, as happened with his family of origin, that expressing needs in a more calm and evenly sewn fashion will result only in his being ripped apart.

Members consider their fears of fragmentation by working through the metaphoric image of the "frayed shirt." Who will notice? Who will care? How will retribution be sought? Will recognition and amelioration be available? Through the lightly disguised pun—frayed for afraid—they raise their own and each other's questions, doubts, and self-preservative strategies. In the course of the session, participants sooth one another by forming reassuring bonds conducive to more confidence, less trepidation, and added cohesion, both personal and collective.

Several group members suggest to Maria that, although empathizing with her self-effacing, they don't really understand why she puts the material of encounters under a microscope and views matters out of their normal proportion. Disavowing Maria's anticipation of criticism, Art says he only stares at women he finds attractive. In talking through Simon's presenting problem, the group encourages him to speak with his landlady in an assertive, yet nonconfrontative manner. The members believe that by so doing, he might work out a fair compromise—salvaging his wardrobe as well as his ongoing relationship with her.

Simon's "frayed under the collar" image serves as an apt metaphor for members' varied concerns and interpersonal struggles. Each participant contributes a particular story of a similar cloth. Transferentially, the group seeks to work around feelings of being awash, stuck, or tattered in the housing of the collective matrix. The group, regressing with the addition of Simon as a new and scared member, is aptly depicted as a spinning washer. While the purpose of the process is to come clean by sharing in the group's revolutions, Simon expresses concerns about the danger of being singled out, caught up, and injured within the process. Can the washer be trusted to function and be maintained properly? It is yet unclear to him if the possible damage resulting from the risk of engagement will be substantial or negligible. Does the fraying represent structural damage or rather reveal an alterable vulnerability inherent in inordinate self-consciousness? Do narcissistic injuries result from the rending of one's personal cover or from exaggerated sensitivity to rifts in the ongoing fabric of experience? Will this group experience recapitulate or repair' the splits and hurts accrued in the members' primary family groups?

Simon, as group spokesperson, wonders if the group leader and the group-as-a-whole, as landlord and landlady respectively, will acknowledge damage, make amends, and take precautions such that undue fragmentation won't result from liberal use of the common pool. Can one's most precious matter be confidently put into the mix? At an even more symbolic level, the washer image might be seen as a metaphor for the group-as-womb. How will members emerge from this birthing process with its churning, pulling, spinning liquidity—newly cleansed or worse for the wear?

Members contribute to the impetus or actual formation of the shared image and then take back from their creative handiwork implications and personalized perspectives. Migliorati (1989) addresses this simultaneity between collective and individualized symbols when stating, "The unity of the image produced . . . represents the group, whilst, the multiplicity of use constitutes the contributions of single members" (p. 197). Jacobson (1989), describes how the group becomes a cultural object.

> *Each individual has a mental representation of "the group," but a process occurs in which each individual's representation comes to approximate those of the other group members. What is meant here by the "group" is these shared aspects of members' representations, the area of overlap between them. In this sense it is a shared representation. Its being shared is crucial to the feeling of belongingness engendered by having that representation, and no representation inconsistent with it, as a guide. Moreover, it is in its being a shared representation that the "group" is experienced as not quite self or other, but both. (p 482)*

Frey-Rohn (1990), following Jung (1976), suggests that such metaphoric images serve as mediators capable of bringing disparate and seemingly opposite elements into a *tertium quid*, that is, a third space or new symbolic arrangement (p. 265). Group development is thereby marked by constant joinings under a common sign and subsequent separations out in particularized perceptions. Surely the question of how to accommodate to consensual reality while still maintaining individualized perspective is of universal import. Winnicott (1965, 1971) elaborates on the value of imaginary productions as necessary transitional objects closing the gap between inside and outside, between self and other, between patient and psychotherapist, and in this context between the individual and the group.

Private and Public Symbols

The distinction between private and public symbols and the varying attentions required at covariant levels of meaning are also finely elucidated by Firth (1973).

> *An anthropologist is concerned to find out what a given symbol corresponds to in the general understanding and operations of a body of people. He seeks if not consensus at least the highest common factor in referents. He does this because he is looking at symbols as bases for or expressions of common action; the element of communication of meaning is dependent upon the possibility of shared understanding. A psychologist . . . may be interested in this too, but he is also interested in the departure of the symbol from the consensus, with the cues it offers to individual development. (p. 208)*

A group leader functions as an anthropologist—building and interpreting the therapeutic culture when exploring the collective renderings of his or her charge. He or she also functions as a psychologist—charged with rendering help to individuals within the medium of that common culture. When individuals join a group, they contribute their particular problems to the mix, and in a real sense, what is problematic to one becomes problematic to all. Similarly, what is worked out for all becomes a remedy for each. The group and the individuals it comprises are never clearly dichotomized.

In the normal course of the group life, members become more attentive and responsive to each other and to their common culture. They discover universalities of experience, similarities, and differences of perception, empathic resonances, and a diversity of approaches to the group's shared tasks and goals. These intimate, intricate, and often subtle experiences together can be manifestly expressed in the form of creative configurations. Srivastra and Barrett (1988) suggest that key metaphoric images are "at the foundation of the group's collective view and common construal of disparate experiences" (p. 37). The group's overt realities as well as its latent potentials can be so depicted. The group comes to develop a language expressible in symbols of interaction and in self-reflective images. The arousal of these mental images can bring members together, stimulate formative energies, foster insightful recognitions, while moving the shared process to richer levels of engagement and re-vision. The group therapist's task is to listen actively and watch attentively for those spontaneous images that arise as collective representations (Durkheim, 1974; Levy-Bruhl,1985), and bear such immediate relevance and cultural importance, in order to foster the ameliorative potentials inherent in the symbolic domain.

- Amelioration 3. *Group processes take on meaning, and individual dynamics can be transformed within the group culture by discovering and developing apt images, metaphors, and symbols of the shared experience.*

The Elaboration of Emergent Images

The initial emphasis in working with emergent images is to stay within the confines of the word-picture itself. Interpretive and reductive conclusions should be resisted, while attention is focused on the image content and its inherent transformational potentials. By elaborating the image, the therapist allows various members' creativities and imaginative capacities to be brought into play (Shorr, 1983). Suggestions may be made to change or sharpen the mental picture so as to better reflect the affects and circumstances eliciting its occurrence. By walking around the image to see its various sides, shades, and contours, a more encompassing perspective becomes possible (Mattoon, 1978). What does the image look like to the various members? What differing perspectives can be shown? Members are able to readjust their personal positions and perceptions to account for these other points of view.

By extending the image in a process of active imagination, implications are drawn out, and the symbolic content is allowed to develop, to change, and to transform in response to the group's projective, interpretive, and assimilative needs (Hannah, 1981). Can participants add anything new to the developing picture? What is happening, for them, in the image? What is about to happen as a consequence of the developing scenario? How do members feel about the way the picture is evolving?

Within such an open-ended and phenomenological exploration, the psychotherapeutic process takes on poetic license. When the group stays within the metaphoric confines of the presenting image, linguistic embellishment becomes central to the analysis and the further construction of meanings. How does this image explicate, talk about, and depict the many aspects of the current group scene? What sensual qualities of the image touch the experience being reflected? By taking the image and its symbolic significance seriously, we can also take each experience as far as possible, exploring, exploiting, and predicting various subtleties of sequence, plot, and potency. By working with the full picture as presented, creative relationships can be pushed as far as language, common sense, and intuition will allow. The analogy implied in the image can reach asymptotic limits when the emergent talk approaches the essential tale.

The last step in the exploratory process looks to the formative past for etiological antecedents. Following Freudian understandings and genetic causality (Freud, 1964; Horowitz, 1970), the processes motivating image formation now come under specific therapeutic analysis. The urges, motives, defensive structures, object relations, memories, fantasies, group-level transferences, or historical events that provide source material for the arising image are probed. What in the group process has caused this image to appear? What spurred this expressive change? What are the inherent qualities of the image (i.e., aggressive, compliant, remorseful, etc.)? What conflicts are implied? What overdetermined personal experiences or social adjustments account for this particular image form?

Anticipating ameliorative transformations, the therapist can also ask, What changes in individual patterns or in group adaptations are needed to resolve the presenting problem or impasse? What directions are suggested for working through? Through free association, secondary elaboration, and subsequent interpretation, the therapist relates the emergent imagery to the group's focal conflicts and to the individual member's intrapsychic and interpersonal life adjustments. The imaging process itself, treated as a fully motivated dynamic, becomes the messenger to be halted, frisked, and relieved of its overdetermined meanings before being sent on its symbolically unencumbered way.

Expected Sequence in Working with Spontaneous Images

Images arise spontaneously, yet a regularity in the process of image formation and elucidation can be outlined. The working sequence is generalized as follows:

1. An individual, interactional, or group-level problem or conflict is presented or enacted.
2. The presence of misunderstanding, fear, defensiveness, resistance, impasse, or dysfunctional problem solutions leads to frustration, confusion, chaos, demoralization, and/or disequilibrium within the group.
3. The sudden emergence of a metaphoric or symbolic image characterizes heretofore diffuse, abstract, unorganized, or underutilized energies and trends; the group intuitively recognizes the relevance, power, and prescience of the image.
4. The group is encouraged to actively develop the image through a brainstorming process that includes imaginal elaboration, circumambulation, active imagination, amplification, and poetic license to call out the inherent metaphor by particularizing its essences and implications for the current situation or problem.
5. The symbolism of the image and its evoking circumstances are gener-

alized by the therapist and related to common situational, developmental, groupwide, or universal concerns, which the members are then encouraged to discuss and explore within this wider context.

6. Members are now engaged in free association, secondary elaboration, and interpretive analysis of the phenomenology and etiology of the original problem, impasse, or resistance with one eye on the formative past and one eye toward the transformative future.

Clinical Vignettes

Working with Depression

Terry, a 36-year-old woman, suddenly had her engagement broken off by her fiancé. She is stunned, enraged, and depressed. With an air of desperation, Terry talks about all the dreams that have gone down with the relationship, and of everything she is doing to get over her dysphoric feelings quickly. The group is very responsive to Terry's sadness and her anger at her ex-fiancé, but has difficulty relating to her efforts to stay afloat. Whenever Terry exposes her losses and her floundering self-healing plans, the group remains silent and members appear cringingly uncomfortable. The therapist suggests that there is something about the quality of Terry's sadness and restorative attempts that makes it difficult for the members to respond empathically to her.

The group members are encouraged to explore their paucity of reaction by expressing how they actually feel when Terry demonstrates her sadness and distress. The group's imagery is expressly cultivated by asking: How do you picture Terry at these times? How do you see her? Paul, an obsessive young man, identifies a sense of paralysis and helplessness in Terry's demeanor. With sudden intuitive force, Rosa suggests that "its like Terry is in quicksand." The more she struggles, the sooner and the faster she seems to go down.

The group is reluctant to engage with Terry, within this desperate thrashing, for fear of being grabbed and submerged within her grief. They suggest that her various frantic attempts to remain on the surface of her feelings just engender panic and push her down faster and further. The members also begin to realize that Terry is blaming herself and the group for the failure of her relationship, and is acting as if to drag everyone under with her. With the quicksand image as a guide, the group helps Terry look at her pique of misappropriated projections and activities, which ultimately result in her remaining immersed, stuck, and sinking within her own depression. They can now reach a hand toward a member who has had the ground pulled out from under her.

Through Terry's experience and its encapsulation in imagery, other members are able to grasp their own sinking and suffocating reactions to hurt and loss. Rosa suggests that perhaps facing the feelings and just waiting them out would be a better strategy than struggling so. Paul wonders if maybe the work that needs to be done now involves developing internal supports rather than grasping for external handholds. The group goes on to expressly explore Terry's and their own responsibility for the drowning of her relationship. They look into Terry's pattern of relating with her ex-fiancé and with the group, a pattern that leads to dangerous and quixotic disappointments.

Working with Anxiety

Some sessions later, Rosa appears very shaky. She reluctantly relates that she has just taken her comprehensive exams for her master's degree and is unsure if she has passed. The group queries Rosa about the test, encouraging her to explain the relevant details and to talk about her particular concerns. Rosa is very tentative, and the group becomes impatient when she is not more forthcoming. Rosa appears on the verge of crying, but tries resolutely to be still so as not to let loose her tears. The image occurs to the therapist that Rosa is holding her feelings and fears like "a glass of water filled to the brim. If she moves forward she might spill."

Kevin develops the image further by suggesting that if, in fact, it is water that is contained, what's the danger? He says, "Its more like she's carrying sulfuric acid." The therapist incorporates this elaboration by suggesting that Rosa is crossing the threshold of her profession. If she is carrying her fears with benign liquidity, spilling and failing the comprehensives will just be water under the bridge. She will take them again. However, if she is full of turbulent acidity, any overflow may seem to corrode her chances of traversing from the present into the future. She may fear that "bridges will be burned and there may be no other way across."

The other group members associate to the glass-of-acid image by relating to the risk, terror, and vulnerability of crossing difficult transitional bridges in their own lives. What are they facing? How do their feelings come across? What are they holding in for fear of ruinous chemical reaction? With the glass-of-acid image as a guide, Rosa and the group are more able to speak directly of the churning anxieties inherent in being put to the test. Rosa can recognize and explore the extent of her vulnerability, as well as her attempt to suppress and contain her fears, lest they destructively spill out of control. The group can explore with Rosa the origin, meaning, and current utility of this self-contained stance. Rosa can see how holding in her feelings eats away at her, and she can experiment with other ways to soothe her turbulent insides.

The image of corrosive liquidity also suggests that Rosa needs a milk-based lining to neutralize her anxieties. Using the water/acid/milk transformation as a symbolic guide, the group can explore with Rosa if lapses in mothering contribute to her lack of confidence and fears of change. By so responding, the group provides the nutrient base and containing substance so necessary to help her pass over this transitional period.

Working with Group Disillusion

By amplifying an image, comparisons and similarities can be drawn to known cultural, mythical, and historical forms and antecedents (Jung, 1976). What motifs, scenarios, or universal concerns does the image suggest? What modern contexts are brought to mind? Usandivaras (1986) goes so far as to suggest that "in each session a myth is created, a myth which has to be discovered and deciphered in order to understand what [is] happening at the deepest level of the group" (p. 197). Hidden agendas can then be elucidated within the symbology of predetermined cultural patterns. In a distinct act of narrative retelling, the history and mythology of the human group helps illuminate what is going on in the psychotherapy group.

A long-term therapy group in its fourth year was struggling with a number of members simultaneously considering termination. Wanting to exit yet stay attached, Ward asks for a 6-month leave of absence to concentrate on his graduate studies. Lisa discusses her impending move to marriage and a new geographic area. Of late, she had been steadily distancing herself from the group, yet she appears afraid to make a formal break. Group members consider these matters in muted tones and with an evident lack of energy and involvement.

With obvious dependency, Lisa expresses her concern that even after moving, she will need the group. Jokingly, she suggests that the other group members might see her jogging back across country to attend a session. Jane quickly quips that she can easily picture Lisa as "a group marathon runner." With the presentation of the marathon image, the group spirit begins to lift, as preconscious recognitions dawn. The marathon, as a modern event, carries many ready connotations of fitness, perseverance, and determination. In ancient Greece, the messenger reaching Marathon signaled a Persian invasion, thus allowing the polis to secure its defenses and battlements. The runner, upon completion of the task, terminates while the city group is preserved. In this moving image, Lisa, who speaks of leaving, is actually seen running toward the group. In dual symbolic significance, she works out her last gasp of participation, serving the collective function of mobilizing the remaining members for reengagement and a continuance of their therapeutic struggles.

The therapist highlights the emergent image by suggesting that "this long-term group effort, at times, assumes marathon proportions." Who will finish this race? Who will drop out? What are appropriate grounds for leaving? What pace is required in order to stay involved? What does it feel like to tire and work through fatigue? How does one know, in fact, if his or her therapy course is run? The symbolic resonances inherent in the marathon image energize the group, while stimulating an in-depth exploration of the current, heightened dynamics around stopping or moving on.

Ward and Lisa now directly consider the meaning and timing of their impulses to leave. One of Ward's continuing complaints is lack of available energy. His compulsive and single-minded strivings often lead to mental and physical exhaustion and subsequently result in failed mastery and goal attainment. With the marathon image as a guide, the group helps Ward realize that he is approaching graduate school in the same driven manner that led to his dropping out of medical school in a heap of demoralized debility. He sprints where a steady jog is more the required pace. Suggestions are made that perhaps a more metered approach might be advisable, and if so, members wonder if Ward really needs to leave group to succeed in his studies.

Lisa, on the other hand, is encouraged to consider the anachronistic fears that impede her from cleanly cutting the umbilicus stretching across the finish of her time in the group. In the course of this discussion, she comes to realize that despite her anxiety about moving on with her life, she is doing quite well and feeling much better. The group points up the strides Lisa has made in her time here. In fact, on exploration, Lisa realizes how little she currently relies on the group, on the therapist, or for that matter, on her parents for security and direction. The path of the group discussion now turns toward the sadness of taking leave, the inherent loneliness of the long-distance runner. Over a number of sessions, plans are made for cutting the chord in a formal termination.

Lisa's and Ward's talk of leaving is initially demoralizing and contagious for the remaining members. The others now expressly wonder if they can stay the course. Working within the symbolic scenario of the marathon image, the therapist encourages various group members to assess where they are in own their therapy progress: "How do you feel about how far you've come? How much farther do you need and wish to go? What landmarks and milestones remain to be passed?"

As the various group members explore their commitments and reservoirs of available energy, necessary adjustments are made to carry themselves toward completion. New leaders quicken their participatory pace and come to the forefront, as the reformed pack moves on together. The sudden appearance of the marathon image and its supplementary forms tangibly helps the group focus, hold, and work through this transitional period in its communal life.

Expressive junctures or turning points in a group are often "marked by ritualistic signs" (Whitaker & Lieberman, 1964, p 117). Such a sign may, in fact, be the occurrence of a particularly striking image or figure of speech. Like a key symbol in a dream series or a resounding cultural production, the marathon image, with its symbolic implications, guided this therapeutic process for some time through a sequence of crisis, termination, and renewal.

Induction and Translation

In many ongoing psychotherapy groups, the therapist usually waits for evocative images to arise spontaneously within the context of the session.

The process can be helped along by periodically asking members how they see or visualize themselves, each other, or the group-at-large. In the normal course of the dialogue, suggestions can be given to picture particular persons or events. Fromm (1955) champions pulling for pictures as a way of stimulating associations.

> *Let us assume that you have analyzed the patient's relationship to his father, but want more unconscious material than he has offered in his associations; you tell the patient "now concentrate on the picture of your father, and tell me what is the first thing that comes to your mind." I might draw your attention to the fact that there is a certain difference between asking the patient, "What comes to your mind about your father?" and the second way of telling him "visualize your father now, and tell me what is on your mind." There seems to be only a slight difference in wording. However, there is a great difference in effect. (cited in Shorr, 1978, p. 96)*

Once an image is stimulated or naturally arises, there is considerable debate as to whether it is necessary and useful to translate it into more verbal generalities. Some believe that imagery work is a direct form of communication with the less-than-conscious processes or the right hemisphere of the brain. To communicate by way of visual metaphor bypasses conscious censorship and resistance and allows the therapist and the group direct access to deeper, more primitive levels of the psyche. These clinicians believe that translation takes away from the therapeutic effect of the work. One does not have to interpret a painting to be touched and moved by its significance or relevance. Representative of this school of thought is the work based on Milton Erickson's hypnotic techniques (Erickson, Rossi, & Rossi, 1976; Bandler & Grinder, 1979; Haley, 1973; Watzlawick, 1978), which revert to the time-honored use of stories, metaphors, allegories, and parables to convey messages. These approaches often involve purposely confusing the client or bypassing the conscious mind of the client so that symbolic messages might gain direct access to his or her unconscious.

Many times, without the participants' conscious recognition or avowal, poignant images can serve as a direct impetus to change. In these instances, translation may actually reduce change potentials. Whether or not to translate depends both on the current state of affairs, the ongoing context of the shared experience, and the psychological makeup of particular clients gathered together. More cerebral members may readily seek and relate to translations, but then may intellectualize the work—robbing it of the lubricating effect. An unprocessed image may serve to create a dissonance that engenders a change in a time-worn perception or behavior. Participants with more hysterical styles may require some translation to pin down messages and insights, thereby helping them realistically hold and structure their experience. In a group context, the therapist needs to determine what type of group culture or shared ego state best describes the collective, before deciding what interpretative tactic fits membership needs. Is the group-as-a-whole seemingly confused and in need of some direct, concretization of experience? Or is the group rather overprocessed and in need of direct experience or affective stimulation?

Katz (1983) argues for the nontranslation of metaphors when egos are too fragile or affects and impulses too powerful to be faced directly. He suggests that work within a metaphor allows for the parallel processing of latent and manifest meanings. Premature interpretations can lead to increased defensive maneuvers, such as isolation and withdrawal, regressive symptoms, stringent denial, or actual flight. Katz suggests that sometimes the metaphor represents a "safe middle ground" that allows discussion that is neither too intellectualized nor too primitive. He argues that work within the metaphor has the advantage of promoting active consideration of problems amid an atmosphere of emotional vitality and relatedness. Since metaphors can be understood and worked at many levels, they are the perfect expressive medium for the diverse circumstance and varied egos found in the group therapy settings.

In this mobile and mechanical society, the car has arrived as a powerful symbol of self. In a new group of ego-disturbed patients, members use the car image to symbolize their concerns about their upcoming therapeutic journey. A member with distinct borderline features begins a session by complaining about her vehicle. She reports that it is always breaking down. The car image becomes an apt metaphor for self-images of the others, as well as for early group hesitancies, concerns about the leadership, and questions about the mechanics of the therapeutic process. A second member, a very controlled man who speaks in a monotone, drones on that he is afraid that the brakes on his car will fail. A third member, with strong paranoid tendencies, vehemently warns that you have to be careful who you let work on your car. "They just might keep it too long and do unnecessary work." A fourth member demands that "the authorities fix the car properly."

In this case, the therapist chose not to translate or amplify the car metaphor, but rather let it diagnostically signal and preconsciously carry members and meanings along. The metaphor was already being expanded and particularized in the natural course of the discussion. As an apt linguistic device, the car image moved the group toward active consideration of evident anxieties. To translate would have been too directly exposing for this particular group. At a later time in the collective's progress, the car image might be reconjured and more closely inspected. Sometimes translation will speed the journey; in other instances, it can bring proceedings to an abrupt, frightening, and unnecessary halt.

A Contextual Model for Working with Emergent Images in Groups

Expressive language remains a prime medium of exchange in the psychotherapy group, but not every session produces the opportunity for depicting the process metaphorically. Many sessions may go by with the therapist functioning more in the workman-like role of managing the interactions and monitoring the discussion. During these times, group talk may be much more concrete, issue, or event oriented. Material may flow easily or may choppily follow the varied associations of the members.

Other sessions may be predominated by an emotional climate that binds the group in common or uncommon feeling. Here, the leader more acknowledges and works with the affect in the room, as various members display and work around their sensitivities. Should a poignant mental image present to the therapist's mind or in the member's communication, then this visualizable figure of speech can be utilized to focus and clarify the emerging, affect-laden picture. If not, the group is helped to stay in the moment for the time being.

Still, the rightful place of imagery, metaphor, and symbol within the ongoing context of the group session can be anticipated. Imagistic interventions are ceremonial in the sense of bringing together, punctuating, celebrating, and ritually moving the working process ahead. As such, within a psychotherapy context, the emergent image form of most value has proven to be the spontaneous thought or utterance that succinctly captures and aptly expresses the ongoing, operative individual, interpersonal, and/or group-as-a-whole dynamic.

Shaping Circumstances

The contextual utility of the emergent orienting image may be understood by first specifying the nature of the session in which it appears. The group enters the room with some *shaping circumstance* in mind, be it overtly or covertly recognized and acknowledged. The circumstance may be a boundary issue, like the therapist's upcoming vacation, an absent member, or an impending addition or termination. Other shaping circumstances may involve a distinct member crisis, due to injury, sickness, job loss, or any extreme change in circumstance. Similarly, unfinished business from a previous session, including unresolved conflicts or heightened emotions, carry over into the next meeting. Prototypical phase behaviors, such as formative pressures, groupwide resistances, or competitive strivings, can also underlie the discussion and shape the interactions within the room. Thus, the shaping circumstance is anything brought in over the session boundary that serves to create a subtext or dialectical imperative. Members may be fully aware of and freely speak to what is brought into the room, or they may merely feel its unspoken tug while conforming to its hidden agenda.

Bipolar Themes

As the members begin to talk together and freely associate, *bipolar themes* arise that serve to develop and specify issues and conflicts around the shaping circumstance. For example, a long-standing member's sudden decision to leave group may trigger a consideration of independence versus dependence, loyalty versus liberty, or acting on impulse versus thinking through and planning. A member's unresolved anger from a previous session might usher in ambivalent concerns about aggression versus passivity, sadism versus masochism, power versus weakness, dominance versus submission, or protection versus exposure to harm.

The themes and subthemes that arise in response to a particular group's shaping circumstance differ according to which nuclear concerns and behavioral repertoires various members bring with them to group. The potential for exploring any bipolar theme also reflects on the group history. What issues can and have already been discussed? What groupwide ambivalences have been raised and previously worked out? What depth of inquiry has been achieved? Certainly, a heterogeneous group mix, a cohesive and trusting environment, and a good prior working history greatly enhance a group's ability to consider its ready, bipolar contradictions, discrepancies, and complimentary relations.

Talking Points

In order to come up with synthetic and synergistic solutions to the various activated, bipolar themes, a number of *talking points* are formulated. The content of the discussion focuses on a series of unresolved, often existential questions for which members seek to negotiate or discover answers. For example, talking points around anger innervation may include such questions as: Can I survive other people's rage? Is it appropriate to express myself so forcefully? Am I like my father if I freely give vent to my emotions? Will the group shatter if we all say what we really feel? Is anger a primitive, bestial expression that should really be tamed? Such questions reflect the curiosities, cognitive capacities, experiential histories, and current need states of the various members. These interrogative talking points may freely come up in conversation, be openly pointed out by the therapist, or preconsciously inform and direct the dialogue as unspoken backdrop.

Depending on the phase of the group's development, the quest for answers may take the form of imploring the leader as expert to provide solutions (dependency culture), running from questions or fighting about answers (fight/flight culture), or joining together to come up with facile suggestions, advice, or collusions in the hopes of creating a better internal or external world (pairing culture). In a more developed group, the members may readily take on the inquisitive task in a less stereotypical, fantasied fashion. They may be able to accept the realistic challenge and necessity of working within the ambiguity and ambivalence of the collective process.

Particularizations of Experience

In order to avoid undue abstraction, or barren, hypothetical communications, members bring their real lives into the room, thereby infusing the discussion with personal relevance. Various *particularizations of experience,* suggestive of larger ambivalences and life concerns, are presented to the group for consideration, deliberation, and resolution. Raw material and pertinent contents are provided as members talk about experiences both in an out of group. "Let me tell you all how this plays out in my life." "My anger at my wife was so great last night, I was afraid I'd throw a chair through the television." "Sometimes when I ride down the street I imagine that I could press a button on the dashboard and blow my enemies away." "Last week, in here, I was so frightened by your anger that I didn't want to come tonight." "I'm so angry at myself for letting you bully me."

Organizing Image or Metaphor

Sometimes out of this admixture of shaping circumstances, bipolar themes, talking points, and individual particularizations of experience, an *organizing image or metaphor* spontaneously appears. This image simultaneously contains and expands the experiences being considered in the room. The containing function encompasses the production of concrete summary or cultural symbols that capture and express the inherent energies and present concerns. The expansive function turns around the image's ability to suggest a direction for further work, while pointing the way toward transformations of underlying impasses. Synthetic symbolic compromises can lead to real solutional progress. Working out in imagination is often a prelude to working through in reality.

Some emergent images are situationally bound, that is, tied to a particular discussion of a specific psychotherapy group, at a given moment, in a certain session. Other symbolic forms may link the current discussion to more universal and less time-bound concerns. Jung (1976) suggests that evolving images may resemble figures and themes from mythology or ancestral history. The individuals in the group may actually be playing out a collective universal script. Experience in the therapy room, while unique to time and place, may also transcend idiosyncratic relations and temporal parameters by presenting a variation of a common time-worn theme. Certainly anger and fear of aggression make for a basic, universal human by-play.

Nor is the emergent form of the image a fixed product. The shape of the symbol or comparative metaphor is overdetermined by the constraints of the proximate situation; the knowledge and experience of the immediate contributor; the existent cultural forms available in superordinate settings; relevant pictures of reality presented by parallel current events; and the linguistic and receptive capacities of the members. Given similar formative energies, symbolic vehicles analogous in meaning will arise.

Again, assume that a group is struggling with explosive feelings. Depending on the intensity of the affect present and the connotations currently activated, a range of apt images may suggest themselves. For example, the prevailing image can be of a gas main blowing up, a kettle boiling over, or a caged lion escaping from the zoo. The concrete picture portrayed in these images varies considerably as to scene and seriousness, but the structural and dynamic meanings remain similar. The operative comparison in this series of suitable images is that of compressed and dangerous energies suddenly escaping confinement.

Subsequent Symbols

Sessions following one in which a metaphor has emerged may continue under the sign of that image or may change the picture in order to develop *subsequent symbols* more applicable in furthering the exploration or switching the channel. In each case, the fashioning of forms from the group's concerns is a cultural event. Such forms truly express *collective representations* yet remain available to the whole of the group as common touchstones and concrete products of the shared work. Any group can be followed and summarized by attending to its collection of shared symbols, comparative metaphors, extant images, transformative motifs, guiding scenarios, and mediating myths.

Exploring Maturational Issues

Shaping Circumstance

A young adult group is concerned about Cathy's imminent departure after many years of membership. Amidst her strong intention to leave, the group is uncertain about her readiness. Several other participants are making hesitant strides to get on with their own lives.

Bipolar Themes
Independence vs. Dependence
Certainty vs. Hesitation
Maturity vs. Immaturity

Talking Points
- Am I growing up too fast?
- Can I really take care of myself?
- Is it possible to change my life circumstances?
- Can I make it in the outside adult world?
- Can I make it without this group?
- To whom am I responsible: myself, my parents, my friends, the therapist, or the group?

Particularizations of Experience

Maria speaks of the complexities of the independence/dependence theme. She describes trying to adapt to starting nursing school at age 24, living in a dorm, and falling back on her parents for support. This long-range educational plan has somewhat curtailed her present liberty. While at long last working toward financial independence by pursuing a professional career, she has had to take a step backward in lifestyle and self-sufficiency to achieve this goal. While in greater contact with her nuclear family, Maria again feels the regressive need to get her father's approbation.

Lilly, an immature 20-year-old college sophomore, identifies with the dilemma of being in suspended animation between the world of her parents and that of her peers. She struggles each weekend with whether to bravely face the new world of school or to go home where she already has a secure place waiting. Lilly reports that some of her dilemma revolves around guilt about leaving her divorced and depressed mother alone.

Members also talk of their here-and-now group experiences. Cathy is planning to leave the group after a 5-year stay. Participants have questioned her loyalty, of late, since for the past months she has seemed marginally interested and moderately involved in the shared process. The group also wonders aloud if Cathy is ready to leave, given her quiet demeanor and seeming difficulty in opening up to the relationships in the room. In a nondefensive manner, Cathy acknowledges the current state of her participation. She also realistically considers what changes she has made in the group, while looking at the unfinished shape in which she goes on to face the outside world. Cathy states that she is as ready now as she is likely to be later.

Nick, soon to be the most senior group member, directly expresses his sadness at Cathy's imminent departure. He considers his own progress and level of maturity, and wonders for how much longer the group will meet his needs. Nick speculates on the frivolities of youth and ponders the leadership hierarchy amongst the remaining members. He is both attracted by and worried about inheriting senior-member status. For him, this feels like a graduation from the student to the student-teacher role. He wonders if he is ready.

Organizing Image or Metaphor

Suddenly, and with great esthetic conviction, Maria visualizes the group as a "safe cocoon," a respite from so many internal and external pressures. After encouraging a group discussion of this metaphoric vehicle, the therapist pulls together member responses and amplifies the meaning of the image as a summary symbol for the group's overriding collective concerns. In essence, the protective group environment is about to open and release a member, more or less formed, into the outside world. The other participants struggle with this opening up of the boundary, inferring many personal meanings about their own maturational readiness.

By considering the cocoon image together, the group is brought back under a common symbol—if only for a time—to consider the groupwide implications and the individualized meanings and connotations of leaving safe havens. The group is expressly depicted as that transitional space that aids members in gaining maturity. Each member is further invited to carefully examine his or her own incubation, pupal stage, secure wrappings, and ready moves. Do the various members have the right and/or sufficient developmental resources to grow up, go out, and move on? Can those not ready to leave stay enraptured within the process long enough to nurture their own goals and acheive maturity?

Exploring Immobility and Shame

Shaping Circumstance

A long-standing, stable group has been dealing with the sudden onset of multiple sclerosis in one of its male members. In this particular session, James shakily comes to group supported by the crutches that mark his rapid deterioration. After the preceding session, James had to be helped into his car by two other members, Kitty and Ernie. Ernie has transported James to this session.

Bipolar Themes
Mobility vs. Immobility
Shame and Denial vs. Acceptance of Change
Dependence vs. Independence
Disintegration vs. Intactness
Viability vs. Being Rendered Inessential

Talking Points

- How does one know enough about the future to proceed with any certainty or conviction?
- How much control do we really have in life?
- Who will protect me from pain, illness, and injury?
- To what extent am I responsible for my disabilities and difficulties?
- How damaged or intact am I?
- What is the minimum expected of me to be a functional member of society in general and this group in particular?

Particularization of Experience

James talks about his difficult decision of whether to get hand gears installed in his car. He speaks of not wanting to face this change of capacity. He reports being most reticent about considering other implications around care, confinement, and personal viability. He reports how his family's ready ministrations protect him from confronting the full extent of his disability.

Joan empathizes with James's position and talks of her own ambivalence and "emotional paralysis" when facing upcoming life decisions. She can't seem to mobilize herself to take an active hand in breaking off a destructive relationship: "I'd rather leave it to him."

Helen reveals indecision about whether to leave her religious order. The possibility of change comes 20 years after leaving her mother's home to join the "mother-house." Helen reports that lately she's felt unhealthfully dependent on the sisterhood. With frustration, she complains, "I can't even get the order to give me a working car." Helen is quickly approaching her fortieth birthday and does not know where she resides in her life.

Kitty talks of being stuck socially. She believes she should date, yet she experiences awkwardness and anticipatory anxiety around social settings. Kitty wonders if relational injuries are making it impossible for her to move on with her life.

Taylor reveals that he needs an operation on his knee. A single man living alone, he is coming to realize that he has no one upon whom he can depend. He talks of how this dilemma became clear when the hospital required that someone accompany him to the procedure, and he couldn't think of who might help him out. Having based his life on self-sufficiency, Taylor begins to reexamine the real implications of his isolation and considers his emergent fears of remaining alone.

Ernie talks of how helping James to and from the group has been both frightening and rewarding. Characteristically, Ernie makes it a point not to get too involved in other's lives. However, he finds that he rather enjoys being called on and depended on.

Organizing Image or Metaphor

The group's ongoing discussion is empathic and warm. Members verbally support James while looking at their own versions of his situation. Much affect is stirred.

Out of the talk, James clarifies his sentiments when he suddenly says that he feels "stuck in limbo." This image becomes a rallying point for the group-as-a-whole. Everyone relates to the uncertainty denoted by the emergent metaphoric image.

Limbo is defined as: "a place or state of oblivion to which persons . . . are . . . relegated when cast aside, forgotten, past, or out of date"; a place of imprisonment or confinement; and "a state of being or place midway between two extremes" (bipolar themes) (Urdang, 1972). These various denotations, elaborated in the group, well express the concerns and present situations of the membership.

The therapist asks the religious participants, Helen and Ernie, for amplification of the theological meaning of *limbo*. On the border of heaven and hell, limbo is the place where unsaved infants are sent. The regressive and vulnerable connotations of members' various dilemmas thereby come to light. Issues around life passage, control of one's destiny, guilt for indiscretions and imperfections, and fear of being judged as imperfect are now openly elaborated and discussed. The theme of limbo also bespeaks the prevalent defense of using naivete and innocence as a way of not taking responsibility and facing up to difficult life choices. It is as if the group has maintained an unconscious collusion by agreeing that, "if we don't look at our situations and rather leave them to chance, perhaps higher powers will make everything turn out all right." "If we don't act, we can't be judged, by ourselves or by others, as having made a mistake." Members now collectively and individually question this passive, irresponsible strategy.

Certainly, the group itself, as a transitional space, is "halfway between heaven and hell." Members bring their shameful, less than perfect parts—for a finite time of trial and reprieve—before moving on to face their individual fates.

Spontaneous and A Priori Images

Levi-Strauss (1988) proposes a structural approach to symbolic understandings. Each image presents a way of depiction couched in particular codes, paradigms, or systems of expression. In symbolic relations, a superimposition takes place, a layering of forms, as one expressive display comes to stand in for another set of experiences. Providing an imagistic term from an alternate descriptive system instills creative tension and opens up metaphoric possibilities. "The metaphor rests on an intuition that these terms connote the same semantic field when seen from a more global perspective" (p.194).

This is exactly the process that takes shape in the psychotherapy group. An image arises, appropriated from a parallel paradigm to describe an otherwise undecipherable set of shared circumstances. The emergent image carries within it an inherent set of forms, terms, relations, and transformations. Each word-picture evokes motifs and scenarios suggestive of progression or regression, danger or triumph, evasion or enhancement. Each image holds, within pictorial confines, its own natural extension or diminution. This imminent depiction presents a panorama of qualities for combination, elaboration, and analysis. When working with any particular image, it is preferable to stay within its perceptual language. For in psychotherapeutic dialogue, as in other creative expositions, it is not helpful to mix and match metaphors.

Symbol systems are not biased toward particular hermeneutic decodings. Neither reductive nor expansive views fully characterize the field of symbolic relations. Levi-Strauss (1988) argues that symbolic images have no ultimate, intrinsic, or generalized meanings. Just as the image form can take infinite shapes, so image meanings can express the infinite variety of human activity, at multiple levels of explanation. In fact, the connection between literal experience and figurative expression is not based on any hierarchical relations. Meanings are not transferred by derivatives of lesser or greater importance, and so the symbolic image does not translate up or down. Rather, the image evocatively suggests a self-contained linguistic structure from which to explore a set of experiences.

Supplying an image for a group proforma, as in guided or directed imagery, may not provide the most expressive or timely symbolic paradigm. By attending to and developing emergent images, the group has the advantage of flexible occurrence—the right picture for the right circumstances. Bachelard (1969), in pointing out the prescience and phenomenological potency of fresh images, suggests,

> *Because of its novelty and its action, the poetic image has an entity and a dynamism of its own; it is referable to a direct ontology. . . . By its novelty, a poetic image sets in motion the entire linguistic mechanism. The poetic image places us at the origin of the speaking being [for] the image has touched the depths before it stirs the surface. (pp. xii, xix)*

Within the ongoing group process, some degree of organization is always straining to materialize. Less than conscious processes are already subliminally equating experiences and prefiguring in concrete and expressible representations. Letting a key image arise from within the group's experience makes use of these existent formative processes. The group can then move along by way of its own metaphoric understandings and symbolic codes. The ultimate referent for the group experience becomes the semantic and experiential field itself, which, by definition, requires linguistic expression, perceptual elaboration, and cultural transformation. Within the interactive matrix of the group, the unspeakable is spoken, the literate arises from solecistic, and order comes out from chaos.

An Ending Story

After 5 years in group, Terry was terminating tonight. As part of an informal weaning process, she returned for a last session after a 2-week, end-of-the-summer vacation. Originally beginning treatment to extricate herself from a sadomasochistic relationship, the group saw Terry through two dysfunctional relationships, including a broken engagement. She was now in a marriage with a man substantially different from the others. The current relationship certainly appeared, through her eyes, warmer and more equal in both power and affection. In her mid–30s when initially seeking treatment, Terry longed for a family of her own amidst, at times, overwhelming anxiety and despair that she would never find the right relationship to allow this to happen.

Initially Terry was rather timid in group, afraid to express herself lest she be jumped or ganged up on. She was especially wary of the men, given her familial configuration of a powerful and at times cruel father and a capitulating, inept mother. Terry experienced in group what she also felt at work—a lack of confidence in her ability to adequately express or stand up for herself. She did not believe that she had the intelligence or vocabulary to argue or make her point effectively. This downplaying of her aptitudes was appreciably complicated by a job in a professional setting and an attraction to powerful men with narcissistic and grandiose tendencies. When overwhelmed or overpowered, Terry readily broke into tears. By default, others would inevitably feel sorry and seek to take care of her. She greatly resented this condescension.

Gradually, Terry emerged as a leader—the participant most attuned to the group's subtle emotional context. In time she was able to articulate ideas and display affects with equal facility. Her progress in the group was readily apparent and served as a model for others. She worked hard and took risks, exposing her vulnerabilities while cultivating her strengths, thereby holding forth a norm and standard for the group. As Terry came to feel better about herself, less vulnerable and more in control of her emotions, her choice of partners changed. She no longer needed to gain her sense of worth vicariously by being with a powerful man. In the process, she was able to stand up to the other group members, including the male therapist, with honestly, integrity, and firmness. The final issue she wished to work on before leaving group was getting pregnant. In one particularly poignant session, Terry admitted and talked through some difficulties in intimacy that kept her somewhat distant from her new husband, despite her obvious love for him.

In the last group session, Terry came in beaming, looking familiar yet different. The group talked with fondness and sadness of her imminent departure. Terry told us that she had some news she wanted to share with the group before leaving. "I just found out today that I'm pregnant." This joyful declaration seemed to everyone involved a magical punctuating event, symbolically bringing to an end her group participation with the hope of the future secured. After closing with the other members, Terry turned to the therapist and said, "If you were writing a book, this would be a good story with which to end." She, herself, felt a sense of completion with her therapy and wanted to give some good news and special meaning back to the group and to the therapist as a parting gesture.

Terry had not been informed that the therapist was just finishing a book on group therapy and could not have known that he was, in fact, looking for a suitable vignette about coming to closure. The various members went on to express how Terry would be remembered within the group as part of its intimate history, at once inside and out. As the final minutes arrived and the session came toward its close, the therapist amplified the group's sentiment by using Terry's own book image as the expressive vehicle. "Terry is, in fact, inexorably written into the 'book of life' that is this group, a ready allusion to her lasting impression and her saving grace." For the group history and its culture is truly made up of the contributions of all those members, both past and present, who wrote their lives into the collective text, giving narrative meaning to the work in progress.

PART SIX

Conclusion

To know something by way of mythos is to narrate a compelling story of dramatic force, plot, and denouement. To change by way of novel processes means to restructure the plot lines that reflect the stories of our lives.

A striking resemblance can be found between the mythic thinking evident in tribal groups as studied by anthropologists and the projective processes found in training and therapy groupings as specifically addressed by the object relations school. Many mythic processes and prelogical projections underlie the small-group advance, as members move from a logos of small-group participation to a mythos of small-group culture. These primitive processes and their modern forms can be elucidated (Chapter Fourteen).

As it coalesces, the group itself discovers the capacity for conceptualizing its shared concerns by way of common myths and rituals. A developmental sequence can be described that reflects both the small group's advance and the evolution of the larger human culture. This final chapter comes full circle by suggesting an appreciation of small groups' more dramatic structures and primitive processes through a journey of discovery. Mythic allusions provide creative mediation, bridging the seeming divide between the past and the present and the individual and collective experience. Implications for the future of the human group can be drawn (Chapter Fifteen).

Olmec Buried Offering of Figurines in Ritual Scene (ca. 800 B.C.) (jade and limestone, height 5 1/2" × 20" × 14") Collection, National Museum of Anthropology, Mexico City. © Lee Boltin, photographer.

CHAPTER FOURTEEN

The Mythos of Small-Group Culture:
Object Relations and Primitive Processes

The accumulated misfortunes and sins of the whole people are some-times laid upon the dying god, who is supposed to bear them away for ever, leaving the people innocent and happy. The notion that we can transfer our guilt and sufferings to some other being who will bear them for us is familiar to the savage mind. It arises from the very obvious confusion between the physical and the mental, between the material and the immaterial. Because it is possible to shift a load of wood, stones, or what not, from our own back to the back of another, the savage fancies that it is equally possible to shift the burden of his pains and sorrows to another, who will suffer them in his stead. Upon this idea he acts, and the result is an endless number of very unamiable devices for palming off upon some one else the trouble which a man shrinks from bearing himself. In short, the principle of vicarious suf-fering is commonly understood and practised by races who stand on a low level of social and intellectual culture. (Frazer, 1922/1963, p. 624)

How far have we actually come from the aegis of tribal wonder and era of native truths? Striking parallels exist between primitive tribal rela-tions infused with primordial mythic perceptions (Levy-Bruhl, 1985; Cas-sirer, 1955) and more modern small-group object relations informed by pre-logical projective processes (Ashbach & Schermer, 1987; Ganzarain, 1989). The collective dynamics plied in an ancillary age operate still below the surface until revived in consortium, as members are called upon to respond to ever-pressing existential demands in a context of ever-present situational anxieties.

Both the tribal member and the modern group participant must find ways of working out innermost preoccupations by externalizing them in milieu. Simultaneously, group members must forever accommodate to the ambiguities of the outside world, internalizing that which was previously separate, unassimilated, and confusingly distinct. Both there and here, we find in the group a place of heightened sensitivity—an effervescent forum that stimulates the production of evocative fantasies, effusive ritual enactments, ready symbolic transpositions, underlying mythic formulations, and a bevy of socially inspired collective representations.

Primitive notions of time, space, and relation still provide a geometry of imagination—a dramatic framework and semiotic system for participating in and encoding complex relationships on the level of culture (Jules-Rosette, 1990). The efficacy of such mystical and cultural reality is not judged by any outside objective criteria but rather by the force with which certain understandings impinge on consciousness, demanding representation, meaning attribution, and emotive response. Cassirer (1955) explains, "Long before the world appeared to consciousness as a totality of empirical things and complex of empirical attitudes it was manifested as an aggregate of mystical powers and effects" (p. 1).

Mythic thinking represents a primitive form of relating with many modern parallels that speak to origins and attempt to reconcile basic existential paradoxes and contradictions (Kessing & Kessing, 1971). Primitive conceptions about the natural order impose a structure on thought, captivate the imagination, and lend impetus to psychomotor potentials. Schermer (1991b) suggests that myths are no longer considered "archaic vestiges," as if they were merely "distortions, regressions, and/or historical traces." Rather mythology has been rediscovered as a form of representation "that exists in all cultures in all times and whose themes may also be universal."

The dynamics of enculturation ultimately combine a logos of small-group structure with an evolving mythos of small-group participation. To move by way of logos is to cultivate encompassing understandings and rational guidance systems. To change by way of logical processes means to question and alter the reasons, rules, structures, and conscious motives configuring and propelling actions. To move by way of mythos is to invent compelling stories of dramatic force, plot, and denouement (Howard, 1991). To change by way of mythic processes means to perceive anew and restructure the plot lines that follow and fashion the enactment of our lives. Culture can be defined by both its organizational proclivities and its dramatic formulations. In the process of becoming a group, whether tribal or developed, internal processes and external realities fuse, merge, and mingle within a growing cultural medium, leading to ready transpositions of time (now and then), space (here and there), relation (close and distant), and self (I, you, they, us, and we).

Group Development and the Self-Other Continuum

In reality, there is never a completely separate individual. As a primary bonding, the mother-child dyad reflects on later social adaptations to family, peers, love objects, and society-at-large. Kohut (1971, 1977) appeals to this primitive truth when purporting that, from infancy onward, we all need others as "self-objects" reflecting back to us the essence of our personhood (Harwood, 1983; Tuttman, 1984; Weinstein, 1987). By so doing, an adaptive self-consciousness is fostered and supported, giving shape to our evolving characterological style and effecting the accuracy of our perceptual apparatus. As in mythological reckoning, external spaces are composed in accordance with a ready store of internal representations and subsequent insights about the intimate nature of relationships between self and other. Structure, whether on the level of the society or the person, is equated with destiny.

Mirroring of Self and Others

When a group convenes, distorted, near, or farsighted refractions may reflect a vulnerability of internal structure, most visibly manifested as relational problems. Perceptual confusions or misguided projections can take the form of personal illusions, social misperceptions, interpersonal distortions, and misinformed transactions (Ganzarain, 1989, p. 16). Attempts at mind reading or manipulation may result from difficulties in understanding or dealing with the self-other bond. Object relations theory focuses on the internalization and transformation of formative interpersonal relations into stable or unstable, accurate or inaccurate, and self-satisfying or dysphoric psychic configurations. The resulting personality becomes the sum of one's mode of perceiving and relating to the world of others.

Consider the case of Arthur, who was very finely attuned to group members' negative assessments. He searched every eye in the room for any glimmer of hostility or instance of unflattering judgment. Coming from a chaotic alcoholic family, Arthur learned to guard against his father's sudden and inexplicable bouts of rage. These hurtful outbursts were often misdirected at him when Arthur asserted any independence of thought or action. Arthur internalized this punitive parental response and experienced his own "badness" with painful authority. Not surprisingly, he also complained of recurrent difficulties in risking or sustaining initiative.

As group members increasingly took on the role of fair-minded self-objects for him, a softer and more accurate sense of self and other was mirrored. Arthur came to learn that not all criticism reflected badly on him as a person. A less than positive reaction did not have to be so chilling or carry murderous intent. While particularly sensitive to others' overt reactions, Arthur realized that he did not necessarily interpret subtle motivations correctly.

Pines (1983) describes the mirroring process in group psychotherapy as it reflects on needs for feedback and confirmation.

> *Mirroring, in group therapy, can be considered as the impact of information about the self that is derived through social interaction and relationship in the setting of the small group. The structure of the group is the mirror's setting, its boundaries of time and space the mirror's frame. The backing, the opacity which transforms the sheet of glass into a reflective surface, is the analytic culture which steadily promotes reflection and understanding of unconscious processes. The mirroring process is the steady to-and-fro rhythm of externalization and internalization, me in you and you in me. (p. 5)*

More dramatically, Moreno (1953) defines *interpersonal relations* as "a meeting of two: eye to eye, face to face. And when you are near I will tear your eyes out and place them instead of mine, and you will tear my eyes out and place them instead of yours, then I will look at you with your eyes and you will look at me with mine" (p. xxxi).

Members within the "hall of mirrors" (that is, the group) constantly need to see and be seen with new eyes. Mental imagery provides a ready language of projective screens with which to register perceptions and reflect understandings. The source material for the formation of images can be oneself, one's relations, or the quality of a particular group interaction or event.

When a schizoidal member was particularly withdrawn and tongue-tied during a session, she was invited to speak her thoughts. This appeal to her verbal skills proved fruitless and embarrassing for her. The therapist noted that Charlene, while sometimes at a loss for words, was exceptionally skilled at conceiving and constructing models and crafts. She was asked to picture what she might build to represent the group at this time. Closing her eyes, she remained silent for a couple of minutes before saying that she pictured a "jungle gym" with metal bars connected up so that people could climb and play together.

An astonished laugh came from Sam, who had also tried the exercise and came up with the exact same image. Others in the group readily viewed and concurred with this apt depiction of the current dynamic interaction. The group was, in fact, engaged in spirited parallel play. Through the image, Charlene experienced and demonstrated her connection with the process and once again felt like an important part of the group.

The group's ongoing dialogue concerned sexual relations. Given Charlene's boyish appearance and gender confusions, on a deeper level, the "jungle Jim" image-pun likely reflected homosexual feelings and masturbatory urges of which she was yet ashamed to speak about directly. Sam, an acknowledged gay man, intuitively perceived Charlene's perspective, even before she described it in words. A special alliance arose between the two, which in time extended to the whole of the group configuration, as members moved amongst themselves—hand over hand and ascent amidst descent.

Forms of Psychopathology

With elegant parsimony, Dosamantes-Alperson (1986) suggests that forms of psychopathology can be recognized as permutations of the self-other continuum, ranging from mystical union to violent separation. In psychotic-like adaptations, the self-other interface is so precarious, overwhelming, tentative, fragile, or frightening that the individual personality lives in constant danger of disintegration, fragmentation, and/or ego diffusion. Schizophrenics talk and listen to themselves when addressing or hearing from persecutory others. They thereby lose their privacy along with their individual integrity.

In borderline conditions, a wary merger and hostile alliance ensues between I and thou. The self is forever experienced as at risk of encroachment, while the possibility of sudden nonexistence constantly looms as a frightening specter. Extreme attempts at self-confirmation may precipitate ill-conceived, hysterically tinged, nihilistic enactments reflective of a chaotic inner world. Paradoxically, the self is thought to be protected from extinction when either impulsively splitting off or insistently drawing others in across a supercharged interpersonal boundary (Kibel, 1991).

In narcissistic conditions, other persons are responded to as servant selves, sought after as they provide various restitutive and protective functions for the ego—whether the needs be for affirmation, confirmation, comfort, tension release, or benign care. A sense of identity, albeit in vulnerable constitution, is maintained and solidified by keeping select others in their proper holding or mirroring position. Narcissistic injuries result when the other, by choice or constraint, fails the test of availability or reflects back less than positively.

In neurotic adaptations, more independence is granted to the self and to the other person, introducing inherent problems of loss. Depressive anxiety becomes a manifestation of wary sadness engendered by fears of or anger over the absence of relation and intimacy. With more tolerance for ambivalence, members come to realize that they can hate and wish to destroy the very persons they most love—a shocking revelation and a grievous isolation.

Psychopathology becomes a social phenomenon based on real or imagined mergers and cutoffs (Shapiro, 1990). Boundary confusions, chaotic attachments, injurious abandonments, or loss of consortium result from varied adaptations to the self-other bond. Barring fixation or regression, a developmentally inspired series of transformations is normally followed, as individuals progress from a paranoid-schizoid to a more depressed position (Klein, 1985), from less integrated to more integrated, and from a dependent to an independent and/or interdependent stance.

The group, too, as a fantasied maternal entity, requires perceptual orientation and behavioral enactment along the self-other continuum. Simply put, members must decide how much they see themselves as separate and apart from the collective, and how much they can conceive of being an intimate piece of the larger picture. Certainly modern Eastern societies and primitive tribes can be seen to relate to communal living in a more holistic way, whereas the Western adaptations of developed nations emphasize a more staunch individuality. Whichever cultural pattern is espoused, orientation to collective living is not without fear and trembling (Kierkegaard, 1843/1954). Greene (1983) suggests,

> *The most intensive group-induced anxiety for the participant, recapitulating the fears associated with the early developmental sequence of psychological differentiation, is the annihilation of the sense of self, either through engulfment or fusion with the collectivity, at one extreme, or through isolation from and abandonment by the group, at the other extreme. (p. 4)*

The psychotherapy group, proper, blends individuals into interactional amalgams of literal and figurative arrangement, however close or distant. Like the individuals who compose it, the group itself can become disoriented, suspicious, and disintegrated; confused, inconsistent, and enraged; panicked, vulnerable, and self-conscious; or sad, solicitous, and dependent. The whole of the developing enterprise reflects back on the cohesion, maturity, and structural continuity of the involved participants, who then again affect the integrity of the ensuing collective endeavor.

Genesis as a Guiding Principle

Mythology is also oriented toward origins, but not individual origins; rather, it is oriented toward social and interactive origins—humans in nature, humans in group. Campbell (1988) reminds us that there are two aspects to mythology. "There is the mythology that relates you to nature and the natural world, of which you are apart. . . . And there is mythology that is strictly sociological, linking you to a particular society. You are not simply a natural man, you are a member of a particular group" (pp. 22-23).

Each shared human experience or common life occurrence is thought to be intimately related to a preceding event, a formative innovation of either cosmic or sociological implication. Genesis becomes an explanatory principle par supreme, ceremoniously mimicked in various rites of initiation and passage. Speculations about a group's origins and primary experiences becomes the self-reflective mirror through which members see themselves and against which they judge the authenticity and ethical validity of their actions. A group's real or imagined history takes on mytho-religious fervor, as members seek to return to ancestral precedents, quasi-religious maxims, and time-honored traditions as a security measure and as a way of gaining inspiration for the future. In the antiquity of group relations, religion and society are not separate spheres, but rather blend together in mythopoetic essence, as the profane, by mimetic inference, is made over into the sacred (Eliade, 1959).

A seasoned therapy group was struggling to incorporate two new members. In participants' families of origin, the arrival of a sibling may or may not have marked a joyous occasion. Yet, in addition to these personal reference points, the group has its own history of inclusions to turn upon for comfort and guidance. Every successful group develops a host of public rituals of cultural transformation, including those for incorporating strangers into their midst. Here, when faced with two new entries, the most long-standing member, as tribal elder and group historian, remembers and recounts how other newcomers were welcomed and how inevitable anxieties about changes in composition were managed. Stories are passed down about the most famous arrivals, tales that at times go back further than any existing member's tenure in group. Such collective recollections tell of an assortment of characters and a plurality of group incarnations.

Some newcomers, it is told, entered with silence and reserve, whereas others made a more vocal and immediate impression. In a spontaneously inspired, yet culturally determined go-around, current members give testimonials about their own induction into the group. As a ceremonial gesture, an attempt is made to answer questions about "how we do things here." Experienced members talk of the creative essence of the group process, and describe their more individual reactions to the ameliorative efforts inherent in the collective experience. The message communicated to the newcomers contains assurances that the group culture is diverse enough to incorporate many kinds of people, but forewarns that each in his or her own way is expected to adapt to existing group norms. This ritualized edification serves both to orient new members and rejuvenate the old guard.

In an act of reciprocity, new members are invited to share their reasons for joining the group. They, in fact, do talk of personal histories and current motives for participating. The group-as-a-whole's overall self-satisfaction with this transformational process seemingly reflects on how well its current performance recapitulates the cultural mores that direct such transitions. Thus, the group history, with its inherent mythology about bringing in new members, serves as the collective self-object for individual reflection and sociological enactment.

This particular group also devised the ritual of leaving the seat closest to the door for any new member. This welcoming gesture hearkened back to many new and anxious arrivals, including those of the existing members, who, upon entering for the first time, wished to have escape close at hand.

Certainly fairy and folktales, parables, allegories, reminiscences of elders, or formal myths reflect the history of a culture in forms that can be reinvented or modified in response to novel circumstance. Such scenarios conform to a storied structure that often begins, "It happen that . . . ," "In the beginning," or the ubiquitous "Once upon a time."

Mythic thought draws no fine distinctions between historic and/or universal processes (that which is timeless and forever) and particular representations of these processes (that which comes in time and is for now) (Cassirer, 1955). In the life of the tribe, guiding principles and formative verities are present and active in every instance of human interaction, spurring transcendent thoughts and shaping concrete behaviors. The sociocultural prototype becomes a courted and worshipped structural form. Every individual choice point, each path to be followed, traces the contours of a societal ethos divined in relation to the whole. Empathic resonance is maintained with that which came before, that which is larger than the self, that which is general or eternal, and that which reflects on ultimate meanings and purposes. Personal action becomes at once an intimate conglomeration—an instance of freely initiated individuality, a repetition compulsion, a part of a collective enterprise, and a reflection of sociological or cosmic consensus. The group member rarely operates out of his or her cultural context, historical and foundation matrix, or metaphysical universe.

Primitive Processes and Modern Forms of Enactment

Participation Mystique

The transformation of members' internal structure, as reflected in personality (face shown to the world) and as an instance of character development (edifice of beliefs, perceptions, and action potentials), is taken up as the legitimate business of the group. Participants' familiar expectations and idiosyncratic perceptions take their usual form in response to common problems that demand immediate collective decision making. As members reenact and reexperience their privately inspired object relations within the group setting, alternative rituals, competing visions, and more workable self-other compromises can be engendered. Thus, the collective, as a distinctive cultural phenomenon, becomes a place of personal reflection (members unto themselves) and a space for unified recollection (members with each other and with the group-as-a-whole).

When participants take part in the procession of the group, they engage in a special joining within the larger fabric of society. With everything changing around it, the tribe, clan, or psychotherapy group becomes the stable referential center and the proper way station from which to exhort, weather, and mirror the chimera. Members look to each other for support and consensual reality. Participants inexorably weave themselves together in ritualistic habits and normative proclivities, inventing common operating procedures, subscribing to shared ethics, and purporting prevalent metaphysical beliefs. By assuming a collective identity, the members temporarily diffuse individual conflicts by giving them over to the group for resolution. A participation mystique and reverence of such unanimity ensues. To live in consort is to move in unison, serve a collective role, and bear up under a responsibility to one's reference group.

However, members can also be ill-served and the group swept away by a restrictive solution or trend. At times, the collective response may recreate a pathological or psychologically dangerous position for a particular member. Here, the therapist must question the group's unanimity by challenging its behavior.

A therapy group focused all its attentions on John, a member with hysteroid tendencies. John became increasingly agitated in the process. The leader interrupted this participation mystique by observing, "One person in here is being asked to be the patient while the rest of the group assumes the role of wise doctors. Surely others have problems to consider; John is not alone in his distress."

Or consider the case of a process group where one participant continually volunteered, to his own detriment, to lead the way into every dangerous interpersonal territory. The facilitator identified the stultifying pattern by challenging the ongoing norm of participation. "This group consistently lets Billy be its martyred hero, its leader at the point—first to fight and first to fall." The group, when shaken out of its seemingly unmodifiable, trance-like encounter, could now examine its process. Billy could come to understand his identification with heroic and ultimately tragic figures, while the other members might ponder the insufficiency of working out their own authority issues and failures of initiative through Billy.

The test of the heuristic value of such interventions is what transpires amongst the membership afterward. Is the process formulation embraced, defended against, elaborated, or facilitatively engaged to analyze or revise a collective trend?

Joan, a new member of an ongoing group, seemed to ascribe to a different norm of attendance than the older members. While all the other participants came religiously every week, Joan's presence was punctuated by absence. When available, she involved herself appropriately, but often appeared lost or confused by what had transpired while she was gone. When asked about her motivation, Joan claimed a new job and busy schedule precluded more consistent participation. The other members seemed to accept this answer and accordingly held her to a lesser standard.

Difficulties with commitment and inconsistent relationships marked Joan's interpersonal history. Outside others often became disillusioned with her for not following through on dates and times. Yet, she reported that, so often, she was given the benefit of the doubt. Joan, a very attractive women who had worked as a cheerleader for a professional basketball team, speculated that for many years she "got by on her looks alone"—perhaps as a modern form of goddess worship. Now she was discontented with being accepted for superficialities and wished to experience more honest, lasting, and truer relationships. The group's "letting her slide" was, in reality, not very helpful to her.

Conversely, many of the other group members made indiscriminate and unquestioned commitments. Once they agreed to participate, they carried on with noncritical availability. Many remained stuck in nonproductive habits and habitats. On the level of wish and self-importance, Joan's behavior was actually attractive to them. At least she was able to "put herself above others' expectations." Yet, members' acceptance of Joan's aloof behavior was not helpful to them, by failing to assert their needs or change the nature of their limited relationship with her.

Both Joan and the group were caught in the throws of a nonproductive participation mystique. Each participant played a slightly different part depending on their unique history. Yet, no one seemed free to question the group's dysfunctional pattern. The collective became caught up in an automatic, often unconscious way of relating. The therapist sought to disrupt this staid configuration, as a form of interaction that only brought with it more of the same. Consequently, he pointed out to the group that there seemed to be two sets of standards in the room, one lax and one stringent. He wondered aloud, how it was decided who would be held to which norm.

As a consequence of this intervention, Joan talked about how much she is allowed to get away with, while exploring her actual commitment to this group. She came to realize that much of her confusion in relationships came from her intermittent attention to them. The other members looked at how much they just accepted from others, with the inevitable consequence of feeling abused or taken for granted. They then explored how others' needs and expectations so clearly shaped their behaviors. For many of the members, this pattern of unqualified acceptance was mediated by a sense of their own lack of intrinsic attractiveness—an attractiveness mistakenly believed to be enhanced by merely "going along with the crowd."

Customs, Rites, and Rituals

Participation mystiques can take the form of proscribed rituals. These conventional practices, patterns, or behaviors are often carried out as a systemic observance—a form of public worship or reverence. Equivalently, rite is defined as the performance of a divine or solemn service as established by law, precept, or custom. Many therapy groups develop spontaneous customs like members showing up a little early and chatting amongst themselves before the official session begins. While important information may be exchanged and significant contacts made or sustained, the room often goes quiet when the therapist walks in. The solemn silence marks an acknowledgement of the leader's presence and ceremoniously begins the official group session.

Consider, alternately, the ending ritual of a largely chronic schizophrenic population on a ward in a veterans' psychiatric hospital. This group met daily in social contact sessions. Many of the patients, despite medication, were barely oriented to time and place. Yet under the tight orchestration of the staff psychologist, the group proceeded through its series of soliloquies and tentative interactions spearheaded by the more manic patients.

Mr. Thomas, an elderly gentleman and long-time resident, always sat in unflinching, expressionless, catatonic stupor until the end of the session approached. Then, like clockwork, he pulled his antique watch on a chain out of his vest pocket and subvocally counted off the last 30 seconds of the hour. In his apparent role as group time keeper, Mr. Thomas then uttered the now legendary words, "Time's up," after which all the patients immediately stood and ambled out of the ward room.

A session occurred when the old man was absent. The group proceeded as usual until the last minutes of the hour, when noticeable agitation spread throughout the membership. Patients stopped talking and glanced at each other in confusion and seeming desperation. Though the clock on the wall was readily apparent to all, without Mr. Thomas, the group had no conception of how to end the session—no alternate termination ritual.

Acting Out and Acting In

To become an intimate part of an overall process means losing and finding oneself simultaneously, as characterized by the operative motifs of *sacrifice* and *rebirth*. In this blending of perspectives, subject and object, self and other, and inside and outside lose their considerable distinctiveness. According to the law of participation "all things, beings or whatever are in some fashion linked together" even to include the past with the present, the animate with the inanimate, the timely with the timeless (Levy-Bruhl, 1985, p. xiii). Through this metaphysical joining, the group wishes to dissolve all diversity within and without its bounds.

A group organized around messianic fantasies agreed with the exaggerated sentiment,"If everyone came to a group like this one, then the world would function so much better." Such a leap of faith proffered a situationally helpful, cohesion-making, collective belief in the value of the current proceedings, while also reflecting a more collectively inspired primitive and grandiose desire for self-importance and participatory fusion.

The unanimity involved in a group's beliefs and subsequent actions can be facilitative or resistive.

A newly composed group came together as one to astutely avoid conflict, while engaging each other in pollyanna fashion. In an attempt to break this restrictive consolidated front, the therapist suggested, "The group seems to be ascribing to the myth of utopia. All will be well here if we carefully avoid disagreements or conflicts." This said, the group continued for a time in the avoidance mode, but now without the protection of its repressive ethos. Change inevitably came, sooner than later, because the therapist precipitated a conflict that ultimately could not be denied.

Members of utopian societies often believe that, in time, the world at large can be brought within its sphere of influence. Paradoxically, to maintain this stance often requires careful separation from the world at large. In cult settings, no one is allowed to speak to contradictions or introduce controversial perspectives that challenge the group's overall structure or ritual. For a group to develop past its preconceived, intransigent notions, information must cross permeable collective barriers in two directions—inside out and outside in. Only then can helpful exchange be fostered. Through an accustomed dance of projections and introjections, the microcosm and the macrocosm do become as one. The world inside the group comes to resemble the world outside, while the world outside changes in response to the progression of internal transformations, both individual and collective.

In time, members may report that "somehow things are different for me out there." The timid participant may act more courageously, the withdrawn person may join a club or make a friend, the battered spouse may stand up for himself or herself. For, after all, both tribal and therapy groups take place within the larger world, just as the larger world is transposed inside the group as reflected in the members' psyches and interpersonal relations (Ashbach & Schermer, 1987). The interaction of a working group constantly juxtaposes "acting in" with "acting out" in overlapping sequences of adaptation and assimilation.

Primitive Processes and Modern Forms of Perception

The Preeminence of Collective Thoughts and Shared Beliefs

As tribal or small-group members come together, so individual minds tend to approach collective thoughts. Personal fantasies pool in a common reservoir, finding there a level of cultural articulation. In sociological elaboration, Durkheim (1974) insists on the preemptive role of communal thoughts and consensual beliefs whenever attempting to comprehend humans in society. "We must . . . explain phenomena that are a product of the whole by the characteristic properties of the whole, the complex by the complex, social facts by society" (p. 29). Shared viewpoints give a group its shape and motility, while providing the individual with a deep well of cultural referents from which to draw upon for reflective thought and personal action. Bion (1977) likened a group's holistic, mythic structure to "a membrane of consciousness," capable of capturing, storing, and making available contextual narratives necessary to explain and rework the individual's and the collective's formative experiences.

Levy-Bruhl (1985), in *How Natives Think,* describes this ancient proclivity.

> *As far back as we can go, however primitive the races we study, we shall never find any minds which are not socialized . . . not already concerned with an infinite number of collective representations which have been transmitted by tradition, the origin of which is lost in obscurity. (p. 24)*

Members find expression and the group evolves and changes by formulating and effecting such shared notions of self, other, and world. A metaphysics of natural and social reality is stipulated and perpetuated. Kibel (1990) suggests that some accepted customs and common beliefs turn out to be helpful and others prove inaccurate or constraining.

> *Small psychotherapy groups create a culture of their own and therefore become like mini-societies with their own mythology. For exam-*

ple, group members invariably believe that patients who are more ver-
bal and interactive get better, whereas relatively quiet members don't.
However this isn't always the case.

Consider the experience of a young-adult group meeting in the context of a long-term private psychiatric hospitalization. Through most of its course, the group displayed two classes of members: leaders and followers—dramatic participants and their more silent admirers. Among the prominent were a young couple, Fran and Larry, who started dating half-way through their tenure in group. The collective often focused their attentions on conflicts between the two.

For the first 26 sessions, Ben remained virtually silent. When Larry's condition suddenly deteriorated and he left group for a closed unit and more intensive individual care, the group initially struggled without him. Then, remarkably, Ben stepped into the vacant leadership role, with an authority and a sensitivity of which Larry was incapable. As the sessions proceeded, it became clear how much vicarious learning Ben had absorbed and was now able to put into practice. He learned from Larry both what to do and what not to do in order to successfully sustain relationships.

Part of the facilitator's role is to help the group search for and challenge dysfunctional myths, practices, or uniform beliefs. In this example, it became clear that more was not necessarily better than less. While Fran and Larry monopolized, they didn't gain as much from the process as did Ben in his watchful silence. It also became evident that the extragroup contact between Fran and Larry was not constructive, since it created a special relationship that dominated sessions. The unbridled intensity that poured into the sessions likely contributed to Larry's relapse. Yet, the membership supported this lovers' tryst in the hope of finding intimate salvation through the chosen pair. With this revelation in mind, the therapist could have directed the group to look to its less evident resources, while evening out its participatory practices. The facilitator might have clarified the effect of the out-of-group contact and interpreted the group's vicarious wishes for Fran, Larry, and themselves.

At other times, culturally inspired initiatives, mutual understandings, and socially endowed perceptions are helpful to collective adaptation. These newly conceived points of view can be suggested or reinforced by the therapist, as members find comfort in coming up with similar experiences. Paradoxically, by finding enough in common, participants are free to express more personal and less articulate perceptions and affects.

When a long-term group went through a radically rapid turnover in its membership, newcomers hesitated in bringing up personal experiences of an abusive nature—experiences apparently too terrible to admit in public. Although central to various members' psychodynamics, these traumata were seemingly off limits, hidden behind a veil of shame and secrecy. The revamped group had yet to develop acceptable forms and norms by which such powerful memories and their sympto-matic sequelae might be accessed, expressed, and thereby externalized and dif-fused.

Finally, Dorothy, impelled by private dreams and violent visions, talks of "seeing herself lying in bed and being repeatedly stabbed by a male invader." She reveals, that as a child, she slept with heavy covers as battlement and protection. Dorothy wonders aloud if she had been sexually abused within her family. Other members now respond with care and in kind. Bert, the chronologically oldest group member, talks of the loose sexual boundaries within his own family of origin, and tells the newly composed group of his recent turn to homosexuality. Margaret reveals, for the first time, her 25-year-old fear of serious illness and the long-standing practice of avoiding intrusive doctors. As members open up to each other in the presence of the therapist, the culture is transformed by developing a language permissive of expressions of safety and danger pertinent to both in- and out-of-group experi-ences. As the session ends, the therapist summarizes developments by suggesting, "Today we have come together, in trust, to form a 'secrets society,' a place where the unthinkable can be thought and where the unspeakable can be spoken."

Transitional and Transferential Phenomena

Forceful and unique conceptualizations of how to conform to the de-mands of social reality are retrievable as particular transformative images, metaphors, symbols, or rites of passage. In primitive mentalities, both an-cient and modern, these artfully executed words, objects, and actions are believed coincident or identical with the things, people, or processes for which they stand.

Seeing or touching an image brings to mind and to life a host of pri-mary attributes, characteristics, and essences. The idol becomes the god incarnate, the talisman radiates with its source of its power, while the fetish is thought to hold those qualities it is carefully fashioned to embody. In a unification between subject and inanimate object, statues are viewed with awe-inspiring reverence and effigies are burned in flagrant disrespect.

In intimate acts of symbolic interactionalism and sympathetic magic, the tribal group engages in moving representational scenarios—whether ex-pressed as traditional dance, meticulous ceremony, or overdetermined ha-bitual activities performed with exquisite mimetic sensitivity. These enact-ments are fashioned to keep self and other, inside and outside, finite and infinite enjoined and on course by a crafted force of imagination no less convincing than real, proximate, tangible, and causal relations.

The medium often becomes more than merely the message. The com-munication is transformed by its receiver into identity with the communicator. To criticize is to be critical, whereas to idealize is to be ideal. No fine distinctions are made between states and traits, behaviors and persons, actions and actors. In the process, members can lose the ability to differentiate what one does from who one is. Remember the fate of the purveyor of bad news who is killed when too closely associated with the malevolent omen he or she carries. Or consider, instead the conveyor of good tidings.

Peter missed a month of group while he went on a cross-country journey of initiation and renewal. His absence was viewed with considerable ambivalence. On the one hand, the group envied Peter's freedom; on the other, they resented his leave taking. Upon receiving a "postcard from the edge" of the Grand Canyon, Peter's presence was directly reintroduced into the group. The members felt soothed and tangibly touched, rejoined with their missing member. The transitional object, though made only of paper, stood in for Peter in essence, spirit, and body. Through its mediation, others vicariously shared his adventure by being included in his thoughts and deeds.

In contrast to the laws of logic, representations become synonymous with the thing represented. Symbols become equated with the reality, circumstance, or person spurring their occurrence. Segal (1957), reiterated by Ashbach and Schermer (1987), suggests that patients, especially in groups, often reify symbols. The "as if" relation between the representation and what it represents may be superseded. As a consequence, the group members respond to the leader as an actual father, participants become competitive siblings, and the group-as-a-whole is enticed to act as would a real mother.

Transferences onto the leader can be personally or archetypically inspired. Certainly the leader can be seen as a transposed parental or authority figure. The leader can also be fit into the transpersonal role of "wise old man or woman," "primal father," "great mother," "shaman," "hero", "demon," "witch," or "fairy godmother." When under the spell of an archetypal symbol, particular members and/or the group-as-a-whole may respond with an urgency beyond usual capacities for persuasion or endurance.

The flesh-and-blood leader may gain inordinately in charisma and attributed power, when merged with the group's more primal identifications. The "hero myth" (Rank, 1932; Campbell, 1949) signifies just such an emergence of the individual from within the group, first through merging with collective needs and later by transcending consensual visions. The group embraces its heroes—even following them through hell if need be—when circumstance or necessity mandates quick or powerful change. Then, the strong words of a leader to his or her group may result in an immediate collective reaction with little lapse in time between instruction and compliance. The hero serves as a "transformational object," leading his or her group to deeper levels of cultural and creative evolution. Bollas (1987) points out

> *the phenomenon in adult life of the wide-ranging collective search for an object that is identified with the transformation of the self. In many religious faiths, for example, when the subject believes in the deity's actual potential to transform the total environment, he sustains the terms of the earliest object ties within a mythic structure. (pp. 15–16)*

Usandivaras (1986) equates the evocation of groupwide archetypal symbols and roles (Jung, 1969) with Foulkes' (1965) notions of being caught up in primordial experiences. Here, the leader can, in fact, function in the sensitive and often prescient role of shaman by either facilitating or challenging powerful shaping forces—forces larger than any one member or any particular group.

Schermer (1991b) suggests that "object relations theory seeks to analyze these transferences whereas anthropology accepts transference as a normative social phenomenon." Yet, to amplify a universal image or transpersonal transference implies not only analyzing it, but also identifying with its cultural, historical, mythical, and literary referents. How has the has the symbolic image or role been evoked and what has it meant across time and circumstance? In what way is the present situation suggestive of a more general or existential context? Symbolic images often serve to connect inner experience with outer reality by transforming inert tendencies into overt acts.

The Intimate Connection Between Perception and Emotion

In mythic thinking, emotive and perceptual systems are inexorably linked. Seeing, if only in the mind's eye, is experienced directly as feeling, believing, and being so. Levy-Bruhl (1985) suggests that, "the primitive actually has an image in his mind and thinks it's real, but also he has some hope or fear connected with it, [believing wholeheartedly] that some definite influence emanates from it, or is exercised upon it" (pp. 37–38). Such unquestioned perceptual certainty can present as compelling visions, haunting hallucinations, sure-fire delusions, or hypnotic inducements.

More positively and more reasonably, *literal images* work as practice actions, such as when a group leader suggests skill-enhancing social images for mental rehearsal and adaptive performance, as in assertiveness training.

Cybernetic images and *creative visualizations* (Silva, 1977; Gawain, 1978) instill the power of positive thinking as evident in cognitive behavior modifications (Beck, 1969) and the uses of imagery techniques in immunology (Simonton & Simonton, 1974). *Figurative images* create mental representations of experience as apt phenomenological descriptors. *Semiotic images* present picture puzzles as contextual metaphors. *Perceptive metaphors, suggestive viewpoints,* and *compelling analogies* can all lead to an adaptive changes in feeling and in behavior.

In primary process, images of night and day dreams are often accorded more affective immediacy and respect than logical, waking narratives.

A long-standing group seemed carried away by its anger at one another. Fights and misunderstandings broke out indiscriminately, as members appeared out of control with their misdirected rage. No amount of reasoning helped resolve the conflict. Alice suddenly remembered a dream from the previous evening. She is driving to work and loses the breaks on her car. Stunned, Marie interrupts by saying that she has had a recurrent dream for years in which she is driving blindfolded and can't reach the steering wheel or the brakes. The precipitous dream material, which well characterizes the ongoing encounter, allows the collective to come together to begin to regain control of the group vehicle, while anticipating and avoiding imminent collisions.

The group dream provides perceptive images for insight into the collective experience (Greenson, 1970; Kolb, 1983). Images reflect on both the dreamer and the social context that spurred its occurrence. Keys to decoding the group dream lie in both the personal meanings for the dreamer and the implications for the group-as-a-whole.

Real-life and dream-life can impinge on the sanctity of the therapeutic circle. While not usually sharing personal news with his groups, the therapist made exceptions in the case of "major life events" (i.e., birth, death, marriage) and occurrences that might directly effect his availability (i.e., absences, injury, changes in practice). During a particularly precipitous time in the leader's life, two births were imminent. A baby was due to be born, and a book was soon to be published. Both events would likely call the therapist away for the last bit of intensive labor.

Most groups and members took the news well enough, offering congratulations and probing their own reactions to the news. However, the therapist's most vulnerable group reacted as if either the messiah had arrived or tragedy had struck. Dave, who idealized his father to his own detriment, felt instant gratification that the therapist might both father a child and write a book. Glassy-eyed, he pronounced, "I feel like I'm getting so much more from you now." In contrary fashion, Mary expressed her annoyance that the leader "would presume to know something about groups," when he had on a particular occasion, some years ago in this group, said something that hurt her. Amy became instantly despondent. With prompting, she admitted feeling jealous of both the unborn child and of the therapist's love for his wife. She felt that any caring for others meant that he did not care for her at all. Amy was left abandoned and destitute.

In response to such contradictory and dysphoric responses, the therapist absorbed members' distress and felt ashamed, crazy, and unreal. Images of Jesus with the lepers filled his thoughts. He ended the session by saying, "Today, I realize how difficult it is to be who everyone needs me to be." Yet, this emotional disclosure did not assuage the distress he felt. The leader went to sleep still distraught and disorganized.

That night he had a dream that his long-dead grandfather appeared to him as he was sitting with a group of unrecognized others. In real life, this grandfather had been the person in his life who made him feel most special, most accepted. Yet, the last times they were together were quite difficult; the old man was so senile as to not even recognize his beloved grandchild. In the dream, the therapist anxiously watched his grandfather approach, fearing that he would still be confused. After initial greeting, the dreamer was relieved to find a kind, smiling, and coherent figure. But then the old man pulled out some papers that were filled with seemingly undecipherable symbols. Now the dreamer worried that his grandfather was crazy. Yet their contact brought considerable relief and dissipation of tension. As pages were turned, the "wounded healer's" turmoil seemed to alleviate.

The dreamer woke refreshed and intact. The dream served to calm him and restore his equilibrium. On re-visualizing the dream, the therapist realized that while his grandfather was a short and stocky man, the figure in the dream was tall and thin, though with his grandfathers eyes, face, and mannerisms. The dream personage was actually an amalgam of his grandfather and himself. This group-inspired dream, later shared with the therapy group, brought insight into the character of the members' hurts. Faced with real or imagined injury, they were unable to soothe themselves. Rather they carried their hurts as increased dependency and decreased self-confidence when idealizing others (Dave), long-standing slights and grudges (Mary), or reinforced feelings of being unloved (Amy). After acknowledging the emotional reality of various members' responses, and apologizing for overloading them with news, the theme of "self-soothing" became the focus for many sessions to follow. The dream, as a distinct product of the group experience, affected the psyche of the therapist who received a vision of comfort for himself and an ameliorative message for his community.

In primitive societies, prophets, shamans, and seers are engaged to penetrate the unseen stream of time and consciousness in order to recollect the past as well as predict the future. In the modern culture of the therapy group, members, with the help of the facilitator, look into the meaning of their less than conscious processes. Dream-time is still thought to link the tenses in one unbroken chain of events. Such metaphysical in-viewing is imbued with radiant significance, as an enlivened instance of the transcendental unity of apperception (Cassirer, 1955, p. 111). At peak moments and in sacred epochs, intuitions of the whole and contemplations of complete cycles of experience appear fully grasped. Creative visualizations seek to encompass the larger picture, and cultivate the synergistic potential for changing mind, body, and world in ensemble. Ever since Joseph interpreted the pharaoh's night vision, dreams have held the promise of reflecting the emptiness or fullness of the societal experience (Mann, 1950).

Primitive Processes and Modern Forms of Psychic Relation and Exchange

The Exchange of Parts and Feelings

A group in a primitive state of relating is capable of ritual transference, or the moving around of psychic components. Ready exchanges are possible between the self and its internal representations through a panoply of external transactions. Through archaic processes such as splitting, projection, introjection, identification, and projective identification, that which is native can be pushed out and viewed as strange, while that which is other can be taken inside and experienced as familiar (Klein, 1946). M. Klein (1985) describes this very human tendency. "We are inclined to attribute to other people—in a sense put into them—some of our own emotions and thoughts. . . . By projecting oneself or part of one's impulses and feelings into another person, an identification with that person is achieved" (p. 10).

In simple projection, expectations or impulses are "put on" others who may remain independent and unaffected. In projective identification, the recipient of projections rather "takes in" and "acts upon" these transferable parts and processes. Horwitz (1985), quoting Segal (1973), suggests that the external object (or person) "becomes possessed by, controlled, and identified with the projected parts" (p. 25). The donor, by making these resonant characteristics external, can manage and reconfigure himself or herself at a distance by imaginatively interacting with various ego ideals or shadow personae.

The projection and possession lasts until the receiver rejects the transplant or the originator takes his or her own material "back inside," reclaiming the misplaced and integral parts of his or her own characterological structure. Horwitz (1985) suggests, "When projective identification occurs, the group therapist [for one] has the experience of being manipulated to play a part in someone else's fantasy" (p. 23). The psychotherapeutic task is then to absorb, understand, and shake oneself free from this numbing state, often accomplished by the leader giving the material and unwanted role restraints back to the group and/or its members through interpretations (Bion, 1961).

Afraid of being left alone (a fate equated with existential demise), Candice maintained a frenetic social schedule; yet close involvement also proved threatening. When intimate with any one man, Candice felt overwhelmed by his needs and again experienced the dreaded loss of self. Her compromise was to create love triangles where she went back and forth, as her relations with any one man became either too distant or too close for comfort. This strategy was not without pain; chaotic interactions, hurt feelings, and somatic distress followed the acting out of internal conflicts.

After years of demonstrating this pattern, Candice was notably disgusted with herself and yet unable to overcome her bouts of ambivalence. She reported her pain and her predicament to the group as a familiar and unsolvable dilemma. The group members struggled to be patient and facilitative. At the same time, the therapist was aware of becoming increasingly intolerant and judgmental, a position connected with feelings of helplessness and frustration. Nothing that he or the group could do or say seemed to much matter.

Candice wondered aloud if therapy was helping her. While wondering the same, the therapist experienced this legitimate question as somehow manipulative and hostile. Some certain response seemed to be called for from him. Suddenly, his distemper broke as he realized the position of any number of Candice's other men, unable to matter and unable to hold her. He didn't feel as if this stance was truly his own, but assumed that it was rather induced in him to reenact Candice's conflict and paradoxically resolve it by recapitulation in the therapy.

The therapist was projectively identifying with Candice's self-loathing and notable lack of control when being pressured to give up or reject her. If acted on, he might take over responsibility for her bind and decide that, in fact, therapy wasn't working. Instead, he reflected back empathically the nature of Candice's success at putting her feelings and her potential for action into others and thereby truly losing herself. He wondered aloud what would happen if he and the group did not accept the rejecting role and rather encouraged Candice to face her conflicts with courage and insight, staying within the group relationship long enough to work through her fears.

How similar this projective exchange of psychic material is to a shamanistic trance, where the sensitive tribal member unknowingly "takes on" others' concerns, or where the medicine man deliberately "takes over" the tribe's worries until that time when they can be returned and incorporated in altered, processed, and ritualized form. The human drama has always been acted out in a cathartic interaction between protagonist and audience, between perpetrator and victim, between leader and follower, and between active party and passive yet vicarious participant (Moreno, 1953; Rioch, 1975a).

Various role formations such as scapegoating or martyrdom also allow internal and external objects and attributes to be moved from person to person, from member to group, and from group to member (Perera, 1986; Colman, 1989; Gadlin, 1991). Scheidlinger (1982) retells the biblical myth of the scapegoat.

> *According to the Old Testament (Leviticus, 16:8–10), in the ritual Day for Atonement, one of two goats was chosen by lot and symbolically laden by the High Priest with the sins of the Jewish people. The thus-burdened goat was sent into the wilderness alive to placate Azazel, a demonic being. In later days, the goat was pushed over a cliff near Jerusalem to certain death. The other goat, reserved for the Lord, was sacrificed as a burnt-offering in the temple. (p. 132)*

Unfortunately, not only animals but people can be recruited for the scapegoat position. A member can be loaded up with the group's dysphoric projections and sacrificed in session or actually pushed so far off on a lonely ledge that he or she will certainly drop out of sight.

Totemic Relations and Oral Incorporation

Group participation can stimulate or cultivate a variety of superstitions, including a studied regression involving an identification with the animal forces of our prehuman endowment. In antiquity, power and strength were believed to emanate from totemic relations (Freud, 1946; Levi-Strauss, 1963). Various animals were believed to be guardian spirits for the tribe in recognition of the power of lower forms and as an incantation to our instinctual heritage. Men's and women's mystery rites, practiced in small groups, often invoked animals as mediators equidistant between humans and gods.

Consider the power of a mythological animal for 6 sexually abused latency-age girls who met weekly in a psychoeducational context. As an act of cohesion making, the therapist asked them to pick a name for their group. After much spirited debate, they chose "the Unicorns." This identification with a magical, horned, horse-like creature was overdetermined by many aspects of the abuse experience. Traditionally, the unicorn symbolizes the protection of young maidens in their virginity, a companion sign of feminine purity and chastity often associated with the Virgin Mary (Cooper, 1978). Here, the invocation of the unicorn as totem bespoke the need for a renewed protectorate in the group in prelude to the reinstitution of innocence.

Respect for our animal heritage can lead to seeking out potent parts—the rabbit's foot, the tiger's tale, the fish egg—in order to assimilate valued characteristics. By so doing, humans act out the wish to harness luck and strength by possessively mastering libidinal and aggressive urges. In reality, the worshipped animal can be held in ritual abeyance, like the sacred cow of the Hindus. In fantasy, the relationship becomes more complex, as that which is idealized is often killed and consumed in instances of hunting magic. Such primitive processes can be found in actual cannibalism or in more modern symbolic sacrament. Oral incorporation fosters a primary identification, a unity of prey with prayer, as a collectively inspired, unconscious bid for cultural continuance (Saravay, 1978).

Even that which is most loved is often the object of such envy, hostility, or sacrifice (M. Klein, 1985). In modern groups, compromise must also be reached between the savage and the civilized, between the wish to consume and the need to conserve. The special or unattainable qualities of others are often coveted and imaginatively taken inside in intimate attempts at self-satisfaction and self-aggrandizement. Ganzarain (1989) suggests that "love must mitigate the hate for objects and guilt must be overcome by resolving in healthy ambivalence while tolerating sadistic impulses and satisfying greedy parts" (p. 45). Oral incorporation, rather than simple imitation, remains the highest form of flattery.

To prevent hurtful exclusions, members must ultimately be taken inside the body of the group, with their issues digested and metabolized so as to provide the nutrients and the bulk necessary for the survival and continuance of the whole. If the group is properly fed, then members can be incorporated anew in the belly of the experience and born again through the collective womb. It is likely no accident that interactive conversation is referred to as "chewing the fat," whereas alternative perspectives are viewed variously as "easy to get one's teeth into" or "hard to swallow."

Fragmented Images and Part-Processes

Following the principle of *pars pro toto,* people can be represented by incomplete or partial images (breasts, faces, tempers), which come to stand in for their whole essences in intimate fantasies, whether of sexuality, love, or aggression. All physical characteristics (i.e., strength, weakness, or visual acuity), body parts (i.e., hair, teeth, or hands), or metabolites (i.e., nail filings, blood, spit, or excrement) can take on symbolic significance. Members easily speak of not seeing clearly, having a hair-raising experience, or feeling like shit. Truncated organs (i.e., heart, stomach, or spleen) as well as isolated organic processes (i.e., incorporation, digestion, expulsion, inspiration) can also be conjured up in mysterious interaction with other part-objects or distilled dynamics, sometimes in confabulated and often in creatively imaginative ways (Dosamantes-Alperson, 1986).

Pieces of physicality or emotion stand in for basic wishes, fears, and impulses directed toward oneself or significant others. For example, in Klein's (1946) paranoid-schizoid position, "Imaginary objects experienced as sensations, images, forces, and part-objects such as breast, penis, or womb" terrorize the individual in bouts of persecutory anxiety and splits between good and bad (Ashbach & Schermer, 1987, p. 39).

Betty, when faced with negative feedback, however mild or constructive, literally saw her father's wagging finger pointing out her inadequacies. She would then tend to obsessively focus on her own less than perfect body parts—the size of her nose, the curve of her chest. Don reported having heated imaginary discussions with the therapist, focusing on the group leader's mouth, as a violent profusion of moving teeth, lip, and jaw. Sharon, who had difficulty staying away from a dysfunctional relationship, told the group how she idealized her ex-partner by visualizing his unbending posture as a sign of strength. When doing so, she neglected to remember that it was this same rigidity that contributed to their demise as a couple.

Such fragmented images are often highly stylized, engendering disintegration into excited and confused states. Partial psychic contact stimulates surrealistic perspectives that often lose sight of larger realities, whether of whole persons or of full experiences.

After a number of years in a mixed-adult group, Jim finally told the story of how he came to be a member. During a frightening session, Doris related that she was being followed by and receiving phone calls from a veritable stranger whom she dated on a few occasions. She reported being afraid to go home, believing that he was watching her from a distance. Doris was terrorized by the vision of an intruder present in fleeting shadows and partial images. She considered changing her phone number or even moving.

Jim was noticeably uncomfortable as the story unfolded. Suddenly, with pressured speech, he revealed being arrested as a "peeping Tom." With great shame, he told the group the story of how he was caught looking in neighbors' windows. Jim explained that in individual therapy, prior to joining the group, he came to realize his need to see for himself what an intimate relationship looked like, having no clue from his parents or his own distant marriage. Although not condoning his action, neither did the group reject Jim, as he had feared.

The discussion evolved into a consideration of feeling out of control when particular parts of one's personality or need structure gained undue influence over the whole of one's behavior. As the session wound down, Jim expressed his relief at the group's acceptance of him despite his lapse of judgment. He said how hard it was to "let his skeleton out of the closet." The skeleton image is a ready symbol for split off, deadly parts too disturbing to expose in public. Spurred by Jim's act of courage and the group's understanding, in the weeks that followed other members revealed hidden experiences, fragmented images, and buried part-processes that had been carefully concealed. Containing the revelations required a collective sensitivity for what it is like to penetrate one's protective layer and expose inner structure to others. The therapist sought to reinforce the members' progress by suggesting that they return next week, bringing "both their sensitive skin and their underlying bones."

Part-object visualizations in the form of personality characteristics or interpersonal potentials can also provide reassurance and feelings of security, if not longing.

During one poignant session, group members talked of carrying comforting parts of each other between sessions—Joe's calm, Jo Anne's sensitivity, Bill's assertion, Tina's optimism—conjured up in times of pressing crisis or confusion. Participants then compared their enlivened fantasies about the therapist, images that were sometimes summoned and sometimes unbidden. One member reported hearing the therapist's assuring voice and cool advice in times of high anxiety. Another reported having a partial vision of sitting in the therapist's lap, encircled by comforting arms and sustained by enveloping protection. A third member reported fleeting sexual fantasies that never came into clear focus and rarely encompassed the whole of the therapist's person.

Part-object relations have the power to torment or entice, with a current and captivating force capable of obscuring more holistic perceptions and assessments.

Primitive Processes and Modern Forms of Spatial Relations

Sacral Boundaries and Metaphorical Space

Ashbach and Schermer (1987) suggest that "metaphors of psychological distance can be thought of as derivatives of primitive spatial relations in which physical space, emotions, and object relations are fused rather than separate dimensions of experience" (p. 51). Such relations can be described by bipolar topographical concepts such as in-out, up-down, close-far, inside-outside.

Stiers (1987), based on the earlier work of Schutz (1966) and Yalom (1985), relies on such spatial metaphors when describing how groups actually move through three distinct phases. First, in the *in-out* phase, members are preoccupied with the boundary that separates what is inside from what is outside the group. Participants question and act out their feelings about staying within the confines of the collective experience. Primitive anxieties about participation often imply a more personal confusion and concern with the limits, integrity, and the permeability of one's personal space and territorial imperative.

If a safe enough place can be created in the process, then the group moves to a *top-bottom* phase, where issues of control, dominance, and power come to the foreground. Here, members often attribute aggressive feelings to the therapist, who is seen as sadistically depriving. With time, anger toward the formal leader is expressed more directly, setting off reactive guilt and depressive fears of retaliation.

If the therapist can withstand the attack and endure the hate, then the group can progress to the *near-far* phase. At this point, the collective becomes predominately concerned with intimacy and closeness. Progress involves acknowledging and accepting a host of feelings, first toward the therapist and eventually toward each other. Significant others come to be viewed more as a totality, encompassing both good and bad aspects.

In primitive mentality, whether of the race or of the individual, space and content are intimately related. Each space has a distinctive tonality and each place brings objects, subjects, and topics together by merging separate essences into conglomerations of desire and practicality. Group boundaries inclusive of self/other and containing a synthetic mixture of various dualities of human nature become sacral enclosures (Cassirer, 1955). The whole of the group or primitive community becomes a self-contained village, a field of forces or dreams (Lewin, 1951).

The collective also precipitates out into a pooled distillate of persons, affects, and issues (Bion, 1970). Each object or constellation can be identified by the space it occupies, as well as by the territory it maintains on the periphery as a protective zone or defensive buffer. A group forms when separate and protected spaces are shared in common in an area of mutual play—neither self nor other, but rather one and the same (Jacobson, 1989, p. 479). In the therapeutic community, members constantly negotiate with their group about how much and what kind of space they require as a mean distance.

Charlene described her position within the group as like being in her own "telephone booth," separate but able to observe others more freely moving about and interacting. This personal symbol also accurately depicted how Charlene negotiated her territorial needs outside the group. She went through life literally closed off from others. It took another member, Lauren, to point out Charlene's obvious desire for making and receiving contact, for Charlene described herself as if encased in a phone booth, not a closet. And phone booths have phones, opening up a line of communication to the outside, albeit at long distance. Charlene later thanked Lauren for calling on her and drawing her into conversation.

Spatial relations take on symbolic significance, whether tunneling beneath the surface, rising to the occasion, or becoming firmly entrenched in the here-and-now (Sallis, 1987). Both horizontal and vertical inquiry are possible, as when investigating equidistant relations or when exploring the deeper core or genesis of transactional proclivities. Ashbach and Schermer (1987) reiterate that "groups, like inner phantasies, are experienced in spatial terms" (p. 51). Each direction holds its own mystical properties and possibilities, whether seeking to be right, wishing to come out on top, struggling to hold one's center, or scurrying so as not to appear downcast or left behind.

Following principles of spatial causality, illness becomes a matter of possession—bad elements entering into and contaminating good objects—toxic contents poisoning pure forms of matter and relation. The relevant diagnostic questions become: What malady has possessed the individual, the relationship, or the group-as-a-whole? What bad influence has overcome or infused itself, claiming the intrapsychic or interpersonal territory as its own? Healing entails overcoming, diluting, or pushing out atavistic and foreign forces by way of the intercession of good objects, pure intentions, or palliative remedies. Dysphoric world views must also be exorcised to regain an emptiness from pathology, so that positive or more accurate images and perceptions can be introduced. Thereby, a fullness of native essence is regained.

Geertz (1966) reminds us of the necessity of accounting for spatial discontinuities, missing pieces, and empty spaces. "The problem of cultural analysis is as much a matter of determining independencies as interconnections, gulfs as well as bridges" (p. 65). Transmuting internalizations allow for favorable qualities, gleaned one from another, to be incorporated into the self as a way of filling gaps in experience (Shapiro, 1990). Change ensues with this deconstruction and reconstruction of internal and external spaces.

The *"potentiating space"* (Winnicott, 1971) or *"facilitating environment"* (Bollas, 1987) that is the group is composed of both subjective and objective elements—"I" and "we" simultaneously as "homo duplex" (Durkheim, 1974, p. viii). As a transitional place, the group becomes a fluid crucible for the breakdown and consummation of all manner of seeming contradiction—a place of magical transformations and creative equilibrations (Dosamantes-Alperson, 1986). Durkheim (1974) suggests, "A chemical synthesis results which concentrates and unifies the synthesized elements and by that transforms them. Since the synthesis is the work of the whole, its sphere is the whole. . . . It is in the whole and it is by the whole" (pp. 26, 29). During distinct rites of passage and bouts of spatial magic, the resultant collective changes in shape, developing and transitioning from one sacral ring to another. New space is constructed out of old space by transforming from the inside out. Members further their personal growth by recombining within alternative social contexts in response to varying circumstantial necessities. Maturity comes with the ability to manage oneself over time in a variety of places.

Ritual Transference

Violating the law of noncontradiction, people or things can be experienced in more than one place at one time (Levy-Bruhl, 1985). In distinct acts of translocation, the group space brings dispersed objects together. Satellite members not actually in the room can be in the group. Brought forth from within the minds of members, these invisible yet transcendent others continually influence current relationships. For example, in a long-standing group formed with supportive intent, participants continually ask after one another's family members. The extended group certainly includes Ann's husband, John, and her two children, Andy and Karen, as well as Mary's sister, Lauren, along with Bill's teenage brother, Sam, among others. Prior members continue to populate the group as ancestors and guiding spirits, materializing as their special insight, warning, or influence is needed.

In acts of ritual transference, personal properties and characteristics are moved from the familial to the interpersonal sphere, while keeping their overdetermined form by faithful recreation within current circumstances. Tom's father continues to haunt him, as evident in his reactions to Jim, a man of similar mannerisms. The therapist continuously takes on the shifting qualities of Lynn's overbearing brother and Eric's distant father. In the transitional space of the group, real persons become an amalgam of fantasy and reality, as inside and outside, past and present personages are viewed simultaneously in one and the same visage.

The Reconciliation and Differentiation of Opposing Tendencies

As a developing yet finite creature, nomadic humankind led a scenic existence while wandering in preoccupation. A variety of natural rhythms, day-to-night, love-to-hate, hot-to-cold, rest-to-restlessness, came alive as an animated arrangement of spiritual forces imbuing the seen and unseen universe with energy, meaning, and direction. In the context of the modern collective, one might similarly ponder the undulating relationship between individual/group, self/other, leader/follower, internal/external, content/ process, dominance/submission, and insider/outsider. Schermer (1991) suggests that "all human development parallels the symbiosis/separation-individuation process and, in groups, the fusion/individuation dilemma. . . . Self psychology and object relations provide complementary theories that allow both tracks to be understood and elaborated in group."

Certainly, to be reconciled, paired opposites require mediation or messenger, some hypothetical construct, process, or person traversing and connecting up otherwise polarized attributes. The world as we know it initially presents itself to us in the form of basic oppositions or paradoxes (Kant, 1929). Pythagoras conceived of the universe as a series of dichotomies to be harmonized (Bly, 1990). Yet, conceptual opposites do more than merely repel or attract, they also blend together within complex relationships evident in many synthetic symbolic configurations (Durkheim, 1974; Needham, 1978). Neumann (1973), in mythic allusion, describes the uroboric snake swallowing its own tale as a visual representation of the reconciliation of opposites and contradictions, and as an instance of the wholeness attainable through creative revolution.

Consider the tension when a young-adult group composed largely of struggling street-wise members was joined by three agemates who all worked for industry and held high-paying jobs. The newcomers represented an action oriented, "go-get-it" philosophy. In the second joint session, one of the new cadre complained that if people really wanted to get better they would talk more about their problems. The experienced members coached patience and recommended the value of the slow unfolding and subtle richness of the process. A split was occurring between the old and new subgroups.

The facilitator suggested that perhaps both approaches held merit, and that the group task was not to choose one over the other. Rather, the essence of the challenge was to create an environment that could contain and utilize both patience and impatience, action and contemplation, old and new. Evolving cultures regularly rely on prophetic or enjoining visions to bring together, in interpenetration and predilection, otherwise irreconcilable aims and devices.

Other dyadic conceptions like reality/fantasy, good/bad, masculine/ feminine, and active/passive also present a constant conjunctive challenge, an ultimate joining as if in spiritual mating or cosmic union. Levi-Strauss (1962) agrees that "the human mind operates according to binary logic, and that a fundamental feature of all cognitive models, civilized as well as primitive, is a schema in terms of which seemingly inherent (and irreconcilable) oppositions are resolved" (paraphrased in Levy-Bruhl, 1985, p. xxxvi).

Structuralism, as a discipline, seeks to discover the basic elements by which social life is bifurcated and the resultant forms into which it is then refused as mythic motif. By devising a unanimity of perception and storied configuration, seemingly polar opposites can be brought into context as a working dynamic.

Adrian, an overtly depressed and restricted woman, tended to look at the world as either black or white. In group, she either fully agreed with or couldn't tolerate others' opinions. Her therapeutic work largely involved suspending such judgments and developing an habitable place between extremes. Adrian had to become comfortable with gray before she could allow color into her life.

A similar differentiation and reunion compose the intimate work of all group psychotherapy. Participants present differing pictures of reality. Disparate situations, selective perceptions, and particularized life experiences must be amalgamated into a viable collective with its own emergent and encompassing cognitive forms, explanatory codices, and descriptively apt literary device. Not withstanding the diverse configuration of roles and personal attributes, the group must somehow create a unity of perception by bringing and holding its members and all they represent together in compromise, if not in unison.

The simplest compromise formation comes as a merging, one with the other, wherein individual distinctiveness melts away. Yet, as described earlier, this fused condition represents a most primitive, undifferentiated form marked by catastrophic loss of individual uniqueness and structural integrity. Other primitive attempts at reconciliation of differences include "splitting" basic elements apart or "projecting" out what doesn't readily fit together. More complex solutions to personal diversity and existential ambiguity can be found in the fashioning of homologies, correlations, symmetries, and complementarities, as well as in all manner of collective metamorphosis, synergy, transformation, symbolic interaction, and creative mediation. Durkin (1981, p. 15) describes the group's process of intimate recombination as a "dialectical dance" between elementary (individual) and complementary (collective) forms. Ashbach and Schermer (1987) explain,

> *Complementarity is a systems model that is useful in reconciling two diametrically opposed points of view. . . . Complementarity is conceptually related to paradox, contradiction, and asymmetry in nature and man. It therefore resembles both transpersonal, existential, and religious insight and at the same time the nature of myth, metaphor, and primary process thinking. (p. 21)*

Conversely, in the process of primitive differentiation, the cosmos or the culture is redivided and categorized into a hierarchy of forces, a pantheon of gods and demons. Each deity or devil—whether personal or social—represents various functions and coincides with particular natural forces and emotional proclivities. Aphrodite symbolizes love, Pan fuses humans with their animal nature, while Apollo ushers in the light of reason with the daily concourse of his winged chariot. Just so, each group member represents, holds, and acts out particular proclivities for the collective. The roles assumed and the characteristics demonstrated serve as an expressive integration of individual offerings with collective needs and presses. Adrian holds the group's critical edge, Ann represents the ability to get along with a diversity of people, and Bill amplifies a striving for betterment—though hopefully not in mutually exclusive possession.

Dosamantes-Alperson (1986) describes how "psyche as an emerging organization evolves through an active and ever more complex interchange with significant others and becomes increasingly more differentiated as a separate psychic entity by a slow process of gradual individuation" (p. 201). All comparative relations require unanimity prior to separation. Uniqueness follows from universality. Only by being seen together can humans ultimately be told apart. The ultimate goals of psychotherapy become cultivating the ability to lose oneself by joining with the whole, while also bolstering individuality by finding one's unique position in the group.

Word Magic, Insight, and the Art of Interpretation

The group leader, like the ancient sphinx, embodies and bestows the sacred art of word magic through interpretation, thereby coming closest to unraveling the mysteries of nature and the vagaries of being human. Yet, true insight might be differentiated from word magic by the necessity of working through its implications, rather than merely absorbing its message through contagious, hypnotic-like processes.

Like the solutions to puzzles or mazes, the truth in an interpretation is often encapsulated in its seemingly unfathomable character. The target of revelation can be the obvious or the unforeseeable, as analyzable material is actually called out of the unspoken and unseen void of heretofore hidden relations. Ganzarain (1989) alludes to distinctive acts of wonder when describing how the facilitator "may sometimes focus attention on the interactions taking place, within each member's mind, [or] between the self and the [invisible] group-as-an-entity" (p. 3). Interpretations are conjoining events, crossing time when linking the past to the present; crossing space when linking there with here; crossing relational bounds when linking inside with outside; crossing contextual meanings when linking the concrete with the abstract; and crossing levels of organization when linking the individual with the group.

A group composed of managers and workers seemed at cross purposes, pulling in different directions while displaying no great empathy for one another's priorities. Part of the problem seemed to be that the expectations of both subgroups were unrealistically high. The group consultant experienced the process as akin to listening to different languages being spoken and heard, thus nullifying communication and endangering the completion of the shared task. He suggested to the gathering as a whole, "This group had best find a common and realistic perspective, lest like the Tower of Babel our lofty pursuits crumble to the ground as members disperse in misunderstanding to the far corners of the company."

Suggestions to the group can be phrased in speculative language, "It could be . . . , It might happen that . . . , It seems like. . . ." Here, observations of the present are used to conjecture about the future. Yet, especially when addressing individuals, the cloak of mystery should not be stripped away precipitously to render reality naked while prematurely exposing stark aspects of inner and outer experience. The group leader, like the shaman or medicine woman, must be careful when conjuring up the underworld, sensitive to the dangers of reviving bad contents or evil spirits and inducing only shame, guilt, or contamination. Ganzarain (1989) suggests that the leader must "rather hold, contain, question in a way that allows patients" to take up matters as they are capable of assessing and reintegrating split-off parts (p. 44). Mania and grandiosity can result from too great an infusion of mana or sacral energy, while neurasthenia, exhaustion, and deflation can signal too meager a dose of elementary force or collective vision.

The Place of Primary and Secondary Processes

Perhaps mental evolution, especially as stimulated by social participation, has not evolved so far past its more archaic manifestations. In fact, leaders are ever invested with inordinate powers. We are just as likely to use each other and our collective forums as objects and containers to store or shake out intrapsychic or existential problems during bouts of massive projection. Our sports teams still invoke totemic powers by calling upon our animal heritage, at least in spirit or for mascot (Campbell, 1988). And even our first families consult the stars for guidance and inspiration. In this so-called modern era, logos and mythos coexist and intermingle, as societal groupings call upon both reason and fantasy in order to render up an enlivened and evolving culture, one in tune with the world about and consistent with the world within.

On the whole, humankind reaches beyond its animal heritage through fusion, identification, and later metaphoric imitation of totemic forces. Instinctual energy is projected outward and an effulgence of animistic energies infuse the world with charged significance. The brain's repetitive firings are hammered into habitual human actions and later sculpted into meaningful enactments, rituals, ceremonies, and dramatic symbolizations of experience. Primitive awe is transformed into an overwhelming sense of spirituality and later manifest as magico-religious fervor, culminating in the scientific spirit.

A recognition of stability engenders an appreciation of change, process, periodicity, and pattern. Humans watch nature and understand themselves; they watch themselves and see into their world. Memory images are repeated in oral history and elaborated in recurrent mythological motifs, often assuming archetypal importance. The aesthetic appreciation of natural phenomena sparks human intercession and artistic creation. Humans notice, appropriate, copy, combine, invent, record, and finally critique their own work. Each objectification of nature spurs further subjective advance. The "I" emerges from the "not-I." The "not-I" conforms to the "I."

The psyche asserts its independence in conjunction with and opposition to worldly matters, including most importantly intercourse with significant others. The human group becomes a source of comfort and a base from which to venture out (Ettin, 1987). The therapy or process group, consistent with its primitive underpinnings, transforms into a space of sacral relationships wherein objects are imbued with significance, judgments transform into social ideals, and normative structures emerge out of moments of high intensity and meaning attribution. Individuals are induced to surpass private uncertainties marked by the lonely striving of egos in isolation. No longer do members merely engage in autistic, idiosyncratic manifestations of personal fantasies, but rather together fashion collective fantasies about the group, its inhabitants, and the world outside.

Group culture evolves as symbol systems develop and maintain their collective aspect. Through the group's rites of passage and symbolizations of experience, a birthing process ensues, which Durkheim (1974) characterizes as so many "supreme moments of social synthesis, creativeness, [and] oneness" (p. xxvi). The modern group becomes a place of enactment and change, a special space for imitation and practice action—a place out of time and a time immemorial. By fostering a sense of groupness, transcendental possibilities are created. For as Durkheim (1974) argues, changing the whole is easier than changing representative parts in isolation. "The greater the intensity of social life, the greater the probability that out of this crucible of ideas some new ideal will emerge, an ideal which will act as a catalyst of emotion and as a purified reflection of this unique historical moment'' (p. xxv). Such potency comes in the form of novel collective realizations and symbolic and behavioral transformations.

Bolman and Deal (1984), writing about modern organizations, suggest that ''to cope with confusion, uncertainty, and chaos, humans create a variety of symbols. *Myths* provide explanations, reconcile contradictions, and resolve dilemmas (Cohen, 1969). *Metaphors* make confusion comprehensible. *Scenarios* provide direction for action in uncharted and seemingly unchartable terrain (Ortner, 1973)'' (p. 151). Dunphy (1974) suggests that through these *shared fantasies,* groups give voice to their otherwise unspeakable attitudes, perceptions, and feelings about leaders, each other, and about the tasks at hand. Common understandings and practices, although derived from a pooling of individual fantasies, provide a collective text and ongoing narration that can be read, recorded, and reedited enroute. Here, myth becomes ''a shared, rather than individual fantasy, built up over time out of events in the history of groups and incorporating elements of the individual fantasies of members'' (p. 311).

The resultant succession of fantasy themes, enhanced by primitive conceptualizations, and culminating in specific collective representations, help further the process and content of the evolving group culture. Whatever their transformational form, primary processes as represented in creative imagery and symbolic reckoning is essential to the evolution of the shared culture.

Yet to provide adequate socialization for its members, the group must also prepare participants for life outside the collective enclave. Kibel (1990) raises the question of whether ''group therapists must convert the social structure of the group from its naturally occurring one, i.e. one which resembles primitive society, into a new social structure, one that is more closely analogous to present day society, in order to help patients adapt to the demands of real life situations.'' He goes on to wonder if being helpful implies doing more than merely reexperiencing archaic adaptations, timeless myths, and homogeneous perceptual proclivities. Perhaps the group must rather transcend its primitive aspects in order to reach a new order based on more modernly conceived secondary processes.

One might argue, however, that it is necessary to go back before going forward, become unified before becoming separate, while retaining to the end the ability to fit within a more encompassing societal context in fantasy as well as in reality. The ameliorative medium of the small group does not necessarily have to mimic the larger society from which it springs, but only support its legitimate aims while transforming its inherent potentials. It is possible to send a member back to real life fortified by a knowledge of his or her own and the group's prototypical history of adaptive problems and resolutions. This intimate experience allows for flexibility based on personal insight and relational powers accumulated through successfully participating in the very primary process of cultural evolution. Whether we wish it or not, we are never so far removed from our infancy as a person or a race to risk the hubris of formulating our logos while neglecting our mythos.

CHAPTER FIFTEEN

The Evolution of the Human Collective:

A Myth for Modern Times

The aborigine of Australia live in the tradition of the walkabout. These native Australians believe that the land was created by totemic ancestors in the process of laying down songlines across the vast out- back. Each feature of the environment was sung into existence at the exact moment when it was reached along the track, seen for the first time, and melodically named, thereby calling it out of the void. To rediscover these original imprints in epic journey is to make a most personal and fundamental self-transformation (Chatwin, 1987). Like- wise, the Machiguenga Indians of Peru believe that by incessantly traversing the rain forest in intimate walking groups, and by never settling too long in one place, they keep their vitality as a people. By moving on with such regularity, the sun is aided in crossing the sky while demons large and small are outdistanced (Llosa, 1989).

The very process of mythologizing may have actually begun as newly cognizant humankind glimpsed the phases of the moon and thus discovered periodicity while speculating about eternal recurrence (Marschack, 1972). An appreciation of progressive and regressive change was spawned by look- ing out in wonder at the animated forces of nature. Storied formulations and fantasied relations were likely invented to grasp and reiterate these cyclical occurrences. For example, watching the transformations of the lu- nar cycle might have suggested myths about a heroic sequence encompass- ing birth, growth, fullness, decay, disappearance, and renewal.

By analogy, the remarkable passage and the regular concourse of hu- man existence was elevated to a cosmic plane. The ages of humankind were thought to mirror the movement of the heavens, presenting a cosmologically inspired schemata of normative parallels. Cognitive capacity likely matured with just this recognition and evocation of periodicity, pattern, and process (Marshack, 1972, p. 40). As humans became capable of meaningfully dividing time, they were then able to organize experience by thinking in phases, stages, and sequential elucidations. Recognition of periodicity spurred subsequent novel participation as humans became "narrators of the passage." A creative place in the firmament was secured by so depicting the inexorable progression of life.

Campbell (1988) suggests that mythologizing, while ultimately reflecting on the infinite wisdom of the ages, was soon pragmatically applied to the human life cycle and the social experience. While the

> *themes are timeless . . . the inflection is to the culture. . . . Mythology has a great deal to do with the stages of life, the initiation ceremonies as you move from childhood to adult responsibilities . . . the maturation of the individual, from dependency through adulthood, through maturity, and then to the exit; and then how to relate to this society and how to relate this society to the world of nature and the cosmos. . . . The myth tells me . . . how to respond to certain crises of disappointment or delight or failure or success. The myths tell me who I am (pp. 11,15, 32).*

Mythic content becomes pedagogic—instructive to living—by establishing precedents and exemplary reactions to authority figures and to peers over the course of human development (Dunphy, 1974). Possible paths and actions, taboos, rewards, and dangers inherent in such interactions are pointed out (Ashbach & Schermer, 1987).

In attempts to understand the intricacies of human nature, do we not still imagine and engage in fantastic journeys spawned by primitive needs and directed by creative speculations about the psychosocial advance? Process and psychotherapy groups assume their enlightened powers just so, by moving through the psychic terrain and encountering objects and obstacles in line and litany. The movement of the group itself is life affirming. The shared participation is bonding. The general possibilities are ancient and boundless, while the particulars of each journey remain idiosyncratic and analyzable.

Every group excursion is thus familiar and extraordinary—a recurring exploration of varying scope, pain, and beauty. Main paths are timeworn, marked by recognizable milestones and predictable dynamic proclivities, mediated within transitional symbolic terrains. The group facilitator, like any seasoned guide, knows generally what to expect in passing and basically how to cover the heights and depths traveled from beginning to end. By calling out to each other enroute—"What do we see and what must we do?''—this small group of interrelated participants resounds the rhythms and tones necessary to operate harmoniously within the world of nature amidst a world of people. Insights are born up by the very acts of motility and interaction. With a sense of anticipation and a penchant for mythologizing the group experience, members move on together into the rarely visited inner continent.

The Group Life Cycle

Various modernly wrought linear progressive models of group development (Kellerman, 1979) turn back to phylogeny (Neumann, 1973, Slater, 1966), ontogeny (Gibbard, Hartman, & Mann, 1974; M. Klein, 1985), psychosocial epigenesis and life cycle (Erickson, 1950; Mills, 1964; Mann, Gibbard, & Hartman, 1967; Rosenfeld, 1988), existential necessity (Tuckman, 1965; Lacoursiere, 1980), and preOedipal and Oedipal myths (Applebaum, 1963; Durkin, 1964; Bennis & Shepard, 1974; Saravay, 1978; Stiers, 1987) for a rough cognitive mapping of the regularities of the psychosocial advance. Yet more than just merely a straight line to the future, the group's life cycle can also be viewed as a search for homeostasis—a moving in and out of alignment, a pendular back and forth swing poised around the fulcrum of relevant human themes. Both micro-cycles and macro-cycles make for circles within circles, ripples upon ripples, and waves of momentum amidst particles of truth.

The very notion of the group presents a paradox—comprising, at once, a traditional form and a transitional phenomena. We might wonder alternately: "How can our group formations remain permanent enough to maintain their timeless structure? How can our human collectives accommodate enough to changing circumstances and constituent members in constant flux?" Kellerman (1979) suggests that the relevance of the ongoing group process stems from "an attempt to create an enduring social structure as a reworking of historical reference points" (p. 66). The history to be reexplored can be that of the individual, the nuclear family, or even the human group-as-a-whole. Progression simply implies negotiating the vortex of time and space with greater facility for free locomotion, more accurate descriptive abilities, and a finer structural integration of emergent territories, both personal and cultural.

The Parameters of Small-Group Culture

Culture carries both conservative and progressive connotations. A group's static character, stage, or phase of development can be equated, at any one point in time, with its current norms, aims, operational procedures, defensive structures, linguistic/symbol systems, myths, and emotional proclivities. A more active sense of culture is suggested when attempting to transform collective experiences by specific care and development. With interactive sociological implications in mind, culture becomes the "sum total of living built up by a group of human beings and transmitted from one generation to another" (Urdang, 1972).

Kessing and Kessing (1971) suggest that analyzing and/or codifying a culture means elaborating its general principles—its underlying axioms and givens, the theorems, corollaries, and guiding principles that influence the subsequent shape of inherent relationships—making wholes out of parts by bringing recurrent patterns to light. By following the ongoing grouping process, particular collective manifestations can be recognized in the "intricate web of interlocked symbols and meanings on many levels" that naturally arise within the course of events (Ashbach & Schermer, 1987, p. 315).

Small process and psychotherapy groups can be approached as distinct cultural mediums. Jacobson (1989) reiterates that "a psychotherapy group is a small society with a therapeutic purpose, so this experience of the group is a cultural experience" (p. 476). Each group displays a unique collective personality and a normative patterning all its own. Yet, diverse groupings also conform to certain universal principles inherent in joining, forming, and maintaining collective enclaves. The particular form in which material emerges and configures may vary across instances and settings, whereas constituent forces and their underlying significance remain constant. Guided by the centrality of perceptual/cognitive processes as organizing phenomena, a developing schema of small-group relations can be introduced as a series of unfolding cultural imperatives.

- **Cultural Imperative 1:** Regression sets the stage for involvement.

Groups form, become whole, and remain cohesive by members joining together to go through, in discussion and in vitro, a developmental sequence that represents basic orientations to life, task, self, and other.

This grouping process represents a continual quest for "self out of other," stimulating ontogenetic, developmental imperatives. An inherent regression fosters a return to preOedipal object relations, preverbal primary processing, a preoccupation with the personal past, and the innervation of individual defenses and projective mechanisms. Members re-create or rediscover in the group their formative relations and nuclear family dynamics as repetition compulsions. A return is made to an earlier and more primary means of organizing the world, as basic psychic structures are exposed in response to collective demands. Members are also provided with an opportunity for growth by expanding capacities and repertoires when filling in gaps in experience—seeing and doing in ways that are different from how they characteristically respond to irrepressible personal needs. Individual movement and psychological growth occurs as members are swept up in the group's developmental sequence. Participants become responsive to the problems and initiatives created by being together.

The grouping process also represents a continual quest for "certainty out of uncertainty," and thus phylogenetic, existential imperatives are stimulated. An inherent regression stipulates a return to prelogical relations; mythic, archetypal, and pictorial processing; a preoccupation with the historical-cultural past; and the innervation of collective defenses and animistic projective device. The problems that arise in the modern group are not new for the human collective as a whole. Recent incarnations recall age-old dilemmas and prior resolutions. To solve problems of survival, security, and satisfaction, people have always formed into groups and sought collective solutions. Each modern instance of grouping falls back on the history of the race and re-creates, by way of image, symbol, myth, and ritual, prototypical human experiences. Metaphorically, the modern process or therapy group becomes a social unit with the capacity to summon ancient truths. By attuning to the archaic level of the group advance, the modern collective is informed by the cultural and sociological adaptations that preceded it.

• **Cultural Imperative 2:** Cohesion is found around a central focus.

The capacity for consolidating available energies while working together in groups depends on the willingness and ability to locate issues of common concern. Central foci are often manifested as emergent collective themes, familiar contents, recurrent motifs, or communal problems.

The group's social life is initiated and maintained through finding a central focus for collective attentions. This centrality may emerge in the idealization of a leader, or as a shared task, common theme, collective vision, or consensual agreement about the nature of current realities. The group progressively develops its sense of orientation and purpose by moving toward more pointed explorations of its pressing common concerns.

A universal need for human connection is met by working in unison. Feelings of security, familiarity, cohesion, and "esprit de corp" are stimulated when seeing matters through together. A sense of "we-ness" emerges and further solidifies the attentions of the membership, so that the group itself takes on instrumental meaning and worth.

During the interaction of any such group, specifiable themes can be identified by informally factor analyzing the discussion (Whitaker & Lieberman, 1964; Srivastra & Barrett, 1988). The therapist or group consultant may wonder at any point in the proceedings, "How is the process being personified? Through what person or set of circumstances is the group finding its center?'' The essence of the ongoing progression can be extrapolated by attuning to individual and collective preoccupations as manifest in members' expressive utterances and the group's evolving cultural forms.

- **Cultural Imperative 3:** The group develops a perceptual/linguistic frame.

Collective themes or motifs are progressively represented by shared visions, familiar fantasies, common images, recurrent symbols, compelling scenarios, significant myths, and interactive roles and rituals. These metaphoric figures and forms express pertinent aspects and/or the affective essence of the communal experience.

As the group advances, it moves through cycles of specificity. Within its developing perceptual/linguistic frame, psychic elements are continually collected and reflected. Pooled perceptions become recognizable as pictures of reality that are developed further, exposed, traded, and transferred in a continual process of material configuration, projection, containment, and introjection. Ashbach and Schermer (1987) reiterate that ''an integral part of the analysis of group is an examination of the ways in which the collective imagery and shared imaginative productions of the group provide a linking and transforming medium between the intrapsychic and the sociocultural contexts'' (p. 209). Migliorati (1989) proposes that such emerging ''relational images'' are ready amalgams of individual introspection and the formative forces of the interpersonal field. The psychotherapy or human relations group can work with just these pieces and pictures of reality, as expressed and experienced in varied perspectives on the common experiences. By so doing, the group's overall agendas, both overt and covert, are clarified.

- **Cultural Imperative 4:** Particular sequences are organized around some specific narrative device.

Within any one session or therapeutic sequence, the group may preconsciously and automatically organize around some central image, metaphor, fantasy, or myth as a narrative device for realizing, collecting, conserving, and representing the formative energies in the room.

Each session becomes a bonafide unit of experience. As such, its organizational needs can be recognized by the membership coming up with some centrally emergent image, fantasy, or myth as a summary process or compromise formation. Frey-Rohn (1990) suggests, ''Not infrequently, some things [can] be bridged in the symbol which, when viewed in a logical perspective, would seem to preclude each other and present an insoluble conflict on a practical level'' (p. 265).

Imagistic and narrative forms are packed with meaning, memory, and emotion. Describing the group culture means exploring both its collective representations along with the feeling tone, climate, and overall atmosphere surrounding transactions. By looking to the group's expressive device, a ready appreciation is gained about how members experience themselves, each other, the facilitator, and the whole of the process at any point in time. A group evolves with the active engagement of perceptual parameters, often externalized behaviorally by the evocation of rituals and norms that express what members "see," "feel," and "do," as usual, helpful, or possible.

• **Cultural Imperative 5:** Individuals become catalysts for their group.

Individuals serve as group mediums or spokespersons when they spontaneously offer up the suggestive language necessary to focus the group's attention on common experiential referents and visions.

The group as an organizational entity utilizes its chief resource, the membership, to raise and express its viewpoints and affects. Participants provide both the raw data of the group experience and the perceptual/cognitive organization of the material at higher levels of integration. The group facilitator, as special member, is in the forefront of soliciting varied perspectives, culling out common concerns and contributing and interpreting individualized and groupwide symbolic expressions. He or she also highlights adaptive myths and fantasies, while challenging dysfunctional symbolic adaptations or enactments. With time and experience, members take over some of the group leader's expressive, assimilative, critical, and interpretative functions.

Any particular emergent image, myth, fantasy, or otherwise culturally overdetermined content, while an immediate product of its creator, is ultimately a synergistic event spawned from the raw material of the group involvement. Such metaphoric expressions serve a collective and communicative function as soothsayers for the shared experience. The contributor of a fantasied production, whether a member or the leader, serves as group spokesperson, that participant most sensitive, expressive, or vulnerable to the presenting affect, issue, or operative theme.

Firth (1973) suggests that transfer of meaning from the private to public domain is evident when symbols are seen to have a social or an organizational effect on the conglomerate. In these cases, private reveries transform into public revelations. As such, the individual contributor's authority comes to surpass that of idiosyncratic experience, and in a real sense, he or she talks to and for the collective. Firth (1973) explains how "the significance of private symbols may be thought to lie in the degree to which they express experiences or feelings of what may be called the audience. . . . The initial visionary acts as a trigger . . . one might say a catalyst'' (pp. 236–238).

- **Cultural Imperative 6:** The group is transformed by changing collective representations.

The group and its members can be transformed by evolving and changing collective representations, enactments, and other shared visions of reality, thereby reshaping the ongoing group culture.

Members continue in their roles as purveyors of alternate realities, while the group-as-a-whole remains a collective vehicle for formulating consensual truths. The group serves its members by continuously containing and framing current events. Pictures of reality are changed in the process, transformed in line with the actual or required parameters of the common experience. The group as a "hall of mirrors" begets more stable, accurate, and artistic visions and enactments. The group as "collective workshop" forges more adaptive behaviors and interactions.

Dosamantes-Alperson (1986) suggests that recent advances in object relations theory have helped legitimize the use of spontaneous mental images as direct reflections of relational capacities. She argues that when patients' images are specifically attended, a whole host of emotional meanings, defensive postures, cognitive styles, practice actions and internalized self-other relationships are revealed. Similarly, Ganzarain (1989) recommends working in groups with just those mental images and fantasies, which reflect patients' internalized perceptions and outward expectations of persons and situations. In part, the working-through process involves checking inner visions against outer signs, comparing myths with the events that stirred them. Members can contrast their personal views with the overview provided by the whole of the group and change accordingly.

- **Cultural Imperative 7:** The group develops on overriding culture.

Group culture, in toto, comprises all the collective's operative and evolving procedures, perceptions, motifs, myths, ritual enactments, historical precedents, and affective understandings in their current state of metamorphosis, interactive expression, and transmission.

Group culture comes to include all of its logistical and procedural developments, leadership dimensions, and role requirements, along with more artistic, fantastic, imagistic, and mythical productions. As groups formalize a complex of recurrent, shared meanings and creative possibilities, symbolic and linguistic systems consolidate further.

Various symbolic paradigms, recurrent motifs, and ritualized activities make up any group's collective essence. The group-as-a-whole's emergent personality reflects its history of representations and transformations and expresses its unique and up-to-date world view. Such operative beliefs, motifs, and action potentials are capable of being culturally transmitted inside and outside the formal group setting, signifying and instilling a "new order."

- **Cultural Imperative 8:** Members' involvement increases as they find their place within the group.

The drive to participate in the group's enculturation grows when members find that they have importance and bear influence. This continual discovery enlivens interactions and provides the fertile ground for further cooperative, comparative, and creative endeavors, both inside and outside the therapeutic or human relations frame.

The act of becoming a participant in a group engenders both playful and serious exchange—an infusion of perceptions and a unity of experience. When members contribute their pictures of reality to the collective matrix, they provide the group with needed pieces with which to fill in the puzzle of life.

Seemingly irreconcilable points of view, however, can still result in narcissistic injuries for that member who sees the world differently and feels his or her basic perceptions challenged. Such conflicts can be worked out in milieu by bringing individual visions and actions into context. Groupwide viewpoints are adapted to accommodate personal perspectives, as specialized vantage points useful in keeping the group aware of difference and attuned to subtlety. By so doing, the parts and the whole come into greater alignment.

- **Cultural Imperative 9:** The small-group culture reflects on the outside world.

As the collective experience becomes richer, more complex, and increasingly inclusive, individuals are provided with a flexible and powerful forum for progressively reconstruing themselves, each other, the group-as-a-whole, and the world-at-large.

As a direct result of participation in the collective process (whether in the human relations movement, a psychotherapy group, or a sociopolitical matrix), pictures of reality can be reformed. A vibrant juxtaposition occurs between joining/accommodating and separating/differentiating with respect to the varied stimuli and shaping circumstances provided by the whole of the experience. In this inevitable move toward enculturation, members develop increasingly articulate means of expression and more facile forms of participation. They have an opportunity to master the skills necessary to act in consort with others. By viewing the world together, individuals learn to see through a clearer, more accurate, and versatile lens. By hearing each other out and going through things together, creative compromises are reached.

Emergent cultural forms become the structural frame upon which the group and its members fashion current and future perceptions and interactions. In this socialization process, cultural reality comes to supersede and shape individualized experience.

> *A social system presents the individual with institutionalized channels and models of action. It provides him with . . . a conceptual framework. . . . [Neither random nor idiosyncratic], "the pattern, the grammar of thought of a certain society is connected with its historical development and with the structure of society and of its system of values, which is something other than the structure and development of individual minds. (Durkheim, 1974, pp. xxii, xxxiii)*

The framework that evolves in the group, whether represented by prevalent myths or pressing realities, can provide members with prototypical experiences that they can then transfer to the "real outside world," thereby transforming the larger culture. Societal introjects, as cultural byproducts, encapsulate a vision of how the world is, how it came to be, how it currently functions, and how it can be changed. This intimate knowledge, transmitted within and between cultures in the form of particular myths, beliefs, ideals, shared fantasies, recurrent stories, or epic or cautionary tales, serve as guideline and orientation. Creativity is certainly in evidence as particularly adroit formulations, discovered in the group and transposed to outside life, combine and proliferate elemental and emotive forces in new and often startling ways.

Mythic Allusions to Small-Group Advance

Various collectively inspired theories (Slater, 1966; Hartman & Gibbard, 1974; Shambaugh, 1985), derived from human relations experiences and student study groups, rely on fantasy and mythic material to follow collective evolution through a seemingly inevitable series of progressive interactions, dilemmas, and paradoxes. Hartman and Gibbard (1974) go so far as to suggest, "In small experiential groups, individuals often develop and express fantasies, hopes and beliefs which become myth-like and which assume great importance for the group-as-a-whole in maintenance of group equilibrium" (p. 315). Gibbard, Hartman, and Mann (1974) go on to state,

"We regard group fantasy activity . . . as adaptive if not crucial to group process and structure" (p. 271).

More than by meaningful coincidence, the thematic content manifested in small-group evolution, upon amplification, is also found to correspond to larger societal issues evident in psychological, phylogenetic, political, and religious epigenesis. Particular motifs, myths, fantasies, concrete images, and collective representations arise in the service of identifying and describing each and every group's current events, shared aims, and unique place on a continuum that ranges from an undifferentiated aggregate to an integrated collective forum.

Slater (1966) believes that large or small, every group moves from a matriarchal merged mass, through dependency on a patriarchal leader, to a more egalitarian differentiation of roles and behaviors in the eventual service of equality, fraternity, and interdependence. Collective fantasies arise and depict this progression. Neumann (1973) instructs that group transition is made possible through establishing and changing the unconscious bonds that bind participants into a serviceable union. Axiomatic is the conviction that by following any group's cultural representations and by interpreting evident symbolic interactions, the collective advances and enriches in meaning, scope, and adaptive capacity.

From Separate Individuals to a Merged Mass

Out of a state of alienation, individuals draw together to confront common dangers and figure upon the workings of the external world. Rosenfeld (1988) suggests, "Seriality is at the origin of every group, understood as the moment in which every individual is a 'series'—alone, isolated, a number without a specific place or order in the group. When the group becomes constituted, a fusion among its [separate] members occurs" (p. 14).

In the group's beginning, this primitive human collection can be said to exist only as a convergence of unconscious bonds and plethora of silent mergings. Individuals gather as one in a seeming intrauterine-like connectivity—common in context, yet to be separated out by conscious intents or vocalized contentions. Jacobson (1989) describes how "out of what was previously merely a global and diffuse sense of being, there comes an experience of creating an object," a group (p. 479). Slater invokes Bion's (1961) concept of this initial grouping as stimulating fantasies of the insides of the mother—with its fluid warmth, security, closeness, and belonging, as well as its potentials for boundary dissolution, losses of identity and consciousness, and fears of death by constraint or suffocation.

As members identify with a larger whole, a participatory mystique evolves. The shared environment of the early group provides for oceanic feelings of unity (Turquet, 1985), with both the safety and terror inherent in being so held, enveloped, submerged, and undifferentiated. Here we have the stage of mystical fusions and mass contagions—precarious, primary, and preconscious groupings. Hartman and Gibbard (1974) suggest that the positive aim of this primordial phase and symbiotic fantasy is to establish a safe haven where peace, tranquility, and magical fullness envelop all needs and cares. The requirements of primary narcissism are fulfilled, as images of Paradise or Nirvana are evoked. This mystical fusion also defends against more barren ideas of inner hunger, emptiness, and provisional distress.

When a process or psychotherapy group commences, members may initially seek such enveloped protection and anonymity within the still amorphous mass. Like the infant first sheltered inside the mother, subsequently contained at her breast, and later held within the whole of the family, participants often regress by submerging their individuality within the unanimity of the collective. At this stage of "embryonic containment" (Neumann, 1973), however, the group proves incapable of responding to the varied needs and necessities of the so-gathered, thus precipitating a restless frustration in its members. Unrequited personal requirements, coupled with the threat of lost selves, inspire fights and flights aimed toward individual emergence or escape.

In nightmarish fantasy, the group as dragon tightly and greedily holds its members within its cavernous lair. In macrocosm, a period of primitive religion and classic magical beliefs is suggested. With weak and elastic distinctions between subject and object, world and self, it is easy to believe that words, charms, and mimetic mystery rites can directly influence physical forces and coax higher spirits to provide for material needs through a process akin to hypnotic inducement. The primal grouping is organized and maintained by such contagions and mergers of self and other, inside and out. In its most primitive stage, the group itself holds unquestionable great sway over its undifferentiated constituency.

The Overvaluation of the Leader

As a way of surviving and continuing, en masse, the group looks to a leader as its first distinctly separate and specialized participant, an heir apparent brought up to break the spell of silence and shatter the maw of entrapment. Dependent fantasies are transferred from the depersonalized group to the person of the leader—those wishes for freely offered nurturance, succorance, and benign care. Bion (1961) believes that it is as if "the group has met to obtain security from one individual on whom they depend" (p. 66). The group leader is fully expected to provide whatever direction and protection is necessary to keep members safe and keep matters moving.

Fantasies of deification arise as an antidote to immobility and depression (Hartman & Gibbard,1974). Splitting ensues wherein all of the good and powerful is transferred to an idealized leader-figure, while the members inherit the shackles of helplessness, incompetence, and dependency. Some cooperation does become possible as members now join together around their subservience to the deified chieftain. To keep the leader interested, active, and care giving, the group often pushes forth a troubled party from within its midst, in the hopes of seducing the leader's active ministrations (Bion, 1961).

In the therapy or training setting, the god-like figure of the leader— who forged the group out of seriality, and whose unspoken promise coaxed the membership to emerge from its unconscious oblivion when encouraging the open, unfettered expression of basic needs and wants—often disappoints. He or she turns out to be unwilling or unable to lead. Like a "stone deity," the leader is experienced as "reliable and everlasting" but "ungiving and comfortless" (Slater, 1966, p. 9). The group's initial touchstone largely remains inert, silent, and deaf to invocations for direct help, offering instead confusing, incomplete, or seemingly meaningless, random, or oracular interpretations. Certainly if addressed at all, the group is not sung the soothing lullaby it longs to hear.

Instead, the leader wills members to look to each other for satisfaction and enlightenment just at a time when their emotional ties are obviously and solely to him (or her). Myths arise to explain the god or god-like leader's lost voice (Jaynes, 1977). This is the era of archaic religion and nascent consciousness. Kings, upon their death, readily transform into deities (Jaynes, 1977). Personified gods are then placated, prayed and sacrificed to in an obedient effort to summon ancestral wisdom, salvage emotional stables, and attain existential stability.

As an intermediate step from godly to worldly, the group history may be formally compiled and consulted as a bible for insight into what is currently transpiring and what is yet to come. In the alleged absence of a willing or functional leader, the group's formative experiences are referenced as the mystical, totemic basis of human precedent. The protective wisdom of guardian spirits and revelation bearers are actively sought (Neumann, 1973). Myths, legends, parables, and folk and fairytales bind the collective within a union of shared analogies and common perspectives. This is the era of longing and reverence for the past, as manifested in active ancestor worship.

Slater (1966) believes that in both religion and practical necessity, the deity's continued silence is essential to the group's growth and enculturation. Lonely desperation eventually breeds progressive advance, as a cycle of depression, deification, abandonment, and hostility ensues. The hero-leader as mother-slayer now transforms into an unapproachable, unwanted, despicable father ogre. This circumstance hastens the transmuting internalizations described in self-psychology that build ego structure just when self-objects fail.

Comes the Revolution and the Ascent of Heroes

Revolt against the leader is the pivotal point or "lynch pin" in Slater's (1966) conception of group development. Akin to Freud's (1967, 1987) notions about the uprising of the primal horde, a group only consolidates after challenging and deposing its autocratic, paternalistic structure, while incorporating into its body the strength, powers, and prerogatives of that authority.

At first, only rebellious parallel talk and vague threats ensue, as a wide variety of authority figures are denounced as "false prophets." Members express their feelings of dissatisfaction indirectly through passive-aggression, mockery, cajolery, and sarcasm. Initial attempts to actually overthrow the oppressive order may peter out in lone charges or collective scapegoatings (Scheidlinger, 1982). The group may brandish a sensitive member to raise its complaints, only to leave the accuser branded and punished as a paranoid troublemaker. Many a *pharmacos* is heaped with communal sins, maligned, and driven away in misguided or premature manifestations of rebellion and pseudoautonomy. All manner of martyr may be seduced forth to face the leader-now-enemy alone and disarmed by lack of consensus.

Since the facilitator, by design and reality constraints, continues to frustrate the group, in time even the noncommittal join the resistance by giving at least tacit approval to a more directly targeted revolt. Reticent tribes transform into restive tribunals. Members begin to confront the leader by standing up for themselves. The old leader and the wider manifestations of the conservative order are first burned in effigy and later fired in actual conflagrations aimed toward ridding the group of tyranny and repression.

A newly spawned hero-son, or golden bough (Frazer, 1963) is sought—the peer leader who, along with his feminine consort, tries to unmask and undermine the vested and cloaked father, albeit extruding his "mana" or mystic powers (in this case, the awareness and skill to intuit and interpret group dynamics). Enter Luke Skywalker, who, schooled by the gnome wizard Yoda and inspired in cohort with the universal feminine wiles of Princess Leia, brings "the Force" to bear against his heretofore hidden, empathy-less, machine-like father Darth Vader (Villela-Minnerly & Merkin, 1987). With successive attacks, the transference trance is lifted, and the deification fantasy decays (Hartman & Gibbard, 1974b) as the fast falling father figure is eventually overcome and secularized within the process. The populace is thus purified and trapped initiatives are freed up.

In the revolt phase of group development, Slater (1966) identifies symbolic themes around group murder, autonomy, cannibalism, and orgy. Likewise, Freud's (1987) primordial sons return in rebellion to kill and devour the primal father. For the group to survive and advance, the leader must be at once deposed and incorporated, abjectly thrown out, and introjectedly taken back in. A counterdependent stance and a public sequence of   dissatisfaction-plotting-revolt-guilt-expiation-identification-and-independent strivings enacts this process.

The jubilant conqueror usually takes a piece of the fallen leader for souvenir and talisman. Here we have the symbolism of the sacrament, with subthemes of self-feeding, revenge, and synonymous identification. While the god-figure is deemed well dead, members greedily take in and take over his or her roles, rights, and prerogatives. Slater (1966) aptly sums up the dependency-revolt phases. "The killing or sacrifice of those powerful figures effects a redistribution of power. Instead of the power lying in one being, it now flows into every part of the universe. It is made accessible to all" (p. 194).

Neumann (1973) suggests that the transition of power does not always have to be so violent. In fact, built into the leader's role may be the requirement of sharing authority when the group has developed to the point where it can take it on. Certainly, a key leadership skill comes in knowing when to be dominant, when to bow, and when to willingly step aside. Neumann (1973) explains

> *Whereas in a collective composed of incomplete individuals the god-king is the archetypal representative of the group's totality, this figure gradually develops a mediatory function, that is, it gives up more and more of its mana to the group members and is thus disintegrated and "dismembered."* . . . *His divine kingship is continually reduced, but at the same time the incomplete members of the collective, who formerly existed only as instruments of his apotheosis, become complete individuals. (p. 429)*

The new heir apparent in the succession from neutralized queen (great mother) through dethroned king (deified father) is the group itself, which is now able to move on with less dependency, greater solidarity, and an increased ability to function independently of an all encompassing structure or all powerful leader. Freud evokes this overdetermined Oedipal myth as model for the passion play that acts out all generational successions. The group ceremoniously kills off (replaces or outlives) the father-leader and takes possession of the mother-group. An internalized image of the group-as-a-whole replaces the visage of an all powerful monarch, as the paternalistic structure is superseded in both mind and deed.

The Instability of the Postrevolt Era

In actuality, all is not as well as initially anticipated. Every functional advance brings equivalent loss and renewed challenge. The group, now more self-sufficient and no longer solely equated with the stability of the leader, inexorably experiences separation anxiety and renewed fears of disillusion and disintegration. In the postrevolt group, members worriedly wonder: Can we really survive solely through our own interactions devoid of divine or inspired guidance? Slater (1966) beautifully describes every collective's ongoing dilemma: "All 'progress' in groups is necessarily temporary, since it produces the confidence to 'take it a little deeper' either in the sense of increasing personal relevance of [an] issue to individual members or of establishing its connectedness with other group problems. Each 'gain' is weighted with new burdens" (p 94).

Freud (1987) views the overthrow of the leader as an essentially ambivalent act, stimulating both celebration and mourning. Problems of sovereignty and authority arise anew. Infighting often results, as members who have taken an "oath" as bloodbrothers, in order to overcome the primal father, now substitute "fraternity-terror" for the repression of the tyrant's deposed regime (Rosenfeld, 1988). Transitional leaders with pronounced paranoid tendencies may be promoted with the group's hope that they can differentiate friend from foe. A fierce and rigid ethos can arise with collective pressures dictating that "you are either with us or against us." Heads roll when like minds don't so easily come together (Sartre, 1960).

Unintended victims, scapegoats, dropouts, and other casualties of the rebellion and its aftermath bear witness, as the most dependent fail to thrive, while the most independent may be summarily purged in witch-hunts or inquisitions. The group fears that leaving any remnant of the deposed order intact would be cancerous to whole of the body politic. Accordingly, reactionary forces—wolves in sheep's clothing—may be unleashed. Yet, as much as it might wish a fresh start, a group cannot change too completely, by indiscriminately leaving behind all aspects of the old order. Such a group would surely risk extremism or disintegration in the face of uncertain times and lack of available organizational structures.

It is, in fact, possible that chaos rather than coherence may come forth as the stepchild of change. Regression to smaller units of identification, such as tribal, regional, racial, religious, familial, special interest, and/or subgroup loyalties can become the misplaced mortar where bricks once stood. In the new configuration, it is yet to be determined how the boundaries between person, role, right, territorial claim, and governance will actually be redrawn—as a collectivity of vision or as a more partisan parceling of resources. After all that has taken place, will the result of the revolution be unanimity under a flag, factionalism under a banner, or dispersion under the cover of night?

Not so surprisingly, the stability inherent in the dethroned leader's rule is often missed and in some circles even idealized. The deposed patriarch remains, in death or dispersion, a fearsome figure of contempt and a revered object of identification. Religious ceremonies (holidays) evolve as an expression of loss and reverie over the primal father's overcoming and subsequent recreation as a resurrected godhead. Yet still, in times of uncertainty and crisis, old spirits are invoked as the collective regresses in the service of regrouping. The group remains ever susceptible to the ministrations of charismatic and evangelistic leaders, those who claim authority by hearkening back to the old ways. A dictator may be replaced only to anoint a successor with similar powers, thereby resuming a dependent leader-follower format characteristic of the old regime (Rioch, 1975a). More progressively, every society returns to its common traditions and sacred rites, constructing and celebrating celestial holidays as symbolic reminder, renewal, and replacement.

To Dream of Utopia

With the leader newly deposed and the group still frightened and guilty over its destructive power, a fantasy of utopianism may arise (Gibbard and Hartman, 1973). In the renewed order, all is expected to be well and equitable. When resisting the temptation to reinstall a dictator, the new governing union is mandated to rectify the abuses and shortsightedness of the old staid and selfish regime. Aggressive impulses and turbulent times, which so characterized the revolt and its aftermath, are now simultaneously denied or overcontrolled. Further belligerence and competitiveness are consciously banned or unconsciously repressed. The group strives to resume its primordial status as a benign maternal entity, albeit at a more differentiated level of development than was possible in its earlier and primitive state of participatory fusion.

The collective seeks a period of peace, with diffuse feelings of love and warmth evident throughout. Not yet ready to face the anxiety of differences, competition, ambivalent relations, heterogeneity (including heterosexuality), or the active resolution of long-standing problems, members settle for a more child-like chum love for one another—a time of rest rather

than restitution. A fantasied atmosphere of harmony, mutuality, and celebration is fostered, wherein Oedipal, libidinal, and aggressive fantasies are
held in check. The group itself optimistically looks to a new age of innocence and goodwill, a veritable heaven on earth.

By the defense of splitting, the group is now viewed as all good and
the deposed leader and old order is characterized as all bad. It is assumed
that change, whether ushered in by mass uprising, palace revolt, or constitutional congress, will inevitably lead to progressive advance. An enlightened and unifying organizational structure is expected to emerge whole
from the burnt rubble where once stood the edifice of the old regime.

The group's naive and neutered utopian stance may stimulate the fantasy of limitless unity, or even bisexuality, as a mediation in the group's
progress toward autonomy and full maturity (Hartman & Gibbard, 1974b).
In order to avoid competition (sexual and otherwise), that would disrupt
the idealized order by instilling a new hierarchy and power elite, all members are treated as if they are equally attractive and enticing. Participants
are not differentiated by sex or by prowess. Libidinal needs are rather
paired with leftover dependency strivings. Thus, to be well taken care of in
the group is substituted for being competent or sexually viable. Here are
the makings of both the great society and the welfare state. Members may
simply wait to see what the new order can provide.

How, then, will the group perpetuate itself? How will new ideas be
generated and constructive changes be brought to life? What will be the
impetus for maintaining social intercourse if attractions and repulsions cannot be acknowledged and individual resources cannot be demonstrated or
rewarded? Hermaphroditic pronouncements of self-sufficiency and secondary narcissism arise, as Hermes, the quicksilver messenger, and Aphrodite,
the goddess of love, merge to make a perfect union in need of nothing.

Members fantasize that in the benign atmosphere of the group, "I
have all I need to take care of myself, to love myself, and even to reproduce
myself" (Hartman & Gibbard, 1974b, p. 324). Participants may feel that
they don't really need to assume any individual initiative or goal-directed
activity. The group will somehow take care of everything. Just by being
together, in a process akin to osmosis or magical fruition, the collective
will progress. Images and motifs depicting asexual reproduction, twinship
(Kohut, 1977), and conflict-free pairing arise as the vehicle for holding and
transporting the collective away from its unresolved problems. Movement
is expected to occur as if by the orderly procession of Noah's Ark floating
gently on the "wave of the future."

A Period of Renewed Striving and Reformation

As a new stability is found within the group, members find that they
want and need more from each other. What, they wonder, was the ultimate

purpose of managing the revolt and surviving the regressive pulls of the transitional period? What do members eventually get for their trouble and for their courage? Most notably they get each other. Successful postrevolt adaptation, while ushering in an end of innocence that is symbolized by forever exiting the Garden (Hall, 1984), bears the fruit of increased capacity and functional autonomy. Members are now free to bond together: to commune, relate, argue, compete, cooperate, and share experiences.

Slater (1966) suggests that the whole of the group's development to this point has stimulated erotic fantasies. Plunging interpretations "pregnant with meaning" have sought out "fertile minds" in which to plant compelling seeds of thought—a notably phallic-penetrative symbolism. Even the Bible equates "knowing" with intercourse, sexual reproduction, and, by derivation, with cultural and generational continuance. Images of masculine sexual conquest resound throughout the ancient text. "Thy rod and thy staff they comfort me."

As the group no longer tries exclusively to seduce the attentions of the masculine group leader (or more accurately, adopt a paternalistic collective eidos as evident also when the leader is a woman), an objectless vacuum is created within which to reattach pods of libidinous attachments. The fairy-tale treasure brought to the surface by overcoming the mean giant is the shiny coin of sexuality. Evolving themes around "sexual liberation through revolt" and "Oedipal disengagement and group orgy" are spontaneously elaborated, as members move closer to each other. Culturally, the group looks for a viable means of reproduction, planting seedlings that can be cultivated over time.

In this phase of the group's advance, distinctive pairing behavior and reproductive fantasies arise as a way of directly assuring group survival. Fantasies of meaningful togetherness create hope and shared purpose. They yield the collective's manifest creative offspring, its working byproducts, in the form of various aesthetic and cultural realities, generalized understandings, collective representations, universalized truths, and tangible commodities. Once the collective setting is safe enough to openly express sexual and competitive impulses, members rush to know and engage each other in a frenzy, which Slater equates with Dionysian reverie.

The displacement of parents leads ultimately to self-parenting and mating behaviors, as concerns with mortality, renewal, and reproduction set off generational shifts. Such pairing fantasies also defend against the fear of the group's death, ennui, or failure through disengagement (Hartman & Gibbard, 1974b). As a further hedge against personal extinction, the group fosters messianic fantasies (Hartman & Gibbard, 1974b), as the pantheon is populated by displaced solar deities and myths about the coming or return of the great savior—the newly born and ultimate leader who will lead members to everlasting life. In an equivalent macroscopic era, historical religions become preoccupied with moral enlightenment, salvation, resurrection of the deity, and infinite renewal through life after death.

The New Order

As a "new order" dawns, members begin to look more to reason than to faith. They respond more to what is said than to who says it. The previously sacred, now made profane leader is accepted back in memory and/or in reality, to be treated as a special resource whose contributions are assimilated or ignored more on merit than on faith. In processes akin to the alchemical calcinatio and separatio (Edinger, 1985), the group continues to burn off and distill out from the original source (the leader) those abstract principles and useful subtexts that add reality and insight to the shared endeavor. By so doing, valued matters of prime concern are relieved of their impure, living vehicle—the who is replaced by the what. Theoretically, wisdom, influence, and reproductive capacity become available to all.

The group organizes anew, forming itself into legislative, affiliative, and affective bodies with operational rules and standardized procedures for carrying out its work functions and social contracts (Bion, 1961). Neumann (1973) asserts, "When paradise is abandoned, the voice of God that spoke in the Garden is abandoned too, and the values of the collective, of the fathers, of law and conscience, of the current morality, etc., must be accepted as the supreme values in order to make social adaptation possible" (p. 403).

Yet, rules, regulations, and normative expectations can be invoked rigidly; the new society can be held up as an organizational deity. Rosenfeld (1988) describes how an entelechial structure results when legislative and consensual formalities take on a life of their own. Here, the group's aims and means calcify so as to be near immune to innovative modification. Checks and balances, forms and procedures can virtually exclude real change. A collective mind-set can develop that is oblivious to the skills and facilities of its individual assets, thereby disallowing differentiation into suitable or preferable roles. Conformity results when the primary task and/or its means of accomplishment are reified. Fetish-bound, obsessive-compulsive bureaucracies create a group sheltered in formal arrangements to the detriment of more novel accommodations. A managerial function is needed—a brand of consultation capable of helping the group to move again through its ever-necessary transitions.

Soon comes the era of science when even modern religions collapse into organizational hierarchies informed more by worldly than by godly concerns. A pragmatic age of experimentation replaces an era of inspired enlightenment. Clergy become cleric. Wisdom, progress, understanding, and control are worshipped as consensually accepted guiding principles. Slater (1966) suggests that the group is now viewed more practically as an "expanded economy with potentially limitless resources" (p. 162). The collective process inevitably democratizes, as a new heterogeneity arises based in part on equal opportunity, in part on survival of the fittest, and to a lesser extent on social conscience and ethical principle. Neumann (1973) explains, "Whereas formerly . . . only the 'great man' possessed a consciousness and stood for the collective in the role of the leader, the further course of evolution is characterized by a progressive democratization, in which a vast number of individual consciousnesses work productively at the common human task" (p. 434).

Autonomy becomes increasingly linked with the functional, the rational, the consciously intended, and the pragmatic. Slater (1966) summarizes, "In the history of individual, of species, of group, or of any relationship, all is fantasy. Development is simply a matter of rescuing more and more pieces of reality, like bits of dry land emerging from the sea" (p. 144). Similarly, Cassirer (1944) suggests, "Human culture taken as a whole may be described as a process of man's progressive self-liberation. Language, art, religion, science are various phases in this process. In all of them man discovers and proves a new power—the power to build up a world of his own" (p. 228).

The Future of the Human Group

The myth of modernity—escape from autocracy, the assumption of limitless choice, loss of constraint, conquest of nature, idealization of rational advance, and the primacy of human endeavor—may not mark the end of this progression. Although well differentiated and technologically sophisticated, we live in a time of fragmentation, parts out of touch with wholes. Our groupings have become more bureaucratic than beatific, more a business-like investment than a collective inspiration. Toward what ultimate aim do we annex more and more unconscious territory and retrieve more and more serviceable land from inviolable sea? Now when we walk about, calling out the features of our shared environment, it is often in prelude to altering inexorably that which we find.

The recent return of the myth of the great earth goddess Gaia bespeaks the need for a newly wrought unanimity, whether in common markets or in shared ecological concerns (Lovelock, 1989; Bunyard & Goldsmith, 1989; Meyers, 1990). Both in microcosm and in macrocosm, a sacred respect must be garnered for that which needs to remain unchanged, that which is greater than the sum of individual strivings, and that which forever looms beyond the grasp of human understanding.

An appreciation of unending diversity must be wrought into homeostasis by increasing our capacities for creative mediation—as when fashioning responsible wholes reflective and inclusive of their parts. Conversely, character must be carefully composed into culture, with Narcissus ever coaxed to see beyond his own reflection. What in ourselves we give over and what from the outside we take in needs constant and insightful equilibration. Only by renegotiating both real and imagined relationships can particular desires and general needs be reconciled.

Only when holding in mind a larger perspective will we operate in harmony with existential necessities attuned to eternal verities. Perhaps true progress, whether in psychotherapy groups, nature, or society-at-large, involves defining a novel arrangement of parts within a whole, between individual striving and the greater good. Then, the very foundations and applications of our collective habit might assume their rightful sphere of influence.

References

A. K. Rice Institute Brochure (1990).

Agazarian, Y. (1982). Role as a bridge construct in understanding the relationship between the individual and the group. In M. Pines (Ed.), *The individual and the group: Boundaries and interrelations.* New York: Plenum Press.

Agazarian, Y. (1989). Group-as-a-whole systems theory and practice. *Group, 13*(3 & 4), 131–154.

Agazarian, Y., & Peters, R. (1981). *The visible and invisible group: Two perspectives on group psychotherapy and group process.* Boston: Routledge & Kegan Paul.

Ahlin, G. (1988). Reaching for the group matrix? *Group, 21*(3), 211–226.

Ahsen, A. (1977). *Psycheye: Self-analytic consciousness.* New York: Brandon House.

Ahsen, A. (1981). Eidetic group therapy. In G. Gazda (Ed.), *Innovations to group therapy.* Springfield, IL: Charles C. Thomas.

Alexander, F. (1948). *Fundamentals of psychoanalysis.* New York: W. W. Norton.

Alexander, F., & French, T. (1946). *Psychoanalytic theory: Principles and applications.* New York: Ronald Press.

Allen, R. (1966). *Greek philosophy: Thales to Aristotle.* New York: The Free Press.

American Group Psychotherapy Association Committee on History. (1971). A brief history of the American Group Psychotherapy Association 1943–1968. *International Journal of Group Psychotherapy, 21*(4), 406–435.

Angles, P. (1981). *Dictionary of philosophy.* New York: Barnes and Noble.

Anzieu, D. (1984). *The group and the unconscious.* Boston: Routledge & Kegan Paul.

Applebaum, S. (1963). The pleasure and reality principles in group process teaching. *British Journal of Medical Psychology, 36,* 49–56.

Arcaya, J. (1985). Metaphorical analysis and hermeneutical interpretation in analytic group psychotherapy. *Group, 9*(2), 17–28.

Ashbach, C., & Schermer, V. (1987). *Object relations, the self, and the group: A conceptual paradigm.* New York: Routledge & Kegan Paul.

Bach, G. (1954). *Intensive group psychotherapy.* New York: Ronald Press.

Bachelard, G. (1964). *The poetics of space.* Boston: Beacon Press.

Bakewell, C. (1907). Source book in ancient philosophy. New York: Charles Scribner's Sons.

Bales, R. F. (1950). *Interaction process analysis: A method for the study of small groups.* Cambridge, MA: Addison-Wesley.

Balgopal, P., Ephross, P., & Vassil, T. (1986). Self-help groups and professional helpers. *Small Group Behavior, 17*(2), 123–137.

Bandler, R., & Grinder, J. (1979). *Frogs into princes: Neurolinguistic programming.* Moab, UT: Real People Press.

Banet, A., & Hayden, C. (1977). A Tavistock primer. *The 1977 annual handbook for group facilitators.* Washington, DC: A. K. Rice Institute.

Barnes, J. (1986). *The preSocratic philosophers.* New York: Routledge & Kegan Paul.

Beck, A. (1969). *Depression: Clinical, experiemental and theoretical aspects.* New York: Harper & Row.

Beck, A. (1981a). Developmental characteristics of system-forming process. In J. Durkin (Ed.), *Living groups.* New York: Brunner/Mazel.

Beck, A. (1981b). The study of group phase development and emergent leadership. *Group, 5*(4), 48–54.

Beck, A., Eng, A., & Brusa, J. (1989). The evolution of leadership during group development. *Group, 13*(3 & 4), 155–164.

Beier, E. (1966). *The silent language of psychotherapy.* Chicago: Aldine.

Bender, L. (1937). Group activities in a children's ward as methods of psychotherapy. *Amer. J. Psychiat., 93*:1151–1173.

Bender, L. (1979). Paul Schilder's contribution to group therapy. In L. R. Wolberg & M. L. Aronson (Eds.), *Group therapy 1969: An overview* (pp. 1–9). New York: Stratton Intercontinental Medical Book.

Bender, L., & Woltman, A. (1936). The use of puppet shows as a psychotherapeutic measure of behavior problem children. *Amer. J. Orthopsychiat., 6*: 341–354.

Bennis, W. G., & Shepard, H. A. (1956). A theory of group development. *Human Relations, 9,* 415–437.

Bennis, W. G., & Shepard, H. A. (1974). Theory of group development. In G. Gibbard, J. Hartman, & R. Mann (Eds.), *Analysis of groups* (pp. 127–153). San Francisco: Jossey Bass.

Berne, E. (1958). Transactional analysis: A new and effective method of group therapy. *American Journal of Psychotherapy, 12,* 735–743.

Bertalanffy, L. von (1968). *General systems theory.* New York: Brazillier.

Bion, W. (1961). *Experiences in groups and other papers.* New York: Basic Books.

Bion, W. (1970). *Attention and interpretation: A scientific approach to insight in psycho-analysis and groups.* New York: Basic Books.

Bion, W. (1977). Attention and interpretation. *Seven servants: Four works by Wilfred Bion.* New York: Jason Aronson.

Bion, W. (1985). Container and contained. In. A. Colman & M. Geller (Eds.), *Group Relations Reader 2.* Washington, DC: A. K. Rice Institute.

Bly, R. (1990). *Iron John: A book about men.* New York: Addison-Wesley.

Bogdanoff, M., & Elbaum, P. (1978). Role lock: Dealing with monopolizers, mistrusters, isolates, helpful hannahs, and other assorted characters in group-psychotherapy. *International Journal of Group Psychotherapy, 28,* 247–262.

Bollas, C. (1987). *The shadow of the object: Psychoanalysis of the unthought known.* New York: Columbia University Press.

Bolman, L., & Deal, T. (1984). *Modern approaches to understanding and managing organizations.* San Francisco: Jossey-Bass.

Boris, H., Zinberg, N., & Boris, M. (1975). Fantasies in group situations. *Contemporary Psychoanalysis, 11*(1) 15–45.

Borriello, J. (1976). Leadership in therapist-centered group-as-whole psychotherapy approach. *International Journal of Group Psychotherapy, 26,* 149–162.

Borriello, J. F. (1979). Intervention foci in group psychotherapy. In L. R. Wolberg & M. L. Aronson (Eds.), *Group therapy 1979: An overview.* New York: Stratton Intercontinental.

Bradford, J., Gibb, J., & Benne, K. (1964). *T-group theory and laboratory method.* New York: John Wiley & Sons.

Bradford, L. (Ed.). (1978). *Group development.* San Diego: University Associates.

Brown, D. (1985). Bion and Foulkes: Basic assumptions and beyond. In M. Pines (Ed.), *Bion and group psychotherapy* (pp. 192-219). Boston: Routledge & Kegan Paul.

Brown, R. (1965). *Social psychology.* New York: Free Press.

Brown, S. (1978). Freud's primal horde—The symbolic death of the matriarchy? *Journal of Personality and Social Systems, 1*(3), 29-45.

Buchanan, D. (1980). The central concern model, a framework for structuring psychodramatic production. *Group Psychotherapy, Psychodrama and Sociometry, 33*, 47-61.

Budman, S. H., Bennet, M. J., & Wisnewski, M. J. (1981). Short-term group psychotherapy: An adult developmental model. *International Journal of Group Psychotherapy, 30*, 63-76.

Bunyard, P., & Goldsmith, E. (Eds.). (1989). *Gaia: The thesis, the mechanisms and the implications.* Worthyvale Manor, Camelford, Cornwall: Wadebridge Ecological Centre.

Burrow, T. (1927). The group method of analysis. *Psychoanal. Rev., 10*: 268-280.

Burrow, T. (1928). The basis of group analysis or the analysis of the reactions of normal and neurotic individuals. *Brit. J. Med. Psychol., 8*: 198-206.

Campbell, J. (1949). *The hero with a thousand faces.* Princeton, NJ: Princeton University Press.

Campbell, J. (1988) (with Bill Moyers). *The power of myth.* New York: Doubleday.

Canetti, E. (1984). *Crowds and power.* New York: Farrar Straus Giroux.

Cannon, W. (1920). *Bodily changes in pain, hunger, fear and rage.* (2nd ed.). New York: Appleton.

Cartwright, D., & Lippitt, R. (1978). Group dynamics and the individual. In L. Bradford (Ed.), *Group Development.* San Diego: University Associates.

Cassirer, E. (1944). *An essay on man.* New Haven, CT: Yale University Press.

Cassirer, E. (1955). *The philosophy of symbolic forms: Vol. 2, Mythical thought.* New Haven, CT: Yale University Press.

Charlton, W., trans. (1983). *Aristotle's physics 1,11.* Oxford: The Clarendon Press.

Chatwin, B. (1987). *The songlines.* New York: Viking.

Cirlot, J. E. (1971). *A dictionary of symbols.* New York: Philosophical Library.

Cohen, P. (1969). *Theories of Myth. Man, Vol. 4.*

Cohen, B., & Epstein, Y. (1981). Empathic communicaton in process groups. *Psychotherapy: Theory, Research and Practice, 18*(4), 493-500.

Cohn, R. (1969). From couch to circle of community: Beginnings of the theme centered interactional method. In H. Ruitenbeck (Ed.), *Group therapy today: Styles, methods and techniques.* New York: Atherton Press.

Cohn, R. (1972). Style and spirit of the theme-centered interactional method. In C. Sager & H. Kaplan (Eds.), *Progress in group and family therapy.* New York: Brunner Mazel.

Cohen, S. L., & Rice C. A. (1985). Maximizing the therapeutic effectiveness of small psychotherapy groups. *Group, 9*(4), 3-9.

Colman, A. (1975). Group consciousness as a developmental phase. In A. Colman & W. Bexton (Eds.), *Group relations reader 1* (pp. 35-42). Washington, DC: A. K. Rice Institute.

Colman, A. (1989). The scapegoat: A psychological perspective. In F. Gabelnick & W. Carr (Eds.), *Contributions to social and political science* (pp. 31-41). Washington, DC: A. K. Rice Institute.

Colman, A., & Bexton, H. (Eds.). (1975). *Group relations reader 1.* Washington, DC: A.K. Rice Institute.

Colman, A., & Geller, M. (Eds.). (1985). *Group relations reader 2.* Washington, DC: A. K. Rice Institute.

Cooper, J. C. (1978). *An illustrated encyclopedia of traditional symbols.* London: Thames and Hudson.

Copleston, F. (1985). *A history of philosophy: Vol. I Greece and Rome.* Garden City, NY: Image Books.

Corsini, R. (1955). Historic background of group psychotherapy. *Group Psychother., Psychodrama Sociometry, 8*: 219–229.

Corsini, R. (1956). Bibliography of group psychotherapy. *Group Psychother., Psychodrama Sociometry, 9*: 178–249.

Curtis, C., & Greenslet, F. (1962). *The practical cogitator: The thinker's anthology.* Boston: Houghton Mifflin.

Dakyns, H. (trans.). (1897). *The works of Xenophon.* New York: Macmillan and Company.

Day, M. (1981). Process in classical psychodynamic groups. *International Journal of Group Psychotherapy, 31*(2), 153–174.

De Mare, P. (1989). The history of large group phenomena in relation to group analytic psychotherapy: The story of the median group. *Group, 13*(3 & 4), 173–197.

De Mare, P. (1990). The development of the median group. *Group Analysis, 23*(2), 113–127.

Desoille, R. (1965). *The directed daydream.* New York: Psychosynthesis Foundation.

Dosamantes-Alperson, E. (1986). A current perspective of imagery in psychoanalysis. *Imagination, cognition and personality, 5*(3), 199–209.

Dover, K. (Ed.). (1968). *Aristophanes' clouds.* Oxford: Claredon Press.

Dreikurs, R. (1932). Early experiments with group psychotherapy. *Amer. J. Psychother., 13*:882–891.

Dreikurs, R. (1956). The contribution of group psychotherapy to psychiatry. *Group Psychother., 9*(2): 115–125.

Dreikurs, R. (1959). Early experiments with group psychotherapy. *Amer. J. Psychother., 13*:882–891.

Druck, A. B. (1978). The role of didactic group therapy in short-term psychiatric settings. *Group, 2*, 98–109.

Drum, D. J., & Knott, J. E. (1977). *Structured groups for facilitating development.* New York: Human Sciences Press.

Dunphy, D. (1974). Phases, roles, and myths in self-analytic groups. In G. Gibbard, J. Hartman, & R. Mann (Eds.), *Analysis of groups.* San Francisco: Jossey-Bass.

Durant, W. (1954). *The story of philosophy.* New York: Pocket Books.

Durkheim, E. (1974). *Sociology and philosophy.* New York: The Free Press.

Durkin, H. (1964). *The group in depth.* New York: International Universities Press.

Durkin, H. (1976). Toward a common basis for group dynamics: Group and therapeutic processes in group therapy. In M. Kissen (Ed.), *From group dynamics to group psychoanalysis: The therapeutic application of group dynamics understanding* (pp. 19–33). New York: Halsted Press.

Durkin, J. (1981). *Living groups: Group psychotherapy and general systems theory.* New York: Brunner/Mazel.

Durkin, J. (1989). Mothergroup-as-a-whole formation and systemic boundarying events. *Group, 13*(3 & 4), 198–211.

Eco, U. (1984). *Semiotics and the philosophy of language*. Bloomington: Indiana University Press.

Edinger, E. (1982). Psychotherapy and alchemy: VIII. Coniunctio. *Quadrant, 15*(1), 5–23.

Edinger, E. (1985). *Anatomy of the psyche: Alchemical symbolism in psychotherapy*. La Salle, IL: Open Court.

Eliade, M. (1959). *The sacred and the profane: The nature of religion*. New York: Harcourt Brace Jovanovich.

Eliade, M. (1960). *Myths, dreams and mysteries*. New York: Harper & Bros.

Eliade, M. (1988). The eternal return. *Parabola, 13*(2), 4–15.

Elliot, S. (1976). *The theory and practice of encounter group leadership*. Berkeley, CA: Explorations Institute.

Ellis, A., & Harper, R. A. (1975). *A new guide to rational living*. Hollywood: Wilshire.

Erickson, E. (1950). *Childhood and society*. New York: Norton.

Erickson, M., Rossi, E., & Rossi, S. (1976). *Hypnotic realities: The induction of clinical hypnosis and forms of indirect suggestion*. New York: Irving Publishers.

Ethan, S. (1987). Some connections between individual and group psychotherapy. *The Psychoanalytic Review, 74*(3), 373–386.

Ettin, M. (1982). Imagery in client-therapist communications. *The American Journal of Psychoanalysis, 42*(3), 229–237.

Ettin, M. (1983). Principles of time-determined group psychotherapy. *Newsletter of the New Jersey Group Psychotherapy Association, Volume I*, 8–10.

Ettin, M. (1984). Sound theories and theory soundings. In J. Royce & L. Mos (Eds.), *Annals of Theoretical Psychology, 2*, 211–223.

Ettin, M. (1985a) Private eyes in a public setting: The use of imagery in group psychotherapy. *Journal of Mental Imagery, 9*(3), 19–44.

Ettin, M. (1985b) Working through humor with Lou Ormont. *Newsletter of the New Jersey Group Psychotherapy Association, Vol II*, 1–2.

Ettin, M. (1986). Within the group's view: Clarifying dynamics through metaphoric and symbolic imagery. *Small Group Behavior, 17*(4), 407–426.

Ettin, M. (1987). Novel accounts of prehistoric mentality. *Imagination, Cognition, and Personality, 7*(2), 177–197.

Ettin, M. (1988a). By the crowd they have been broken: By the crowd they shall be healed: The advent of group psychotherapy. *International Journal of Group Psychotherapy, 38*(2), 139–167.

Ettin, M. (1988b). Stalking the lost cause: An Aristotelian paradigm for group analysis. *International Journal of Group Psychotherapy, 38*(1), 87–107.

Ettin, M. (1988c). Through the meadow and to the woods: Forty years traversing imaginary terrains. *Imagination, Cognition and Personality, 8*(1), 79–84.

Ettin, M. (1989a). Come on Jack, tell us about yourself: The growth spurt of group psychotherapy. *International Journal of Group Psychotherapy, 39*(1), 35–47.

Ettin, M. (1989b). Points of view: Working with spontaneous images in group psychotherapy. In J. Shorr, P. Robin, J. Connella, & M. Wolpin (Eds.), *Imagery: Current perspective*. New York: Plenum Press.

Ettin, M. (1989c). Strangers in a strange land: Working within the sphere of the remote psychotherapy group. *The Psychotherapy Patient, 6*(1&2), 229–261.

Ettin, M. (1989d). The use and abuse of structure and exercise in ongoing group psychotherapy. *Small Group Behavior 20*(2), 279–286.

Ettin, M., Vaughn, E., & Fiedler, N. (1987). Group process in nonprocess groups:

Working with the theme-centered psychoeducational group. *Group, 11*(3), 177-190.

Ezriel, H. (1980). A psychoanalytic approach to group treatment. In S. Scheidlinger (Ed.), *Psychoanalytic group dynamics: Basic readings* (pp. 109-146). New York: International Universities Press. Original work published in 1950.

Fagan, J., & Shepard, I. (1970). *Gestalt therapy now*. New York: Harper & Row.

Fenichel, G., & Flapan, D. (1985). Resistance in group psychotherapy. *Group, 9*(2), 35-47.

Fidler, J. (1979). *Personal communication*. Rutgers Medical School.

Fidler, J. (1989). *Personal communication*. Robert Wood Johnson Medical School.

Firth, R. (1973). *Symbols: Public and private*. Ithaca, NY: Cornell University Press.

Foulkes, S. (1964). *Therapeutic group analysis*. New York: International Universities Press.

Foulkes, S. (1968). On interpretation in group analysis. *International Journal of Group Psychotherapy, 18,* 432-444.

Foulkes, S. (1975). Problems of the large group: Therapeutic implications. In L. Kreeger (Ed.), *The large group: Dynamics and therapy,* (pp. 33-56). London: Constable.

Foulkes, S., & Anthony E. (1965). *Group psychotherapy: The psychoanalytic approach*. Baltimore: Penguin Books.

Francis, A., Clarkin, J., & Marachi, J. (1980). Selection criteria for outpatient group psychotherapy. *Hosp. & Commun. Psychiatry, 31,* 245.

Frazer, J. (1963). *The golden bough*. New York: Macmillan.

French, T. (1952). *The integration of behavior, Vols. I, II*. Chicago: University of Chicago Press.

Fried, E. (1982). Building psychic structures as a prerequistive for change. *International Journal of Group Psychotherapy, 32*(4), 417-430.

Freud, S. (1915). A case of paranoia running counter to the psycho-analytic theory of disease. *Standard Edition, 14,* 261-272.

Freud, S. (1946). *Totem and taboo*. New York: Vinatage Books. Original work published in 1918.

Freud, S. (1967d). *Group psychology and the analysis of the ego*. New York: Liveright. Original work published in 1922.

Freud, S. (1964). *New introductory lectures on psychoanalysis. vol. 22*. New York: International Universities Press.

Freud, S. (1967). *Totem and taboo*. New York: W. W. Norton & Company.

Freud, S. (1987). *A phylogenetic fantasy: Overview of the transference neuroses*. Cambridge, MA: Harvard University Press.

Frey-Rohn, L. (1990). *From Freud to Jung: A comparative study of the psychology of the unconscious*. Boston: Shambhala.

Fromm, E. (1955). Remarks on the problem of free association. *Psychiatric Research Reports 2,* American Psychiatric Association.

Fromm-Reichmann, F. (1950). *Principles of intensive psychotherapy*. Chicago: University of Chicago Press.

Gadlin, W. (1991). On scapegoating: Classical sources, group psychotherapy, and world affairs. In S. Tuttman (Ed.), *Psychoanalytic group theory and therapy* (pp. 27-44). Madison CT: International Universities Press.

Gans, J. (1990). Broaching and exploring the question of combined group and individual therapy. *International Journal of Group Psychotherapy, 40*(2), 123-137.

Gans, J. (1991). The leader's use of metaphor in group psychotherapy. *International Journal of Group Psychotherapy 41*(2), 127-143.

Ganzarain, R. (1983). Working through in group psychotherapy. *International Journal of Group Psychotherapy, 33*(3), 281–296.

Ganzarain, R. (1989). *Object relations group psychotherapy*. Madison, CT: International Universities Press.

Gawain, S. (1978). *Creative visualization*. Mill Valley, CA: Whatever Press.

Geertz, C. (1966). Person, time, and conduct in Bali: An essay in cultural analysis. Southeast Asia studies. *Cultural Report Studies 14*.

Gemmel, G., & Kraus, G. (1988). Dynamics of covert role analysis. *Small Group Behavior, 19*(3), 299–311.

Gibbard, G., & Hartman, J. (1973). The significance of utopian fantasies in small groups. *International Journal of Group Psychotherapy, 23,* 125–147.

Gibbard, G., Hartman, J., & Mann, R. (1974). *Analysis of groups*. San Francisco: Jossey-Bass.

Glantz, K., & Pearce, J. (1989). *Exiles from Eden*. New York: W. W. Norton & Co.

Gleick, J. (1987). *Chaos: Making a new science*. New York: Viking Press.

Glenn, L. (1987). Attachment theory and group analysis: The group matrix as a secure base. *Group Analysis, 20*(2), 109–117.

Glucksberg, S., & Keysar, B. (1990). Understanding metaphorical comparisons: Beyond similarity. *Psychological Review, 97*(1), 3–18.

Goffman, E. (1967). *Interaction ritual: Essays on face-to-face behavior*. New York: Pantheon Books.

Goodman, M. (l986), Boundaries, group psychotherapy and object relations. *Newsletter NJ Group Psychotherapy Society, 2,* 3–6.

Goulding, M., & Goulding, R. (1979). *Changing lives through redecision therapy*. New York: Brunner/Mazel.

Gray, W. (1981). System-forming aspects of general systems theory. Group forming and group functions. In. J. Durkin (Ed.), *Living Groups*. New York: Brunner/Mazel.

Greene, L. (1983). On fusion and individuation in small groups. *International Journal of Group Psychotherapy, 33*(1), 3–19.

Greenson, R. (1970). Dreams in group therapy: A review of the literature. *Psychoanalytic Quarterly, 29,* 394–407.

Grunebaum, H., & Kates, W. (1977). Whom to refer for group psychotherapy? *American Journal of Psychiatry, 134*(2), 130–133.

Gustafson, J., & Cooper, L. (1979). Collaboration in small groups: Theory and technique of small group processes. *Human Relations, 33,* 155–171.

Haley, J. (1973). *Uncommon therapy: The psychiatric techniques of Milton Erickson, M.D.* New York: W. W. Norton & Company.

Hall, J. (1984). Revolt in the Garden of Eden: An alternative group model. *Group, 8*(4), 29–40.

Hammer, E. (1967). The use of imagery in therapeutic communication. *Journal of the Long Island Consultation Center, 5*(2), 3–12.

Hannah, B. (1981). *Encounters with the soul: Active imagination as developed by C. G. Jung*. Cambridge, MA: Sigo Press.

Hartman, J., & Gibbard, G. (1974a). Anxiety, boundary evolution, and social change. In G. Gibbard, J. Hartman, & R. Mann (Eds.), *Analysis of groups*. San Francisco: Jossey-Bass.

Hartman, J., & Gibbard, G. (1974b). A note on fantasy themes in the evolution of group culture. In G. Gibbard, J. Hartman, & R. Mann (Eds.). *Analysis of groups* (pp. 315–335). San Francisco: Jossey-Bass.

Harwood, I. (1983). The application of self-psychology concepts to group psychotherapy. *International Journal of Group Psychotherapy, 33*(4), 469–487.

Haskell, R. F. (1978). An analogic model of small group behavior. *International Journal of Group Psychotherapy, 28*(1), 7–54.

Hawkins, D. (1986). Understanding reactions to group instability in psychotherapy. *International Journal of Group Psychotherapy, 36*(2), 241–260.

Hearst, L. (1981). The emergence of the mother in the group. *Group Analysis, 14,* 25–32.

Hicks, R. (trans.). (1925). *Diogenes Laertius: Lives of eminent philosophers.* New York: G. P. Putnam's Sons.

Hill, W. F. (1977). The Hill Interaction Matrix: The conceptual framework served rating scales, and an updated bibliography. *Small Group Behavior, 8,* 251–268.

Hobson, R. F. (1959). An approach to group analysis. *The Journal of Analytic Psychology, IV*(2), 139–151.

Hobson, R. F. (1964). Group dynamics and analytical psychology. *The Journal of Analytic Psychology, 9*(1), 23–47.

Horowitz, M. (1970). *Image formation and cognition.* New York: Appleton-Century-Crofts.

Horwitz, L. (1977). A group centered approach to group psychotherapy. *International Journal of Group Psychotherapy, 27,* 423–439.

Horwitz, L (1983). Projective identification in dyads and groups. *International Journal of Group Psychotherapy, 33*(3), 259–280.

Horwitz, L. (1985). Projective identification in dyads and groups. In A. Colman & M. Geller (Eds.), *Group relations reader 2* (pp. 21–35). Washington, DC: A. K. Rice Publications.

Hospers, J. (1967). *An introduction to philosophical analysis.* Englewood Cliffs, NJ: Prentice-Hall.

Howard, G. (1991). Culture tales: A narrative approach to thinking, cross-cultural psychology and psychotherapy. *American Psychologist, 46*(3), 187–197.

Illing, H. (1957). C. G. Jung on the present trends in group psychotherapy. *Human Relations, 10,* 77–83.

Irizarry, C. (1983). Hospital-based therapy groups for medically related problems. *Newsletter of the New Jersey Group Psychotherapy Assoc.,* Vol. I, 4–5.

Jacobson, L. (1989). The group as an object in the cultural field. *International Journal of Group Psychotherapy, 39*(4), 475–497.

James, C. (1984). Bion's "containing" and Winnicott's "holding" in the context of the group matrix. *International Journal of Group Psychotherapy, 34*(2), 201–213.

Janis, I. (1982). *Groupthink* (2nd ed.). Boston: Houghton Mifflin.

Jaynes, J. (1976). *The origin of consciousness in the breakdown of the bicameral brain.* Boston: Houghton Mifflin.

Jules-Rosette, B. (1990). Semiotics and cultural diversity: Entering the 1990's. *The American Journal of Semiotics, 7*(1&2), 5–26.

Jung, C. (1960). *The structure and dynamics of the psyche. Collected works vol. 8.* Princeton, NJ: Princeton University Press.

Jung, C. (1969). *The archetypes and the collective unconscious. Collected Works Vol. 9.* Princeton, NJ: Princeton University Press.

Jung, C. (1973). *Syncronicity.* Princeton, NJ: Princeton University Press.

Jung, C. (1976). *The symbolic life. Collected works, Vol. 18.* Princeton, NJ: Princeton University Press.

Kant, E. (1929). *Critique of pure reason.* London: McMillan.

Kanzer, M. (1983). Freud: The first psychoanalytic group leader. In H. Kaplan & B. Sadock (Eds.), *Comprehensive group psychotherapy.* Baltimore: Williams and Wilkins.

Kaplan, H. I., & Sadock, B. J. (1983). *Comprehensive group psychotherapy* (pp. 8–14). Baltimore: Williams & Wilkins.

Katz, G. (1983). The noninterpretation of metaphors in psychiatric hospital groups. *International Journal of Group Psychotherapy, 33,* 53–67.

Kauff, P. (1979). Diversity in analytic group psychotherapy: The relationship between theoretical concepts and technique. *International Journal of Group Psychotherapy, 29,* 51–64.

Kellerman, H. (1979). *Group psychotherapy and personality: Intersecting structures.* New York: Grune and Stratton.

Kellerman, H. (1981). *Group cohesion: Theoretical and clinical perspectives.* New York: Grune and Stratton.

Kernberg, O. (1975). A systems approach to priority setting to interventions in groups. *International Journal of Group Psychotherapy, 25*(3), 251–275.

Kessing, R., & Kessing, F. (1971). *New perspectives in cultural anthropology.* New York: Holt, Rinehart and Winston.

Kibel, H. (1990). Personal communication.

Kibel, H. (1991). The therapeutic use of splitting: The role of the mother-group in therapeutic differentiation and practicing. In S. Tuttman (Ed.), *Psychoanalytic group theory and therapy* (pp. 113–132). Madison, CT: International Universities Press.

Kibel, H., & Stein, A. (1981). The group-as-a-whole approach: An appraisal. *International Journal of Group Psychotherapy 31*(4), 409–427.

Kierkegaard, S. (1843/1954). *Fear and trembling and sickness unto death.* Princeton, NJ: Princeton University Press.

Kissen, M. (1976a). *From group dynamics to group psychoanalysis.* New York: J. Wiley and Sons.

Kissen, M. (1976b) From group dynamics to group psychoanalysis: Therapeutic applications of group dynamic understanding. In M. Kissen (Ed.), *From group dynamics to group psychoanalysis: The therapeutic applications of group dynamic understanding* (pp. 329–343). New York: Halsted Press.

Kissen, M. (1976c). Some dynamic processes observed during an unstructured group laboratory experience. In M. Kissen (Ed.), *From group dynamics to group psychoanalysis: The therapeutic applications of group dynamic understanding* (pp. 51–64). New York: Halsted Press.

Klein, M. (1946). Notes on schizoid mechanisms. *International Journal of Psychoanalysis, 27,* 99–110.

Klein, M. (1985). Our adult world and its roots in infancy. In. A. Colman & M. Geller (Eds.), *Group relations reader 2* (pp. 1–19). Washington, DC: A. K. Rice Publications.

Klein, R. (1985). Some principles of short-term group therapy. *International Journal of Group Psychotherapy, 35*(3), 309–330.

Koffka, K. (1947). *Principles of gestalt psychology.* London: Kegan Paul.

Kohler, W. (1947). *Gestalt psychology.* New York: Liveright.

Kohut, H. (1971). *The analysis of the self.* New York: International Universities Press.

Kohut, H. (1977). *The restoration of the self.* New York: International Universities Press.

Kolb, G. (1983). The dream in psychoanalytic group therapy. *International Journal of Group Psychotherapy, 33*(1), 41–52.

Kosseff, J. (1975). The leader using object-relations theory. In Z. Liff (Ed.), *The leader in the group* (pp. 212–242). New York: Jason Aronson.

Kron, T., & Yungman, R. (1987). The dynamics of intimacy in group therapy. *International Journal of Group Psychotherapy, 37*(4), 529–548.

Kubie, L. (1961). *Neurotic distortion of the creative process.* Toronto: Ambassador Books.

Lacoursiere, R. (1980). *The life cycle of groups: Group development stage theory.* New York: Human Sciences Press.

Lang, M. (1978). *Socrates in the Agora.* Princeton, NJ: American School of Classical Studies at Athens.

Langer, S. (1974). *Philosophy in a new key: A study in the symbolism of reason, rite and art.* Cambridge, MA: Harvard University Press.

Laplanche, J., & Pontalis, J. B. (1973). *The language of psychoanalysis.* New York: W. W. Norton.

Lazell, E. W. (1921). The group treatment of dementia praecox. *Psychoanal. Rev., 8,* 168–179.

Lazell, E. W. (1930). The group psychic treatment of dementia praecox by lectures in re-education. *U.S. Veteran's Bur. Med. Bull., 6,* 733–747.

Leary, T. (1957). *Interpersonal diagnosis of personality.* New York: Ronald Press.

Le Bon, G. (1977). *The crowd.* New York: Penguin Books. Original work published in 1895.

Leroi-Gourhan, A. (1967). *Treasure of prehistoric art.* New York: Harry N. Abrams, Inc.

Leroi-Gourhan, A. (1986). The religion of caves. *October,* Summer, *37,* 7–17.

Leuner, H. (1969). Guided affective imagery: A method of intensive psychotherapy. *American Journal of Psychotherapy, 23,* 4–22.

Leuner, H. (1981). *Group dynamics presented in guided affective imagery.* Presented at Third Annual Conference of the American Association for the Study of Mental Imagery, New Haven, Yale University.

Leuner, H. (1984). *Guided affective imagery: Mental imagery in short-term psychotherapy.* New York: Thieme-Stratton.

Leuner, H. (1990). Workshop: guided affective imagery in groups. International Congress of Group Psychotherapy, Amsterdam.

Lévi-Strauss, C. (1962). *La pensee sauvage.* Paris: Plon. (Translated as *The savage mind* (1966) Chicago: University of Chicago Press.)

Lévi-Strauss, C. (1963). *Totemism.* Boston: Beacon Press.

Lévi-Strauss, C. (1988). *The jealous potter.* Chicago: University of Chicago Press.

Levinson, D., Darrow, C., Klein, E., et al: (1978). *The seasons of a man's life.* New York: Alfred A. Knopf.

Lévy-Bruhl, L. (1985). *How natives think.* Princeton, NJ: Princeton University Press.

Lewin, K. (1951). *Field theory and social sciences.* New York: Harper & Row.

Lieberman, M. (1990). A group therapist perspective on self-help groups. *Int. J. Group Psychother., 40*(3) 251–278.

Lieberman, M., Yalom, I., & Miles, M. (1973). *Encounter groups: First facts.* New York: Basic Books.

Llosa, M. (1989). *The story teller.* New York: Farrar Straus Giroux.

Locke, N. (1961). *Group psychoanalysis: Theory and technique.* New York: New York University Press.

Lodge, D. (1988). *Nice work.* New York: Viking Press.

Lothane, Z. (1981). Listening with the third ear as an instrument in psychoanalysis. *The Psychoanalytic Review, 68*(4), 487–503.

Lovelock, J. (1989). *The ages of Gaia: A biography of our living earth.* Oxford: Oxford University Press.

Lubicz, R. (1978). *Symbol and the symbolic: Ancient Egypt, science, and the evolution of consciousness.* New York: Inner Traditions International.

Lubin, B., & Lubin, A. (1987). *Comprehensive index of group psychotherapy writings.* American Group Psychotherapy Monograph Series, 2. Madison, CT: International Universities Press.

Luft, J. (1970). *Group processes: An introduction to group dynamics.* Palo Alto: Mayfield Publishing.

Main, T. (1985). Some psychodynamics of large groups. In A. Colman & M. Geller (Eds.), *Group relations reader 2* (pp. 49–69). Washington, DC: A. K. Rice Institute.

Malan, D. H. (1976). *The frontier of brief psychotherapy.* New York: Plenum Medical Book Company.

Mann, D. (1990). Crowding, or the complexity of group relationships. *Group Analysis, 23*(1), 69–80.

Mann, R. D., Gibbard, G., & Hartman, S. (1967). *Interpersonal styles and group development.* New York: Wiley.

Mann, T. (1950). Joseph and his brothers. In J. Angell (Ed.), *The Thomas Mann reader.* New York: Grosset & Dunlap.

Maranhao, T. (1986). *Therapeutic discourse and Socratic dialogue: A cultural critique.* Madison: University of Wisconsin Press.

Marschack, A. (1972). *The roots of civilization.* New York: McGraw Hill.

Marsh, L. C. (1931). Group treatment of the psychoses by the psychological equivalent of the revival. *Ment. Hyg., 15*:328–349.

Marsh, L. C. (1933). An experiment in group treatment of patients at Worchester State Hospital. *Ment. Hyg., 17*:396–416.

Marsh, L. C. (1935). Group therapy and the psychiatric clinic. *J. Nerv. & Ment. Dis., 82*:381–393.

Maslow, A. (1963). The need to know and the fear of knowing. *The Journal of General Psychology, 68,* 111–125.

Mattoon, M. (1978). *Applied dream analysis: A Jungian perspective.* New York: John Wiley and Sons.

McCully, R. (1977). Impressions of a visit to Lascaux. *Quadrant, 10*(1), 39–42.

McDougall, W. (1973). *The group mind.* New York: Arno Press. Original work published in 1920.

Meissner, W. (1978). Theories of personality. In M. Nicholi (Ed.), *The Harvard guide to modern psychiatry.* Cambridge, MA: The Belknap Press of Harvard University Press.

Mesmer, F. (1980). *Mesmerism.* G. Bloch (Trans.). Los Altos, CA: William Kaufmann, Inc. Original work published in 1799.

Meyers, R. (1990). The inner nature of the environmental crisis. *Quadrant, 22*(2), 39–55.

Migliorati, P. (1989). The image in group relationships. *Group Analysis, 22*(2), 189–199.

Miller, E., & Rice, A. K. (1975). Selections from systems of organizations. In D. Colman & H. Bexton (Eds.), *Group relations reader 1* (pp. 43–68). Washington, DC: A. K. Rice Institute.

Millon, T. (1981). *Disorders of personality.* New York: John Wiley & Sons.

Mills, T. (1964). *Group transformation: An analysis of a learning group.* Englewood Cliffs, NJ: Prentice-Hall.

Mintz, E. (1971). Therapy techniques and encounter technique: Comparison and rationale. *American Journal of Psychotherapy, 25,* 104–109.

Mintz, E. (1974). On the dramatization of psychoanalytic interpretations. In L. Wolberg & M. Aronson (Eds.), *Group therapy 1974: An overview* (pp. 175–185). New York: Stratton International Medical Books.

Moreno, J. L. (1932). *Group method and group psychotherapy.* Sociometry Monograph No. 5. New York: Beacon House.

Moreno, J. L. (1937). Interpersonal therapy and psychopathology of interpersonal relations. *Sociometry, 1:*9–76.

Moreno, J. L. (1950). The ascendance of group psychotherapy and the declining influence of psychoanalysis. *Group Psychother.: J. Sociopsychopath. & Sociatry, 3*(1), 121–141.

Moreno, J. L. (1953). *Who shall survive? Foundations of sociometry, group psychotherapy and sociodrama* (2nd ed.) Beacon, NY: Beacon House. Original work published in 1934.

Moreno, J. L. (1957). *The first book on group psychotherapy* (3rd ed.). New York: Beacon House.

Moreno, Z. T. (1966). Evolution and dynamics of the group psychotherapy movement. In J. L. Moreno (Ed.), *The International Handbook of Group Psychotherapy.* New York: Philosophical Library.

Murphy, L. R. (1984). Occupational stress management: A review and appraisal. *Journal of Occupational Psychology, 57,* 1–15.

National Training Laboratories. (1962). *Issues in human relations training. selected readings series, no. 5.* Washington, DC: National Training Laboratories.

Needham, R. (1978). *Primordial characters.* Charlottesville: University Press of Virginia.

Nehamas, A. (1985). Meno's paradox and Socrates as a teacher. In J. Annas (Ed.), *Oxford studies in ancient philosophy, Volume III.* Oxford: Clarendon Press.

Neumann, E. (1963). *The great mother: An analysis of the archetype.* Princeton, NJ: Princeton University Press.

Neumann, E. (1973). *The origins and history of consciousness.* Princeton, NJ: Princeton University Press. Original work published in 1954.

Nietzsche, F. (1968). Thus spoke Zarathustra. In W. Kaufmann (Ed.), *The portable Nietzsche.* New York: The Viking Press.

Ormont, L. (1990). The craft of bridging. *International Journal of Group Psychotherapy, 40*(1), 3–17.

Ortner, S. (1973). On key symbols. *American Anthropologist, 75,* 1338–1346.

Osmond, H., Osmundsen, J., & Agel, J. (1974). *Understanding understanding.* New York: Harper and Row.

Parkin, A. (1981). Repetition, mourning and working through. *International Journal of Psychoanalysis, 62,* 271–281.

Parloff, M. (1968). Analytic group psychotherapy. In J. Marmor (Ed.), *Modern psychoanalysis* (pp. 492–531). New York: Basic Books.

Partridge, E. (1983). *Origins: A short etymological dictionary of modern English.* New York: Greenwich House.

Patterson, T. (1966). *Management theory.* London: Business Publications.

Perera, S. (1986). *The scapegoat complex: Toward a mythology of shadow and guilt.* Toronto: Inner City Books.

Perls, F. (1969a). *Gestalt therapy verbatim.* Lafayette, CA: Real People Press.

Perls, F. (1969b). *In and out the garbage pail.* New York: Bantam Books.

Petrakos, B. (1977). *Delphi.* Athens: Clio Editions.

Pfeiffer, J. (1985). *The emergence of humankind.* New York: Harper & Row.

Pfeiffer, J., & Jones, J. (1975). *A handbook of structured exercises for human relations training* (Vols. 1–5). La Jolla. CA: University Associates.

Pines, M. (1981). The frame of reference of group psychotherapy. *International Journal of Group Psychotherapy, 31*(3), 275–285.

Pines, M. (Ed.). (1983). *The evolution of group analysis.* London: Routledge & Kegan Paul.

Pines, M. (1985). Psychic development and the group analytic situation. *Group, 9*(1), 60–73.

Pines, M. (1989). The group-as-a whole approach in Foulksian group analytic psychotherapy. *Group, 13*(3 & 4), 212–216.

Plato. (1985). Gorgias, Protagoras, Meno, Symposium (a) *Plato: The collected dialogues.* (E. Hamilton & H. Cairns, eds.) Princeton, NJ: Princeton University Press.

Plato. (1987a). Euthyphro, Apology, Crito, Phaedo. *The last days.* (Trans. H. Tredennick). New York: Penguin Books.

Plato. (1987b). Ion, Laches, Lysis, Charmides. *Early Socratic Dialogues* (T. Saunders ed.). London: Penguin Books.

Plato. *Symposium.* (1987c). (Trans. W. Hamilton) London: Penguin Books.

Plato. (1987d). *Theaetetus.* (Trans., R. Waterfield). New York: Penguin Books.

Poey, K. (1985). Guidelines for the practice of brief, dynamic group therapy. *International Journal of Group Psychotherapy, 35*(3), 331–354.

Porter, N. (1898). *Webster's international dictionary.* Springfield, MA: G. & C. Merraim Company.

Pratt, J. H. (1906). The "home sanatorium" treatment of consumption. *Boston Med. Surg. J., 154*:210–216.

Pratt, J. H. (1907). On the organization of tuberculosis classes. *Med. Commun. Mass. Med. Soc., 20*:475–492.

Pratt, J. H. (1908). Results obtained in treatment of pulmonary tuberculosis. *Brit. Med. J., 2*:1070–1071.

Pratt, J. H. (1922). The principles of class treatment and their application to various chronic diseases. *Hosp. Soc. Serv. Quart., 6*:401–411.

Pratt, J. H. (1934). The influence of emotions in the causation and cure of psychoneuroses. *Int. Clin., 4*:1–16.

Pratt, J. H. (1945). The group method in the treatment of psychosomatic disorders. *Sociometry, 8*:323–331.

Prodgers, A. (1990). The dual nature of the group as mother: The uroboric container. *Group Analysis, 23*(1), 17–30.

Rank, O. (1932). *The myth of the birth of the hero.* New York: Vintage Books.

Raphael-Leff, J. (1984). Myths and modes of motherhood. *British Journal of Psychotherapy, 1,* 14–18.

Redl, F. (1980). Group emotion and leadership. In S. Scheidlinger (Ed.), *Psychoanalytic group dynamics: Basic readings* (pp. 15–68). New York: International Universities Press. Original work published in 1942.

Redlich, F., & Astrachan, B. (1975). Group dynamics training. In A. Colman & H. Bexton (Eds.), *Group relations reader 1* (pp. 225–234). Washington, DC: A. K. Rice Institute.

Reik, T. (1948). *Listening with the third ear.* Garden City, NY: Garden City Books.

Rice, A. K. (1969). Individual, group and intergroup processes. *Human Relations, 22*(6), 565–584.

Rice, A. K. (1975). Selections from "Learning for leadership. In A. Colman & H. Bexton (Eds.), *Group relations reader 1.* Washington, DC: A. K. Rice Institute.

Rioch, M. (1970). The work of Wilfred Bion on groups. *Psychiatry, 33,* 56–66.

Rioch, M. (1975a). "All We Like Sheep-" (Isaiah 53:6): Followers and leaders. In A. Colman & H. Bexton (Eds.), *Group relations reader 1* (pp. 159–177). Washington, DC: A. K. Rice Institute.

Rioch, M. (1975b). Group relations: Rationale and technique. In A. Colman & H. Bexton (Eds.), *Group relations reader 1* (pp. 3–10). Washington, DC: A.K. Rice Institute.

Rioch, M. (1975c). The work of Wilfred Bion on groups. In A. Colman & W. Bexton (Eds.), *Group relations reader 1* (pp. 21–34). Washington, DC: A. K. Rice Institute.

Rioch, M. (1991). Personal communication.

Roberts, J. (1982). Foulkes' concept of the matrix. *Group Analysis, 25*(2), 111–126.

Rogers, C. (1961). *On becoming a person.* Boston: Houghton Mifflin.

Rogers, C. (1967). *On encounter groups.* New York: Harper and Row.

Rogers, C. (1987). On putting it into words: The balance between projective identification and dialogue in the group. *Group Analysis, 20*(2) 99–107.

Rosenbaum, M. (1978). Group psychotherapy: Heritage, history, and the current scene. In H. Mullan & M. Rosenbaum, (Eds.), *Group psychotherapy: Theory and practice.* New York: Free Press.

Rosenfeld, D. (1988). *Psychoanalysis and groups: History and dialectics.* London: Karnac Books.

Rosenthal, L. (1983). S. R. Slavson—An appreciation. In L. Wolberg & M. Aronson (Eds.), *Group and family therapy* (pp. 3–7). New York: Brunner/Mazel.

Rosie, J., & Azim, H. (1990). Large-group psychotherapy in a day treatment program. *Int. J. Group Psychother., 40*(3), 305–321.

Roth, B. (1991). Some of the origins of Freud's paper on group psychotherapy: A psychohistorical exploration. In S. Tuttman (Ed.), *Psychoanalytic group theory and therapy* (pp. 287–308). Madison, CT: International Universities Press.

Rothberg, M. (1984). Group centered group psychotherapy. *Newsletter of the New Jersey Group Psychotherapy Society, I,* 4–6.

Rousseau, J. (1987). *The social contract.* New York: Penguin Books. Original work published in 1762.

Ruitenbeek, H. (1969). *Group therapy today: Styles, methods, and techniques.* New York: Atherton Press.

Ruitenbeek, H. (1969). *The new group therapies.* New York: Avon Books.

Russell, B. (1964). *A history of western philosophy.* New York: Simon and Schuster.

Russell, E. (1983). Psychological modes: Elaboration of a sociometric mandala. *Quadrant, 16*(2), 39–55.

Rutan, J. S. (1985). Termination in groups. Lecture in group psychotherapy. Course offered in association with Massachusetts General Hospital and Harvard Medical School.

Rutan, J. S., & Alonso. A. (1978). Some guidelines for group therapists. *Group, 2*(1), 4–13.

Rutan, J. S., & Rice, C. (1981). The charismatic leader: Asset or liability. *Psychotherapy: Theory, Research and Practice, 18*(4), 487–492.

Rutan, J. S., & Stone, W. N. (1984). *Psychodynamic group psychotherapy.* Lexington, MA: Collamore Press.

Sadock, B., & Kaplan, H. (1983). History of group psychotherapy. In H. Kaplan & B. Sadock (Eds.), *Comprehensive Group Psychotherapy.* Baltimore: Williams & Wilkins.

Sahakian, W. S., & Sahakian, M. S. (1966). *Ideas of the great philosophers.* New York: Barnes & Noble.

Sallis, J. (1987). *Spacing of reason and imagination: In texts of Kant, Fichte, Hegel.* Chicago: University of Chicago Press.

Santas, G. X. (1979). *Socrates: Philosophy in Plato's early dialogues.* Boston: Routledge & Kegan Paul.

Saravay, S. (1978). A psychoanalytic theory of group development. *International Journal of Group Psychotherapy, 28,* 481–507.

Saretsky, T. (1977). *Active techniques and group psychotherapy.* New York: Jason Aronson.

Sartre, J. P. (1960). *Critique de la raison dialectique.* Paris: Gallimard.

Scheidlinger, S. (1952). *Psychoanalysis and group behavior: A study in Freudian group psychology.* New York: W. W. Norton & Co.

Scheidlinger, S. (1955). Concepts of identification in group psychotherapy. *American Journal of Psychotherapy, 6,* 661–672.

Scheidlinger, S. (1974). On the concept of the "mother-group". *International Journal of Group Psychotherapy, 24,* 417–428.

Scheidlinger, S. (1980). *Psychoanalytic group dynamics: Basic readings.* New York: International Universities Press.

Scheidlinger, S. (1982). Presidential Address: On scapegoating in group psychotherapy. *International Journal of Group Psychotherapy, 32*(2), 131–143.

Schermer, V. (1985). Beyond Bion: The basic assumption states revisited. In M. Pines (Ed.), *Bion and group psychotherapy* (pp. 139–150). Boston: Routledge & Kegan Paul.

Schermer, V. (1991a). Workshop at American Group Psychotherapy Association Conference.

Schermer, V. (1991). Personal communication.

Schiffer, M. (1983). S. R. Slavson. In L. Wolberg & M. Aronson (Eds.), *Group and family therapy* (pp. 9–20). New York: Brunner/Mazel.

Schilder, P. (1936), The analysis of ideologies as a psychotherapeutic method, especially in group treatment. *Amer. J. Psychiat., 93*:601–615.

Schilder, P. (1939). Results and problems of group psychotherapy in severe neurosis. *Ment. Hyg., 23*:87–98.

Schilder, P. (1938). *Psychotherapy.* I. L. Border (Ed.) New York: W. W. Norton.

Schilder, P. (1940). Introductory remarks on groups. *J. Soc. Psychol., 12*:83–100.

Schindler, W. (1966). The role of the mother in group psychotherapy. *International Journal of Group Psychotherapy, 16,* 198–202.

Schlachet, P. (1979). An interview with Dr. Al Wolf. *Group, 3*(3), 181–187.

Schlachet, P. (1986). The concept of group space. *International Journal of Group Psychotherapy, 36*(1), 33–53.

Schutz W. (1967). *Joy.* New York: Grove Press.

Schwartz, G. E. (1980). Stress management in occupational settings. *Health promotion at the worksite, 95*(2), 99–108.

Segal, H. (1957). Notes on symbol formation. *International Journal of Psychoanalysis, 38.*

Segal, H. (1973). *Introduction to the work of Melanie Klein.* New York: Basic Books.

Segal, H. (1981). *Melanie Klein.* Harmondsworth, Penguin Books.

Shaffer, J., & Galinsky, M. (1974). *Models of group therapy and sensitivity training.* Englewood Cliffs, NJ: Prentice-Hall.

Shambaugh, P. (1985). The mythic structure of Bion's groups. *Human Relations, 38*(10), 937–951.

Shapiro, E. (1990). Self psychology, intersubjectivity, and group psychotherapy. *Group, 14*(3), 177–182.

Shapiro, J. L. (1978). *Methods of group psychotherapy and encounter: A tradition of innovation.* Itasca, IL: F. E. Peacock.

Shaskan, D. (1978). History of group psychotherapy: W.W. II. *AGPA Working Papers,* 1–6. New York: AGPA.

Shaskan, D., & Jolesch, M. (1944). War and group psychotherapy. *Amer. J. Orthopsychiat., 14*:571–577.

Sheehy, G. (1976). *Passages: Predictable crisis of adult life.* New York: E. P. Dutton.

Shelburne, W. (1988). *Mythos and logos in the thought of Carl Jung: The theory of the collective unconscious in scientific perspective.* Albany: State University of New York Press.

Sherwood, M. (1964). Bion's experiences in group: A critical evaluation. *Human Relations, 17,* 113–130.

Shibles, W. (1971). *Models of ancient philosophy.* London: Visions Press.

Shiffer, M. (1983). S. R. Slavson (1890–1981). *International Journal of Group Psychotherapy, 33*(2), 131–150.

Shorr, J. (1978). Clinical uses of categories of mental imagery. In J. Singer & Pope (Eds.), *The power of human imagination: New methods in psychotherapy.* New York: Plenum Press.

Shorr, J. (1983). *Psychotherapy through imagery.* New York: Thieme-Stratton Inc.

Shorr, J. (1986). The use of imagery in group psychotherapy. *Scandanavian Journal of Psychology.*

Silva, J. (1977). *The Silva mind control method.* New York: Pocket Books.

Sime, W. E., & Tharp, G. D. (1982). Managing organizational stress: A field experiment. *Journal of Applied Psychology, 67*(5), 533–542.

Simon, B. (1978). *Mind and madness in ancient Greece: The classical roots of modern psychiatry.* Ithaca, NY: Cornell University Press.

Simonton, O., & Simonton, S. (1974). Management of the emotional aspects of malignancy. Paper presented at the symposium New Dimensions of Habilitation for the Handicapped. Gainesville: University of Florida.

Slater, P. (1966). *Microcosm: Structural, psychological and religious evolution in groups.* New York: John Wiley & Sons.

Slavson, S. R. (1940). Group psychotherapy. *Ment. Hyg., 24*:36–49.

Slavson, S. R. (1951). Current trends in group psychotherapy. *International Journal of Group Psychotherapy, 1,* (7–15).

Slavson, S. R. (1957). Are there dynamics in therapy groups? *International Journal of Group Psychotherapy, 7,* 131–154.

Slavson, S. R. (1964). *A textbook in analytic group psychotherapy.* New York: International Universities Press.

Slavson, S. R. (Ed.). (1971). *The fields of group psychotherapy.* New York: Schocken Books.

Sledge, W. (1977). The therapist's use of metaphor. *International Journal of Psychoanalytic Psychotherapy, 6,* 113–130.

Snell, B. (1982). *The discovery of the mind: In Greek philosophy and literature.* New York: Dover Publications.

Solomon, L., & Berzon, B. (1972). *New perspectives on encounter groups.* San Francisco: Jossey-Bass.

Sorabji, R. (1980). *Necessity, cause, and blame: Perspectives on Aristotle's theory.* Ithaca, NY: Cornell University Press.

Spolin, V. (1963). *Improvisation for the theatre*. Evanston, IL: Northwestern University Press.

Spotnitz, H. (1961). *The couch and the circle: A story of group psychotherapy*. New York: Alfred A. Knopf.

Srivastva, S., & Barrett, F. (1988). The transforming nature of metaphors in group development: A study in group theory. *Human Relations, 41*(1), 31–64.

Stein, A. (1976). Discussion of Yalom's using the here-and-now in group therapy. In *Proceedings of the Third Annual Conference of Group Therapy* of the Group Therapy Department, The Washington Square Institute For Psychotherapy and Mental Health (pp. 36–52). New York: The Washington Square Institute.

Stevens, A. (1982). *Archetypes: A natural history of the self*. New York: William Morrow and Company.

Stiers, M. (1987). A Kleinian analysis of group development. *Group, 11*(2), 67–77.

Stokes, J. (1983). Toward an understanding of cohesion in personal change groups. *International Journal of Group Psychotherapy, 33*(4), 449–467.

Stone, I. F. (1988). *The trial of Socrates*. Boston: Little, Brown.

Stone, W. (1985). The curative fantasy in group psychotherapy. *Group, 9*(1), 3–14.

Sullivan, H. (1953). *The interpersonal theory of psychiatry*. New York: W. W. Norton & Co.

Syz, H. C. (1928). Remarks on group analysis. *Amer. J. Psychiat., 85*:141–148.

Tauber, L. E. (1978). Choice point analysis—Formulation, strategy, intervention, and result in group process therapy and supervision. *International Journal of Group Psychotherapy, 28*(2), 163–184.

Taylor, A. E. (1953). *Socrates: The man and his thought*. Garden City, NY: Doubleday Anchor Books.

Thomas, C. W. (1943). Group psychotherapy: A review of recent literature. *Psychosom. Med., 5*:166–180.

Tuckman, B. W. (1965). Developmental sequence in small groups. *Psychological Bulletin, 63*, 384–399.

Tuckman, B., & Jensen, M. (1977). Stages of small-group development revisited. *Group organizational studies 2*, 419–427.

Turquet, P. (1985). Leadership: The individual and the group. In A. Colman & M. Geller (Eds.), *Group relations reader 2* (pp. 71–88). Washington, DC: A.K. Rice Institute.

Tuttman, S. (1984). Applications of object relations theory and self psychology in current group psychotherapy. *Group, 8*(4), 41–48.

Tuttman, S. (1986). Theoretical and technical elements which characterize the American approaches to psychoanalytic group psychotherapy. *International Journal of Group Psychotherapy, 36*(4), 499–515.

Ulanov, A. (1985). A shared space. *Quadrant, 18*(1), 65–80.

Urdang, L. (Ed.). (1972). *The Random House college dictionary*. New York: Random House.

Usandivaras, R. (1986). Foulkes' primordial level in clinical practice. *Group Analysis, 19*(2), 113–124.

Vassiliou, G., & Vassiliou, V. (1981). Outlining the synallactic collective image technique as used within a systemic-dialectic approach. In J. Durkin (Ed.), *Living groups: Group psychotherapy and general system theory*. New York: Brunner/Mazel.

Vernant, J. (1988). *Myth and society in ancient Greece*. New York: Zone Books.

Villela-Minnerly, L., & Merkin, R. (1987). Star Wars as myth: A fourth hope? *The Psychoanalytic Review, 74*(3), 387–399.

Vlastos, G. (1971). *The philosophy of Socrates.* Notre Dame, IN: University of Notre Dame Press.

Vlastos, G. (1983). The Socratic elenchus. In J. Annas, (Ed.), *Oxford studies in ancient philosophy, Vol. I.* Oxford: Clarendon Press.

Von Franz, M. (1980). *Reflections of the soul: Projection and re-collection in Jungian psychology.* London: Open Court.

Watzlawick, P. (1978). *The language of change: Elements of therapeutic communication.* New York: Basic Books.

Weiner, M. (1983). The assessment and resolution of impasse in group psychotherapy. *International Journal of Group Psychotherapy, 33*(3), 313–331.

Weinstein, D. (1987). Self psychology and group therapy, *Group, 11*(3), 144–154.

Wells, L. (1985). The group-as-a-whole and its theoretical roots. In A. Colman & M. Geller (Eds.), *Group relations reader 2,* (pp. 109–126). Washington, DC: A. K. Rice Institute.

Wender, L. (1936). The dynamics of group psychotherapy and its application. *J. Nerv. & Ment. Dis., 84*:54–60.

Wender, L. (1940). Group psychotherapy: A study of its application. *Psychiat. Quart., 14,* 708–718.

Wertheimer, M. (1912). Experimentelle studien uber das sehen von bewegung. *Z. Psychol., 61,* 161–265.

Wheelwright, P. (1962). *Metaphor and reality.* Bloomington: Indiana University Press.

Whitaker, D. (1987). Some connections between a group-analytic and a group focal conflict perspective. *Int. J. Group. Psychother., 37*(2), 201–218.

Whitaker, D. (1989). Group focal conflict theory: Description, illustration and evaluation. *Group, 13*(3 & 4), 225–251.

Whitaker, D., & Lieberman, M. (1964). *Psychotherapy through the group process.* Chicago: Aldine.

White, R. (1986). *Dark caves, bright visions: Life in Ice Age Europe.* New York: W. W. Norton.

Whitmont, E. (1964). Group therapy and analytic psychology. *Journal of Analytic Psychology, 9*(1), 1–21.

Whitmont, E. (1969). *The symbolic quest: Basic concepts of analytic psychology.* Princeton, NJ: Princeton University Press.

Willeford, W. (1967). Group psychotherapy and symbol formation. *Journal of Analytic Psychology, 12*(2), 137–160.

Wilson, B. (1969). The creative persons' group. In H. Ruitenbeek (Ed.), *Group Therapy Today* (pp. 268–278). New York: Atherton Press.

Winnicott, D. W. (1965). *Maturational processes and the facilitating environment.* New York: International Universities Press.

Winnicott, D. W. (1971). *Playing and reality.* New York: Basic Books.

Winnicott, D. W. (1986). *Holding and interpretation: Fragment of an analysis.* New York: Grove Press.

Wolberg, A. R. (1976). The contributions of Jacob Moreno. In L. Wolberg & M. Aronson (Eds.), *Group therapy 1976: An overview.* New York: Stratton International Medical Books.

Wolf, A. (1949). The psychoanalysis of groups. I. *Amer. J. Psychother., 3*:525–558.

Wolf, A. (1950). The psychoanalysis of groups. 11. *Amer. J. Psychother., 4*:16–50.

Wolf, A., & E. Schwartz (1962). *Psychoanalysis in groups.* New York: Grune and Stratton.

Wolpe, J., & Lazarus, A. (1966). *Behavior therapy techniques.* New York: Pergamon.

Xenophon. (1985). *Memorabilla.* (J. R. Smith, ed.). Salem, NH: Ayer.

Xenophon. (1897). *The works of Xenophon: Vol. III* (Trans. H. G. Dakyns). New York: Macmillan.

Yalom, I. (1970/1985). *The theory and practice of group psychotherapy.* (lst & 3rd editions). New York: Basic Books.

Yalom, I. (1976). Using the here-and-now in group therapy. In *Proceedings of the Third Annual Conference* of the Group Therapy Department, The Washington Square Institute for Psychotherapy and Mental Health (pp. 8–29). New York: The Washington Square Institute.

Zweben, J., & Hammann, K. (1970). Prescribed games: A theoretical perspective on the use of group techniques. *Psychotherapy: Theory, Research and Practice, 7*(1), 22–27.

Name Index

Subject Index

Focus of groups, 11: spatial, 23, 94; temporal, 17, 22–23, 94–95
Formats, group, 9–14, 35, 56–58: and types of groups, 72–73, 102–104
Free analysis, 84–86
Free association, 52, 86
Free-floating attention, 166, 179–180
Freudian psychology, 61–65, 85
Fusion, 380, 397–398, 414: mythical, 415–416

Gaia myth, 424 (see also Mother group)
Gender, of group members, 84
Generalization, to outside of group, 412–413
Gestalt approach, 122
Goals, therapeutic, 56, 73–74, 79, 104–106
Go-around, 86, 164, 237
Gossip, 218
Grandiosity, 400
"Greek chorus," 122
Group analysis, 24–35, 111–147: the British school, 196; Burrow's method, 67–69; causal approach, 314–339; and Socratic technique, 45–52; and spherical properties, 289–313
Group-as-a-whole, 99, 113–114, 126–129, 148–173, 321, 419 (see also Group, definition): Burrow's concept of, 68; and collective representations, 411; diagnosis of, 158, 159, 164–167; and group relations conferences, 215; metaphors of, 194–197; as nascent formation, 25; vignette, 151–152
Group-building approaches, deductive, 113, 148–173: depictive, 113, 174–206; inductive, 122–147, 350–352; and Socratic induction, 54; and theory building, 315
Group-centered leaders, 320
Group, definition, 115–129, 148–149
Group development (see also Phases, group): and building psychic structures, 119; and infant development, 136–137; and individual development, 316; and interpersonal relations, 125; and Kleinian theory, 374, 392; and life-cycle and linear models, 406; and mental imagery, 343; and pendular process, 17; and phases of moon, 404; and progression, 171; and regression, 170; as shared tasks, of Beck, 146–147; as substituting reality for fantasy, 402; through trial and error, 140–142
Group dynamics, 67, 92, 95, 97–98, 265–276, 280–283: in psychoeducational groups, 260–283; interrupted by therapist, 122
Group process, destructive, 6: fragmented, 148–149; group quarantine, 159; grouping trends, 6; and structure, 213–214
Guidance groups, 65, 91
Guided imagery (see Mental imagery)

"Hall of mirrors" (see Mirroring process)
Hallucinations, 385
Harvard Social Relations approach, 214
Here-and-now approach, 23, 68–69, 71, 95, 125, 317–320: Burrow, influence of, 68; and choice point analysis, 320, 322; and

efficient cause, 325–326; and process activation, 317; and process illumination, 317, 322; in training groups, 13
Hermeneutic approach, 166–167, 195, 305, 361
Hero (see Role, group and Transpersonal roles)
Heterogeneous groups (see Composition, group)
Hidden agendas, 235–236, 328–329, 345–346: and shaping circumstances, 354
History, 332, 365, 416: and bipolar themes, 354; Burrow on, 68; and formal causality, 334; as genesis, origins in mythology, 374–376; and group bible, 416; of group therapy, 56–110; history-taking, in preparation, 60; and image formation, 345–346; and social structure, 406; Wolf on, 87
Holding environment, 206, 310: and group as container, 308–312
Holidays, 420
Holistic phenomenon, 150, 374: and Eastern societies, 374
Homeostasis: and group development, 406; and mental imagery, 192
Homogeneity (see Composition, group)
Horizontal analysis of groups, 123, 395
Human relations conferences, 214–216: examples from, 216–232; groups, at, 413
Hunting magic (see Ritual and rite)
Hypnosis, 82: and hypnotic inducement, 385; hypnotic processes, and word magic, 399
Hysteria and hysterical style, 306, 377: and image translation, 351–352

Identification: against the aggressor, 248; and group cohesion, 20
Identity: and group membership, 5–7, 153, 374–375; "I" and "We," 7, 25, 38, 301
Idols, 383
Imagination, forms of, 216–230 (see also Mental imagery)
Impasses, group, 297, 316, 322, 330, 333, 339: individual, 121; and mental imagery, 192–194; working through in ritual, 223
Individual therapy, 18, 22, 56, 63, 66, 68, 76, 79, 82, 86, 91, 119, 289
Inductive logic, 133–134 (see also Group-building approaches)
Inquisitions, 419
Insight, 315, 317 (see also Causal analysis, formal cause)
Internalization and externalization, 372: and the exchange of parts and feelings, 388–390; and totemic relations and oral incorporation, 390–391
International Association of Group Psychotherapy, 96
Interpersonal relations, 122–126, 372
Interpersonal wheel, of Leary, 124
Interpretation, 315: as conjoining events, 399–400; and language, 167–170, 400; linking past with present, 332; and mental imagery, 183–184; and projective identification, 389–390

Interventions, 129–130, 168, 211, 238, 280–283, 318: enhanced by mental imagery, 183–184; effective intervention, 377–378; summary statements as, 320
Intimacy, 301: and mental imagery, 188–189
Introversion (and extroversion), 300
Invisible group approach, 129, 155–164
Isomorphy, of members and groups, 172–173

Jazz improvisation, and imagery, 193
Jungian approach (see also Archetypes; Transpersonal roles): and amplification of images, 349; and archetypal images, 355–356; and collective unconscious, 194; and group as circle, 291, 304; and group space, 304; and imagery techniques, 180; and images as mediators, 343 (see also Mental imagery); and lack of endorsement for group work, 71; Lazell and, 61; and Platonic search for universals, 53–54; and primordial images, 194

Leader-centered groups, 121, 211–212: and charismatic leaders, 153, 420
Leadership, group, 11, 56, 79, 160, 211–214, 232: as content expert and task organizer, 262; and dealing with collusive defenses, 159–160; in Freudian psychology, 64; and group conductor role, 196; and group-as-a-whole, 128–129, 149, 172; and individuals in group, 119–121 (see also Transference); and interpersonal relations, 123–124; and interpretation, 167–170, 399–400; and leader-hero, 417; and leadership style of Schilder, 82–83; and levels of expertise, 9; libidinal ties to leader, 121–122; overestimation of leader, 415–417; and psychoeducational groups, 10; and silent leader, 417; Socrates, style of, 41–45; and structured exercises, 237–239; and systems group therapist, 157, 158; and T-groups, 231–232; and task management, 213; and therapeutic techniques, 107–110
Leadership roles, of members (see also Roles, group and Role formation): defiant, emotional, scapegoat leaders, 161; and member skills, 236; task leader, 154, 233–259
Life-cycle, group (see Group development)
Logistics, group, 3, 5–11, 76–78, 107–110, 367, 370: of Adlerian tradition, 66–67; of Lazell, 61; of Pratt, 58; of Schilder, 84; of Slavson, 92; of Socrates, 36–38; of Wender, 81; of Wolf, 85
Long-term groups (see Time determinants for groups)

Mana, 400, 417, 418
Mania, 400
Marathon, group (see Time determinants for groups): motif, 349–350
Martyrdom, 390 (see also Role, group)
Mascot, 400
Masochism, 219
Matrix, group, 23, 200, 293–294, 299–303, 361, 412 (see also Mother symbolism): as

foundation matrix, group, 7, 376; and group-as-a-whole, 126
Maturation, 300, 421: of "good" group, 171–172; and group-as-a-whole, 156–157; and group space, 396
Meaningful coincidence, 200–221
Median group, 19
Medical education, 10, 56–58, 62
Member-centered groups, 211–212, 412: and interpersonal level of analysis, 122–126
Membership criteria, 8, 19–21, 56, 76, 79 (see also Client selection)
Mental homogeneity, 154
Mental imagery, 176–177, 219–221: in active imagination, 180, 192; as amplified in group, 180, 192, 349; as analogy, 345; and collective process, 340–363; definition and distinctions, 176; elaboration of, 345–346; evocation of, 177–180; and goals of intervention, 180–194; and group imagery technique, of Leuner, 198–199; in guided affective imagery, 178; and inanimate object technique, 182–183; as interventions, 180–194; as provided by therapist, 179–180; and pulling for pictures, 351; and spontaneous and a priori images, 360–361; and structural repair, 175; as structured by therapist, 178; as transitional objects, 343; and translation of mental images, 351–352; in working sequence, 346–347
Mental images, types: cybernetic, 386; daydreams, 386; directed daydreams, 178; figurative, 385; fragmented, 391–392; group dreams, 386; holographic, 172; image-puns, 373; imaginary scenarios, 178, 224, 402; literal, 385; metaphoric, 340–341 (see also Metaphors); organizing, 355–356, 359; poetic, 361; primordial, 194; semiotic, 386; starting, 178; symbolic, 385 (see also Symbols); transformative, 190–192, 383; unbidden, 340
Messianic fantasies (see Fantasies)
Metaphors, 175, 221–222, 402: for the group-as-a-whole, 194–197; of psychological distance, 393; in psychotherapy, 175–176; used by Socrates, 42–43; and translation, 352
Milestone groups, 19–20
Milieu therapy, 18–19, 62, 88, 188, 299, 442
Miracle, 221
Mirroring process, 371–373, 375, 411
Monarch, 419
Monopolizing, vignette, 382
Mother group, 197–206, 215, 309, 418 (see also Mother symbolism): as collective womb, 301; and environmental mother, 297
Mother symbolism, 309 (see also Symbols; Matrix, group): ambivalent mother, 201; bad mother, 201, 203; derivatives of, 197; "good-enough" mother, 311; good mother, 201, 203; great mother, 384, 418; Great Mother, Neumann on, 191, 197; and group as container, 309; and group as insides of mother, 414; and group-as-womb, 191, 343; and matriarchal merged mass, 414; and "mother earth," 197; and

452